CENTRAL THEMES *in*
BIBLICAL THEOLOGY

Edited by Scott J. Hafemann
and Paul R. House

CENTRAL THEMES *in* BIBLICAL THEOLOGY

Mapping unity in diversity

APOLLOS (an imprint of Inter-Varsity Press)
Norton Street, Nottingham NG7 3HR, England
Email: ivp@ivpbooks.com
Website: www.ivpbooks.com

First published 2007

British Library Cataloguing in Publication Data
A catalogue record for this book is available from the British Library.

UK ISBN-13: 978-1-84474-166-3
UK ISBN-10: 1-84474-166-4

Set in Monotype Garamond 11/13pt
Typeset in Great Britain by
Servis Filmsetting Ltd, Manchester
Printed and bound in Great Britain by
Ashford Colour Press Ltd, Gosport, Hampshire

Inter-Varsity Press publishes Christian books that are true to the Bible and that communicate the gospel, develop discipleship and strengthen the Church for its mission in the world.

Inter-Varsity Press is closely linked with the Universities and Colleges Christian Fellowship, a student movement connecting Christian Unions in universities and colleges throughout Great Britain, and a member movement of the International Fellowship of Evangelical Students. Website: www.uccf.org.uk.

To
Lindsey Hafemann
and
Martin Spence

CONTENTS

CONTRIBUTORS

Roy E. Ciampa is Director of the ThM Program in Biblical Studies and Associate Professor of New Testament at Gordon-Conwell Theological Seminary, South Hamilton, Massachusetts, USA.

Stephen G. Dempster is Professor of Religious Studies at Atlantic Baptist University, Moncton, New Brunswick, Canada.

Scott J. Hafemann is Mary F. Rockefeller Distinguished Professor of New Testament at Gordon-Conwell Theological Seminary, South Hamilton, Massachusetts, USA.

Paul R. House is Associate Dean and Professor of Divinity at Beeson Divinity School, Birmingham, Alabama, USA.

Elmer A. Martens is President Emeritus and Professor of Old Testament Emeritus at Mennonite Brethren Biblical Seminary, Fresno, California, USA.

Thomas R. Schreiner is Associate Dean (Scripture and Interpretation Faculty) and Professor of New Testament Interpretation at The Southern Baptist Theological Seminary, Louisville, Kentucky, USA.

Frank S. Thielman is Presbyterian Professor of Divinity at Beeson Divinity School, Birmingham, Alabama, USA.

ABBREVIATIONS

AB	Anchor Bible Commentary	BEvTh	Beiträge zur evangelischen Theologie
ABD	*Anchor Bible Dictionary*	BECNT	Baker Exegetical Commentary on the New Testament
AOTC	Apollos Old Testament Commentary		
BA	*Biblical Archaeologist*	BHS	Biblia Hebraica Stuttgartensia
BBET	Beiträge zur biblischen Exegese und Theologie	*BJRL*	*Bulletin of the John Rylands University Library of Manchester*
BBR	*Bulletin for Biblical Research*		
BCBC	Believers Church Bible Commentary	*BSac*	*Bibliotheca Sacra*
		BSL	Biblical Studies Library
BDAG	W. Bauer, F. W. Dander, W. F. Arndt and F. W. Gingrich, *Greek–English Lexicon of the New Testament and Other Early Christian Literature*, 3rd ed. (Chicago: University of Chicago Press, 1999)	BTCL	Biblical and Theological Classics Library
		CBQ	*Catholic Biblical Quarterly*
		CSIR	Cambridge Studies in Ideology and Religion
		DOTP	*Dictionary of the Old Testament: Pentateuch*

DPL	*Dictionary of Paul and His Letters*	*JSNT*Sup	*Journal for the Study of the New Testament* Supplement Series
EKK	*Evangelisch-katholischer Kommentar zum Neuen Testament*	*JSOT*Sup	*Journal for the Study of the Old Testament* Supplement Series
ET	*Evangelische Theologie*		
ExpT	*Expository Times*	*JTS*	*Journal of Theological Studies*
FCI	Foundations of Contemporary Interpretation	LSJ	H. G. Liddell, R. Scott and H. S. Jones, *A Greek–English Lexicon*, 9th ed. with revised supplement (Oxford: Oxford University Press, 1996)
FOTL	Forms of the Old Testament Literature		
FRLANT	Forschungen zur Religion und Literatur des Alten und Neuen Testaments		
HALOT	*The Hebrew and Aramaic Lexicon of the Old Testament*	LXX	Septuagint
		MT	Masoretic Text
		NAC	New American Commentary
Herm	Hermeneia		
HNTC	Harper New Testament Commentary	NASB	New American Standard Bible
HSMS	Harvard Semitic Monograph Series	NCB	New Century Bible
		NDBT	*New Dictionary of Biblical Theology*
IBC	Interpretation: A Bible Commentary for Teaching and Preaching	NIB	New Interpreter's Bible
		NICNT	The New International Commentary on the New Testament
IEJ	*Israel Exploration Journal*		
Int	*Interpretation*	NICOT	The New International Commentary on the Old Testament
ISBE	*International Standard Bible Encylopedia*		
JBL	*Journal of Biblical Literature*	*NIDOTTE*	*The New International Dictionary of Old Testament Theology and Exegesis*
JETS	*Journal of the Evangelical Theological Society*		
JPSTC	Jewish Publication Society Torah Commentary	NIGTC	New International Greek Testament Commentary
JSNT	*Journal for the Study of the New Testament*	NIV	New International Version

NovT	*Novum Testamentum*	*SJT*	*Scottish Journal of Theology*
*NovT*Sup	*Novum Testamentum* Supplements	SNTSMS	Society for New Testament Studies Monograph Series
NRSV	New Revised Standard Version		
NSBT	New Studies in Biblical Theology	*TDOT*	*Theological Dictionary of the Old Testament*
NTS	New Testament Studies	TNTC	Tyndale New Testament Commentary
OBT	Overtures to Biblical Theology		
OTL	Old Testament Library	*TynBul*	*Tyndale Bulletin*
PNTC	Pillar New Testament Commentary	*TZ*	*Theologische Zeitschrift*
		UBS	United Bible Society
PWCJS	*Proceedings of the World Congress of Jewish Studies*	UBT	Understanding Biblical Themes
RTR	*The Reformed Theological Review*	*VT*	*Vetus Testamentum*
		*VT*Sup	*Vetus Testamentum* Supplements
RSV	Revised Standard Version		
		WBC	Word Biblical Commentary
SBL	Society of Biblical Literature		
		WEC	Wycliffe Exegetical Commentary
SBLDS	SBL Dissertation Series		
SBLSP	SBL Seminar Papers	*WTJ*	*Westminster Theological Journal*
SBLSym	SBL Symposium		
SBT	Studies in Biblical Theology	WUNT	*Wissenschaftliche Untersuchungen zum Neuen Testament*
SHS	Scripture and Hermeneutics Series	*ZAW*	*Zeitschrift für die alttestamentliche Wissenschaft*

Dead Sea Scrolls

CD	Cairo (Genizah text of the) *Damascus (Document)*	1Q33 1QM+	*1QWarScroll*
1QH	*Hôdayôt (Thanksgiving Hymns)* from Qumran Cave 1	4QFlor 4QMessAp	Florilegium *Messianic Apocalypse*
		4QpPS^a	*4QPsalms Pesher^a*
1QM	*Milhamâ (War Scroll)*		

Old Testament Pseudepigrapha

T. Jud   *Testament of Judah*

Papyri

P. Mich. Zen.   *Zenon Papyri,*
University of
Michigan

Ignatius

Eph.   *Letter to the Ephesians*
Rom.   *Letter to the Romans*
Smyrn.   *Letter to the Smyrneans*

Philo

Spec. Laws   The Special Laws

INTRODUCTION

In 2000 several biblical scholars met at Wheaton College in Wheaton, Illinois to discuss the past and future of biblical theology as a discipline in the academy and in the church. It was an exciting conference, one in which veteran biblical theologians such as Peter Stuhlmacher, Daniel Fuller, Graeme Goldsworthy, Elmer Martens and William Dumbrell presented papers, and one in which younger scholars participated as well. This conference proved that interest in biblical theology has not waned in evangelical circles. Indeed, it evidenced a vitality that probably surprised even the participants. The collected conference papers appeared as *Biblical Theology: Retrospect and Prospect* (Downers Grove: IVP; Leicester: Apollos, 2002), and the volume was well received.

After that event the editors of the present volume discussed ways to build upon the stimulating experience of the conference. We agreed that one way we could do so was to gather a group of like-minded scholars to explore biblical themes that contribute to the wholeness of the Bible. We chose people we believed shared our commitment to 'whole-Bible biblical theology', a term we coined for the sort of biblical theology that tries not only to examine the theology of biblical books, which we applaud, or to use biblical categories for discussing theology, which we also applaud. Rather, we wanted to bring together people who saw the need to trace themes and overarching structural ideas through the whole Bible. We wanted to discuss the type of biblical theology Elmer Martens defines as that approach to Scripture which attempts to see Biblical material holistically and to describe this wholeness or synthesis in Biblical categories. Biblical theology attempts to embrace the message of the Bible and to arrive at an intelligible coherence of the whole despite the great diversity of the parts. Or, put another way: Biblical theology investigates the themes presented in Scripture and defines their inter-relationships. Biblical theology is an attempt to get to the theological heart of the Bible.[1]

With these basic principles in mind, we selected the contributors to this volume and met from 24 to 27 April 2003 in Wheaton, Illinois and from 28 to 30 April 2005 at Beeson Divinity School in Birmingham, Alabama to present our research on seven basic themes in biblical theology and to gain the insights of our colleagues. Participants chose the theme they wished to address. This meant that some significant themes would have to be handled by other experts at other times, or were deemed to have been discussed effectively by others in the past. We did not determine the seven most important themes in the Bible and assign them to one another. Individual interests were allowed latitude, but we nonetheless found that the themes the participants chose provided a solid sample of key biblical ideas.

We came together as fellow students of the Scriptures to pursue with one another the ways in which the Bible presents these great themes across the canon. We came together not because we all shared the exact same methodology and opinions. Rather, we came together because we are like-minded when it comes to pursuing the unifying message of the Bible as it unfolded throughout redemptive history. We came together in the awareness that all our efforts are only preliminary in this world, yet certain that the work we were doing would help our understanding of the Scriptures in a way that would hopefully help us teach others more effectively. To pursue the unity of the Bible in a circle of scholars unified by their faith, their commitment to the Scriptures, their dedication to the church and their collegial relationships with one another was a unique opportunity, and we were grateful to be part of it.

As could be expected from the preceding paragraphs, the contributors to this volume share at least three core convictions about the unity of the Bible. First, we are convinced that the Bible *is* a unity because it is the word of God, who is a unified and coherent being, and that a unified biblical theology should thus span the entire range of the Scriptures because they are all part of the written word of God. Though not a uniform opinion, it is common in our age for scholars to write of the many competing 'voices' and various 'theologies'

---

1. Elmer A. Martens, 'Tackling Old Testament Theology', *JETS* 20 (1977), p. 123.

of the Bible. These essays oppose such trends. They seek to uncover the over-arching theology of the Bible as it develops throughout the canon. The themes they treat are studied with an eye to their integration into the whole fabric of the Bible, their use and reuse by the Bible's writers, and thus to their develop-ment across the canon.

Each contributor was allowed to pursue the chosen theme across the Scriptures in the manner they deemed best, but they all pursued that theme in a way calculated to demonstrate biblical wholeness. Stated simply, the contrib-utors do not pit the Old Testament against the New Testament, for they do not think the biblical writers do so. This pursuit of unity does not reject legit-imate diversity. Indeed, it affirms that effective literature utilizes tension and diversity to create its unity. Nonetheless, this diversity contributes to the overall unity; it does not negate it. Tragedy, for instance, must have comic elements to work, but such diversity aids the creation of the whole.

Second, we are convinced that to do biblical theology is not merely to survey the contents of the Bible. In pursuit of an understanding of God and his ways, a biblical theology that spans the canon seeks not only to unpack the content, but also to establish the conceptual unity of the Scriptures as a whole as they unfold in human events. Thus this type of biblical theology endeav-ours to reflect synthetically on the history and significance of the relationship between God and his people and God and his world, past, present and future, as delineated in the Scriptures. To achieve this goal, whole-Bible biblical the-ology does not settle for describing the discrete theological emphases of *indi-vidual* writers or sources. Nor does it settle for focusing on reconstructing the religious experiences or historical events *behind the text* that gave rise to the text. Instead, *biblical* theology seeks its content and coherence in the final proposi-tions and basic ordering of the Old and New Testaments read in their entirety, in their final form, and in concert with one another. As attempted in this volume, *biblical theology* is the study of God's self-revelation to human beings for the purposes of redemption through the interpretation of the events and experiences written down in the Scriptures. This sort of biblical theology affirms that God's self-revelation can never be separated from the historical context in which it was given, and that this context is in concert with the liter-ary record in which it is found.

Third, we are convinced that these days doing whole-Bible biblical theol-ogy most likely should be a collaborative effort. The subject matter of biblical theology and the literature associated with it have grown too complex and the questions too many for most of us to pursue the task by working alone. There will always be dramatic exceptions to this rule. Still, keeping pace with current scholarship in Old Testament, New Testament and Theology, to say nothing of supporting disciplines such as Ancient History, can be a daunting task. Therefore, we met together at the beginning and end of the work and kept in contact in the interim and afterwards. We learned a great deal from one another. We found working in dialogue with one another to be fruitful and encouraging. Of course, readers will have to judge the results themselves.

Finally, we present the results of our research with a certain progression in mind. The first essay establishes 'covenant' as an integrative concept that spans the Bible. Scripture takes shape as two interrelated covenants, so this choice is not astounding, yet it is a vitally important point to make. Based on this introductory principle, we then present essays on God's commands, God's means of atonement, God's sending of servants and God's warning about the Day of the Lord as natural outgrowths of the Bible's covenantal structure. The final two essays, on God's people and the history of redemption, are considered summaries of God's purpose for relating to human beings in a covenantal way. Stated simply, God is in the process of gathering a holy people, which in effect means that God pursues a redemptive mission in our world.

Several people deserve our thanks for their help in this process. Our first meeting was made possible by a grant from Dr Stan Jones, Provost of Wheaton College. Stan is an excellent scholar in his own right, and he supports his faculty members' scholarly pursuits as well as anyone in the academy. We are also grateful for the help and hospitality given us by the staff at Harbor House at Wheaton College, the lovely venue where the meeting took place.

Our second meeting was supported by a grant approved by Dean Timothy George of Beeson Divinity School. Like virtually everything else that occurs at Beeson, this meeting was made possible by endowment funds provided by our benefactor, the late Ralph Waldo Beeson (1900–90). Mr Beeson's generosity and Dean George's faithful leadership, scholarship and churchmanship have combined to make Beeson Divinity School a unique place. Elizabeth Baker made the arrangements for the meeting as part of her ongoing excellent support of Paul House's work. She also painstakingly produced the final draft of the manuscript.

We owe special thanks to Dr Philip Duce, Theological Books Editor at Inter-Varsity Press (UK), for accepting this project and seeing it through to its completion. Such books are hardly mega-sellers, so his patience, support and commitment to this type of biblical analysis are much appreciated.

Most of all, we thank our wives, Debara Hafemann and Heather House, for their enthusiasm for this project. We thank them particularly for showing gracious hospitality during the two meetings. Their love and support for us and for each other has served to strengthen our long-standing and uncommon friendship, as well as our lives of study and teaching, out of which this work was born. They also deserve thanks for keeping us on task by wondering, among other things, what the Bible is if not a unified expression of God's character that expresses his redemptive and loving plan for us all. Heather merits added thanks for donating hours of work spent copy-editing the manuscript.

Twenty years ago, when we were young teachers at Taylor University, our children Eric Hafemann and Molly House used to play together. In July 2006, Eric was married to Lindsey Robison in California and Molly married Martin Spence in England. We rejoice that both couples know and serve the Lord. Now that we are no longer 'promising young scholars', it is a great comfort to know that not even death can separate us from those we love most. We dedicate this book to Lindsey and Martin as a way of welcoming them to our families and as an encouragement to search the Scriptures for transforming truth.

For these and other kindnesses we are very grateful.

Scott J. Hafemann, Gordon-Conwell Theological Seminary
Paul R. House, Beeson Divinity School

1. THE COVENANT RELATIONSHIP

Scott J. Hafemann

At its most fundamental level, the subject matter of biblical theology is the *Bible's* understanding of *God's* character and purposes. This 'theology' is displayed in the developing relationship between God and his people (Israel and the church) and, through them, in God's relationship with the world (the nations and the created order). The primary matrix of God's self-revelation is therefore not private religious experience, but the events recounted and interpreted in the Scriptures that establish and maintain these relationships.[1]

---

1. As James D. Smart, *The Past, Present, and Future of Biblical Theology* (Philadelphia: Westminster Press, 1979), pointed out, the nature of the link between 'theology' as God's self-revelation and 'history' as the discernible nexus of cause and effect is the key question of Biblical Theology. Smart's own answer, advocated by many today, was to follow Barth's separation of theology from history by relocating revelation in the human experience of God reflected in the Scriptures (see pp. 90–92). In contrast, the position taken here is that Scripture is not a record of religious beliefs or experiences in response to a divine revelation outside itself, but is itself divine revelation. In this regard, see the helpful distinction established by John S. Sailhamer, *Introduction to Old Testament Theology, A Canonical Approach* (Grand Rapids: Zondervan, 1995), pp. 13–15, between God's self-revelation in the Bible and religion as a human act in accordance with that revelation. Sailhamer follows

History, not the heart, is the locus of divine revelation. Moreover, since biblical history focuses on God's rescue of humanity from its rebellion against its
creator and sustainer, it can be called the 'history of redemption' or 'salvation
history'. Thus God's relationship with his people within the salvation history
recounted in Scripture is the subject matter of 'biblical *theology*'. To call it 'theology' is especially apropos in that the intention of biblical salvation history is
unequivocally *theocentric*, being focused on God's self-revelation of his righteous character in and through his relationship with his people, the nations and
the world. Biblically speaking, the purpose of theology is doxology.[2]

This means that God's relationship with the world and his people is not a
theoretical abstraction, nor is it fundamentally a subjective experience. Rather,
with salvation history as its framework, this relationship is expressed in and
defined by the interrelated covenants that exist throughout the history of
redemption. This leads to the apostle Paul being able to refer to the various
covenants throughout Israel's history (cf. Rom. 9:4; Eph. 2:12), as well as to
references to the 'old' or 'new' covenant as the two epochs of salvation history.

Nevertheless, although all would agree that there are various individual
covenants throughout the Scriptures, it is significant that the term for covenant
in the Old Testament (*bĕrît*) never occurs in the plural when describing God's
covenants with Israel.[3] Rather, the biblical writers refer either to a specific
covenant or to 'the' covenant between God and his people. This is because the
covenants of the Bible all embody the same fundamental covenant relationship. For this reason, 'covenant' is the biblical-theological concept used to

---

E. Hirsch in tracing the shift from a faith based on the Bible as revelation, to a faith
based on the Bible as a religious response to revelation, to the work of Sigmund
Baumgarten in the mid-eighteenth century.

2. This conviction first came home to me through the teaching of John Piper as
    crystallized in *The Justification of God, An Exegetical and Theological Study of Romans
    9:1–23* (Grand Rapids: Baker, 1983), pp. 90–97, in which he establishes that God's
    righteousness 'consists most basically in God's unswerving commitment to
    preserve the honor of his name and display his glory' in everything he does (p. 97).
    See, e.g., Exod. 14:4, 18; 1 Kgs 8:41–45; Ps. 31:1–3; 79:9; 143:1–2, 11; Isa. 43:6–7,
    21–25; 46:13; 48:11; Jer. 14:7–21; Ezek. 20:9–44; 36:20–32; Dan. 9:7–19; Rom.
    11:32–36; Eph. 1:3–14.

3. As Rolf Rendtorff, *The Covenant Formula, An Exegetical and Theological Investigation*
    (Edinburgh: T. & T. Clark, 1998), pp. 8, 79, has pointed out, though James Barr
    emphasized this point in 1977, it has not been taken seriously enough in
    subsequent scholarship.

explain (1) the essential character of God as King or Sovereign Ruler, (2) the election of a people under his rule who, as his 'adopted' children, live in dependence upon him, and (3) the corresponding nature of God's bond with them as their 'Sovereign Father'. The content of this covenant relationship is thus summarized in what has come to be known as the 'covenant formula', i.e., that YHWH declares, 'I will be God for you [= your God] and you shall be a people for me [= my people],'[4] a mutual belonging between God and Israel that eventually encompasses the nations and consummates history (Ezek. 37:26–28; Zech. 2:11; Rom. 15:10; Rev. 21:3).

This 'covenant relationship', in which the basic categories of kingship (Sovereign Ruler) and kinship (Father) are mutually interpretive,[5] is not static. It is the dynamic, historical arena within which God reveals himself. As such, it provides the interpretive lens for understanding who God is, who his people are and how they relate to one another. Hence, as Rolf Rendtorff has observed, 'covenant' is 'the most comprehensive and the most theologically weighty term for God's attention to humans in the Hebrew Bible'.[6] John Walton concludes that it is the 'single most important theological structure in the Old Testament'; indeed, 'both the Old and New Testament weave their theology on the loom of history with the thread of the covenant'.[7] The covenant relationship con-

---

4. For an insightful treatment of this theme, see Rendtorff, *The Covenant Formula*. See his p. 11 for this literal translation and pp. 50, 73, for his conclusion that the covenant formula is 'at once the unfolding and the endorsement of the . . . covenant', and as such 'the expression of the fundamental relationship between God and Israel'. Rendtorff's study is based on an analysis of the context and significance of the distribution of the three forms of the formula: (A) 'I will be God for you'; (B) 'You shall be a people for me'; and (A) and (B) combined. For a listing of the passages according to these categories, see his pp. 93–94.

5. For the programmatic insight that the concept of 'covenant' in the Bible is based in tribal and family 'kinship' relationships, which later become interpreted in terms of kingship, see F. M. Cross, 'Kinship and Covenant in Ancient Israel', in *From Epic to Canon* (Baltimore: Johns Hopkins, 1998), pp. 3–21.

6. Rolf Rendtorff, *The Canonical Hebrew Bible, A Theology of the Old Testament*, Tools for Biblical Study 7 (Leiden: Deo Publishing, 2005), p. 433.

7. John H. Walton, *Covenant, God's Purpose, God's Plan* (Grand Rapids: Zondervan, 1994), p. 10. In accord with my emphasis, Walton's thesis, p. 24, is that God's sovereign plan is to be in relationship with the people whom he has created, but that people must know God to be in relationship with him. Therefore God has instituted 'as a primary objective a program of self-revelation . . . the mechanism that drives this program is the

sequently provides not only the content but also the context for understanding the revelation-in-relationship and the history-of-redemption within which the biblical narrative and theology unfold.[8] Brevard Childs is right: a scripturally interpreted *Heilsgeschichte* and the notion of the covenant are the two key categories for constructing a biblical theology.[9]

This does not mean that the 'covenant relationship' is the one, central theme of the Bible. The attempt to isolate such a theme has proved to be too specific to gain a consensus or too general to be of explanatory power. More appropriately, the concept of the covenant relationship provides the *structure* that serves to integrate the interrelated themes developed throughout the history of redemption delineated in the Scriptures.[10] Like the hub and rim of a wheel respectively, the old (establishment) and new (restoration and consummation) covenants define and hold together the different 'spokes' of divine revelation manifested in the words and deeds of redemptive history. In so doing, the covenant becomes the interpretive lens for seeing clearly the conceptual and historical unity of the Bible in the midst of its diversity.

The covenant concept of the Bible

In 1933 Walther Eichrodt shocked the scholarly world of his day, which emphasized critical reconstructions and the disunity of the Old Testament, by arguing

---

covenant, and the instrument is Israel. The purpose of the covenant is to reveal God.' See his pp. 26, 29 and esp. 31–43 for his fourteen key texts in support of this thesis.

8. For the history of the debate surrounding this complex issue, see Robert W. Yarbrough, *The Salvation Historical Fallacy? Reassessing the History of New Testament Theology* (Leiden: Deo Publishing, 2004).

9. Brevard Childs, *Biblical Theology of the Old and New Testaments: Theological Reflection on the Christian Bible* (Minneapolis: Fortress Press, 1992), p. 92; cf. p. 419.

10. James Barr's conclusion concerning scholarship's search for the centre of biblical theology is instructive in this regard: 'To sum up the question of the "centre," it seems to me that the discussion of it has not been a vain waste of breath, as some have thought, and that valuable results have emerged from it. It is not a matter of reaching a definitive answer, but rather of weighing possibilities for the expression of structure. Whether writers of Theologies define a "centre" or not, they will very likely have to work with some idea of one (or more?), as a simple necessity for the organization of their work' (*The Concept of Biblical Theology, An Old Testament Perspective* [Minneapolis: Fortress Press, 1999], p. 343).

that Old Testament religion is a 'self-contained entity' with 'a constant basic tendency and character'.[11] Moreover, this character was displayed in the Old Testament concept of the covenant, which Eichrodt saw to be an antidote to the 'bloodless abstraction of "ethical monotheism"' and to the 'bloodless abstractions of a rationalist individualism'.[12] After fielding twenty-four years of criticism, Eichrodt retained the 'covenant' as the central concept of the Old Testament, 'by which to illuminate the structural unity . . . of the message of the Old Testament', since in the concept of covenant 'Israel's fundamental conviction of its special relationship with God is concentrated'.[13] The criticisms have not abated, but Eichrodt was right. Yet, to make the case today, three important distinctions must be drawn in speaking of the covenant as the integrating concept of Scripture.

First, we must distinguish between covenant terminology and covenant reality. The relative scarcity of covenant terminology in the canon, together with its uneven distribution, has caused many to doubt its viability as an integrating motif within Scripture, not to mention as its integrating centre.[14] It is important, however, not to fall prey to the fallacy of assuming that a reality can only be referenced if a specific term is used. The explicit use of covenant terminology need not be present for the reality to be presupposed or even in view.[15] The realities associated with covenant, centred on kingship and kinship, often reference the covenant relationship between God and his people, but

---

11. Walter Eichrodt, *Theology of the Old Testament*, Volume 1, trans. J. A. Baker
    (Philadelphia: Westminster Press, 1961), p. 11.

12. Ibid., pp. 12, 17.

13. Ibid., p. 13.

14. According to Accordance 6.4.1 (OakTree Software, November, 2004), *bĕrît*
    ('covenant') occurs in the Old Testament 287 times in 267 verses. These occurrences
    are concentrated in the Law (82 times, 27 times in both Genesis and Deuteronomy),
    Joshua (22 times) and 1 – 2 Kings (26 times), Isaiah (12 times), Jeremiah (25 times),
    Ezekiel (18 times), Hosea (5 times) and Malachi (7 times), and the Psalms (21 times)
    and 1 – 2 Chronicles (30 times). In the New Testament, *diathēkē* ('covenant') occurs
    33 times in 30 verses. Of these, it occurs only 6 times in the Synoptics and Acts
    (none in John), 9 times in Paul, once in Revelation 11:19 and 17 times in Hebrews.

15. A point well made by Gordon Hugenberger, *Marriage as a Covenant, A Study of
    Biblical Law and Ethics Governing Marriage Developed from the Perspective of Malachi*,
    *VT*Supp 52 (Leiden: Brill, 1994), p. 6 (pointing to the reference to the covenant
    with David in 2 Sam. 23:5 and Pss. 89, 132, even though no corresponding
    covenant terminology appeared originally in 2 Sam. 7).

occur without an explicit mention of a 'covenant' per se.[16] For this reason, the covenant relationship embodied in its various covenants may be described in the Scriptures from one or more of its interrelated elements, such as the sovereignty and fatherhood of God, divine election and 'adoption', the people of God as a divinely constituted 'family' or 'bride', the mutual belonging expressed in the covenant formula, the call to obedience to specific commands in response to divine provisions, and God's promises of blessing and judgment.

Indeed, Childs emphasizes that while the classic formulation of Israel as 'the people of YHWH' occurs in a standardized covenant formula (cf. Exod. 6:7; Lev. 26:12; Judg. 5:13; Jer. 11:4; Ps. 95:7),[17] even to speak of 'Israel' is to speak of both the covenant relationship and covenants of the Bible. Israel exists as God's people only because of God's covenant with Abraham (Gen. 12:1–3; 15:1–21). She continues on under the Sinai covenant only due to the promises made to Abraham and his descendants (Gen. 17:7; Exod. 2:24; 6:4–5; Deut. 4:31; 7:12; 29:12–13).[18] Eventually Israel incorporates the Gentiles and finds her own final redemption through the new covenant established by the Messiah, in fulfilment of these same promises to the patriarchs (Rom. 11:17–24, 26–29, quoting Isa. 59:20–21; Jer. 31:33; Isa. 27:9; cf. too Isa. 41:8–9; 51:1–3). Thus it is not overstating the case to maintain that the entire Scripture 'is a record of God's activity in creating and defining Israel' in answer to the question of who will inherit the covenant promises made to 'Israel' as the true, elect people of God.[19]

Second, we must distinguish between the establishing of the formal 'covenants' and the continuing personal relationship they either initiate, presuppose or ratify, and thereafter embody.[20] The covenant itself is the formal

---

16. So Childs, *Biblical Theology*, p. 415, with my own expansion of some of these covenant realities.

17. Ibid., p. 421.

18. Emphasized by Bruce C. Birch, Walther Brueggemann, Terence E. Fretheim and David L. Petersen, *A Theological Introduction to the Old Testament* (Nashville: Abingdon Press, 1999), p. 151. So too Rendtorff, *Canonical*, pp. 438, 443.

19. So David E. Holwerda, *Jesus and Israel, One Covenant or Two?* (Grand Rapids: Eerdmans, 1995), p. 30.

20. For the fact that a specific covenant need not create a relationship, but often presupposes and ratifies an existing relationship, see W. J. Dumbrell, *Covenant and Creation, A Theology of the Old Testament Covenants* (Carlisle, UK: Paternoster, 1984), pp. 13–14, 19, 26, 42–43, 47, 76 (on the Abrahamic covenant), 81, 89 (on the Sinai

and/or ceremonial act, both verbal and/or symbolic, that provides the recognized, 'legal' framework for living within the relationship to which it belongs. As a matter of definition, 'covenant' is not a synonym for 'relationship', although the existence and maintenance of a relationship is central to the covenant itself.[21] A covenant is the formal declaration, sealed with a ratifying oath (whether given in a verbal declaration and/or symbolized in a sign or ceremony), of the parties involved, the framework for the commitments of the relationship it defines. As such, a covenant represents 'an elected, as opposed to natural, relationship of obligation under oath', i.e., it establishes or reflects 'a relationship under sanctions' based on 'a sanction-sealed commitment to maintain a particular relationship or follow a stipulated course of action'.[22] A covenant and the relationship it represents is therefore 'an *elected* vs. natural relationship of obligation – established under divine sanction'.[23]

Against this backdrop, YHWH's covenant with Israel and the church as divine King (Lord) and Father is an extension of the 'natural relationship' that exists within the household-family and tribe (with marriage seen as a covenant) to a nation and people. In other words, the covenant extends the otherwise inherent familial or tribal bonds to those not related by birth or blood ties, so that those within this covenant relationship now belong to God and to one another as 'family'. Election not blood, rebirth not birth, defines the people of God. By virtue of the covenant, God, the King, becomes the 'Father' of his elect 'children', and they become 'brothers and sisters' in the people of God.

---

covenant), 127 (on the Davidic), etc., and Hugenberger, *Marriage*, following McCarthy, pp. 169, 175. McCarthy points to thirteen examples of formal covenants ratifying an existing relationship within secular covenants as well (see Hugenberger, *Marriage*, p. 169 n. 5). In fact, ratifying an existing relationship may be the typical use of covenant making. On the other hand, E. Katsch, Perlitt and Nicholson go too far when they conclude that a covenant *never* establishes a relationship (rightly, Hugenberger, *Marriage*, pp. 169–170).

21. For this important point and its implications, see Hugenberger, *Marriage*, pp. 4, 169–171, 176–177.

22. Ibid., pp. 11, 171 n. 5, quoting M. Kline. Thus Mendenhall could define a 'covenant' as a 'solemn promise made binding by an oath' (quoted by Hugenberger, p. 11 n. 76), while D. J. McCarthy called it 'a union based on an oath' (quoted by Hugenberger, p. 12). For the important addition that a covenant may secure a stipulated course of action as well as a relationship, as in Ezra 10:3; 2 Kgs 11:4; 2 Chr. 23:11; Jer. 34:8–10, see Hugenberger, p. 169.

23. Hugenberger, *Marriage*, p. 171.

As a result, God is now his (adopted) people's 'Divine Kinsman', who is no longer simply a family God (the 'God of the Fathers'), but the ruler of all by virtue of an extended 'kinship-in-law'.[24] In this extended covenant relationship,

> The Divine Kinsman, it is assumed, fulfils the mutual obligations and receives the privileges of kinship. He leads in battle, redeems from slavery, loves his family, shares the land of his heritage (*naḥălâ*), provides and protects. He blesses those who bless his kindred, curses those who curse his kindred. The family of the deity rallies to his call to holy war, 'the wars of Yahweh', keeps his cultus, obeys his patriarchal commands, maintains familial loyalty (*ḥesed*), loves him with all their soul, calls on his name.[25]

Third, we must distinguish between the covenant *relationship* that exists between God as King and Father and his people *throughout* history and the covenant *epochs* that take place *within* history. The Bible divides all of history into two opposing epochs: this age and the age to come. From the biblical perspective, history moves from creation to new creation, from this fallen age to the restored age to come, from the evil kingdoms of this world under the rule of Satan to the kingdom of God. In accordance with this two-age conception, the Bible also divides the history of God's relationship with his people into two main periods of time, the 'old covenant' of this age and the 'new (or everlasting) covenant' of the age to come (Isa. 55:3; 61:8; Jer. 31:31–34; 32:40; 50:5; Ezek. 16:60; 37:26; Matt. 12:32; Mark 10:30; Luke 22:20; 1 Cor. 11:25; 2 Cor. 3:6, 14; Eph. 1:21; Heb. 8:6–10).

The transition from this age to the age to come will take place through the last 'great and awesome day of the LORD' (Mal. 4:5; cf. Isa. 13:6–9; Joel 1:15; 2:1–31; Zeph. 1:7, 14; 2:1–3; Amos 5:18–20; 1 Cor. 5:5; 1 Thess. 5:2; 2 Thess. 2:1–2; 2 Pet. 3:10; etc.).[26] On this 'day', God will decisively judge this evil age and in so doing deliver his people once and for all from sin and its consequences. Through this coming day of judgment, God will establish his unrivalled rule and reign as King and, under his undisputed sovereignty, bring about the new creation and its covenant. This coming day of salvation

---

24. Cross, 'Kinship', pp. 6–7.

25. Ibid., p. 7. Walton, *Covenant*, pp. 21–22, makes the same point by emphasizing that, unlike the earthly suzerain who employed the covenant language in the Ancient Near East as a means of maintaining subservience, YHWH was the sovereign who actually loved his people.

26. See Paul House's essay on the Day of the Lord in this volume.

is therefore often pictured in the Bible as a 'second-exodus' redemption of God's people. Like the first deliverance from slavery in Egypt, with its covenant at Sinai, God will once again rescue his people from captivity (to sin) in order to bring them into his presence as their sovereign ruler, albeit now in accordance with an everlasting 'new covenant' associated with a restored Zion (Jer. 32:36–41; Ezek. 34:25–31; Isa. 2:1–4; 55:3; 61:8; Zech. 8 – 9).

The only, but crucial, modification to this linear development of history is the fact that the first coming of the Messiah was intended to inaugurate the kingdom of God without consummating it.[27] The great second-exodus redemption of God's people from their slavery under the presence, penalty and power of sin takes place first not through the judgment of the world, but through the death and resurrection of the Messiah himself as the suffering Servant of the Lord.[28] Only the substitutionary death and vindicating resurrection of the Christ himself can make the new covenant possible in order that, under its provisions, God's people might be prepared for their final deliverance at the judgment to come. Thus the kingdom of God is here (Matt. 12:28; Mark 1:14–15; Luke 10:9; 13:18–21; Rom. 14:17; Gal. 3:14; Col. 1:13; Heb. 6:5), but not yet here in all its fullness (Matt. 24:30; 25:34; Luke 20:34–35; 1 Cor. 15:20–28; 2 Pet. 1:11; 3:1–13). The new age of the new creation under the new covenant is dawning in the midst of this evil age *without* bringing it to an end (2 Cor. 3:6; 5:17; Gal. 6:15)! This 'overlapping of the ages' is the 'mystery of the kingdom' (Mark 4:1–34).

In this way, the linear development of history presented in the Bible, from creation to new creation, overlaps with and is inextricably tied to the sequential development of the biblical history of redemption, from the old covenant to the new. The covenants and story of the Scriptures match one another. This age and the age to come correspond to the two redemptive epochs within

---

27. For the paradigmatic presentation of this 'inaugurated eschatology', see Oscar Cullmann, *Christ and Time: The Primitive Christian Conception of Time and History* (Philadelphia: Westminster Press, 1964). This perspective was established in the English-speaking world largely through the work of G. E. Ladd; of his many works, for a concise presentation, see *The Gospel of the Kingdom: Scriptural Studies in the Kingdom of God* (1959; Grand Rapids: Eerdmans, 2000). For the biblical-theological implications of this basic two-age structure and its modification with the first coming of the Christ, see Roy Ciampa's essay on the history of redemption in this volume.

28. See Frank Thielman's essay on substitutionary atonement and Stephen Dempster's on the Servant, in this volume.

history, that of the old and new covenants, with their respective bodies of literature. The history of 'this age' is first established, and then re-established, by what may be called the two 'covenants of creation', the first with Adam (and Eve) before the fall and the second with Noah after the flood (cf. Gen. 1:28–30 with 9:1–3, and 1:27 with 9:6). These two covenants with humanity ensure God's *providential* provisions necessary for history itself, in order that God may also establish a *redemptive* covenant relationship with his chosen people. These covenants also prefigure the final judgment to come upon rebellious humanity through the expulsion of Adam and Eve from the garden of Eden and the destruction of humanity from the earth, even as the exile of Israel from the Promised Land makes the same point regarding the judgment of those who break his salvific covenants.

The history of redemption, made possible by the re-established 'creation' after the flood, thus stretches from the covenant with Abraham (Gen. 12:1–3; 15:1–21; 17:1–14; 22:15–18), to the consummation of the new covenant of peace between God and his people (Isa. 54:10; 66:22), to the new creation after final judgment (Isa. 65:17–25; 2 Pet. 3:1–13; Rev. 21:1–8). This 'salvation history' unfolds based on a series of specific covenants, which build on one another and mark out its turning points: from the covenant established between God and Abraham, through the covenant established with Israel at Sinai (Exod. 19 – 24), which together make up the epoch of the 'old covenant', to the 'new covenant' established with the church by the Messiah (Matt. 26:28; Luke 22:20; 1 Cor. 11:25; Heb. 8:6–13; 9:15).[29]

The unity of the Bible is therefore built upon a two-age, two-covenant conception, within which the individual covenants play their respective roles in the unfolding drama of a continuous history of salvation. The various covenants and stages of redemptive history are distinguished by the increasing knowledge of God's unified purposes and the manner of their accomplishment, climaxing in the coming and return of the messianic Son of God (cf. Dan. 9:24–27; 1 Pet. 1:10–12; Heb. 1:1–4; John 1:1–5, 14; 1 John 3:2; 1 Cor. 13:8–13). This is reflected in the fact that the same covenant formula remains the purpose of God from

---

29. Within these covenants between God and his chosen people there are two
    important subsidiary covenants, that of kingship with David (2 Sam. 7:12–14; 2
    Sam. 23:5; Jer. 33:21; Pss. 89, 132) and of priesthood with Levi (Num. 25:12–13;
    Deut. 33:10; Jer. 33:21; Mal. 2:4–7; Neh. 13:29). These covenants establish the
    instruments needed for maintaining and consummating the covenant relationship
    with Israel under the so-called 'Sinai' or 'Mosaic covenant', both of which are
    fulfilled under the new covenant by the Messiah, who is 'priest' and 'king'.

the covenant with Abraham, through the Sinai covenant, to its consummation in the new covenant, since this relationship is the means by which God reveals his glory.[30] The specific content of the covenant provisions, stipulations and promises develops as time goes on, but there remains *one* covenant people, in two epochs, with *one* kind of covenant relationship that spans the individual covenants of redemptive history. This 'unity' reading of the Bible, though highly contested,[31] stands at the heart of the proposal before us.

The covenant relationship

Scripture testifies to one, constant relationship[32] between God and his people throughout redemptive history that is formalized and embodied in its successive covenants. Although disagreement remains over various historical, liter-

---

30. For this point, see Rendtorff, *The Covenant Formula*, pp. 3, 20, 22, 26, 43, 47–49, 69, 80, 88–92, who points to the interrelationship at the key turning points in the biblical canon between the 'covenant', covenant formula, self-identification formula ('I am Yahweh') and recognition formula ('You will know that I am the Yahweh, the Lord').

31. One need think only of the conflict theories of biblical theology embedded in the majority of the paradigms employed for understanding the flow of biblical history, whether in the traditional Lutheran law-gospel perspective, the Reformed understanding of the covenant of works and covenant of grace, or the Dispensational understanding of the dispensations of law and grace. For an overview of the various positions within evangelicalism, see John S. Feinberg (ed.), *Continuity and Discontinuity: Perspectives on the Relationship between the Old and New Testaments* (Wheaton: Crossway, 1988); for a survey of the issue within scholarship at large, see David L. Baker, *Two Testaments, One Bible, A Study of the Theological Relationship between the Old and New Testaments*, rev. ed. (Leicester: Apollos; Downers Grove: InterVarsity Press, 1991), pp. 19–176.

32. This seems more appropriate than talking about one 'covenant' in the Bible; there are various covenants, but one covenant relationship based on one covenant structure. In contrast, Walton, *Covenant*, pp. 44–45, 49, 60, 106–107, 148–149, argues for a single 'covenant' in the Bible made up of 'constituent phases of development' based on the fact that all the covenants have the common purpose of revealing God in order to establish a relationship with Israel and the nations (p. 44). The continuity between covenants exists in that 'each is a part of a single, unified program of revelation' (p. 49).

ary and theological issues surrounding the origin and significance of the biblical covenants, a 'substantial scholarly consensus' exists today concerning 'the major elements that typically comprise an ancient covenant'.[33] Specifically, Hugenberger points out that within Israel's history a covenant always entails (1) a relationship (2) with a non-relative (3) that involves obligations and (4) is established through an oath.[34] Thus the covenant relationship between God and his people is determined by divine election on the one hand (as their 'Father', God 'adopts' his dependent 'children' through acts of deliverance) and by the commitments and stipulations of the relationship on the other. This relationship is then guaranteed by a covenant ratification ceremony, which is centred on the taking of an oath of allegiance to the promises and obligations of this relationship. The specific components of actual covenants and their corresponding ceremonies, although seldom preserved in full, embody these elements.

The biblical covenants did not arise in a vacuum. There were a variety of such treaties or covenants in the Ancient Near East, most likely based on intrinsic, tribal, kinship allegiances.[35] Largely due to the programmatic work of G. E. Mendenhall,[36] scholars have widely recognized that the structure of the covenant relationship as we now have it in the biblical text finds its historical location in affinity with, but not necessarily direct dependence on, the well-known Near Eastern suzerain treaties, starting with the treaties between the Hittite kings and their vassals (c. 1400–1200 BC).[37] In accord with the ele-

---

33. Pointed out by Hugenberger, *Marriage*, p. 11.

34. Ibid., p. 215. An 'oath' can be any sign (verbal or non-verbal) 'which invokes the deity to act against the one who will be false to an attendant commitment or affirmation' (p. 215). Moreover, these oaths need not be explicitly self-maledictory, but can be 'a solemn positive declaration or depiction of the commitment being undertaken' (p. 215).

35. So Cross, 'Kinship', pp. 7–11, 19. 'Often it has been asserted that the language of "brotherhood" and "fatherhood", "love", and "loyalty" is "covenant terminology." This is to turn things upside down. The language of covenant, kinship-in-law, is taken from the language of kinship, kinship-in-flesh' (p. 11).

36. 'Covenant Forms in Israelite Tradition', *BA* 17 (1954), pp. 50–76.

37. For a convenient listing of the fifty-seven examples of such treaties, see J. H. Walton, *Ancient Israelite Literature in its Cultural Context* (Grand Rapids: Zondervan, 1989), pp. 95–107. The modern history of the study of the covenant structure is a complex one in which no consensus exists concerning the origin or development of the various kinds of treaty formulas found in the Ancient Near East and the

ments of the covenant outlined above, these treaties were generally comprised of (1) a *preamble*, in which the sovereign identified himself and sometimes summarized the covenant itself; (2) a *historical prologue*, which gave the historical basis of the covenant, often centred in a great act of deliverance or provision on behalf of the vassal; (3) the *covenant stipulations*, which mapped out the requirements that constitute loyalty to the relationship, by which the covenant is maintained; (4) the *covenant blessings or curses* contingent on keeping or breaking the covenant; and (5) the (often divine) *witnesses* to the covenant.[38]

In the biblical text God takes this treaty form, typically used between a sovereign emperor and his dependent vice-regents, and applies it to his relationship with his people. God's self-revelation thus employs the concept of kingship as the fundamental framework for explaining his divine character and purposes, albeit a kingship modelled on kinship, in which the King was also the committed 'Father' of his people. Biblically speaking, divine kingship ('God') and kinship ('Father') become mutually interpretive (Isa. 9:6–7; Gal. 1:4; Eph. 4:6; Phil. 4:20; 1 Thess. 1:3; 3:11, 13; Rev. 1:6; etc.). As Jesus taught his disciples to pray in Matthew 6:9–10,

> Our *Father* in heaven,
> hallowed be your name.
> Your *kingdom* come,
> your will be done,
> on earth as it is in heaven.

Old Testament. For a helpful survey, in spite of his own historical scepticism concerning the early nature of the covenant concept in the Old Testament itself, see Ernest W. Nicholson, 'Covenant in a Century of Study Since Wellhausen', in his *God and His People, Covenant and Theology in the Old Testament* (Oxford: Clarendon, 1986), pp. 3–117.

38. For the historical span of this treaty-form, see the Hittite treaties presented in William W. Hallo (ed.), *The Context of Scripture, Vol. II: Monumental Inscriptions from the Biblical World* (Leiden: Brill, 2003), pp. 93–106, and the two later treaty inscriptions in Aramaic from Sefire (prior to 740 BC), pp. 213–216. Such evidence, together with the parallels between covenant language and early tribal kinship terminology and concepts, has led Cross, 'Kinship', pp. 17–18, to declare that 'the antiquity of covenant forms, of the language of kinship-in-law, and of religio-military federations of tribes is not in doubt. This has been clear since the discovery of the texts of international treaties of the second millennium.'

For as we have seen in the covenant formula, mutual belonging and 'love', like that between members of a family, becomes the 'glue' holding the covenant relationship between God and his people together (on God's love: Deut. 7:8; 10:18; 1 Kgs 10:9; Pss. 33:5; 146:8; Jer. 31:3; John 3:16; Eph. 2:4; 5:2; 1 John 4:10, 19; etc.; on our love for God: Deut. 6:4; Lev. 19:18; Mark 12:29–31; etc.).

In the ancient world, the ideal king, like the tribal 'father' or kinsman, expressed his love, manifested his power and magnified his rule by providing for and protecting his people (Pss. 68:5; 103:13). So, too, God's acts of deliverance and provision in the past, as well as his promises of blessing for the future, serve to reveal God's glory as the supreme, sovereign, self-sufficient supplier of all things for the sake of his people. God's self-revelation as 'King' is therefore the driving force of redemptive history, from the reign of God over his creation as reflected in humanity's exercise of dominion as his 'image' (Gen. 1:26–27) to the demonstration of his rule over the nations at the exodus (Exod. 15:18), and from the promise of his rule after the exile (Isa. 52:7; Dan. 7:13–18) to the dawning and consummation of the kingdom of God in the first and second comings of the Messiah (Mark 1:14–15; 1 Cor. 11:26; 15:24; 1 Thess. 3:13; 2 Tim. 4:1, 18; 1 Pet. 1:3–9). From the old covenant 'song of Moses' to the new covenant 'song of the Lamb', redemptive history is moving towards the full revelation of God's glory as the 'King of the nations' (Rev. 15:3). Hence, although well known for his emphasis on the covenant as the integrating centre of the Scriptures, Walther Eichrodt rightly points out that 'that which binds together indivisibly the two realms of the Old and New Testaments – different in externals though they may be – is the irruption of the kingship of God into this world and its establishment here'; this is 'the unitive fact' of the Scriptures.[39] The thematic lines of Scripture can therefore be summarized under the following fourfold rubric:

Divine Kingship as Father

via

Creation-Provision-Redemption

for

Humanity

in

Covenant

With great theological import, therefore, the relationship between the

---

39. Eichrodt, *Theology*, p. 26.

divine King and his people is interpreted throughout the Scriptures in terms of a family relationship between a father and his children. The parallel between humanity being in the image/likeness of God as King in Genesis 1:26 and Seth being in the image/likeness of Adam as his father in Genesis 5:3 indicates that God rules over his people as a father relates to his son. Exodus 4:22 makes it clear that Israel is not only God's subject, but also his 'son'. The people of the covenant are not merely those over whom God reigns, they are his 'children' (Ps. 103:13; Isa. 1:2–4; 63:16; 64:8; Hos. 1:10; John 1:12; 1 John 3:1; Rom. 8:16, 21). They thus relate to one another as members of the same 'family' (cf. Lev. 19:17–18; Deut. 15:12–18; Lev. 25:35–38).[40] As an expression of their covenant commitment, the kings of Israel took their place under God's authority as his 'sons' (Pss. 2:7; 89:26–28). So, too, Jesus knew himself sent by his Father as his royal and dependent 'Son' (Mark 1:11; 9:7; John 3:35; 5:19–26), called God 'Abba' (Mark 14:36) and taught his disciples to pray to God as their heavenly Father (Matt. 6:9; Rom. 8:15). In response, the church declared God to be the 'Father of our Lord Jesus Christ' (Rom. 15:6; 2 Cor. 1:3; 11:31; Eph. 1:3; 1 Pet. 1:3; Rev. 1:6) and declared themselves related to one another as brothers and sisters in God's 'family' (Isa. 43:6; 2 Cor. 6:18).

This is a consistent pattern. Reflecting its origins, the covenant relationship in the Bible translates the concept of divine kingship in terms of fatherhood, the category of vassal subjects in terms of sonship, the exercise of sovereignty in terms of love, and the call for obedience in terms of faithfulness within a family. With no diminution of God's absolute sovereignty, the biblical covenant thus becomes not only a political arrangement, but also a familial experience of belonging. Once again, this is the import of the covenant formula. Indeed, this same relationship can be expressed in terms of the relationship between a husband (God) and his wife (Israel), or between Christ and his bride, the church (Jer. 31:32; Hos. 2:16–20; Eph. 5:32).

The threefold covenant structure

The implications of God's covenant relationship with his people can now be drawn. From Genesis 1:1 onwards, divine kingship, expressed in kinship, is revealed through the provisions and providence of creation and new creation, as well as through God's acts of deliverance and protection, judgment and

---

40. So Charles H. H. Scobie, *The Ways of Our God: An Approach to Biblical Theology* (Grand Rapids: Eerdmans, 2003), p. 751.

vindication on behalf of his people. Taken together, this revelation of God's glory is the context within which the faith of his people is understood. God's acts as 'King' and 'Father' bring about a response of childlike dependence from the people of his 'kingdom'. Moreover, God's provisions in the past provide the foundation for trusting his promises for the future. This active reliance on God's promises takes the form of obedience to the 'King's' commands as the organic expression of trust in his sovereignty and love. When one trusts God's word, one obeys his commands. The track record of God's ongoing provisions in the past and present and the corresponding surety of his promises for the future therefore establish and maintain a relationship of mutual faithfulness between the King/Father and his people/children.

This relationship of mutual belonging is codified in covenants in accordance with their provisions, stipulations and promises. The threefold covenant structure of the relationship between God and his people may therefore be outlined as follows:[41]

God's Unconditional Acts of Provision (as King/Father)
by which he Establishes the Covenant Relationship
(The Provisions and Promises of the Covenant,
given by grace in the *past*)

which leads to

The Covenant Stipulations or 'Conditions'
upon which the Covenant Relationship is Maintained
(The Commands of the Covenant,
kept by grace in the *present*)

which leads to

The Covenant Promises or Curses
based on Keeping or Not Keeping the Covenant
(The Consummation of the Covenant Promises or Curses,
to be fulfilled by grace in the *future*)

---

41. I have tried to map out this threefold structure and its implications in *The God of Promise and the Life of Faith, Understanding the Heart of the Bible* (Wheaton: Crossway, 2001). The following section is expanded from chapter 2 of that work. The punctuation of the outline is for reasons of emphasis.

There are several implications of this threefold covenant structure. First, its sequence demonstrates that God, as the Sovereign Ruler ('King'), always takes the first and decisive step in establishing the covenant relationship. As the 'Divine Kinsman' ('Father'), God does so by invading history (and the human heart!) with his great deeds of deliverance and provision on behalf of his people ('family'). In Rendtorff's words, covenant is 'always at God's behest and on his initiative'.[42] Brought about by divine initiative, characterized by benevolence and extended to those who are not by nature his own, these divine provisions are acts of unconditional grace. Hence, to speak of a covenant relationship is to speak first and foremost of God's sovereign, self-determined election motivated by his love. Throughout redemptive history, God takes the initiative in establishing, swearing, keeping and remembering his covenant with his people.

Second, the inextricable link between the three elements of the covenant (Provision, Stipulation, Promise) makes clear that God's great acts of provision and deliverance, from the creation to new creation, together with God's rule over the lives of his people, are not isolated acts of divine power and love. God's provisions never stand alone. Every act of God's provision in the *past* brings with it promises for the *future*. In fact, the history of redemption demonstrates that the promises of God for the future are extensions of what he has done in the past. Moreover, the covenant formula itself reveals that the primary provision and promise of the covenant relationship is knowing God himself. Knowing God is not a means to something else, but all of God's other gifts are intended to bring his people into an ever-growing relationship with God himself. In other words, within the covenant relationship, 'the power, the ready assistance, the faithfulness of Yahweh experienced thus far are offered to the people for their permanent enjoyment'.[43] These provisions and promises (YHWH is *their* God) are the means by which God initiates and sustains their relationship with him (they are *his* people).

Specifically, God's provisions and promises create both the basis and motivation for responding to God with the trust and hope that honour him as one's Lord. God's people depend on God in the present because of his track record of faithfulness in the past; they desire to do so because of his promises for the future. Within the covenant, this response of faith and hope in God and his promises is defined in terms of obedience to a specific command towards God or neighbour as an embodiment of love (see, again, Deut. 6:4; Lev. 19:18;

---

42. Rendtorff, *Canonical*, p. 433.
43. Eichrodt, *Theology*, p. 38.

Mark 12:29–31; cf. Exod. 20:6; Deut. 5:10; John 14:15; 21:15–17).[44] Created by God's past provisions and motivated by his future promises, the commands of the covenant embody the necessary response to the God who provides. These commands express the significance of the life-determining reality of what God has done, is doing, and will do on behalf of his people. The commands of God, as the embodiment of love, are the provisions and promises of God applied to the daily circumstances of life. In other words, love is the direct expression of trusting in God's provision and hoping in his promises. Faith, hope and love are thus shorthand summaries of the covenant stipulations.

Third, the movement within the covenant structure from historical prologue to covenant blessing indicates that the focus of the covenant relationship is on the future. On the one hand, in the words of Jon D. Levenson, 'the function of the prologue is to ground the obligations of Israel to YHWH in the history of his gracious acts on her behalf'.[45] Yet, as Levenson points out,

> The revelation of God in history is not, according to covenant theology, a goal in and
> of itself, but rather, the prologue to a new kind of relationship, one in which the
> vassal will show fidelity in the future by acknowledgment of the suzerain's grace

---

44. Cross, 'Kinship', p. 14: 'It should be stressed that adoptive sonship places obligations of kinship on the father, as is generally recognized, and also on the son, which is often forgotten. Kinship obligations are necessarily mutual . . . There are no 'unilateral' covenants in a kinship-based society.' 'The whole design and motivation of the covenanted league was the establishment of mutual obligations' (p. 17). Cross's own surprising distinction, pp. 14 n. 41 and 15 n. 41, between conditional and unconditional promises, based on different types of dynastic clauses in suzerainty treaties, cannot be discussed here. Suffice it to say that this distinction is determined by the content of the promises themselves. I am not convinced that in the case of Abraham and David God makes unconditional promises concerning land and dynasty to future generations based on the covenant faithfulness of their forefather (thus establishing, as Cross puts it, a 'reservoir of grace'). Rather, based on Abraham's and David's keeping of the covenant, God promises that he will continually raise up a faithful remnant who hope in these promises in order that the promises may continue until they are fulfilled (cf. Gen 18:19; 1 Kgs 8:25–26). The 'reservoir of grace' is that God promises to be gracious to their descendants, not that the promise is independent of the faithfulness of future generations.

45. Jon D. Levenson, *Sinai & Zion: An Entry into the Jewish Bible* (San Francisco: Harper and Row, 1985), p. 37.

towards him in the past . . . The historical prologue is only the prologue. It ceases to be at a point when the covenant takes effect. From that moment on, what is critical is not the past, but the observance of the stipulations in the present and the sort of life that such observance brings about.[46]

From this perspective, the commands of the covenant set forth the conditions by which our relationship with God will continue by indicating the ways in which his acts of grace are to be honoured. In doing so, God's commands describe the effects of that grace itself, since to be brought into a relationship with God is to be transformed by it. God's promises (or curses) for the future are therefore dependent upon keeping (or not keeping) his commands in the present, as they flow from what God has done (or not done) in the past and continues to do (or not do) in the present. For, as Elmer Martens has stressed, a 'covenant' is 'an arrangement between two parties in which the greater commits himself to the lesser in the context of mutual loyalty'.[47] So too, Eichrodt: the covenant relationship is always based on God's 'primal act in history', but maintained 'on definite conditions', so that it is always bilateral or two-sided, albeit with the burden for the keeping of the covenant 'unequally distributed', being 'protected by a powerful divine Guardian'.[48] The threefold structure of the covenant, with its divine initiative, provisions and promises of grace, and 'unequal distribution' of commitments, therefore guards against a legalistic distortion of the covenant relationship it embodies. The biblical covenants cannot be degraded 'to the level of an agreement based on mutual service between two partners of equal status'.[49]

Fourth, the fact that the covenant stipulations of faith, hope and love are the essential link between experiencing God's provisions in the past and present and inheriting his blessings in the future signifies that all the promises of God are conditional (Eph. 2:8b: we are saved *through faith*). Nevertheless, there is no such thing as a merited or earned promise in the Bible, in the sense

---

46. Ibid., p. 43.

47. Elmer Martens, *God's Design: A Focus on Old Testament Theology*, 3rd ed. (N. Richland Hills: Bibal Press, 1998), p. 78.

48. Eichrodt, *Theology*, pp. 36–37. See too, Steven L. McKenzie, *Covenant* (St Louis: Chalice, 2000), p. 37: 'The covenantal relationship is best described as "divine commitment and human obligation"' (cf. pp. 39, 50, 120, 140–141). Significant is the fact that both God's commitment and his people's obligation to respond in obedience can be expressed in terms of 'loving loyalty' (*ḥesed*) (p. 141).

49. Eichrodt, *Theology*, p. 44.

of deserving God's blessings by virtue of our own abilities, efforts, ethnic identities, personal accomplishments, feelings or beliefs. In the words of Ephesians 2:8a, we are saved *by grace*. Although all the promises of God are conditional, the provisions of God that make inheriting those promises possible are given unconditionally. These include not only the acts of redemption culminating in the first and second comings of the Christ, but also the provisions in our personal lives needed to fulfil God's covenant conditions. In the words of Ephesians 2:8c, 'this [entire process of salvation by grace through faith] is the *gift of God*. And again, the fundamental provision of God is the presence of God himself. Our lives of obedience are therefore 'fruit of [God's] Spirit', not exercises of our own willpower (Ezek. 36:26–27; Gal. 5:22–23 – note the condition in Gal. 5:21!). In this way, God's commands embody his gifts, since God demands from us in accordance with what he provides for us.

As redemptive history progresses, it therefore becomes clear that an essential aspect of God's deliverance from sin is the provision, through his transforming presence, of the ability itself to respond to his commands in order to inherit his covenant blessings (Deut. 30:1–10; Jer. 31:31–34; Ezek. 11:19–20; 36:25–28; 2 Cor. 3:3–6, 18; 5:17; Heb. 9:15; 10:11–31; Jas 1:5, 16–18; 3:13–18; for the expression of this truth by contrast, see Deut. 29:2–4). God's foundational act of deliverance on behalf of his people is their rescue from the penalty and power of sin, while his presence in their midst becomes his ongoing provision.

Finally, the covenant structure destroys all attempts to define 'faith' as a passive, mental assent to data from the past, or as an emotional attachment centred in private, religious 'experience'. The inextricable link between the provisions, stipulations and promises of the covenant reveals that to live in relationship with God is to respond with Spirit-determined obedience to God as the expression of one's ongoing trust in God. In Jesus' words, 'If you love me, you will keep my commandments' (John 14:15). Thus, 'Whoever says "I know him" but does not keep his commandments is a liar, and the truth is not in him' (1 John 2:4; cf. 4:20). This obedience, therefore, is not something added to faith; it is the organic expression of faith itself. In other words, the commands of God simply make it clear what trusting God looks like in concrete circumstances. Hence, every command is an implicit call to trust God's provisions and promises. In this regard, although this point cannot be developed here, the organic relationship between the covenant stipulations of faith, hope and love themselves means that where one exists all exist (1 Cor. 13:13; Gal. 5:5–6; Col. 1:3–5; 1 Thess. 1:2–6; 5:8; 1 Pet. 1:3–9, 21–22; Heb. 6:9–12; 10:19–25; Jas 2:14–26).

The common approach to the Bible that divides it into two messages, a 'law message', in which God demands something *from* us, and a 'gospel message', in which he gives something *to* us, is therefore inaccurate. Although we may wrongly try to prove ourselves or to earn God's favour with our own efforts (self-justification), the covenant relationship never begins with the commands of God or the efforts of humanity as the precursor to receiving his blessings. We are not called to obey God in order to gain what we do not have, but in response to what we already possess. The commands of God do not establish the covenant relationship, they reflect it. Biblically speaking, the covenant relationship always starts with the great acts of God in the past that embody and lead to his provisions in the present and his promises for the future. Only then, sandwiched between what God has done for us in the past and what he promises to do for us in the future (including our ongoing life with God 'in between'), do we find the commands of God for our lives now. As Goldsworthy puts it, 'In both Testaments the demand to be holy stems from the prior saving activity of God.'[50] This is true whether we are talking about God's relationship with Adam in the garden, with Israel in the wilderness and Promised Land, with Jesus throughout his earthly life, or with the church throughout the world.

The 'covenant' at creation

God's relationship with Adam and Eve established in the garden of Eden provides the basis and contours of the relationship between God and his people throughout history. There we see that God's provisions of creation for Adam and Eve in the *past* (Gen. 1:3–25, 29; 2:8–14) were the foundation upon which they were to obey him in the *present* (Gen. 1:26–28; 2:15), the result of which would be continuing in his covenant blessings in the *future* (Gen. 2:16). As we have seen, this interplay between the past, present and future in relationship to God is at the very centre of biblical theology.

Within this context, God's Sabbath rest after his creative activity indicated that, having conquered chaos, he was now reigning over his creation for the good of his people, having given them *everything* they needed to fulfil their mandate (Gen. 2:1–3). Like a sovereign sitting upon his throne, God's 'rest' was the expression of his control over his kingdom and the sufficiency of his

---

50. Graeme Goldsworthy, *Gospel and Kingdom, A Christian Interpretation of the Old Testament* (1981; Carlisle: Paternoster, 1994), p. 64.

completed provision. Hence the covenant stipulations that flowed from God's provision, both positive and negative, were not opportunities to earn from God something they did not already have. Rather, they were an expression of what dependence on God would look like in view of his pronouncement that what he had made for Adam and Eve was 'very good' (Gen. 1:31), that is, sufficient to meet their needs.[51] As long as Adam and Eve trusted God for their future, in view of what he had already provided for them in the past, they could exercise dominion over the earth. In contrast, to eat of the tree of the knowledge of good and evil would be a declaration of independence[52] flowing from a discontent with God's provisions and a lack of dependence on the promise of their sufficiency as embedded in God's Sabbath rest.

Whether we call the relationship between God and Adam and Eve at creation a 'covenant' relationship or not, since the specific word 'covenant' is not used in Genesis 1–3, the point to be made is that humanity did not initiate this relationship. God's command to Adam and Eve in 1:26 was not only self-determined, but also based on his acts and word of provision (Gen. 1:3–31). Furthermore, God's acts of provision were sovereign and free acts of grace. Nothing forces God to create, provide, rescue or deliver his people. In turn, God's commands flow from his gifts of grace. And, as Genesis 2:17 makes clear, God's promises of blessing or curse are based on the keeping or breaking of his commands as they reflect the reality of God's provision. Adam and Eve therefore reflect the reality of the invisible God as those created in his image (Gen. 1:26a) as they exercise the dominion made possible by dependence on their sovereign Lord (Gen. 1:26b).

The fact that Adam and Eve exist in this relationship with God explains why, as those created in the image of God, they reflect this relationship in their 'marriage covenant' with one another.[53] In line with this, Abraham's 'deep

---

51. John H. Walton, *Genesis*, NIV Application Commentary (Grand Rapids: Zondervan, 2001), pp. 65, 136, 138.

52. So too, Goldsworthy, *Gospel and Kingdom*, p. 50.

53. For both Genesis 2:23–24 and Malachi 2:14 as references to marriage as a covenant, and its implications, see Hugenberger, *Marriage*, esp. pp. 152–165. See especially the parallels between the covenant-ratifying declaration formulae of 2 Sam. 5:1; 1 Chr. 11:1 and Gen. 2:23 (Hugenberger, p. 167). As Hugenberger, p. 202, points out, in Gen. 2:23 Adam is taking a covenant oath and speaking to God as his witness, not to Eve or himself. The meaning of the oath in Gen. 2:23 therefore is: 'I hereby invite you, God, to hold me accountable to treat this woman as part of my own body' (Hugenberger, p. 165). This is the biblical basis for Paul's

sleep' at the time of the covenant ceremony in Genesis 15:12 may recall Adam's 'deep sleep' at the time of his 'marriage' to Eve in Genesis 2:21.[54] God's subsequent relationship with Israel as his people, based on their 'creation' at the exodus, is also understood in terms of a marriage covenant (cf. Hos. 1 – 3 ; Isa. 43; 49; 51; 62; 63; 54:5–8; Jer. 2; 3:1–3; 30; Ezek. 16; 23). Israel's breaking of their marriage vows with one another, as well as their intermarriage with foreigners, can consequently be taken as an indication of their corresponding lack of covenant faithfulness to YHWH (Mal. 2:10–16; Prov. 2:17). The words of Malachi 2:10, 14–15 are therefore framed in the terms of the creation context and 'covenant' mandate of Genesis 2:24. Conversely, the church, brought about by the dawning of the new creation under the new covenant, is identified as the renewed 'bride' of Christ in fulfilment of the marriage mandate from Genesis 2:24 (Eph. 5:31–32). The use of the husband/wife analogy to describe the relationship between God and his people is unique to the Bible in the ancient world.[55] Moreover, this use of the marriage covenant as a way of explaining and evaluating the relationship between God and his people under both the old and new covenants supports the conclusion that God's solemn declaration of divine provision and corresponding command in Genesis 1:28–30 are best understood as delineations of the covenant relationship between God and humanity created from the beginning.

The example of Abraham

The life of Abraham is the patriarchal, and hence foundational, model of what it means to live in a covenant relationship with the 'God of our fathers' (Deut. 26:7; 1 Chr. 12:17; 20:6; Acts 3:13; 5:30; cf. Rom. 4; Gal. 3). In an act of undeserved mercy designed to redeem humanity after the judgment of the tower of Babel (Gen. 11:7–9), God appeared to Abraham when he was an idolater in Ur and called him to go to Canaan (Gen. 11:31–32; 15:7; Josh. 24:2–3; Acts 7:2). Once in Canaan, he would inherit the land and become the father of a great nation through whose blessings from God the other nations of the earth would be blessed (Gen. 12:1–3). Whereas fallen humanity had tried to make a

---

corresponding affirmation in Eph. 5:28 that 'husbands should love their wives as their own bodies. He who loves his wife loves himself.'

54. I owe this suggestion to Michael Dauphinais and Matthew Levering, *Holy People, Holy Land, A Theological Introduction to the Bible* (Grand Rapids: Brazos, 2005), p. 49.

55. Hugenberger, *Marriage*, p. 178.

'name' for itself with a city and the tower of Babel (Gen. 11:4), now God promises to make a 'great name' for Abraham (Gen. 12:2). But Abram stopped in Haran, halfway to the Promised Land of divine blessing (Gen. 11:31). In his continuing mercy, God therefore steps in once again to bring Abram to the final destination to which he had originally called him. In calling Abram a *second* time to go into Canaan (Gen. 12:1), God was following up on his prior act of having invaded Abram's life with yet another act of grace. As the apostle Paul would later put it, God's people can be sure that 'he who began a good work in you will bring it to completion', all the way to the day when Christ comes to judge the world (Phil. 1:6; see Deut. 31:6; Heb. 13:5). Abraham reaches the Promised Land not because of his great commitment to God, but because of God's great commitment to him (cf. Deut. 15:1–21; 17:1–21).

Clearly, then, the call of Abraham and the continuation of his covenant relationship with God are both acts of sovereign, unconditional election and grace. All we learn about Abraham while he was still in Mesopotamia is that he was a pagan who worshipped other gods (Josh. 24:2) and that, before he left for Haran, God himself brought Abram out of Ur (Gen. 15:7; Acts 7:2). God did not rescue Abram from idolatry because of who Abram was, but in spite of who Abram was! Apart from God's saving acts in his life, Abram would have remained an idol worshipper in Mesopotamia. And if God had not continued graciously to intervene in Abram's life, he would have died in Haran with his father, Terah (Gen. 11:32).

Abraham and Sarah subsequently learned to trust God's promises through the ups and downs of their lives, even the promise of a miracle son to come in their old age. Thus, when eventually called to sacrifice Isaac, Abraham's willingness to do so was not an irrational leap into the dark, but the only sensible response to the God who had invaded his life with his presence. By means of some 'theological arithmetic', Abraham surmised that if God himself called his own promises into question (cf. Gen. 17:16–19; 21:12), then God would have to raise Isaac from the dead in order to keep his covenant commitment (Gen. 22:1–6, 8; Heb. 11:19). For when Abraham named the place where he attempted to sacrifice Isaac 'The Lord will provide' (Gen. 22:14), he was declaring the fundamental promise of the covenant relationship.

On his part, Abraham's steps of faith-obedience throughout his life, brought about by God's transforming presence and circumstantial provisions (sometimes even miraculously so), fulfilled the covenant stipulations. Abraham's life illustrates that 'faith' is not 'believing the unbelievable', but trusting in God's word because of the track record of God's faithfulness. Moreover, such faith always 'goes public' in acts of obedience, since biblical faith is not mental assent to data from the past or a passive reception of the actions of others, but an active dependence on God for one's future. And to 'bank one's hope on the promises of God', rather than on one's own ability to provide for oneself, inevitably determines one's behaviour.[56]

An alleged 'faith' that does not express itself in obedience is, by definition, not a true faith (Jas 2:21–26; Heb. 11:17; Gal. 5:6). Abraham's faith is expressed in his actions, from his leaving Ur and Haran to his leaving his servants with wood and knife in hand. His binding Isaac and laying him on the altar, like Abraham's denying the birthright to Eleazar and Ishmael, indicates that, no matter what the consequences, God was to be taken at his word and obeyed. For this reason, Genesis 15:6 is not the initiation of Abraham's covenant relationship with God, nor the first time he has responded to God in faith – it is the summary statement of a principle that describes the pattern of Abraham's life ('Abraham . . . believed the LORD') and God's evaluation of it ('and he counted it to him as righteousness').[57] In the same way, God declares in Genesis 26:5 that he will keep his covenant promises to Abraham 'because Abraham obeyed my voice and kept my charge, my commandments, my statutes, and my laws'. This is no contradiction in terms; it merely reflects the organic unity of faith-obedience and the persevering character of genuine faith within the covenant relationship. And so the New Testament can speak by way of illustration of Abraham being justified at four (!) different times in his life: when he left Ur/Haran in Genesis 12:4 (Heb. 11:8), when he later trusted God for an heir instead of turning to Ishmael in Genesis 15 (Rom. 4:1–3), when he subsequently trusted God for an heir in his and Sarah's old age in Genesis 17 (Rom. 4:19), and when he offered Isaac upon the altar in Genesis 22 (Jas 2:21).

Accordingly, Paul recognizes that Abraham is the 'father' or patriarch of all those 'who also walk in the footsteps of the faith that our father Abraham had before he was circumcised' (Rom. 4:12). From beginning to end, it was Abraham's faith alone that constituted him 'righteous' in relationship to God, inasmuch as faith is the only right response to God's covenant provisions and promises (cf. Rom. 4:3, quoting Gen. 15:6).[58] No self-generated or 'natural'

---

56. I owe this definition of 'faith' and its organic expression in hope and obedience, which plays such an important role throughout this essay, to the programmatic study of the nature of biblical faith in Daniel P. Fuller, *The Unity of the Bible: Unfolding God's Plan for Humanity* (Grand Rapids: Zondervan, 1992), pp. 251–402.

57. So too, Dumbrell, *Covenant*, pp. 54–55, 64–65, 67–69.

58. Ibid., pp. 53–54; and Mark A. Seifrid, 'Paul's Use of Righteousness Language Against Its Hellenistic Background', in D. A. Carson, Peter T. O'Brien and Mark A.

human distinction or achievement (i.e., 'works') can constitute one just in God's sight (Rom. 4:4–5). God justifies the ungodly (Rom. 4:5). Not even circumcision, the old covenant mark of God's chosen people, justifies one in God's sight, since it is clearly 'the seal of the righteousness that [Abraham] had by faith while he was still uncircumcised' (Rom. 4:11). Anyone who 'shares the faith of Abraham', whether Jew or Gentile, therefore becomes part of the 'offspring' promised to Abraham by God's grace in Genesis 12:1–3 (Rom. 4:16).

The Sinai covenant

Israel's deliverance from slavery in Egypt extends the same covenant relationship to Israel as a people that was established at creation and re-established with Abraham. As part of the unbroken history of redemption, the Sinai covenant, like the Abrahamic covenant before it, 'must be part of God's purpose to make for himself a people on the basis of his grace'.[59] Hence, in explicit fulfilment of God's promises to Abraham (Exod. 2:23–25; 6:1–9), 'Sinai is dependent upon the covenant with Abraham and is an exposition of it.'[60] Like the call of Abraham, the exodus thus calls Israel as a nation to respond in trust-obedience to the God who saved her (see below). Rather than establishing a different covenant way of relating to God, 'Sinai fits into a God-Israel relationship in which obedience is already an integral component.'[61] This is confirmed by the fact that the covenant formula declared to Abraham in Genesis 17:7–8 as the purpose of God's covenant with him is repeated in Exodus 6:7 and Deuteronomy 7:6–8 as the purpose of the deliverance of Israel from Egypt.[62] Moreover, the covenant formula appears only twice as an explicit and direct

Seifrid (eds.), *Justification and Variegated Nomism, Vol. 2: The Paradoxes of Paul* (Grand Rapids: Baker, 2004), pp. 39–74, 60–61, who argues both linguistically and contextually that the 'reckoning of faith as righteousness' in Paul's use of Gen. 15:6 in Rom. 4:3–5 is not an acceptance of faith as something it is not, i.e., an 'imputation' ('as if it were righteousness'), but 'a recognition of faith for what it is' (p. 60).

59. Goldsworthy, *Gospel and Kingdom*, p. 61.

60. Ibid., p. 62.

61. Birch et al., *Theological Introduction*, p. 151, pointing to Exod. 15:26; 16:4; 19:5.

62. I owe this parallel to Rendtorff, *The Covenant Formula*, pp. 21, 23, 65: these texts provide 'the unfolding and continuing endorsement of the promise of the covenant given to Abraham' (p. 21).

explication of the term 'covenant', once at its first occurrence in Genesis 17:7 and then again at its last use in Deuteronomy 29:13, with the link between Abraham and Sinai in Exodus 6:7 functioning as the 'bridge' between them.[63]

In fulfilment of God's promises to Abraham, the delineation of the covenant itself in Exodus 19:3–6 and 20 – 24 thus becomes a foundational explication of the threefold covenant structure as applied to Israel's relationship with God. God's bearing Israel to himself 'on eagles' wings' (19:4) leads to the covenant stipulations in response, the doing of which will mean the inheritance of God's promise and the fulfilment of his purpose for the nation. In the words of Exodus 19:5–6,

> Now therefore, if you will indeed obey my voice and keep my covenant, you shall be my treasured possession among all peoples, for all the earth is mine; and you shall be to me a kingdom of priests and a holy nation.

This text and its context make clear that Israel's redemption is an extension of God's sovereign right as Creator and that the covenant stipulations are once again framed by God's provision in the past, his presence now (see Exod. 19:9; cf. 24:45) and his promises for the future.

The movement from the historical prologue of God's deliverance from Egypt and the presence of his glory to the corresponding covenant stipulations is recapitulated in the famous 'prologue' of Exodus 20:1–2 and the ten 'words' that follow. Here, too, the Exodus passage recalls the Abrahamic covenant, focusing on the revelation of God's glory and his deliverance from Ur that likewise grounded the covenant stipulations with Abraham (cf. Gen. 15:7 with Exod. 20:1–2). Understood covenantally, the commands of God merely apply his character, power and promises to specific situations. For, to quote Martens again, the historical prologue in Exodus 20:2 illustrates that

> the prior relationship which will form the framework for the law is the salvation by Yahweh of his people. The deliverance is the basis for obedience. The Ten Words are given to a people freed from bondage, and must be viewed in the context of redemption. The issue is not to establish a close relationship but rather to perpetuate it . . . It must not be thought that observance of the Ten Words is God's appointed way for humankind to establish acceptance with God. Far more does the covenant

---

63. Ibid., p. 69.

context invite us to consider the law as a way of expressing or maintaining the relationship that has already been established.[64]

We are not surprised, therefore, when this same historical prologue grounds not only the 'ten words', but also the 'book of the covenant' in Exodus 20 – 24 and the 'holiness code' summarized in Leviticus 11:1–47 and 26:1–46 (see Lev. 11:45; 26:13). Nor are we surprised to find the same covenant formula affirmed as the purpose of the covenant (see Lev. 11:44–45; 26:12). The three-fold covenant structure, based on God's redemption of Israel from slavery and the subsequent track record of his faithfulness in providing for his people in the wilderness, is then repeated throughout Deuteronomy's summary of Israel's covenant with the Lord.[65]

The historical development within the Bible does not proceed from a creation order with humanity based on obedience to a qualitatively different order with Abraham based on faith, only to return to an obedience-based relationship with Israel. Rather, God's original covenant relationship with humanity before the fall based on creation is re-established with both Abraham and Israel as an act of redemption. Theologically, and from the perspective of the Torah as a whole, God's relationship with humanity in the garden of Eden is therefore understood from the perspective of the covenant with Israel and vice versa, so that the Sabbath as the climax of creation is made the sign of the covenant with Israel (Exod. 20:8–11; 31:12–17). Deuteronomy's focus on Israel's covenant relationship with God, now carried on in terms of the Sinai covenant (Deut. 4:9–14, 23; 5:1–2), casts its interpretive shadow all the way back to creation (Deut. 4:32–33; 5:12–15 [in which the exodus replaces God's rest at creation as the foundation for keeping the Sabbath, cf. 5:12–13 with Exod. 20:8–11]; 32:6–8). Conversely, Deuteronomy also looks all the way forward to Israel's restoration after the exile (Deut.

---

64. Martens, *God's Design*, p. 79. For Martens' delineation of this same covenant structure in Joshua 24 and in the book of Deuteronomy, see pp. 79–83. In this light, Martens, p. 79, warns us about the wrong-headed, 'legalistic and harsh' connotation that the term 'commandment' carries in our culture. In view of the Old Testament designation of the 'Ten Commandments' as the ten 'words' (Exod. 20:1; 34:28; Deut. 10:4), Martens suggests that 'if Exodus 20 is viewed against the ancient Near Eastern covenant stereotype, the harsh color of "commandment" is quickly softened to "rightful response".'

65. See, e.g., Deut. 6:20–25; 7:2–9; 10:12 – 11:32; 13:5; 15:15; 23:14; 24:17–18; 26:5–11, 16–19; 27:9–10; 29:1–15; 30:15–20.

4:29–31; 30:1–10). Israel's relationship with God does not start with creation and move forward, but begins with Israel's own experience of God as King and Father at the exodus (Exod. 4:21–23; 13:14–16; 15:18), from which she learns that God is also the universal God of gods and Lord of lords (Deut. 10:17).[66]

As it was at creation, so too at Sinai, the sign of God's covenant promise to exercise his sovereignty on behalf of his people is once again the establishment of the Sabbath, since the Sabbath is God's declaration of the sufficiency of his provisions and of his ongoing commitment to meet the needs of his people (Exod. 31:16). Keeping the Sabbath is therefore a symbolic, public demonstration of one's dependence on God to lead, guide and provide for his people. Hence the practice of the Sabbath is instituted even before Israel reaches Sinai (Exod. 16:22–30), thereby indicating that the Sinai covenant itself is not the means of creating a relationship, but the ratification of a relationship already established. Beginning already with the manna in the wilderness, Israel's repeated failure to keep the Sabbath by not trusting in the Lord thus revealed her persistent, hardened heart of unbelief. Israel was different from the nations around her symbolically (she did not work on the Sabbath), but not really (she did not trust in YHWH, which the Sabbath was intended to symbolize). Indeed, Ezekiel declares that Israel broke the covenant by profaning the Sabbath in the wilderness before Sinai (Ezek. 20:13; cf. Exod. 16:27–30), after Sinai (Ezek. 20:16, 20–21), and during Israel's history in the land (Ezek. 22:8, 26; 23:38), the latter two of which lead to God's judgment in the exile (Ezek. 20:23–24; 24:1–14). In turn, Israel's future restoration will entail a return to a proper keeping of the Sabbath (Ezek. 44:24; 45:17; 46:3–4).

Jesus' declaration that as the Son of Man he is 'lord of the Sabbath' (Mark 2:28) is to be understood in this light. Through the forgiveness of sins (Mark 2:10), the circumstantial provision of what is needed for his disciples to follow him (Mark 2:25–26) and the showing of mercy (Mark 3:1–5), the Son of Man, like YHWH under the old covenant, is committed to meeting the needs of his people in accordance with his sovereignty. In turn, under the new covenant, God's people will respond in faith, thus truly keeping the Sabbath. As a result, the old covenant symbols become a matter of preference, but are no longer obligatory (Rom. 14:5–6; cf. this to circumcision as well in 1 Cor. 7:19 and to 'kosher' constraints in Rom. 14:2–6). The inauguration of this renewed 'Sabbath relationship' through the Messiah will one day be consummated in

---

66. See, too, Eichrodt, *Theology*, p. 33, following O. Procksch, for this important point.

the full Sabbath rest still to come for those who keep the new covenant through their dependence on God (Heb. 4:1–13). It is to this new covenant reality that we now turn our attention.

The 'new covenant'

The pivotal passage concerning the 'new covenant' is Jeremiah 31:31–34. My understanding of the argument of the text, with the explicit and implicit logic of its constituent propositions highlighted, runs as follows:

v. 31   'Behold, the days are coming,' declares the LORD, 'when I will make a new covenant with the house of Israel and with the house of Judah.

v. 32a   *Specifically,* I will not make it like the covenant which I made with their fathers. . .

v. 32b   *since* they broke this covenant of mine

v. 32c   *even though* I was a husband to them,' declares the LORD.

v. 33a   *'The reason the new covenant will be different in this regard is that* this is the covenant which I will make with the house of Israel after those days,' declares the LORD, 'I will put my Law within them, and I will write it on their heart.

v. 33b   *The result of this new covenant will be that* I will be their God, and they shall be my people.

v. 34a   *The ultimate consequence of this new covenant relationship in which I am their God and they are my people is that* they shall not teach again each man his neighbour and each man his brother saying, 'Know the LORD,'

v. 34b   *because* they shall all know me, from the least of them to the greatest of them,' declares the LORD.

v. 34c   *'The basis for all of this is that* I will forgive their iniquity, and I will remember their sin no more.'

The initial thing to note concerning the 'new covenant' promised in Jeremiah 31:31–34 is its need.[67] When he smashed the tablets of the covenant stipulations

---

67. For a fuller exposition of this summary, see my *Paul, Moses, and the History of Israel. The Letter/Spirit Contrast and the Argument from Scripture in 2 Corinthians 3*, WUNT 81 (Tübingen: J. C. B. Mohr [Paul Siebeck], 1995, and Paternoster, 2005), pp. 129–135. For a detailed study of the promise of the new covenant from Jer. 31:31–34 within its canonical context (and its relationship to Ezek. 11 and 36), in which it is maintained that this promise occupies the very centre of the Old Testament,

after Israel's idolatry with the golden calf, Moses demonstrated that the Sinai covenant had been broken from the beginning (Exod. 32:19). God delivered Israel as a people from slavery circumstantially, but she was largely still enslaved to sin; in a word, she remained 'stiff-necked' (Exod. 32:9; 33:3, 5; 34:9; Deut. 29:4), with an 'uncircumcised heart' (Deut. 10:6; Jer. 4:4; 9:25–26; Acts 7:51; cf. Ezek. 20). The history of Israel as a people under the Sinai covenant was consequently marked by faithlessness.[68] God therefore declared through Jeremiah that under the present covenant not even the intercession of Moses, not to mention Jeremiah himself, could avert God's wrath and the eventual judgment of the exile (Jer. 15:1; cf. 9:12–16; 11:14; 14:11; 26:8–11; 36:23–25, 31). For, as Jeremiah declares,

> From the day that your fathers came out of the land of Egypt to this day, I have persistently sent all my servants the prophets to them, day after day. Yet they did not listen to me or incline their ear, but stiffened their neck. They did worse than their fathers. (Jer. 7:25–26)

Despite the chance to repent offered to the nation (cf., e.g., Jer. 26:1–3; 36:1–3, 7; etc.), there was therefore no longer any hope for the people in their present condition. What was needed was nothing less than a new beginning, a 'new covenant', under which Israel would be decisively changed in her relationship

---

representing as it does the 'perspektivische Fluchtpunkt' (perspectival point of departure) for the Old Testament, see Christoph Levin, *Die Verheißung des neuen Bundes in ihrem theologiegeschichtlichen Zusammenhang ausgelegt*, FRLANT 137 (Göttingen: Vandenhoeck & Ruprecht, 1985). Levin's central thesis is that the promise of the new covenant combines with God's fundamental promise to Israel that 'I am the Lord, your God' to encompass all of the promises of the Old Testament (p. 12). Hence Levin concludes that the promise of the new covenant in Jer. 31 is not principally and qualitatively new in contrast to the past; rather, it is a renewal of God's intended relationship with Israel, which had been lost due to Israel's history of unfaithfulness (cf. pp. 138–141). The covenant promised in Jer. 31:31–34 is 'new' in the sense that it is a radical break with the past, but it is not new in its structure, content or purpose. In this latter case it is a 'renewal' (cf. pp. 140–141). These central points are fundamental to the position argued here.

68. For the motif of the 'stubbornness' of Israel's evil heart in relationship to the perpetual disobedience of the people, see Jer. 3:17; 7:24; 9:13; 13:10; 16:12; 17:23; 18:12; 19:15; 23:17. For the point that the covenant people and their leaders have continued to break the covenant, see Jer. 2:8; 5:31; 6:13, 17; 10:21; 14:18; 23:13–14; 27:16; 28:2; etc.

to God. Such a 'new' covenant would be the divine answer to the perennial problem of Israel's hard-hearted rebellion. Jeremiah 31:31–34 thus looks to a future in which Israel's present state of rebellion and 'stubbornness' will no longer undermine her covenantal relationship with God.

Second, Jeremiah 31:32–33 describes the nature of this 'new covenant' by contrasting it to the Mosaic/Sinai covenant made with the fathers at the exodus (cf. Jer. 11:1–6). This former covenant is rehearsed in Jer. 11:3–5, followed by the grim news that both the fathers 'when I brought them up out of the land of Egypt' (Jer. 11:7) and the Israel and Judah of Jeremiah's own day (Jer. 11:9–10; cf. 22:9–10) have broken this covenant 'in the stubbornness of [their] evil heart' (Jer. 11:8). They consequently stand under the wrath and judgment of God (Jer. 11:11). Hence the essential difference between the new covenant and the Sinai covenant is the fact that the new covenant will not be broken like the previous one. God, like a 'father', remained faithful to his covenant commitments in the old covenant; the people did not. In short, the new covenant, as an 'everlasting covenant that will never be forgotten' (Jer. 50:5; cf. 32:40), is a 'renewed' covenantal relationship.

The reason for this confidence concerning the new covenant is given in verse 33. Unlike the Sinai covenant, God declares that in this new covenant he will place his law 'within them' and 'write it on their heart'. Writing the law on their hearts is the reversal of the present situation, in which the sin of Judah is 'written with a pen of iron; with a point of diamond it is engraved on the tablet of their heart' (Jer. 17:1). In the context of Israel's stubborn rebellion from the exodus onwards, this can only mean that under the new covenant Israel's rebellious nature will be fundamentally transformed so that her hardened disobedience will be replaced with an obedience to God's covenant stipulations. The metaphor of the law written on the heart thus corresponds to the new covenant promise found in Ezekiel 11:19–20 and 36:26–27 of a new 'heart of flesh' and the pouring out of the Spirit, by which God will cause his people to obey his statutes. The law 'within' and 'written on the heart' are images for a people who accept God's law as their own and obey it willingly, rather than reject it as foreign or obey it only externally.[69]

---

69. On the theme of the law written on the heart, W. J. Dumbrell, *End of the Beginning: Revelation 21 – 22 and the Old Testament* (Grand Rapids: Baker, 1985), pp. 91–92, rightly points to Deut. 6:4–5; 10:16; 11:18 to show that the law was always intended to be in the heart, and to Ps. 40:8; Isa. 51:7 to show that doing the will of God depends on the placing of the law in the heart. Hence 'Jer. 31:33 may plausibly be viewed as simply saying Yahweh is returning to the idealism of the Sinai period in the New Covenant relationship' (p. 92).

As a result of keeping God's covenant stipulations, their relationship with YHWH will be maintained, rather than repeatedly broken.

The consequence of this 'new covenant', unlike that of Sinai, will be the realization of the relationship between God and his people promised to Abraham and initiated with Israel, once again summarized in the covenant formulary, 'I will be their God, and they shall be my people' (31:33b). This pledge picks up and underscores the covenant relationship of the Bible, occurring in various forms around twenty-five times in the Bible.[70] More important than its frequency is the fact that the covenant formula unpacks in summary form the covenant relationship ratified in the redemptive covenants of the Scriptures, from the covenant with Abraham (Gen. 17:7) to the Sinai covenant (e.g., Exod. 6:7; 29:45–46), and from the summaries of Deuteronomy (e.g., Deut. 4:20; 29:12–13) to the promise of the new covenant (Jer. 24:7; 31:33; 32:38–40; Ezek. 36:26–28; 37:26–28).

Here, too, we see the unity of the Bible. Jeremiah 31:31–34, like the Sinai covenant before it, equates the past establishment of the covenant relationship with its future realization after the exile; the former is restored in the latter. This equation is also prefigured in the past–future link regarding the covenant formula found between Exodus 29:45 and Leviticus 26:12 and between Leviticus 26:42 and 26:45. This correspondence reflects the fact that there is no difference in the covenant formula or its constituent structure when it is related to the patriarchs, exodus, Sinai or new covenant.[71] Indeed, the covenant formula of mutual, kinship-type belonging, 'God as the God of Israel and Israel as the people of God', occurs in only two basic contexts within the history of redemption: in the establishment of God's relationship with his people through Abraham and Sinai under the 'old covenant' and in the eschatological restoration of this relationship with Israel (and the nations) after the

---

70. Besides the texts listed here, Martens, *God's Design*, p. 72, points to Lev. 26:12; Deut. 26:16–19; Jer. 7:23; 11:4; 24:7; 30:22; 31:1; 32:38; Ezek. 11:20; 14:11; 36:28; 37:23. Cf. Rom. 9:25–26; 1 Pet. 2:9; Rev. 21:3.

71. Rendtorff, *The Covenant Formula*, pp. 80–81, quote from p. 83. Rendtorff argues that the same covenant relationship established with Abraham is called to remembrance and confirmed 'whenever new presuppositions or constellations arise' (p. 81). Thus in Exod. 6 the foundation laid with Abraham in Gen. 17 is extended to the people of Israel (p. 83) and to the nations in the new covenant. Therefore 'there can in fact really be no other further covenant', as reflected in the fact that the covenant is already called 'everlasting' at its foundation with Abraham in Gen. 17:7, 19 (p. 83). As its fulfilment, in Exod. 31:16 the Sinai covenant is also called 'everlasting'.

exile.[72] The first is based on the exodus from Egypt in fulfilment of the call of Abraham, in which God established his intention to dwell among his people, although this covenant was broken by all but a remnant. The second is based on the promised 'second-exodus' redemption of Israel from the exile, in which God will finally fulfil his purpose of dwelling with his people as a whole. Rendtorff therefore concludes that the covenant formula is used as the 'first and last cornerstones' of the Old Testament canon.[73]

The covenant formula makes explicit that within the covenant relationship, whether inaugurated or realized, God and his people belong to one another in mutual obligation. YHWH's declaration to be Israel's God underscores that he is committed to them in a way unlike his commitment to any other people (Gen. 15:1; Exod. 19:5–6; 33:13–16; Deut. 33:29). In turn, their identity as 'his people' points to the exclusivity with which they must trust in him for their future (Exod. 20:1–6; Deut. 6:4). And the two sides of this covenant relationship are inextricably related. For, as Martens concludes, 'In the demand which can be heard in the "my people" of the formula there shines through the initiative of God in taking for himself a people,' just as 'in the promise, "I will be your God" . . . there is implicit also the demand that Israel recognize no God but Yahweh.'[74] So at the same time that it brings forth God's demand, the covenant formula leaves no doubt that the obligation of being God's people is always grounded in God's prior acts of deliverance and redemption.

Third, the line of thought from Jeremiah 31:32–33 represents yet again the threefold structure of the covenant relationship. In the new covenant, as in the Sinai covenant before it, keeping the law, made possible by God's prior act of redemption (cf. Jer. 31:1–40), is what maintains the covenantal relationship between God and his people. Rather than suggesting that the law is somehow negated or reinterpreted within the new covenant, Jeremiah 31:31–33 emphasizes just the opposite. The law written on the heart is the Sinai law itself as

---

72. Cf. its use in regard to the Sinai covenant after the first exodus in Gen. 17:7–8; Exod. 6:7–8; 29:45–46; Lev. 26:11–12; Deut. 4:20; 7:6; 14:2 and in regard to the future eschatological restoration of Israel after the 'second exodus' from exile in Jer. 24:7; 31:31–34; 32:38–40; Ezek. 11:20; 34:24; 36:26–28; 37:21–28; Zech. 8:1–8. So Scott Hafemann, *Second Corinthians*, NIV Application Commentary (Grand Rapids: Zondervan, 2000), p. 284. This was first pointed out to me by James Scott, 'The Use of Scripture in 2 Corinthians 6:16c–18 and Paul's Restoration Theology', *JSNT* 56 (1994), pp. 73–99. See also Rendtorff, *The Covenant Formula*, pp. 89–90.

73. Rendtorff, *The Covenant Formula*, p. 89.

74. Martens, *God's Design*, p. 86.

the embodiment of the will of God. The contrast between the 'old' and new covenants is not a contrast between a covenant with and without an external law; nor is it a contrast between two different kinds of law. Rather, the contrast between the two covenants is a contrast between two different conditions of the people who are brought into these covenants and their correspondingly different responses to the same law. Furthermore, there is absolutely no synergism in the new covenant, as if our obedience were added to God's grace. The mutuality of the covenant relationship is not a partnership in which we add our willpower to God's grace. As the metaphor of the 'law written on the heart' in Jeremiah and its decoding in Ezekiel 11:19–20 and 36:26–27 indicate, the very ability to keep the covenant, like its establishment, is the direct and continuing result of God's transforming presence, manifested in his Spirit. The new heart granted by God is not an enablement for covenant-keeping. Instead, it is the cause of covenant-keeping.

Fourth, verse 34 states both the result and ground of this new covenant transformation of God's people. As a result of having God's law written on their hearts, the people of the new covenant will have no need to be taught to 'know' the Lord, since they will all know him. The transformed heart, which is essential to the new covenant, thus provides the conceptual transition from verse 33 to verse 34, since in Old Testament anthropology the 'heart' is not only the seat of volition and desire, but also the organ most often associated with the function of understanding and intellectual knowledge.[75] Under the new covenant there will no longer be any distinction within the covenant community between those who know and do not know the Lord, i.e., between those who do and do not have a transformed heart. By definition, all those who belong to the new covenant community will do so by virtue of their transformed heart.

Unlike the role played by the prophets and the other members of the remnant under the old covenant, in the new covenant community there will no longer be any need to admonish 'one's neighbour', that is to say, others

---

75. Hans Walter Wolff, *Anthropology of the Old Testament* (Philadelphia: Fortress, 1974), pp. 46–47, 51, pointing to Deut. 29:3; Prov. 15:14; and Ps. 90:12. It is thus significant that the use of the 'heart' occurs most often in the Wisdom literature (99 times in Proverbs; 42 times in Ecclesiastes), and second in the 'strongly didactic Deuteronomy' (51 times) (p. 47). As that which describes 'the seat and function of reason', the heart 'includes everything that we ascribe to the head and the brain – power of perception, reason, understanding, insight, consciousness, memory, knowledge, reflection, judgment, sense of direction, discernment' (p. 51).

within the covenant community, to enter into a covenant relationship with the Lord. The people of the new covenant, all of them, will stand in continuity with the faithful remnant of the old covenant. Those delivered from the penalty and power of sin by the death and resurrection of Christ and the pouring out of the Spirit will enter into the covenant relationship first established with the faithful remnant of Israel. In Romans 4:9–17, 23–25, Abraham is therefore the example of faith and the father of all who believe, while in 2 Corinthians 3:18 Moses' experience of the Lord in the tent of meeting is identified with the experience of all Christians. In Romans 11:1–6, the 7,000 who did not bow their knee to Baal are paralleled to the present-day remnant of believing Jews, and the long list of the faithful from the Old Testament in Hebrews 11 illustrates the definition of faith itself (cf. Heb. 11:1).

Fifth, the foundation of the new covenant is the fact that, despite her past sin, a new possibility for the forgiveness of Israel's iniquity will be opened up so that God will 'remember their sin no more' (v. 34). The changed condition of God's people, and their resultant obedience to the covenant, together with the promise that the covenant community will no longer be a mixed multitude of believers and unbelievers, are both based upon the divine forgiveness that makes the new covenant possible. Here, too, Jeremiah's promise of the forgiveness to come corresponds to the new covenant declarations in Ezekiel 36, this time to the promise that, as with the ritual cleansing of the priests under the old covenant, God will one day 'sprinkle clean water' on all his people so that they 'shall be clean from all [their] uncleannesses' (Ezek. 36:25).

Finally, the promise of the new covenant points to the first coming of the Messiah as the turning point of redemptive history. In fulfilment of this promise, he is the centre point of history. Without the life and death of the Christ, there would be no new covenant, nor would the remnant of believers under the old covenant have experienced the forgiveness of sins declared and symbolized in the old covenant sacrificial system. Planned by God before creation, but manifested in the midst of history, the cross of Christ is applied retroactively to the saints of the old covenant as well as proactively to those of the new as the sole foundation for the life of faith (Rom. 3:21–26; 1 Pet. 1:17–21; Heb. 10:1–22). The history of redemption therefore hinges on the inauguration of the new covenant through Christ's life, death and resurrection. As the corollary to the establishment of the new covenant, Jesus' enthronement as the messianic Son of God at his baptism not only identifies him with his people as they confess their sins, thus previewing the cross, but also inaugurates the kingdom of God, which is declared and demonstrated throughout his subsequent ministry (Mark 1:9–11, 14–15). Its consummation is then

foreshadowed at the transfiguration of Jesus as God's Son (Mark 9:7), proclaimed symbolically at his 'triumphal entry' into Jerusalem as the 'Son of
David' (Mark 11:1–10), effected by the death of the Son on the cross (Mark
15:39), and ratified by his resurrection and enthronement as the Son of God
at the right hand of the Father (Rom. 1:4).

Paul: an apostle of the new covenant

The apostle Paul joins the other apostles in his role as a messenger of the
redemption and the reality of the Spirit brought about by the Christ (1 Cor.
15:1–11). As such, in fulfilment of Jeremiah's promise, he understands
himself to be 'a minister of a new covenant' (2 Cor. 3:6; cf. 1 Cor. 11:23–26).
The context of this statement is instructive. Paul has just finished contrasting his ministry of the Spirit, who is at work in the heart of the Corinthians,
with the old covenant ministry of the 'writing' that took place on the stone
tablets of the law (2 Cor. 3:3; cf. Exod. 24:12; 31:18; 32:15; 34:1; Deut. 9:10).
In doing so, Paul pictured the Corinthians' new identity in Christ in terms of
the 'new covenant' imagery of Ezekiel 11:19 and 36:26–27: the Corinthians,
as Christ's 'letter', have been written not with 'ink', but with the Spirit, not on
tablets of 'stone', but on 'tablets of human hearts' (2 Cor. 3:3).[76] Under the
old covenant, the locus of God's activity was in the law; in the new age
promised by Ezekiel 36:25–27, God will be at work in human hearts by the
power of the Spirit. The Corinthians need look only at their own transformed lives for proof that the new age of the new covenant has dawned (cf.
Joel 2:28–29; Isa. 32:15; 44:3; 59:21; and the use of Jer. 31:31–34 in 2
Cor. 3:6).[77]

    If Moses is the 'law-giver' who mediates the Sinai covenant as a result of

---

76. In 2 Cor. 3:3c Paul establishes *two* contrasts, not one: a contrast between the two
    means of writing (human agency of ink versus the divine agency of the Spirit) and a
    contrast between the two *spheres* of the writing (the old covenant tablets of the law
    versus the new covenant 'tablets' of the human heart). This reading differs from
    the common attempt to read 3:3c as a single contrast between writing with ink on
    tablets of stone (!) and the Spirit's effect on the heart. To do so mixes Paul's
    metaphors to the point of self-destruction.

77. For a development of this argument in detail, see my *Suffering and Ministry in the
    Spirit. Paul's Defense of his Ministry in 2 Corinthians 2:14 – 3:3* (Grand Rapids: Eerdmans,
    1990; reprinted, Paternoster, 2000).

the exodus, Paul is the 'Spirit-giver' who mediates the new covenant as a result of the 'second exodus' that has come about through Christ. Like Moses, Paul is called to be mediator between God and his people. Unlike Moses, the essential content and context of Paul's ministry is not the law given to a hard-hearted people (2 Cor. 3:12–14), but the Spirit poured out to a forgiven people of transformed hearts (3:7–11). Whereas the law without the Spirit remains merely a 'letter' that kills, the power and presence of the Spirit 'gives life' by transforming God's people into his own image (2 Cor. 3:6, 7, 18).[78]

Paul's ministry of the Spirit in fulfilment of Jeremiah's promise (2 Cor. 3:8) leads him to allude to the call of Jeremiah himself in 2 Corinthians 10:8 and 13:10 in order to underscore his call to be a servant of the new covenant. In the former text, Paul tells the Corinthians that the Lord gave him apostolic authority 'for building you up and not for destroying you'. In the latter, Paul closes his letter by introducing a verbatim inclusio to 10:8 when he asserts that in confronting the rebellious in Corinth he is acting in accordance with the 'authority that the Lord has given me for building up and not for tearing down' (13:10). The reference to Jeremiah is clear. For, in calling Jeremiah, the Lord had declared,

> Behold, I have put my words in your mouth.
> See, I have set you this day over nations and over kingdoms,
> > to pluck up and to break down,
> > to destroy and to overthrow,
> > to build and to plant.
> > (Jer. 1:9b–10)[79]

Despite the positive and negative content of his call, due to Israel's covenant unfaithfulness Jeremiah's subsequent ministry was focused on the divine judgment to be meted out in Israel's exile.[80] Yet the promise of a new covenant was

---

78. For Paul's argument from the Old Testament in 2 Cor. 3:7–18, see my *Paul, Moses, and the History of Israel*, pp. 189–436.

79. Cf. Jer. 24:6; 38:27–28; 42[LXX 49]:10; 45[LXX 51]:4[34] for the continuation of this theme, and esp. LXX 38:27–28; 49:10; 51:4, where the related vocabulary of 'to tear down' and 'to build up' found in Paul is used.

80. As Stephen G. Dempster, *Dominion and Dynasty: A Theology of the Hebrew Bible* (Leicester: Apollos; Downers Grove: InterVarsity Press, 2003), p. 160, points out, 'This note of doom is sounded at the beginning of Jeremiah's call with four of the six verbs that describe his task as a prophet . . . "to uproot, to destroy, to tear

also intimated in Jeremiah's call (cf. 'to build and to plant'). In short, 'Looking back on the failure of the covenant at Sinai, which has led to the judgment of exile, Jeremiah announces a new covenant.'[81]

Paul's statement in 10:7–8 thus reflects his conviction that the new covenant restoration of God's people, announced by Jeremiah by way of prophetic sign (cf. his buying land during the Babylonian siege, Jer. 32:14–27), has now taken an eschatological step forward, including its extension to the nations, as in Corinth. Paul's role as a 'servant' of the new covenant, detailed in 2 Corinthians 3:4–18, is now explicitly tied to Jeremiah's role as a prophet of the new covenant. In 2 Corinthians 2:16 – 3:18, Paul argued that he was called like Moses, but with a distinctively different ministry from that of Moses. So, too, Paul argues in 10:7–8 that he was also called like Jeremiah, but with the distinctively different ministry to come that Jeremiah himself had announced. In this way, both the law and the prophets find their goal in Paul's ministry, made possible by the inauguration of the new covenant brought about by the coming of the Messiah.

This is why Paul's role as a minister of the new covenant is to mediate the Spirit, since Paul's primary purpose as Christ's apostle is salvation, not judgment (cf. 1:11, 23–24; 2:3; 3:6–11, 17–18; 4:6, 13–15; 5:13–15; 6:2). Although Jeremiah and Paul were called both to save and to judge, the accents of their respective ministries have been reversed. Jeremiah anticipates this 'role reversal' when he introduces the promise of the new covenant in 31:27–28 as follows:

> Behold, the days are coming, declares the LORD, when I will sow the house of Israel and the house of Judah with the seed of man and the seed of beast. And it shall come to pass that as I have watched over them to pluck up and break down, to overthrow, destroy, and bring harm, so I will watch over them to build and to plant, declares the LORD.

> down, and to smash . . . (1:10)" . . . Jeremiah, whose call resembles those of Moses and Samuel, had a mission that was largely negative . . . The prophetic task of destruction constitutes the main theme of Jeremiah's activity. It was a wrecking ministry, a ministry of demolition. . .' In fact, God's uprooting of what he had planted in Judah, now beginning to take place through his prophet, functions in Jer. 45:4–5 as an introduction to the oracles against the *nations* in chapters 46 – 51. Thus, 'this judgment of Judah, expressed in tearing down and uprooting, has been a prelude to *universal* judgment' (Dempster, p. 163, emphasis mine).

81. Ibid., p. 159. Cf., too, Jer. 24:6–7; LXX Jer. 38:27–28; 49:10.

Given the new covenant context and content of Paul's ministry, it is only natural, then, that the Jeremiah theme of 'building up' becomes a common description of Paul's call to plant churches and to strengthen the faith of believers (cf. 2 Cor. 3:9–10, 12, 14; 8:1; 14:3, 5, 12, 26; Rom. 14:19; 15:2, 20; 1 Thess. 5:11). The establishment of Israel and the intended restoration of the nations, both 'torn down' under God's judgment in the exile, are now being 'built up' as a result of the divine 'yes' to God's promises in Christ (2 Cor. 1:20). It is of note, however, that whereas Paul adopts Jeremiah's language of building up Israel and restoring the temple and applies them both to the church in Corinth, he does not pick up the language of God once again planting Israel in the land after the exile, although this too is inextricably linked to the new covenant promise of Jeremiah 31:31–34 (cf. Jer. 31:1–26; 31:38–40; 32:36–44). This may reflect Paul's conviction that the church is not yet the consummation of the new covenant promises. The coming of the Christ and Paul's ministry as his apostle are not the 'climax of the covenant',[82] but its penultimate anteclimax. The kingdom will be consummated only when the Christ returns.

The church as the family of the new covenant

As the corollary of his self-understanding, in 2 Corinthians 6:14 – 7:1 Paul addresses the church in Corinth as the 'family of God' (kinship) living between the first and second comings of the Messiah (kingship).[83] At the heart of this

---

82. Contra one of the central points of N. T. Wright's programmatic works; see my review of his *The New Testament and the People of God* (Minneapolis: Fortress, 1992) in *JETS* 40 (1997), pp. 305–308.

83. This paragraph and the next are taken in large measure from my *Second Corinthians*, pp. 279–289. The reality of the church as the 'children of God' is a common theme in the New Testament. Cf. Mark 3:33–35; 10:30; John 1:12; 11:52; 1 John 3:1–2, 10; Rom. 8:14–19, 21; Eph. 5:1; Phil. 2:15; Heb. 2:10–11; 12:7–10; Jas 1:2, 16–19; 4:11; 5:7; 1 Pet. 1:17; 2 Pet. 1:10; etc. The corollaries to this conception are, on the one hand, the 19 explicit references to 'God the Father' in the New Testament and the 12 uses of 'God and Father', and, on the other hand, the pervasive theme of the mutual love that members of God's people are to have for one another. In our present passage, Paul links the concept of the church as God's 'children' with their identity as 'the temple of the living God' (6:16) due to their reception of the Holy Spirit (2 Cor. 3:3; cf. 2 Cor. 3:16; 6:19). For the development of the temple motif throughout biblical theology, see G. K. Beale, *The Temple and*

understanding, therefore, is the covenant relationship that exists between God and his people. In line with this, in 2 Corinthians 6:16 Paul applies the covenant formula from Leviticus 26:11–12 to the church in Corinth. Now, however, Paul formulates it in the third person ('I will make my dwelling among them and walk among them, and I will be their God, and they shall be my people'), rather than the second, as in the original text ('I will make my dwelling among you . . . and will be your God. . .'). This alternation is not Paul's own doing, but derives from his conflation of Leviticus 26:11–12 with the new covenant promise of Ezekiel 37:27 ('My dwelling place shall be with them. . .').[84] By interpreting Leviticus 26:11–12 in terms of Ezekiel 37:27, Paul is reflecting his conviction that the original covenant promises and the expectation of Israel's restoration after the judgment of the exile are continuing to be fulfilled in the Corinthian church! Moreover, in combining these texts Paul brings the law and the prophets together to make his point, unified as promise and fulfilment. Thus, 'Paul's conflation of Leviticus 26:11–12 and Ezekiel 37:27 intentionally reflects this correspondence between the Sinai covenant of the first exodus and the new covenant of the "second".'[85]

In 2 Corinthians 6:17–18 Paul draws the scriptural conclusion (note the 'therefore' [*dio*] of 17a) that flows from a covenant relationship with God: three commands from Isaiah 52:11 ('go out . . . be separate . . . touch no unclean thing') and three ensuing promises from Ezekiel 20:34 (LXX), 2 Samuel 7:14 and Isaiah 43:6 ('then I will welcome you, and I will be a father to you, and you shall be sons and daughters to me'). Paul's application of these commands to the Corinthians again demonstrates that he sees the beginning fulfilment of the promised restoration of God's people already taking place in the establishment of the Corinthian church. If the Corinthians are part of God's new covenant people, then they too, like Israel, must separate from unbelievers (now, however, within the church). The 'covenant prologue' of their

---

  the Church's Mission: A Biblical Theology of the Dwelling Place of God (Leicester: Apollos; Downers Grove: InterVarsity Press, 2004).

84. I owe this insight to James Scott, 'The Use of Scripture', p. 82. As he points out, the conflation of these two texts is confirmed by the Septuagint rendering of Lev. 26:11, which reads 'covenant' where the Hebrew text says 'dwelling'. Moreover, Scott, p. 82, points out that Lev. 26:12 is often used in Jewish tradition typologically in the context of the return from exile and the restoration of the broken covenant (cf. Jubilees 1:17, which combines Lev. 26:12 with Zech. 8:8 to refer to the new covenant).

85. Hafemann, *Second Corinthians*, p. 284.

redemption in Christ, by which they have become the 'temple of God's Spirit' (6:16b; 7:1a), leads inextricably to the corresponding 'covenant stipulations' of purity (6:14–16a; 7:1b).

In accordance with the covenant structure, the threefold commands of 6:17abc lead directly to the threefold promises of 17d–18, which are also a conflation of Old Testament texts.[86] In its original context, Ezekiel 20:34 is God's promise of welcome to those who will return home from the exile after their 'second exodus' deliverance.[87] If Isaiah 52:11 calls God's people to 'come out' from the world, then Ezekiel 20:34 indicates that God will 'welcome them in' when they do so. Its combination with the promise of a Davidic Messiah from 2 Samuel 7:14 points to the Jewish expectation that this restoration from exile would take place through and under the reign of David's long-promised 'son'.

Knowing that the Messiah would bring about this 'second exodus' deliverance of God's people, Paul goes on in 6:18 to quote the adoption formula from 2 Samuel 7:14. But he now makes it plural ('sons') in accordance with the previous texts and combines it with the reference to 'daughters' from Isaiah 43:6 (cf. 49:22; 60:4), where Israel's 'second exodus' restoration is expressed in terms of the rescue of 'sons and daughters'. As a result of this collage of texts, God's promise to become the 'father' of David's 'son', who came to be seen as the Messiah, is expanded to include all of God's people as his 'sons and daughters'.[88] Here, too, Paul is thinking covenantally. Scott has shown that the statement 'I will be a father to you, and you shall be sons and daughters to me' is an 'adoption' formula that is specifically used in Scripture to indicate the covenant relationship between God and his people.[89] In

---

86. As Scott, 'Use of Scripture,' p. 86, points out, this becomes evident in the Greek text, where Paul's use of the crasis-form 'and I' (*kagō*) in v. 17d is best understood to be the combination of the 'and' (*kai*) from Ezek. 20:34b (LXX) and the 'I' (*egō*) of 2 Sam. 7:14a (LXX).

87. For the use of the verb 'to welcome' as a promise of deliverance from exile, see Hos. 8:10; Mic. 4:6; Zeph. 3:19, 20; Zech. 10:8, 10; Jer. 23:3; Ezek. 11:17; 20:34; 22:19, as adduced by Scott, 'Use of Scripture', p. 85 n. 51.

88. Ibid., p. 88.

89. Ibid., pp. 87–88, where he points out that the *adoption* formula in 2 Sam. 7:14 corresponds to the *covenant* formula used in 2 Sam. 7:24, and that Jer. 31:1 (*covenant* formula) corresponds to 31:9 (*adoption* formula). So, too, Jubilees 1:24 applies the *adoption* formula of 2 Sam. 7:14 to the Israel of the return from exile as an extension of the *covenant* formula used in Jubilees 1:17. Cf. the use of 2 Sam. 7:14 in

fulfilment of this covenant relationship, established by Jesus as the messianic 'Son' of God, the Corinthians are promised that they too, as God's 'sons and daughters', will participate in the consummation of God's salvation (for the corresponding use of the concept of 'adoption' [*huiothesia*], cf. Rom. 8:15, 23; 9:4; Gal. 4:4–5; Eph. 1:5). The church can therefore be regarded as the 'family' of God, brothers and sisters 'in Christ'. Once again, kingship and kinship are united.

Paul's point is as clear as it is stark. Since the Corinthians are now God's new covenant people in fulfilment of the prophets' hopes (vv. 16c–16e), they must separate from the unbelievers among them (17a–c) in order to continue within the covenant as God's 'sons and daughters' in anticipation of God's future deliverance. This call to purity is necessitated by the fact that the kingdom is here, but not yet here in all its fullness. Hence 2 Corinthians 6:16c–18 reflects the same covenant structure and 'already but not yet' eschatological tension that is characteristic of the Bible as a whole.[90]

Conclusion: the new covenant 'sermon' of 2 Peter 1:3–11

Our survey has shown that the covenant relationship at the heart of the Bible is expressed not only in explicit references to the covenant and its covenant formula, but also in the mode of argumentation found throughout the Scriptures. To illustrate this point, we conclude by looking at a delineation of the threefold covenant relationship from the end of the canon as found in 2 Peter 1:3–11.

The key to this passage is the role of verses 3–4 in relationship to what follows. Although there is a long commentary tradition which considers verses 3–4 to be part of the opening greeting in verse 2, it seems more appropriate to take these two verses to be the opening of the body of the letter, as reflected

---

the Qumran text 4QFlor. 1:11–13, where it refers to the Davidic Messiah, and T. Jud. 24:1–3, where the adoption formula is applied to both the Davidic Messiah and the eschatological people of God. In the New Testament, cf. too Rev. 21:3 (*covenant* formula) with Rev. 21:7 (*adoption* formula); and John 20:17.

90. For the working out of the basic biblical structure of promise – inaugurated fulfilment/promise – consummation in relationship to every major biblical theme, in which the inaugurated fulfilment of the Old Testament promises in the New Testament become themselves promises to be fulfilled with Christ's return, see the encyclopedic work of Scobie, *The Ways of Our God*.

in the punctuation of the Nestle Aland[27] text. Though not unattested in later Christian literature,[91] such a lengthy expansion of the greeting is rare in ancient letters and would be unique among the New Testament epistles. It would also be highly unusual both theologically and rhetorically to begin the body of a letter with the inference and imperatives of verses 5a–7b without the prior indicative to support them that verses 3–4 provide. To do so in this case would subvert the crucial theological structure of the text in which, as in the rest of the Bible, the imperatives never precede the indicative realities upon which they are based and from which they organically derive. Moreover, 1:3 is a genitive absolute construction, the regular placement of which is before the main clause that it modifies,[92] thereby also indicating its forward-looking relationship to verse 5a. As attested in the papyri, such genitive absolutes 'may often be seen forming a string of statements, without a finite verb for several lines', just as we find here.[93] As Bauckham rightly observes, 'The connection with v. 2 is largely stylistic, whereas the connection with vv. 5–7 is fundamental to the flow of argument.'[94]

This decision is confirmed by the threefold covenantal structure that emerges once verses 3–4 are aligned with verses 5–11. It is not surprising that this structure is found in 2 Peter 1:3–11, since scholars have pointed out that this Old Testament covenant structure became the basis for a standard homiletic pattern in early Jewish and Christian literature.[95] The argument of 2 Peter 1:3–11 thus runs as follows:

---

91. See Ignatius, *Eph.* 1:1; *Rom.* 1:1; *Smyrn.* 1:1.

92. So Nigel Turner, *Syntax*, Vol. III of *A Grammar of New Testament Greek*, ed. J. H. Moulton (Edinburgh: T. & T. Clark, 1963), p. 322. For further substantiation of this point, see Richard J. Bauckham, *Jude, 2 Peter*, WBC 50 (Waco: Word, 1983), p. 174.

93. Quoted from Moulton as found in A. T. Robertson, *A Grammar of the Greek New Testament in the Light of Historical Research* (Nashville: Broadman, 1934), p. 513. Robertson himself points out that such strings of phrases are less common in the New Testament. This is evidence of the elevated style of 2 Peter.

94. Bauckham, *Jude, 2 Peter*, p. 173.

95. Cf., ibid., p. 173, where Bauckham recognizes that vv. 3–11 'appear to follow' this pattern and points to the work of K. Baltzer, *The Covenant Formulary* (Baltzer: Oxford University Press, 1971), as support for its Old Testament backdrop and to that of K. P. Donfried, *The Setting of Second Clement in Early Christianity*, NovTSup 38 (Leiden: E. J. Brill, 1974), for its development in the early church. Bauckham himself does not develop this insight further.

1. The Historical Prologue (vv. 3–4);
2. The Covenant Stipulations (vv. 5–7, 10a);
3. The Covenant Promises and Curses (vv. 8–9, 10bc–11).

This covenant structure also explains how the promises that accompany an entrance into the eternal kingdom of God in verses 4 and 11 can be conditional, based on doing the commands of verses 5–7, while at the same time being expressions of grace, having been granted in accordance with one's calling and election as declared in verses 3 and 10. On the one hand, both the stipulations and the promises of God are grounded in the prior act of God's (or perhaps Christ's) calling and made possible by his presence and power as described in verses 3–4: 'His divine power has granted to us all things that pertain to life and godliness. . .' This 'historical prologue' precedes and supports the covenant stipulations and its promises. Hence the acts of divine deliverance, the fulfilment of the ensuing commands and the reception of God's promises are all expressions of God's sovereign grace and election. On the other hand, inasmuch as the focus of these stipulations is on the still unfulfilled promises of God, the promises remain conditional. One must maintain the covenant relationship with God by keeping his stipulations in order to inherit his promises.

The covenantal structure of this passage indicates that salvation is wholly dependent upon the grace of God's calling and election as its only sufficient condition, while at the same time being dependent on the response of those who have been called as its necessary condition. However, since the fulfilment of the covenant stipulations and inheritance of the promises are both made possible by God's saving activity, past, present and future, the conditional nature of the promises of God cannot be perverted into a 'covenant of partners' in which obedience to the covenant stipulations becomes an independent basis for inheriting God's promises. This would be to add the covenant stipulations to the historical prologue in some kind of functional equivalence. Nor can the obedience described in verses 5–7 be viewed as our contribution to the process in a divine-human synergism.[96] God's grace and calling do not enable

---

96. In commenting on v. 5, it is therefore important not to speak of the believer's diligence 'as something brought in alongside of what God has already done (vv. 3–4)', or to conclude that 'the Christian must engage in this sort of *cooperation* with God in the production of a Christian life which is a credit to Him', as is often done (quotes from D. Edmond Hiebert, 'The Necessary Growth in the Christian Life: An Exposition of 2 Peter 1:5–11', *BSac* 141 [1984], pp. 44, 45, quoting

obedience. Rather, they bring it about. Obedience to the covenant stipulations is the inextricable expression of the calling and election of God in the lives of his people. The indicatives of the historical prologue (vv. 3–4) thus lead by nature to the imperatives of the covenant stipulations (vv. 5–7), which in turn lead to the indicative promises of future blessing or curse (vv. 8–11).

In accordance with its covenant structure, the explicit purpose of 2 Peter 1:3–11 is to summarize the covenant relationship that exists in Christ between God and his people in order that it might be continually 'remembered', even after Peter's death (2 Pet. 1:12–15). Indeed, this call to 'remember' Peter's teaching is itself a distinctly covenant act (cf. the inference in 1:12a and Num. 15:39; Deut. 8:2; 15:15; 24:18; etc.). The writing and reading of Peter's letter is therefore in keeping with the Old Testament provisions concerning the necessity of preserving the covenant and its stipulations for future generations. It is this necessity of 'remembering' the covenant that leads Peter to write his 'testament' as an epistle to his churches in order to call them to faithful endurance as they await 'the coming of the day of God' (2 Pet. 3:12). Such 'remembering' links Peter's readers to the faithful covenant partners found throughout the Bible.

Michael Green as well; emphasis mine). Nor should one conclude, as does Frederick W. Danker, '2 Peter 1: A Solemn Decree', *CBQ* 40 (1978), pp. 64–82, that the letter 'establishes a dynamic reciprocity between three benefactor-entities: Peter, representative of apostolic tradition, the writer's community, and Jesus Christ' (p. 80). Rather than possessing 'a partnership in benefaction' or exercising 'reciprocity between Benefactor and Recipients' (p. 81), the covenant structure indicates that the benefaction in view in vv. 1–11 is completely one-sided, with God's people in total dependence upon him as recipients. There is no doubt that this section reflects a solemn tone also found in imperial decrees; but this merely reflects the subject matter common to both, i.e., a 'solemn call to faithful allegiance to One whom the Christian community would recognize as the greatest Benefactor of the ages' (p. 65).

2. THE COMMANDS OF GOD

Thomas R. Schreiner

Introduction

In this essay the theology of law (*tôrâ* and *nomos*) in the Scriptures will be presented, but I shall particularly focus on the law in terms of the role of God's commands in the life of the covenant people, since that is the way the term 'law' is most often used in the Scriptures. The word 'Torah' (*tôrâ*) may designate instruction in general (e.g., Ps. 78:1; Prov. 1:8; 3:1), instruction that likely comes from the Pentateuch (e.g., Mal. 2:6–8), or the book of the law attributed to Moses (2 Kgs 22:8; cf. Josh. 23:6), which may refer to Deuteronomy, or to the Pentateuch more widely.

In the majority of instances the Torah refers to what the Lord commanded Israel to do. Thus the focus is on what the law commanded, although we should immediately add that the law is the gift of the covenant Lord and hence should be viewed within the covenant relationship as a gift rather than a burden. The emphasis on doing what the Torah commands is evident, for the word 'Torah' is often linked with doing the statutes, commands and judgments God prescribed (e.g., Gen. 26:5; Deut. 4:8; 17:19; 30:10; 1 Kgs 2:3; 2 Kgs 17:13; 2 Chr. 19:10; Ezra 7:10; Neh. 9:14; 10:29; Jer. 44:10; Amos 2:4; Mal. 4:4). The emphasis on the commands of the law is also evident in the verbs that are used with 'Torah': walking in the law (e.g., Exod. 16:4; Josh. 22:5; 2 Chr. 6:16; Pss. 78:10; 119:1; Jer. 26:4; 32:23); keeping the law (e.g., Josh. 23:6; 1 Chr. 22:12; Ps. 119:44); doing the law (e.g., Deut. 27:26; 28:58; 29:29; 31:12; Josh. 1:7; 23:6; 2 Kgs 17:37; 2 Chr. 33:8); obeying the law (Isa. 42:24; cf. Ezra 7:26); transgressing the law (Dan. 9:11). Further, there are numerous cases where the law refers to cultic practices that are to be carried out (e.g., Lev. 6:9, 14, 25; 7:1, 7, 11; Num. 6:13; 19:14).

As such, the prescriptions of the law, individually and taken as a whole, constitute the covenantal demands for Israel. When Israel entered into covenant with the Lord, as the covenant Lord he demanded that they keep his law (Exod. 19:5, 8). Hence the law and the Sinai covenant are closely related in the Old Testament, since the Mosaic law constitutes the requirements of the suzerain Lord in the Sinai covenant (cf. Deut. 29:21). The cursings of the covenant stem from a failure to keep the law specified by the covenant (Lev. 26; Deut. 26 – 28), while at the same time Israel will be blessed for keeping the law.

The same pattern is evident in the New Testament. The word 'law' (*nomos*) may refer to the Pentateuch, as in the phrase 'the law and the prophets' (e.g., Matt. 5:17; 7:12; 22:40; Luke 16:16; John 1:45; Acts 28:23; Rom. 3:21), and related thereto to what is written in the law (Luke 10:26; John 10:34; 12:34; 1 Cor. 9:8; 14:34; Gal. 4:21[1]), so that the term virtually has the meaning 'Scripture' in these instances. Many scholars believe that in some texts Paul also uses the word 'law' to refer to a principle, rule or order in general (e.g., Rom. 3:27; 7:21, 23, 25; 8:2), although this is vigorously disputed.[2] Most often, Paul uses the term *nomos* to refer to the Mosaic law, and he especially uses the term with reference to the commands of the law.[3] For instance, Paul emphasizes

---

1. The second use in this text.

2. In support of a reference to the Mosaic law, see Peter Stuhlmacher, *Paul's Letter to the Romans: A Commentary* (Louisville: Westminster/John Knox, 1994), pp. 66–67; C. T. Rhyne, *Faith Establishes the Law*, SBLDS 55 (Chico: Scholars, 1981), pp. 67–70. Supporting a reference to a principle or a norm are Heikki Räisänen, *The Torah and Christ: Essays in German and English on the Problem of the Law in Early Christianity*, ed. A.–M. Enroth (Helsinki: Finnish Exegetical Society, 1982), pp. 48–94; Douglas J. Moo, *Romans 1 – 8*, WEC (Chicago: Moody, 1991), pp. 251–253.

3. The words 'Torah' in the Old Testament and 'law' in the New Testament are used primarily in contexts in which God's people are called upon to 'do' what the law enjoins. For this view, see Stephen Westerholm, *Perspectives Old and New on Paul: The 'Lutheran' Paul and His Critics* (Grand Rapids: Eerdmans, 2004), pp. 297–340. The emphasis on 'doing' in the law does not necessarily indicate legalism or a negative view of the law, for the parenesis in the epistles (and elsewhere in the Scriptures) demonstrates that God's people are to live new lives as a consequence of God's saving grace.

that the law must be obeyed (Rom. 2:13, 25–26; 8:4; 13:8–10; Gal. 5:14). In the same way, Paul regularly links the law with disobedience, showing that human beings have failed to do what the law prescribed (e.g., Rom. 2:12, 23, 25, 27; 3:20–21, 28; 4:15; 5:20; 7:5, 7–9; 1 Cor. 15:56; Gal. 2:16, 19; 3:10; 5:3). Since Paul's view of the law is especially prominent in the New Testament, his use of the term takes on particular importance.

Given the usage of the term 'law' in both the Old Testament and the New Testament, where the emphasis lies particularly on doing or keeping the law (especially for those in a covenant relationship with the Lord), it seems justified when speaking of the theology of the law in the Scriptures to focus particularly on what the law commanded. Moreover, we should note that in most instances in the New Testament the law refers specifically to what is demanded in the Mosaic covenant. Therefore, New Testament authors move rather easily from speaking of the law to covenant (e.g., Gal. 3:10–18; Heb. 7 – 10), since the former is contained in the latter.

Creation to Abraham

The term 'Torah' does not occur in the creation account, but God commanded Adam and Eve to refrain from eating the fruit of the tree of the knowledge of good and evil (Gen. 2:16–17; 3:2–3).[4] The command is rooted in the context of God's provisions at creation as an expression of his relationship with Adam and Eve, showing that God's commands are for the good of human beings and are an expression of his love. God had created a world that was exceedingly good (Gen. 1:31), planted a garden in Eden, breathed life into Adam and Eve, and situated them in this delightful paradise. The prohibition must not, therefore, be construed as an abstract negative, so that we think of it primarily as what God denied Adam and Eve. Such a perspective reflects the view of the serpent (Gen. 3:1), who focuses on restrictions when addressing Eve and also promises them that they will be like God if they partake (Gen. 3:5). Instead, the prohibition must be interpreted in the light of God's lavish and beneficent care bestowed on Adam and Eve. When Adam and Eve received the command, they had every reason

---

4. Stephen G. Dempster remarks that the prohibition given to Adam and Eve 'can be seen in some ways as an encapsulation of the commandments given later at Sinai' (*Dominion and Dynasty: A Theology of the Hebrew Bible* [Leicester: Apollos; Downers Grove: InterVarsity Press, 2003], p. 63).

from their experience of God's goodness to believe that God intended the command for their good.

One of the key points of biblical theology with respect to the law thus surfaces in the temptation and fall of Adam and Eve. Eve transgressed God's command because she doubted God's goodness and believed that the forbidden fruit was in fact nourishing, beautiful and the path to wisdom (Gen. 3:6). Both she and Adam fell prey to idolatry in the desire to be like God, deciding for themselves what was 'good and evil' (Gen. 3:5), and thereby worshipped the creature rather than the Creator (cf. Rom. 1:18–25). Scholars debate the meaning of the phrase 'knowledge of good and evil'. Elsewhere in the Bible the knowledge of good and evil is possessed by God (Gen. 3:22), by angels (2 Sam. 14:17), and is given to Solomon in answer to prayer (1 Kgs 3:9). But young children and the old do not have it (Deut. 1:39; Isa. 7:15; 2 Sam. 19:35).[5] It seems to follow that Adam and Eve were jettisoning childlike dependence upon God by tasting the prohibited fruit. The crucial point for biblical theology is that disobedience to God flows from failure to trust God. All obedience flows from trusting God (Rom. 1:5; 16:26), and conversely 'whatever does not proceed from faith is sin' (Rom. 14:23). Adam and Eve transgressed God's command because they believed they would find happiness independently of God's wisdom expressed in his commands; as creatures they therefore displaced the Creator.

Another theme relative to the law can also be traced to the sin in the garden. Scholars continue to debate whether Paul himself, Israel, or Adam is the subject of the narrative in Romans 7:7–11. Even if Paul refers to himself, his experience with the law mirrors the experience of Israel and in turn Adam.[6] This explains why the language of Romans 7:7–11 fits remarkably well with Adam's sin in the garden. Hence it may cast light on the prohibition against eating from the tree of the knowledge of good and evil.

If it were not for law, Paul says – and he must have in mind the prescriptions of the law (i.e., what the law forbids and enjoins) – sin would not be experienced as rebellion (Rom. 7:7). Paul adduces as evidence the specific

---

5. So Daniel P. Fuller, *The Unity of the Bible: Unfolding God's Plan for Humanity* (Grand Rapids: Zondervan, 1992), pp. 182–183. It seems that the old do not have such knowledge since senility is setting in, so they revert in a sense to being children.

6. I am still persuaded that Paul himself is primarily in view, although a remarkably good case can be made for a reference to Adam. For a discussion of these verses, see Thomas R. Schreiner, *Romans*, BECNT (Grand Rapids: Baker, 1998), pp. 356–370.

injunction against coveting. This command brings to consciousness the fact that certain desires are forbidden, just as the injunction against eating from the prohibited tree raises a standard unknown previously. Sinful desires, however, cannot be assigned to the law which exposes sin as sin, as if the law of God bears responsibility for human evil itself. Paul insists that God's command is holy, righteous and good (Rom. 7:12). God does not give any injunctions contrary to his character or out of malice to human beings.

Paul explains that God's commands provided the bridgehead for sin, so that the desire for sin was precipitated by the commands given (Rom. 7:8). Sin is therefore unmasked as rebellion against God. So verse 9 sums up the life of Adam (and Paul) in a remarkable way. He was alive before the prohibition arrived. With the advent of the prohibition, sin sprang to life, Adam (and Paul) transgressed God's command, and he died.

Paul's reflection on sin and coveting yields two insights that are important for a biblical theology of law. First, sin is not merely the transgression of the law, although it surely includes such transgression (1 John 3:4). It arises from a desire to contravene God's law as an expression of his wise sovereignty over his creation, and hence sin is revealed to be rebellion. In other words, coveting, as Paul informs us elsewhere, is idolatry (Eph. 5:5; Col. 3:5). Still another way of putting this is that the first and tenth commandments teach the same thing, for coveting means that something besides God is first in one's heart. Faith, on the other hand, finds God to be the treasure of one's heart, and thus willingly submits to his commandments in dependence on his word. Therefore faith glorifies God (Rom. 4:17–22), for faith views him as the source of joy.

The second insight is that the commandment intended to bring life ended up producing death (Rom. 7:10). The fault does not lie in the law, for it is perfect, but the problem is traced to human rebellion, as the story of Adam and Eve reveals. The same truth emerges in the history of Israel, since the nation failed to keep the Sinai covenant. Indeed, Paul's discussion in Romans 7:7–11 indicates that what was true for Adam, Israel and Paul himself is also true for every person. No one left to him- or herself can be righteous before God, since the law reveals that all sin and fall short of God's glory (Rom. 3:23).

In the period between Adam and Noah human beings are not under the Mosaic law. Still, Genesis emphasizes consistently that God was pleased with those who obeyed him. What is featured in the story of Abel, Enoch and Noah is that they lived righteously by doing God's will (Gen. 4:4; 5:23–24; 6:8–9, 22; 7:5). They offered sacrifices, walked with God and lived blamelessly. Nevertheless, it is also obvious that Noah was a sinner (Gen. 9:20–21). Noah's blamelessness, then, is not to be equated with sinlessness, and yet it is clear from his obedience that he was rightly related with God. Indeed, we could even say that he was rightly related to God *because* of his obedience, for we learn from Hebrews 11:4–7 that Abel, Enoch and Noah all obeyed by faith. Faith inevitably manifests itself in obedience, so that faith is the seed and works are the fruit. Those who genuinely trust God obey him, and without such obedience, as James teaches, they are not in the right before him (Jas 2:14–26).

In the biblical storyline the flood and the tower of Babel represent the next two major events. In each case the Lord judges human beings because of their failure to obey him. Those who spurn God's will face his fierce and just judgment, yet the Lord is also gracious to human beings and enters into a covenant with Noah, promising not to destroy the world before his saving plan for the world comes to pass (Gen. 9:8–17).

Abraham

The next major account in the biblical storyline is the life of Abraham. The narrative in Genesis portrays Abraham's faith in God during his sojournings in and out of the land of promise (Genesis 12 – 25). Clearly his faith was imperfect, and there were a number of missteps along the way. New Testament authors, however, are not concerned with Abraham's failures, for they are not even mentioned. They consistently salute Abraham for his faith (cf. Rom. 4; Gal. 3; Heb. 11). Indeed, Genesis 15:6 informs us that Abraham was right with God because of his faith (cf. Rom. 4:3; Gal. 3:6).

Abel, Enoch and Noah should not be distinguished from Abraham on the matter of righteousness, as if they had a right relation with God on the basis of works whereas Abraham was right in God's sight by faith. Abraham too obeyed God, an obedience that likewise stemmed from his faith. Hebrews 11:8–9 illuminates the relationship between faith and obedience in the life of Abraham, explaining that 'by faith Abraham obeyed' and travelled to the land of promise. Faith and obedience are distinct, but remain undivided. The author of Hebrews forges the same connection relative to the sacrifice of Isaac (Heb. 11:17–19). The obedience rendered on that occasion can be traced to Abraham's faith. Hence Hebrews operates in the same orbit as James, who insists that genuine faith manifests itself in works (Jas 2:21–24). Nor does such an emphasis contradict Paul, since Romans 4:17–22 demonstrates that Abraham's faith was dynamic and persevering, not passive.

It could be objected that the approach taken here relies unduly on the New Testament in explaining the Old Testament, but the New Testament evidence is adduced here to suggest that the New Testament authors themselves read the Old Testament organically and respected the progress of the history of redemption. Canonical biblical theology is based on the conviction that the interpretation offered by the New Testament fits what the Old Testament itself teaches, so that the New Testament writers are not guilty of imposing an alien interpretation upon the Old Testament storyline. The interpretation offered in the New Testament fits with the narrative about Abraham in Genesis. Abraham obeyed in leaving his homeland and in travelling to the land of promise (Gen. 12:1–3), but such obedience flowed from his belief that God would bless him. Abraham's life of faith contained ups and downs. For example, he resorted to lying about his wife (Gen. 12:10–20; 20:1–18), and he and Sarah conspired to produce an heir by their own wisdom (Gen. 16:1–4). On the other hand, Abraham trusted God for his future and hence he allowed Lot to choose first the place where he wished to dwell (Gen. 13:1–18). Abraham also trusted God for his safety and rescued Lot from enemy forces, refusing at the same time to enrich himself (Gen. 14:1–24). When God promised as many offspring from his body as the stars of heaven, Abraham believed God (Gen. 15:1–21). Abraham kept God's command in applying the covenantal sign of circumcision for those in his household (Gen. 17:1–27). The narrative of Genesis emphasizes that Abraham was chosen for the purpose of establishing righteousness among his descendants in order that the promises to Abraham might be fulfilled, since the promise can only be given to those who keep the law/covenant (Gen. 18:17–19). Most remarkably, he obeyed God when he was willing to sacrifice Isaac (Gen. 22:1–18). The account of the sacrifice of Isaac is particularly important, for there the narrator states that the whole world will be blessed 'because you have obeyed my voice' (Gen. 22:18). Indeed, the first use of the term 'Torah' appears in Genesis 26:5. God promises Abraham that the whole world will be blessed through him because of his obedience: 'I will multiply your offspring as the stars of heaven and will give to your offspring all these lands. And in your offspring all the nations of the earth shall be blessed, because Abraham obeyed my voice and kept my charge, my commandments, my statutes, and my laws' (Gen. 26:4–5). Abraham's obedience, however, can never be sundered from faith, for the narrator emphasizes both themes in his explication of the life of Abraham.[7]

---

7. John H. Sailhamer maintains that Abraham's obedience here cannot mean that Abraham kept the Mosaic law, as was typically argued in rabbinic exegesis. Rather, says Sailhamer, the author of the Pentateuch contrasts Abraham and Moses, demonstrating that Abraham kept the law because he lived by faith (*The Pentateuch*

Sinai covenant

One of the key questions for biblical theology is how one understands the Sinai covenant relative to the Abrahamic covenant, and this question becomes particularly pressing in understanding the law. One must begin with the narrative in Exodus in which the first eighteen chapters relay the story of God's deliverance of his people from Egyptian bondage. Their redemption functions as a fulfilment of God's covenant with Abraham, Isaac and Jacob (Exod. 2:24; 3:6, 15–16; 4:5; 6:8). Hence it is correct to conclude that segregating the Sinai covenant absolutely from the covenant with Abraham is a mistake, since the former fulfils the latter.[8]

Furthermore, the storyline is foundational for understanding the giving of the law on Mount Sinai. Before the covenant is established, Yahweh reminds Israel how he carried them 'on eagles' wings' and freed them from Egypt (Exod. 19:4). Before the Ten Commandments are enunciated, Yahweh proclaims, 'I am the LORD your God, who brought you out of the land of Egypt, out of the house of slavery' (Exod. 20:2). The following commands are clearly not a means to earn favour with God, nor is keeping them necessary to establish a relationship with Yahweh. God fulfils his promise to Abraham by liberating Israel from Egypt, and his gracious redeeming work precedes any commands. The law must be interpreted within the context of grace, since God gives commands to people he has redeemed freely and chosen solely because of his great love for them (Deut. 7:7–9). There is no basis, then, for thinking that the Mosaic covenant is a legalistic covenant.

The Sinai covenant, however, did not lead to all the blessings promised if Israel would obey the stipulations of the covenant (Exod. 19:5–6). There is a foretaste of the problem with the Sinai covenant at the golden calf incident, where the breaking of the covenant was symbolized by the breaking of the

---

as Narrative: A Biblical-Theological Commentary [Grand Rapids: Zondervan, 1992], pp. 66–71). Hence, according to Sailhamer, life under the law is characterized by lack of faith in contrast to Abraham and the promised new covenant where faith leads to obedience (ibid., pp. 72–78). It seems to me, however, that Sailhamer drives to a conclusion that is not clearly verified by the biblical text. He is right to say that Abraham did not keep the Torah, since the Torah was introduced at Sinai, and Abraham did not live under the Sinai covenant. But Sailhamer wrongly cuts the cord between faith and obedience in the Sinai covenant.

8. T. Desmond Alexander, From Paradise to Promised Land: An Introduction to the Main Themes of the Pentateuch (Grand Rapids: Baker, 1995), pp. 82–83.

tablets (Exod. 32:19). The Sinai covenant promised blessings for those who obeyed and curses for those who transgressed it (Lev. 26; Deut. 26 – 28). The breaking of the covenant does not indicate that the Sinai covenant was legalistic or that the covenant was bereft of grace, but it reveals an internal problem with Israel in that they violated the stipulations of the covenant. The problem was not with the *commands* of the covenant, but with the *people* of the covenant.

The stories about the wilderness generation recorded in Numbers confirm what was adumbrated in the golden calf incident. Most of the wilderness generation did not trust in and therefore obey Yahweh (Num. 14:10–12; 1 Cor. 10:5). Again and again they murmur, complain and fail to trust his word. Finally, they do not believe his promise that he will sustain them in entering the land of promise (Num. 13 – 14). As a consequence the wilderness generation is judged, so that they wander in the wilderness for forty years. Their disobedience is no trifle, for the disobedient ones fail to receive the promise of land given to Abraham, Isaac and Jacob (e.g., Exod. 13:5, 11; Num. 14:23; Deut. 1:8, 35). In the New Testament their disobedience corresponds typologically to the final judgment (1 Cor. 10:1–12; Heb. 3:7 – 4:13; Jude 5). The author of Hebrews, of course, draws on Psalm 95:7–11 to make this very point. Their failure to keep God's law, therefore, led to damnation.[9] The commentary in Hebrews proves to be very helpful, because it specifically states that Israel had an 'evil, unbelieving heart' (Heb. 3:12). Those who were disobedient did not enter God's rest (Heb. 3:18; 4:6, 11). But their disobedience had its roots in unbelief (3:19; 4:2–3). The oscillation between disobedience and unbelief in Hebrews demonstrates that the two are intimately related, and we have good reasons to conclude that they failed to obey because they failed to believe (cf. Ps. 78, particularly v. 32). On the other hand, we see that Abraham (and Moses, Joshua, Caleb and the generation who inherited the land under Joshua) obeyed God and were blessed because they believed.

The incident with the golden calf forecasts the bulk of the history of Israel, and demonstrates the curse that comes from the failure to keep the Torah. Except for a remnant, Israel lacked a circumcised heart. Hence they failed to keep God's law. The blessings and cursings of the covenant (Lev. 26; Deut. 26 – 28) presage Israel's disobedience in that Deuteronomy 26:45–57 intimates

---

9. Perhaps some individuals who were initially judged repented and were saved, although the latter is never stated. Miriam, Aaron, Moses, Joshua and Caleb seem to be exceptions to the rule. In any case, New Testament authors draw the connection from the event as a whole and do not consider exceptional cases.

that the curses will indeed come (see also Deut. 4:25–31). Any doubt about the spiritual state of Israel is removed in subsequent verses. Moses announces that 'the LORD has not given you a heart to understand or eyes to see or ears to hear' (Deut. 29:4). As a nation Israel was physically delivered from Egypt, but all their eyes were not opened spiritually. They are called upon to love the Lord, to walk in his ways and to fear him. They must circumcise their hearts (Deut. 10:16). But in actuality their hearts are stiff-necked and resistant, as was evident in the incident of the golden calf (Deut. 9:1 – 10:11).

Since most of Israel has not been transformed by God's grace, Moses knows that the people will experience both the blessing and the curse (Deut. 30:1). They will abandon the Lord, serve false gods and break the covenant with God (Deut. 31:16). In response, God will bring the curses of the covenant upon them (31:17–18). Moses was commissioned to write his song because God knew about Israel's apostasy in the coming days (Deut. 31:19–22). Israel would continue to be stiff-necked and rebellious, and hence they would certainly depart from God and his ways (31:24–29). The song of Moses indicted Israel as a crooked generation who did not truly know the Lord, and hence they were not genuinely his children (32:5). God had lavished his grace upon Israel by choosing them to be his people, by rescuing them from Egypt, by restoring the covenant after the golden calf and by sustaining them in the wilderness. Israel, however, will forsake the Lord and turn to idolatry (32:15–18). In consequence, the curses of the covenant will be unleashed upon them, and they will be driven into exile. The root problem is that Israel as a whole does not truly know God and is no different from Sodom and Gomorrah (32:32). Only Lot and his daughters escaped Sodom's demise, and only a remnant will survive Israel's exile. Indeed, they are the seed of the serpent rather than being the seed of the woman (32:33). Nevertheless, God will not utterly abandon his people, but promises to circumcise their hearts in the future (30:6), and then Israel will love and obey the Lord (30:7–8). The Abrahamic covenant will thereby be fulfilled and the new covenant established.

One of the fundamental differences between the old covenant and the new is illustrated by the above discussion. The Sinai covenant is a gracious covenant, but the new covenant is inherently superior to the old covenant in terms of its consequences. Only in the new covenant does God's grace grant to all covenant members a heart to keep God's law and to do his will, whereas under the old covenant most of Israel remained uncircumcised in heart (cf. Ezek. 11:18–19; 36:26–27; Jer. 31:31–34). In other words, none of the members of the new covenant lack inward renewal and transformation (in contrast to the old), for the genius of the new covenant is that all the members of the covenant community truly know the Lord and have received forgiveness of sins (Heb. 8:7–13; cf. Jer. 31:31–34).[10] God's saving promises will, therefore, not be fulfilled through the Sinai covenant, but will be realized in the new covenant.

The subsequent books of the Old Testament demonstrate that the old covenant did not produce a circumcised heart in most of the people, just as Moses indicated would be the case in the book of Deuteronomy. In Joshua, Israel remains faithful to the Lord and the Torah, but by the time of the Judges the nation has slipped considerably. The cycle of evil, judgment, the raising up of a deliverer, and then a fresh return to wickedness repeats itself again and again throughout the book (Judg. 2:11–23). Deep corruption permeates the nation. Saul, the first king, replicates the history of Israel, for he began well and then hardened his heart against the ways of the Lord. David, unlike Saul, was a man after God's own heart, although even he fell dramatically at the high point of his reign. Unlike Saul, he repented and turned from his evil. Under Solomon Israel reached its pinnacle, but he forsook the first commandment and turned aside to other gods, representing the course of the nation as a whole. The nation was then divided into two kingdoms, Israel and Judah. The books of 1 and 2 Kings recount the reigns of various rulers in both the northern and southern kingdoms. The kings in the north without exception abandoned the Lord and failed to obey him. The kings in Judah, on the other hand, have a mixed record. Some of them were pleasing to the Lord, but the history of the people as a whole was a downward spiral. At the end of the day both kingdoms were judged by the Lord for their failure to keep God's law and were sent into exile – Israel by Assyria in 721 BC and Judah by Babylon in 586 BC.

The prophetic literature unpacks the elements of this survey of the history of Israel. It is well accepted in Old Testament scholarship that the prophets contain covenant lawsuits (cf. Hos. 4:1; Mic. 6:1–2).[11] The prophets, who represent the faithful remnant, call the Lord's judgment down upon Israel and Judah because they have failed to conform to the stipulations of the covenant.

---

10. I would argue that those who fall away from the covenant community were never truly saved. See Thomas R. Schreiner and Ardel B. Caneday, *The Race Set Before Us: A Biblical Theology of Perseverance and Assurance* (Downers Grove: InterVarsity Press; Leicester: Inter-Varsity Press, 2001).

11. E.g., H. B. Huffmon, 'The Covenant Lawsuit in the Prophets', *JBL* 78 (1959), pp. 285–295.

The covenantal curses threatened in the Sinai covenant (Lev. 26; Deut. 27 – 28) are heralded against both Israel and Judah, and the prophets frequently proclaim that Israel has failed to keep the Torah.

Hosea may be adduced as a test case. He indicts Israel for 'swearing, lying, murder, stealing, and committing adultery' (Hos. 4:2). Clearly, these sins violate the Sinai covenant and more specifically the Ten Commandments (Exod. 20:2–17). Even though Hosea does not specify violation of the Torah here, the reader is expected to understand these charges against such a backdrop. Of course, the entire book of Hosea complains that Israel is guilty of spiritual adultery, and spiritual adultery is nothing less than a violation of the first commandment of the Torah, for Israel's whoredom signifies a forsaking of the living God. Indeed, the second commandment which prohibited idols was violated as well, and Hosea frequently calls attention to this sin (Hos. 4:12–13, 17; 8:5; 10:1, 5–6; 11:2; 13:2). Israel's violation of the first commandment is not an isolated phenomenon, for, as was noted above, Hosea 4:2 mentions that the Sinai covenant was being violated in terms of other sins. Indeed, Hosea mentions elsewhere murder (Hos. 6:8–9), stealing (Hos. 7:1) and adultery (Hos. 4:14; 7:4). The reason for judgment in Hosea is summarized in 8:1: 'they have transgressed my covenant and rebelled against my law.' Here the close relationship between the law and the covenant is evident, which demonstrates that the law represents the stipulations of the covenant. The covenant curses will come because of Israel's failure to keep the law. Similar themes also occur in the other prophets. Ultimately both kingdoms are sent into exile because of failure to do God's will as it is expressed in the Torah.

New covenant

Exile, however, is not the final word. The Lord promises a new exodus in which Israel will return from Babylon (e.g., Isa. 11:15–16; 40:3–11; 42:16; 43:2, 5–7, 16–19; 48:20–21; 49:6–11; 51:10). He will pour out the blessing of his Spirit on his people in the days to come (Isa. 44:3). When the Spirit is poured out, there will be, so to speak, a new creation (Isa. 32:15). When the Spirit is poured out (Joel 2:28), nations who oppose the Lord will be defeated and the Lord will vindicate and restore his people (Joel 3:1–21). Both Jeremiah and Ezekiel anticipate a return from exile (Jer. 30 – 33; Ezek. 36 – 37). Tucked into these chapters is the promise that the Spirit will be given to God's people so that they will obey the Torah. Ezekiel calls this new work of God a 'covenant of peace' (Ezek. 34:25; 37:26) that will last for ever. The Lord will cleanse his

people from uncleanness and put his Spirit in them so that they keep his law.
They will therefore inherit his promises (cf. Gen. 18:17–19; Ezek. 36:25–27; cf.
11:18–19). Clearly this is part of the covenant of peace in which God's people
are enabled to keep his law (37:24).

Jeremiah depicts the same reality, but he labels it the 'new covenant' and
'everlasting covenant' instead of the 'covenant of peace' (Jer. 31:31–34;
32:40).[12] The new covenant fulfils the command to circumcise the heart
found in Deuteronomy (10:16; cf. Jer. 4:4; 9:25–26), for in the new covenant
God writes his law on the hearts of his people and definitively forgives their
sins. The old covenant was ineffective because Israel broke the covenant
through disobedience (Jer. 31:32). The majority of those in Israel failed to
keep God's law and were sent into exile because they did not have the Spirit.
In contrast, Jeremiah and Ezekiel emphasize that in the new covenant *all*
God's people (i.e., every member of the new covenant community) will
keep the law through an interior work of God himself. The new covenant
also promises that full and final atonement for sins will be accomplished
(Jer. 31:34), suggesting that the sacrifices offered under the old covenant
could not secure forgiveness in and of themselves, since they pointed
forward to Christ's atonement. The glory of the new covenant is not that
God's people are freed *from* keeping God's law, but that they are empowered to put it into practice.[13] Most fundamental of all, though, is the forgiveness of sins achieved under the new covenant, which Hebrews locates
in the atonement of Jesus Christ (Heb. 10:15–18).[14]

New Testament

In the New Testament I have chosen to begin with Hebrews instead of the
Gospels. Hebrews is selected for the starting point because in my judgment it
represents most clearly the differences between the New Testament and the

---

12. Ezekiel also speaks of an everlasting covenant (Ezek. 37:26).

13. In my view the law that is fulfilled is the law of Christ, see below.

14. A question arises at this juncture. Do the expressions of joy in God's law in Psalm
    19 and 119 contradict the claim that Israel failed to keep the law? It seems that the
    most satisfying answer is that these psalms represent the experience of the
    remnant. The remnant did not find the law to be a burden or onerous, but a joy.
    The righteous, who were circumcised in heart, did not sigh when considering the
    Torah, but found it to be the delight of their hearts.

Old Testament relative to the law. Luke-Acts is examined next, since it contains both a Gospel and the history of the early church. Not surprisingly, the Pauline writings receive the most attention, for Paul says much about the law and his teaching on the law is a matter of controversy. I conclude with James and Matthew, inasmuch as they are often considered to promote a Jewish-Christian view of the law in the New Testament.

Hebrews

The author of Hebrews engages in a sustained argument against Christians reverting to the Aaronic priesthood and the levitical sacrificial cultus in order to maintain their ties to Judaism for the purpose of avoiding persecution.[15] He does not claim that the Mosaic covenant was somehow a mistake from its inception. Instead, he hangs his argument on salvation-historical realities. Now that Christ has arrived as the Melchizedekian priest, a return to the levitical priesthood would constitute a denial of Christ's sacrifice. The Aaronic priests and the Old Testament sacrifices are not rejected as such; they are viewed typologically. The Old Testament priesthood and sacrifices pointed to and anticipated the sacrifice of Christ. They are the shadows, but he is the substance. Old Testament sacrifices cannot bring permanent forgiveness, for brute beasts are offered, but Christ's sacrifice is fully and finally atoning, since he is a willing and sinless sacrifice. The repetition of Old Testament sacrifices reveals that they do not remove sin for all time, whereas the once-for-all sacrifice of Christ definitively and finally atones for sin (Heb. 9:15 – 10:18).

The author of Hebrews maintains that a change of priesthood also constitutes a change of law (Heb. 7:11–12). Indeed, he claims that the law did not bring perfection and was weak and useless for such a purpose (7:18–19). In context it is clear that his point is that the law does not provide a full and final atonement for sin. He proceeds to argue that the promise of a new covenant indicates that the Sinai covenant is now obsolete (Heb. 8:7–13). Once again, the focus is on the failure of the law to provide final forgiveness, inasmuch as its purpose was to point to Christ. A regular feature in Hebrews is the corresponding contrast between the stipulations and/or punishments of the Sinai covenant and what is required now for those belonging to Christ (Heb. 2:1–4; 9:6–10, 15–24; 10:26–31; 12:25–29; 13:9–12). Indeed, the very first verses of the letter contrast the definitive revelation given in the last days in the Son with

---

15. The situation addressed in Hebrews is disputed. See the discussion in William L. Lane, *Hebrews 1 – 8*, WBC 47A (Dallas: Word, 1991), pp. li–lx; Harold W. Attridge, *The Epistle to the Hebrews*, Herm (Philadelphia: Fortress, 1989), pp. 9–13.

the partial and preliminary revelation given under the old covenant (1:1–3). The contrast between Moses and Christ articulated in 3:1–6 is similar in this regard.

It seems quite evident that the author of Hebrews believes that the new covenant has displaced or, perhaps better, 'fulfilled' what was promised in the old. Now that the end of the ages has arrived, a return to the old covenant would lead to final destruction. The author is strikingly severe and dogmatic. Those who return to the regulations and sacrifices of the old covenant will be damned, for to do such is to reject the work of Christ on the cross (cf. Heb. 6:4–8; 10:26–31; 12:25–29). Hence he can say that no sacrifice for sins remains for those who turn away from Christ's sacrifice (Heb. 10:26). This is another way of saying that those who turn back to the levitical cult have shut themselves off from any possibility of forgiveness.

The author of Hebrews does not charge the Mosaic covenant with legalism, nor does he find fault with the specific prescriptions in the law per se. Rather, the Mosaic covenant and law had a typological and salvation-historical function. The tabernacle points to the true tabernacle in heaven where God dwells (cf. Heb. 8:1–6; 9:1–10). The Old Testament sacrifices and regulations anticipate the sacrifice of Christ and the era that has dawned in the new covenant (Heb. 9:11–14, 23–28; 10:1–18). Old Testament sacrifices also point to the need to share with others and to praise God (Heb. 13:15–16). The promises of land and rest in the Old Testament forecast the heavenly city and the Sabbath rest prepared for the people of God in the age to come (Heb. 3:7 – 4:13; 11:9–10, 13–16; 12:22; 13:14).

Is there any continuity between the Old Testament law and the New Testament fulfilment of Christ in Hebrews? The author cites the new covenant promise of Jeremiah 31:31–34 where the law will be written on the hearts of believers (Heb. 8:7–13). The author does not work out what the law written on the heart would mean in terms of giving specific prescriptions from the law. He clearly believes there is a place for commands and injunctions, as is evident from the parenesis in chapter 13. At the same time there is the remarkable discontinuity in terms of intention. The Sinai covenant had a distinctively different purpose from the new covenant, for all members of the new covenant community have received internal transformation, while the majority of the members of the old covenant did not.[16] The author of

---

16. The remnant serves as an exception, but what impressed the biblical writers is that the vast majority of those who were under the old covenant did not do God's will. Their failure to obey verified the inadequate character of the Sinai covenant.

Hebrews also emphasizes the inadequacy of the old covenant in this regard, since cleansing of sins has been achieved once for all through the death of Christ. The forgiveness of sins promised in the new covenant has been realized through Christ's definitive sacrifice on the cross, and not in the sacrifices prescribed in the old covenant.

Luke-Acts

It is well known that Jervell argues that Luke's view of the law was the most conservative in the New Testament.[17] It is striking that both in the Gospel and in Acts there are many references to the observance of the law, from Jesus' parents keeping the law at his birth (Luke 2:22–24) to Paul's observance of the law in Jerusalem for the sake of the Jews (e.g., Acts 16:3; 18:18; 21:26). But such observance of the law should be interpreted within the framework of redemptive history.[18] Jesus kept the law because he lived under the law. Paul followed the prescriptions of the law when he was in Jerusalem, or when he was working with Jews (esp. Acts 16:3), to facilitate the spread of the gospel. Luke can scarcely be understood to demand wholesale adherence to the Mosaic law, for the Jerusalem Council concluded that circumcision was not required of Gentile converts (Acts 15:1–35). Furthermore, the Cornelius incident implies that Old Testament food laws are not required for Christians (Acts 10:1 – 11:18). Luke does not provide a detailed explanation of the reason for the change, for such was not his purpose in writing. Still, it seems fair to say that he follows a redemptive-historical framework. The fulfilment in Christ frees believers from the necessity of observing the Mosaic law. On the other hand, Jewish believers need not overreact and spurn the Mosaic law if observing it opens up opportunities in ministering to Jews who keep the law.

Other hints of discontinuity crop up in Acts. Although scholars have often overread Stephen's words about the temple in Acts 7 as if he dismisses the temple altogether, it does seem that Stephen reduces the temple to a subsidiary role now that Christ has arrived. In Acts 13:38–39 Paul contrasts belief in Jesus with the Mosaic law. The latter did not provide forgiveness of sins and

---

17. Jacob Jervell, *Luke and the People of God: A New Look at Luke-Acts* (Minneapolis: Augsburg, 1972). For quite a different analysis of the law in Luke-Acts, see Stephen G. Wilson, *Luke and the Law* (Cambridge: Cambridge University Press, 1983).

18. See the important essays by Craig L. Blomberg, 'The Law in Luke-Acts', *JSNT* 22 (1984), pp. 53–80; Mark A. Seifrid, 'Jesus and the Law in Acts', *JSNT* 30 (1987), pp. 39–57.

justification, whereas those who believe in Jesus are forgiven and justified. It seems that these verses run along the same lines as Hebrews. Forgiveness of sins comes only through the death of Jesus, not ultimately from the Mosaic law, although in the old era forgiveness was granted through the sacrificial cultus.[19] Otherwise, the death of Jesus is superfluous (cf. Acts 2:38; 3:19; 17:30; 20:21; 26:20).

Another instructive text is Acts 15:10–11. Here Peter contrasts the yoke of the law with believing in Christ. He specifically identifies believing in Christ with grace. Indeed, Peter says that neither the present generation of Jews nor the fathers have been able to bear the law's yoke. He probably means by this that Israel has consistently failed to keep God's law.[20] Salvation does not come through keeping the law, since all have sinned, but by the grace of God in Christ. A right relation with God, says Peter, is now obtained by believing in Christ, and hence circumcision as a sign of the old covenant should not be imposed on Gentiles as necessary for salvation – contrary to the position of those Jews who insisted that circumcision was necessary for salvation (Acts 15:1).

Paul

The apostle Paul's view of the law has been the subject of controversy since the time of his ministry, and debate over his theology shows no signs of abating. Paul, like the author of Hebrews, clearly views the Sinai covenant as a temporary covenant that is no longer in force.[21] This is particularly evident in Galatians 3 – 4. In Galatians 3:15–18 he emphasizes the temporal interval between the Abrahamic and Mosaic covenants, the latter commencing 430 years after the former. Furthermore, Paul contrasts the law with the promise, identifying the Abrahamic covenant with promise and the Mosaic covenant with law. What he means by this contrast will be explored shortly.

Galatians 3:19–20 is notoriously difficult, but the only point that needs to be observed here is that the law is in force only until the promised seed arrives. Now that Christ has come, the era of the law has ended. The provisional role of the law is also expressed through the image of the peda-

---

19. I would suggest that the sacrificial cultus in the Old Testament provided forgiveness in that it anticipated and pointed to the promised atonement of Christ.

20. So John Nolland, 'A Fresh Look at Acts 15.10', *NTS* 27 (1980), pp. 105–115.

21. Paul, like the author of Hebrews, focuses on the prescriptions of the law, and he has these especially in mind when he speaks of the Sinai covenant.

gogue in Galatians 3:23–25. What Paul intends in using the metaphor of the pedagogue is the subject of intense debate. It is quite doubtful that he calls attention to the role of the law as an instructor or tutor, as if he focuses here on the law's role of convicting people of sin and hence leading them to Christ, since Paul speaks here in terms of salvation history, not individual experience with the law. I have argued elsewhere that the term that captures best what Paul means is the word 'babysitter'.[22] The law, i.e., the Sinai covenant, functions as an authority during the time of spiritual infancy. But a new era of salvation history has dawned, so that people are now to put their faith in Christ for salvation. The law, as verse 24 says, has functioned as our pedagogue 'until Christ came' – understanding the *eis* here as temporal. Now that faith in Christ has come, the time of living under the law has elapsed (Gal. 3:25). All those who have faith in Christ live as spiritual adults (Gal. 3:26).

The argument in Galatians 4:1–7 is quite similar. Before heirs reach maturity, they are legally no different from slaves. The stewards and guardians here represent the era of the law under which Israel lived. The time under the law, described as a period of infancy, is also a time of slavery. Life under the law ended up being no better than paganism ('the elements of the world'),[23] for Israel failed to obey the Torah and experienced exile. Now a new period of salvation history has arrived with the coming of God's Son, Jesus Christ. He has liberated his people from slavery to sin through his death on the cross and made them spiritual adults.

The interim character of the law is confirmed by 2 Corinthians 3. The Mosaic covenant is described in terms of its ministry in verses 7–11. The new covenant is characterized as one that 'remains' (*menon*), whereas the Sinai covenant 'has ended' (*katargoumenon*), signifying that the Sinai covenant is

---

22. Thomas R. Schreiner, *The Law and Its Fulfillment: A Pauline Theology of Law* (Grand Rapids: Baker, 1993), pp. 77–80.

23. Gal. 4:3, 9. This is my translation here. For this understanding of the elements, see E. Schweizer, 'Slaves of the Elements and Worshipers of Angels: Gal. 4:3, 9 and Col. 2:8, 18, 20', *JBL* 107 (1988), pp. 455–468; James D. G. Dunn, *The Theology of Paul the Apostle* (Grand Rapids: Eerdmans, 1998), pp. 107–108. For the view that they are spiritual beings, see Clinton E. Arnold, 'Returning to the Domain of the Powers: *Stoicheia* as Evil Spirits in Galatians 4:3, 9', *NovT* 38 (1996), pp. 55–76. For the view that the reference is to the regulations of the law, see Linda Belleville, '"Under Law": Structural Analysis and the Pauline Concept of Law in Galatians 3:21 – 4:11', *JSNT* 26 (1986), pp. 64–69.

obsolete now that the new covenant has commenced.[24] Verse 13 is the subject of much controversy, but it seems that the glory that comes to an end on Moses' face symbolizes the character of the Mosaic covenant, so that the words *to telos tou katargoumenou* should be translated 'the outcome of what was being brought to an end'. If such a reading is correct, it provides more evidence for the transitory character of the Sinai covenant. It seems that the ministries of Moses and Paul (and the old and new covenants) are intertwined here, so that Paul's ministry is superior to Moses' ministry because of the superiority of the new covenant to the old. The new is inherently superior, since the Spirit is granted to *all* members of the new covenant community, whereas the majority of the members of the old covenant lacked a circumcised heart.

Within this framework, Paul establishes a series of contrasts between the new covenant and the Sinai covenant. I have already noted that Paul contrasts the promise of the Abrahamic covenant with the law of Moses in Galatians 3:15–18. Moreover, he teaches that those who depend on works of the law are under a curse, and that no one can be justified by law (Gal. 3:10–11). Indeed, he goes further and asserts that 'the law is not of faith' (Gal. 3:12). In the allegory of Galatians 4:21–30 the Sinai covenant is contrasted with God's new work in Christ. The Sinai covenant leads to slavery (4:24–25), and the Jerusalem of Paul's day lives in bondage. Those who belong to the heavenly Jerusalem enjoy freedom, and believers are the children of this mother who corresponds to Sarah rather than Hagar. The freedom of those who are now part of the heavenly Jerusalem contrasts with the slavery of those still choosing to live under the Mosaic covenant.

Romans 4:13–16 contains remarkably similar themes. The promise of Abraham is contrasted with the Mosaic law. The promise is not received through the law, but through the righteousness of faith. If those who keep the law receive the promise, then faith is emptied of its significance and the promise is nullified. The law cannot lead to life, for the violation of the law evokes God's wrath, and everyone violates some part of the law. Thus the

---

24. The meaning of the participle *katargoumenon* and the following *katargoumenou* is debated sharply. For a survey of various views, see Murray J. Harris, *The Second Epistle to the Corinthians: A Commentary on the Greek Text*, NIGTC (Grand Rapids: Eerdmans, 2005), pp. 283–285, 290–292, 299–300. It seems to me that in both vv. 7–8 and v. 11 the contrasts indicate that the term denotes the cessation of the Mosaic covenant.

promise is not based on law but on faith, and hence the promise will be secured for all those who are the seed of Abraham.

How should we explain Paul's negative statements on the law, declarations that seem to separate the Mosaic law from faith? This is one of the most difficult questions in biblical theology, and one that has puzzled interpreters over the centuries, leading to significant disagreements on how to explain the relationship between the Testaments. It seems to me, however, that the best solution is one which takes into account salvation history, which entails the intentional salvation-historical superiority of the new covenant to the old. I begin by saying something about salvation history. Paul writes from the standpoint of the fulfilment of the covenant in Christ. The new age has dawned and the old age has passed away. Christians are now a new creation in Christ (2 Cor. 5:17), and believers, as was argued above, are no longer under the Mosaic covenant. The Mosaic covenant was not intrinsically legalistic, but was instead a nationalistic covenant.

The new perspective on Paul has something valuable to contribute here. The Mosaic law established a wall of separation between Jews and Gentiles.[25] Indeed, God intended such a separation, since the law marked off Israel from the nations, although it was wrong for the Jews to take pride in themselves because they were separated from Gentiles. A diverse body of literature in the Second Temple period, including the New Testament and both Jewish and Gentile writings, testifies to the cultural/religious divide between Jews and Gentiles. In the literature of the day certain Jewish boundary markers come to the forefront, such as circumcision, purity laws and the Sabbath. In Ephesians 2:11–22, the wall of separation has been removed between Jews and Gentiles. The distinction between the two cultures has been erased through the cross of Christ. The new age has arrived in which Jews and Gentiles are fellow citizens in the people of God (cf. also Eph. 3:5–6).

This salvation-historical shift is crucial for Paul's theology. The Jewish teachers in Galatia who desired to impose the Mosaic law on Gentiles were therefore travelling backwards in redemptive history, and therefore interpreted the old covenant in a manner Paul considered erroneous.[26] They denied the

---

25. For representative work on the new perspective, see J. D. G. Dunn, 'The New Perspective on Paul', *BJRL* 65 (1983), pp. 95–122; idem, 'The Justice of God: A Renewed Perspective on Justification by Faith', *JTS* 43 (1992), pp. 1–22; N. T. Wright, *The Climax of the Covenant: Christ and the Law in Pauline Theology* (Minneapolis: Fortress, 1991).

26. It seems that the Jewish teachers in Galatia advocated the same view as the Jews described in Acts 15:1. Both insisted that circumcision was required for salvation

very purpose for which Christ came, and insisted that Gentiles must become Jews to be part of the people of God. By doing so they reified the Sinai covenant and made it the standard for salvation, instead of seeing that the Mosaic covenant always pointed towards the fulfilment in Christ, and that it would be superseded by the new covenant.

They also seemed to miss the point made in Genesis 15:6, Numbers 14:10–12 and Psalm 95:7–11 that salvation came by faith in the Old Testament, not by adherence to the law's demands. It is important to remember that these Jewish teachers believed Jesus was the Messiah. Paul is not responding to Jewish opponents who denied that Jesus was the Christ. Nevertheless, these Jewish teachers were convinced that keeping the laws prescribed in the Old Testament was required for salvation (cf. Acts 15:1). In effect, even though the Messiah had come and the new covenant had been inaugurated, they believed that the Sinai covenant still remained the standard for salvation. Paul opposes such a theology root and branch, because it denied the all-sufficient nature of the work of Christ on the cross. According to Paul, the cross functions as the replacement and fulfilment of circumcision (Gal. 1:4; 2:19–21; 3:1, 13; 4:4–5; 5:11, 24; 6:12, 14, 17).[27] If one must keep the Sinai law to be saved, then Christ died for nothing (Gal. 2:21; 5:2), for the law itself would then provide the means of forgiveness with its animal sacrifices. Therefore, if Old Testament sacrifices are sufficient to atone for sin, there is no need for the sacrifice of Christ.

The above observations, incidentally, explain why Paul insists that one must obey the law perfectly to be saved (Rom. 1:18 – 3:20; Gal. 3:10; 5:3). Some scholars disagree with this claim, arguing that the Sinai covenant never demanded perfect obedience.[28] In one sense the law does not demand perfect

---

(Gal. 5:2–6; cf. Gal. 2:3–5). These teachers likely demanded that Christians observe the entirety of the Old Testament law (cf. Gal. 4:10, 21; 5:18; 6:13). Paul's defence of himself in Galatians 1 – 2 suggests that they discredited the legitimacy of Paul's apostleship as well.

27. Cf. Peder Borgen's two articles in support of this conclusion. 'Observations on the Theme "Paul and Philo": Paul's Preaching of Circumcision in Galatia (Gal. 5:11) and Debates on Circumcision in Philo', in S. Pederson (ed.), *The Pauline Literature and Theology* (Göttingen: Vandenhoeck & Ruprecht, 1980), pp. 85–102; and 'Paul Preaches Circumcision and Pleases Men', in M. D. Hooker and S. G. Wilson (eds.), *Paul and Paulinism: Essays in Honour of C. K. Barrett* (London: SPCK, 1982), pp. 37–46.

28. For discussion of this issue, see Thomas R. Schreiner, 'Is Perfect Obedience to the Law Possible? A Re-examination of Galatians 3:10', *JETS* 27 (1984), pp. 151–160;

obedience, since sacrifices are provided for atonement under the Sinai covenant. On the other hand, the very need for atonement confirms in another sense that perfect obedience is required, since apart from sacrificial atonement such infractions remain unforgiven. In any case, Paul demands perfect obedience of those in Christ who return to norms of the Mosaic covenant, since the fulfilment of that covenant has now come in Christ (cf. Gal. 5:2–6). Now that Christ has come, Old Testament sacrifices no longer atone for sin and those who demand obedience to the law must therefore revert to the terms of the Sinai covenant for salvation (minus its provision for forgiveness!). I have already noted this argument in the epistle to the Hebrews. Those who return to the levitical cult will face eschatological judgment, for they are denying Christ's sacrificial work on the cross. Similarly, Paul threatens judgment upon those who desire to revert to the Mosaic covenant. If they submit themselves to the stipulations of the Sinai covenant, then they are required to observe the law perfectly, for animal sacrifices no longer provide atonement for sin.[29] One either relies upon the Sinai covenant for salvation with all that it entails (without its Old Testament sacrifices, since they point to Christ), or one trusts in the work of Christ on the cross alone.

Hence Paul's negative statements about the law stem in part from the place he occupies in redemptive history. He is not intending to say that the Sinai covenant itself demanded perfection to be saved (except insofar as the law's demands show that sacrifices are needed for atonement), or that it was a legalistic covenant. His point is that reverting to the Sinai covenant now that Christ has come denies the fulfilment of the covenant in Christ and places one in the impossible position of having to do everything the law says to be saved, apart from its provisions for forgiveness. Since all sin, all need atonement. Those who do not accept Jesus as their atonement have no atonement. Their position is hopeless.

The inherent efficacy of the new covenant must also be taken into account. In Judaism there was the proverb, 'The more Torah, the more life.'[30] Paul, on the contrary, in one of the most shocking things he ever wrote, maintained that the giving of the law precipitated sin (Rom. 5:20; Gal. 3:19). The Jewish

---

idem, 'Paul and Perfect Obedience to the Law: An Evaluation of the View of E. P. Sanders', *WTJ* 47 (1985), pp. 245–278.

29. For a similar understanding on this matter, see A. Andrew Das, *Paul, the Law, and the Covenant* (Peabody: Hendrickson, 2001), p. 144.

30. M. Aboth 2:7. This is a standard Jewish view. See also Sirach 17:11; 45:5; Baruch 3:9; 4:1; Psalms of Solomon 14:2; 2 Esdras 14:30; 2 Baruch 38:2.

teachers advocating the Sinai covenant likely believed that the law was necessary to curb sin. As Moisés Silva argues, they believed that the Torah was a
source of life.[31] Paul's negative comments on the law counter the notion that
the law itself provides the ability to do what is pleasing to God. In Galatians
3:21 he acknowledges that if the law could grant righteousness, then righteousness would have been through the law. Contrary to the Jewish teachers,
however, Paul asserts that the law is not the source of life. The Sinai covenant
did not provide the internal grace and transformation for all Israel that is
bestowed upon all members of the new covenant (2 Cor. 3). This insight aids
a proper understanding of Galatians 3:12 and Romans 10:5 as well. When Paul
says that the law is not of faith, we should not understand these verses to say
that the Sinai covenant teaches works righteousness or that the Mosaic
covenant is intrinsically legalistic. Nor is it likely that Paul corrects the teachers' exegesis of Leviticus 18:5 by proposing an alternate interpretation of the
verse, since we have no example of Paul correcting misinterpretations elsewhere.[32] Paul simply reflects the demand of the covenant that human beings
must keep its prescriptions to live. The problem is that the Sinai covenant did
not provide for the majority the grace to keep what was prescribed, and such
a view is confirmed by Moses' words about the majority of Israel in
Deuteronomy and the history of Israel as recorded in the remainder of the
Old Testament.[33] Israel failed to do what the law demanded, and hence experienced the curses of the covenant.

---

31. Moisés Silva, 'Is the Law Against the Promises? The Significance of Gal. 3:21 for
     Covenant Continuity', in William S. Barker and W. Robert Godfrey (eds.), *Theonomy:
     A Reformed Critique* (Grand Rapids: Zondervan, 1990), pp. 153–167.

32. Previously this view seemed the most promising to me, especially as it was
     explained by Silva. See n. 31 above. For a similar view, see John Murray, *The Epistle
     to the Romans: The English Text with Introduction, Exposition, and Notes. Chapters 9 – 16*
     (Grand Rapids: Eerdmans, 1965), vol. 2, pp. 249–250; Hans Hübner, *Gottes Ich und
     Israel: Zum Schriftgebrauch des Paulus im Römer 9 – 11*, FRLANT 36 (Göttingen:
     Vandenhoeck & Ruprecht, 1984), p. 93.

33. Cf. here James M. Scott, '"For as Many as Are of Works of the Law Are under a
     Curse" (Galatians 3.10)', in Craig A. Evans and James A. Sanders (eds.), *Paul and the
     Scriptures of Israel* (Sheffield: JSOT Press, 1993), pp. 187–221. It seems to me,
     however, despite Scott's helpful comments on the Old Testament context, that he
     misinterprets Gal. 3:10. For a critique of Scott on Gal. 3:10, see Seyoon Kim, *Paul
     and the New Perspective: Second Thoughts on the Origin of Paul's Gospel* (Grand Rapids:
     Eerdmans, 2002), pp. 134–140.

The citation of Leviticus 18:5 in both Romans 10:5 and Galatians 3:12 reflects Paul's salvation-historical view of the Mosaic covenant. The Sinai covenant was gracious in that it was given to people whom God had rescued from Egypt in fulfilment of his promises to Abraham. And yet we should also observe that the stipulations of the law focus on the obedience demanded of God's people, most of whom were unregenerate. The law was given mainly to people who were stiff-necked and who had not been transformed by grace, and the law itself lacked the capability to change the hearts of people. Indeed, the law has the opposite effect. Those who do not have the Spirit rebel against the law, and their sin takes on the character of wilful transgression (Rom. 7:5, 7–25). The history of Israel testifies to the weakness of the law. Because of their constant violation of the law, both the northern and southern kingdoms were sent into exile. In Romans 2:17–29 Paul indicts the Israel of his day for failing to keep the very law they treasure and teach. The fundamental charge raised against Israel here is not legalism, but failure to do God's will as it is expressed in the law. Legalism is defined here as the view that human works function as the ultimate basis of one's salvation on the last day. What is remarkable is that sin has co-opted the law and employed it, so the effect is that the coming of the law has led to more sin rather than less (Rom. 5:20; 7:5, 7–25; Gal. 3:19).

Some interpreters suggest that Galatians 3:19 actually teaches that the purpose of the law is to restrict sin.[34] Paul does speak of the law restricting sin in 1 Timothy 1:8–11, but in the 1 Timothy text he likely has in mind the swift punishment meted out to law-breakers that restrains the desire to sin (cf. Rom. 13:1–7). In Galatians, however, he addresses Jewish teachers who were convinced that the law was the pathway to life. Paul reflects on Jewish history and Scripture, concluding that the law enslaved rather than liberated. The law did not grant life because it was not accompanied by the Spirit, but Scripture documents that all under the law are imprisoned under sin. During the era of the law people were captive to sin (Gal. 3:23). Indeed, to be under the realm of law, i.e., the old era of salvation history, is to be under sin (Gal. 5:18; cf. Rom. 6:14–15). Paul portrays life under the Sinai covenant and the law as a period when Israel was 'enslaved under the elements of the world' (Gal. 4:3).[35] Freedom from the curse of the law and bondage to the law comes only through the substitutionary death of Christ (Rom. 3:21–26; Gal. 3:13; 4:4–5).

---

34. David J. Lull, '"The Law Was Our Pedagogue": A Study in Galatians 3:19–25', *JBL* 105 (1986), pp. 481–498.

35. This represents my translation.

One of the major themes of Galatians is that believers who have been for-given through Christ's death now enjoy the life-giving Spirit. If they walk in the Spirit and are led by the Spirit, they please God (Gal. 5:16, 18). The con-trast between the Spirit and the law in Galatians supports the theme that those who lack the Spirit cannot keep God's law (Gal. 5:18). Romans 7 should be interpreted similarly. Sin utilizes the law to produce even more sin for those who are in the flesh (Rom. 7:5), i.e., those who are in the old Adam and are therefore unregenerate. Human beings do not have the inherent capacity to be changed by the law, and hence the law does not restrain sin, but multiplies it.

On the other hand, Romans 8 celebrates the transforming work of God's Spirit, for those whom the Spirit indwells keep God's law (though not perfectly, since believers live in the interim between the already and the not yet); and 2 Corinthians 3 points in the same direction.[36] The letter represents the law without the Spirit (2 Cor. 3:6). The commands of the law put to death those who lack the Spirit, and such is the history of those who lived under the old covenant and all human beings who encounter the law as sons and daughters of Adam. Hence Paul can describe the Mosaic administration as one of death and condemnation (2 Cor. 3:7, 9), since such was the effect of the law for those who lived under the Sinai covenant.[37] By contrast, the Spirit brings life, glory and righteousness for *all* those who are united to Christ (2 Cor. 3:6–11). The days of slavery to sin have ended with the coming of the Spirit, and now believ-ers enjoy the freedom to do God's will (2 Cor. 3:17; cf. Gal. 5:13–15), although the picture is clouded by the fact that believers live in the interval between the inauguration and consummation of God's promises. Hence they also experi-ence the continuing presence of sin and the death-dealing impact of the law insofar as they still inhabit the old age (cf. Rom. 7:13–25).

Is there any polemic against legalism in the Pauline letters? Since the publica-tion of E. P. Sanders's *Paul and Palestinian Judaism* and the rise of the 'new per-spective' on Paul,[38] many have doubted that any criticism of legalism can be detected in the Pauline letters. How could there be a polemic against legalism if there is sparse evidence of legalism in the Judaism of Paul's day, as Sanders insists? Several things should be said in response. First, Sanders's portrait of Judaism has been questioned in recent scholarship, and there is evidence that

---

36. See the seminal work of Scott J. Hafemann, *Paul, Moses, and the History of Israel: The Letter/Spirit Contrast and the Argument from Scripture in 2 Corinthians 3*, WUNT 81 (Tübingen: Mohr, 1995).

37. Again, the remnant functions as an exception here.

38. For an introduction to the new perspective, see n. 25 above.

Judaism does not fit entirely into the categories he posits.[39] The view of covenantal nomism, as Sanders describes it, needs to be modified, for even though he traces some diversity regarding the law in Second Temple Judaism, he overemphasizes the extent to which covenantal nomism (according to his definition) is present. However, some scholars have overemphasized the polemic against legalism in Judaism, and hence Sanders's work is a needed corrective. Other scholars have wrongly interpreted the demand to obey the law as evidence of legalism, but such a view would put the Old Testament and the New Testament in the legalistic category as well! Sanders has gone too far, however, in denying any polemic against legalism in the Pauline letters. Seeing legalism everywhere in Judaism is a mistake, but seeing it nowhere in Paul's polemic is equally misguided. Second, we need to remind ourselves that Paul's fundamental polemic against Judaism is not legalism, but failure to keep the law (see above). This fits with Matthew 23, where the primary complaint against the Pharisees and scribes is their disobedience.[40]

As a modification of Sanders's views, a number of scholars now argue that Paul criticizes Jewish opponents for their ethnocentricism, nationalism and exclusivism rather than their legalism or failure to observe the law.[41] James Dunn, for instance, argues that 'works of law' in Paul focuses on the boundary markers that separate Jews from Gentiles. We agree that boundary markers and exclusivism concerned Paul, and the new perspective has reminded us that the badges separating Jews from Gentiles played a significant role in the first century AD. It is more likely, however, that 'works of law' emphasizes all the deeds demanded by the law.[42]

---

39. Cf. Mark A. Elliott, *The Survivors of Israel: A Reconsideration of the Theology of Pre-Christian Judaism* (Grand Rapids: Eerdmans, 2000); Friedrich Avemarie, 'Erwählung und Vergeltung: Zur optionalen Struktur rabbinischer Soteriologie', *NTS* 45 (1999), pp. 108–126; Simon Gathercole, *Where is Boasting? Early Jewish Soteriology and Paul's Response in Romans 1 – 5* (Grand Rapids: Eerdmans, 2003); D. A. Carson, Peter T. O'Brien and Mark A. Seifrid (eds.), *Justification and Variegated Nomism*, vol. 1, *The Complexities of Second Temple Judaism* (Tübingen/Grand Rapids: Mohr Siebeck/Baker, 2001).

40. This is rightly emphasized by Moisés Silva, 'The Place of Historical Reconstruction in New Testament Criticism', in D. A. Carson and J. D. Woodbridge (eds.), *Hermeneutics, Authority, and Canon* (Grand Rapids: Zondervan, 1986), pp. 119–121.

41. See n. 33 above and, in addition, James D. G. Dunn, 'Yet Once More – "The Works of the Law": A Response', *JSNT* 46 (1992), pp. 99–117.

42. See the older but still very instructive article by Douglas J. Moo, '"Law", "Works of the Law", and Legalism in Paul', *WTJ* 45 (1983), pp. 73–100.

Moreover, a polemic against legalism cannot be washed out of texts like Romans 3:27 – 4:8; 9:30 – 10:13; Philippians 3:2–11; Galatians 2:16–21; 3:10–14, where we see a contrast between 'doing' and 'believing'. This is scarcely surprising, for the parable of the Pharisee and the tax collector is certainly an indictment against a legalistic mindset (Luke 18:9–14). Those who lack the Holy Spirit begin to think that God is impressed with their observance of the law, even if they are failing to keep it! It is a natural human tendency (not just a Jewish one) to compliment ourselves, at least silently if not publicly, for our own morality. We all have a tendency to compare ourselves to others and to massage our egos with the idea that we are somehow better than they. Jews did not think they were superior to Gentiles merely because they were circumcised and kept the Sabbath; they naturally thought they were morally superior as well (e.g., Rom. 2:17–24).

Furthermore, Paul's criticisms of boasting (e.g., Rom. 3:27 – 4:5; 9:30 – 10:8) suggest that he counters the tendency to boast in one's own works. The contrast between working for a wage and trusting in God points to an indictment of legalism (Rom. 4:4–5). Some apparently believed their observance of the law was sufficient to merit payment. Paul counters that trusting in the God who works for us is the pathway to blessing (cf. Isa. 64:4). Paul distinguishes between his own righteousness from the law and righteousness by faith in Christ (Phil. 3:9). The parallels between Romans 10 and Philippians 3 indicate that the righteousness that was Paul's before his conversion was an illusory righteousness: (1) in Romans 10:2 Paul speaks of the Jewish zeal for the law, and in Philippians 3:6 his own zeal in persecuting the church because of his devotion to the law; (2) in Romans 10:3 the Jews are faulted for seeking to establish their own righteousness, and in Philippians 3:9 Paul contrasts his own righteousness with righteousness that comes through faith in Christ; (3) in both texts Paul speaks of the righteousness that comes from God as a gift (Rom. 10:3; Phil. 3:9); (4) in both texts he emphasizes that righteousness comes from faith rather than obedience to the law (Rom. 10:3–13; Phil. 3:2–9). As Paul indicates in Romans 9:30–33, Israel did not obtain righteousness, because they pursued it the wrong way by works instead of by faith in Christ.[43]

Does Philippians 3:6 contradict the thesis set forth here? Paul claims to have been blameless in the righteousness of the law before his conversion. It should be noted that being blameless is not equated with being sinless. Paul means that he was extraordinarily devoted to what the law demanded. He was careful to practise all its prescriptions and offer sacrifices for the sins he committed.

---

43. For further defence of this interpretation, see Schreiner, *Romans*, pp. 537–540.

It is also imperative to see that Paul describes his pre-conversion view of himself before he realized the depth of God's demand. If Romans 7:7–11 is autobiographical, as I suspect, Paul came to understand that his outward obedience was insufficient. Inwardly he desired to do evil, and the tenth commandment did not merely ban outward actions, but also inward desires. Romans 7:7–11, then, represents Paul's *Christian* reflections upon his pre-Christian life as a Pharisee. Furthermore, Paul declares in Romans 1:21 that sin consists in the failure to glorify and honour God the way he should be honoured. Before Paul's conversion his observance of the law was due to his confidence in the flesh (Phil. 3:3–4) instead of boasting in Christ Jesus. In other words, his 'obedience' did not stem from faith (Rom. 14:23), and hence even while doing 'outwardly' right actions he was sinning. The extent of Paul's sin was revealed to him in his persecution of the church (Phil. 3:6; 1 Cor. 15:9). Paul realized that he was not pleasing God, but instead was a 'blasphemer, persecutor, and insolent opponent' (1 Tim. 1:13). He perceived that his blamelessness was nothing other than his own righteousness (Phil. 3:9). Therefore, Philippians 3:6 should not be understood to say that Paul was truly righteous before God by virtue of his observance of the law.

What role does the law have in the life of Christians for Paul? On the one hand, we have already seen that the Sinai covenant is terminated for Paul. It has come to an end because it is now fulfilled in Christ. The physical temple in Jerusalem is no longer God's dwelling place, but believers in Christ are the new temple due to their union with Christ (1 Cor. 3:16; 2 Cor. 6:16; Eph. 2:22). God is unconcerned about whether believers observe Passover and remove leaven from their houses, for the Passover points to Christ's death (1 Cor. 5:7) and the removal of leaven symbolizes freedom from evil in our lives (1 Cor. 5:8). Those who require circumcision for salvation deny the gospel of Christ (Gal. 2:3–5; 5:2–6; 6:12–13). In and of itself, physical circumcision is insignificant (Gal. 5:6; 6:15; 1 Cor. 7:19). What matters is the circumcision of the heart (Rom. 2:28–29; Col. 2:12) – the circumcision accomplished by the Spirit of God and rooted in the cross of Christ (Phil. 3:3). In the same way, Paul does not believe food laws are obligatory for believers now that Christ has come (Rom. 14; Col. 2:16–23), nor is the Sabbath required in the new era (Rom. 14:5–6; Col. 2:16–17). The requirement of capital punishment for certain sins under the old covenant (cf. Deut. 17:7; 22:20–24) does not apply literally in the new people of God, but is fulfilled when believers expel unrepentant sinners from the church (1 Cor. 5:13).

On the other hand, Paul also seems to carry over some of the moral norms of the law for the Christian. The command to honour fathers and mothers still applies to believers (Eph. 6:2). Those who live in love will not commit

adultery, murder, steal or covet (Rom. 13:8–10; cf. Rom. 2:21–22; 7:7–8). Those
who live according to the Spirit will fulfil the ordinance of the law (Rom. 8:4),
or, as Paul says in Romans 2:26, they will keep the precepts of the law. The obedience of believers is the result of the Spirit's work (Rom. 2:28–29), although
all obedience is still touched and tainted by sin as long as believers live in the
body and await the fulfilment of the promise of final redemption (Rom. 8:10,
23; Eph. 1:14). The prohibition against idolatry still stands, although Paul does
not cite any particular Old Testament text (1 Cor. 5:10–11; 6:9; 10:7, 14; 2 Cor.
6:16; Gal. 5:20; Eph. 5:5; Col. 3:5). Paul believes that some of the standards in
the Old Testament law are normative, although he does not necessarily specify
that they derive from the law: honouring and obeying parents (Rom. 1:30; Eph.
6:1–3; Col. 3:20; 1 Tim. 1:9; 2 Tim. 3:2); murder (Rom. 1:29; 13:9; 1 Tim. 1:10);
adultery (Rom. 2:22; 7:3; 13:9; 1 Cor. 6:9; cf. 1 Tim. 1:10); stealing (Rom.
1:29–30; 1 Cor. 6:9–10; Eph. 4:28); lying (Col. 3:9; 1 Tim. 1:10; 4:2; Titus 1:12);
coveting (Rom. 1:29; 7:7–8; Eph. 5:3, 5; Col. 3:5).[44]

How do we account for Paul's teaching that the Mosaic covenant is obsolete, while still citing commands from the law as authoritative? The moral
norms of the Old Testament law are included in the law of Christ (Gal. 6:2; 1
Cor. 9:21; cf. Lev. 19:18; Mark 12:28–32).[45] Nevertheless, in giving exhortations
to his churches Paul does not often cite specific commands from the Old
Testament, for the heart and soul of his ethic is summed up in the command
to love one another (e.g., Rom. 12:9; 13:8–10; 1 Cor. 8:1–3; 13:1–13; 14:1; Gal.
5:13–15; Eph. 5:2; Col. 3:15; 1 Tim. 1:5), and yet the love command itself hails

---

44. It should be noted that the Old Testament prophets do not often appeal explicitly
    to the moral norms of the law in declaring judgment on Israel, and yet it is clear
    that they believed Israel had violated the norms of the covenant, and there are
    many allusions to the Sinai law. See the brief discussion on Hosea above.

45. In his work on the law, Frank Thielman especially emphasizes discontinuity
    between the Mosaic law and the law of Christ. See *The Law and the New Testament:
    The Question of Continuity* (New York: Crossroad, 1999). Although there is overlap
    between Thielman's view and my own, I see more continuity than Thielman.
    Interpreting the meaning of the law of Christ is quite controversial. For an
    excellent survey of scholarship on the matter, see Todd Wilson, 'The Law of
    Christ and the Law of Moses: Reflections on a Recent Trend in Interpretation',
    forthcoming in *Currents in Biblical Research*. Wilson seems to suggest, although he
    does not finally endorse any view in his essay, a closer connection between the
    Mosaic law (per Gal. 5:14) and the law of Christ. It seems to me that such a
    suggestion is on the right path.

from the Old Testament (Lev. 19:18)! Many have rightly seen, therefore, the injunction to love as the centre of the law of Christ (cf. John 13:34–35).

Love, however, cannot be separated from moral norms. For instance, Paul gives specific and concrete parenesis to his churches, instructing them not to get divorced (1 Cor. 7:10–16) or to commit sexual immorality (1 Thess. 4:3–8; 1 Cor. 6:12–20).[46] He admonishes the idle to get to work (2 Thess. 3:6–13). The man committing incest must be disciplined (1 Cor. 5:1–13). Love for Paul does not float free of ethical norms, but is expressed by such norms. In some ways Paul's ethic is rather general, for he does not give specific guidance for each situation. He realizes that in many situations wisdom is needed to determine the prudent and godly course of action (Phil. 1:9–11; Eph. 5:10; Col. 1:9–11). Paul does not have a casuistic ethic that prescribes the course of action for every conceivable situation, but neither does he simply appeal to the Spirit and freedom without describing how life in the Spirit expresses itself. The notion that Paul appeals to the Spirit for ethics without any ethical norms is contradicted by his parenesis. The Pauline theme of obedience should not be identified as a new legalism, for the new obedience is the work of the Spirit in those who are the new creation work of Christ. The work of the cross is not diminished, for the cross is the basis and foundation for the transforming work of the Spirit in us.

James

The letter of James provides an interesting window into the role of the law in early Christianity. What James means by the law must be discerned by examining his letter inductively. James was likely written by the brother of Jesus, representing the Jewish-Christian wing of the Christian church (cf. Acts 15:13–21; 21:18–25; 1 Cor. 15:7; Gal. 1:19; 2:9, 12; Jude 1). The letter of James is parenetic and clearly teaches that genuine faith must express itself in works. Those who do not practise good works are not justified (Jas 2:14–26). True wisdom manifests itself in godly behaviour (Jas 3:13–18). James identifies the law as 'the law of liberty' (Jas 1:25; 2:12), 'the perfect law' (Jas 1:25) and 'the royal law' (Jas 2:8). The law surely includes the Old Testament, for in James 2:9–11 transgressing the law is connected with failing to keep the commands prohibiting

---

46. See especially the detailed studies by Wolfgang Schrage, *Die konkreten Einzelgebote in paulinischen Paränese: Ein Beitrag zur neutestamentlichen Ethik* (Gütersloh: Gerd Mohn, 1981); Thomas J. Deidun, *New Covenant Morality in Paul* (Rome: Biblical Institute Press, 1981). See also Brian Rosner, *Paul, Scripture, and Ethics: A Study of 1 Corinthians 5 – 7* (Grand Rapids: Baker, 1999).

murder and adultery. The 'law' for James is closely related to the 'word'. Believers were granted new life 'by the word of truth' (Jas 1:18), and hence this word must refer to the gospel of Christ. James speaks of doing 'the word' and not just hearing it (Jas 1:22–23), and such doing of the word can also be described as 'doing' the law of liberty, the perfect law (Jas 1:25). This evidence suggests a close relationship between the 'law' and the 'gospel', if we can put it that way. Remarkably, James enjoins his readers to 'receive with meekness the implanted [*emphytos*] word, which is able to save your souls' (Jas 1:21). The 'implanted word' suggests the new covenant work of God in which the law is written on the heart (Jer. 31:31–34; cf. 1 Thess. 4:9). An allusion to the new covenant would explain the relationship between the 'word' of the gospel and the Old Testament law in James, for the new covenant was inaugurated when the law was written on the heart through the gospel. Another way of stating this is to say that this is James's way of speaking of the law of Christ, and it seems that for James the law of Christ also contains the moral norms of the Old Testament law. It is particularly interesting that James, as a conservative Jewish Christian, says nothing about boundary markers like Sabbath, circumcision or purity laws.[47] The silence on these matters could be interpreted variously, but the keeping of the law in James appears to be rather similar to the Pauline view of the fulfilment of the law, although James does not discuss the law in the same detail as Paul, so we cannot narrow down James's view with certainty.

Matthew

Matthew is often likened to James, in that a Jewish-Christian stance towards the Old Testament law seems to dominate, which some scholars see as contradicting the more 'liberal' viewpoint of Paul. An observation needs to be made at the outset, one which also relates to the Gospel of Luke. If we take Matthew seriously as history, he recounts events that occurred before the death and resurrection of Jesus. Hence in some instances references to the Old Testament law do not necessarily function as admonitions for the church of Jesus Christ after the great redemptive events have been accomplished. We should not conclude, for instance, that Matthew recommends offering Old

---

47. Martin Hengel suggests that James distinguishes moral norms from ritual law and especially exalts the law of love. See *Between Jesus and Paul: Studies in the Earliest History of Christianity* (Philadelphia: Fortress, 1983), p. 174, n. 152. It does seem instructive that James never mentions circumcision, food laws and Sabbath, especially since he ministered among Jews.

Testament sacrifices (Matt. 5:24) or tithing (Matt. 23:23). He simply records what Jesus said to his contemporaries who lived under the Old Testament law.

It has sometimes been argued that Matthew has a legalistic view of the law, since he demands that the righteousness of believers is superior to the right-eousness of the scribes and Pharisees (Matt. 5:20) and even insists on perfec-tion (Matt. 5:48).[48] Such a view must be rejected as too simplistic.[49] The Matthean theology of the law must be interpreted in the light of the entirety of the Gospel, and particularly the theme that Jesus is the promised Messiah. In his death and resurrection he is the one who fulfils all righteousness (Matt. 3:15). The power of the kingdom is bestowed upon those who are followers of Jesus Christ, and those who belong to Christ are not commended for their inherent righteousness, but for their recognition that they are poor in spirit (Matt. 5:3). They are keenly aware that righteousness is not fully theirs, and so they hunger and thirst for the righteousness that is given only through the cross and resur-rection of Jesus (Matt. 5:6). The law, as shall be argued below, is fulfilled in Christ, and Jesus maintains that the law is summed up in the command to love God and one's neighbour (Matt. 22:34–40; see Deut. 6:4–9; Lev. 19:18).

One of the main themes that Matthew advances regarding the Old Testament is that Jesus fulfils Old Testament prophecy. The fulfilment for-mulae in Matthew attest to the importance of this theme in his writing (Matt. 1:22; 2:15, 17, 23; 4:14; 8:17; 12:17; 13:35; 21:4; 27:9; cf. also 3:15; 26:54, 56). The fulfilment cannot be construed, however, as demanding that believers keep lit-erally everything the Old Testament law enjoins. The law points to Christ and is fulfilled in him, and hence the Old Testament law must be interpreted in the light of the Christ event. Matthew 17:24–27 seems to support such an inter-pretation. Israelites were required to pay the temple tax according to Exodus 30:13–16. Jesus, obviously, feels under no compulsion to abide by the require-ment to pay a temple tax. He declares that the sons are free from any such pre-scription. We probably have a hint here as well that the temple was no longer central in God's purposes. This fits with the claim that Jesus is greater than the temple (Matt. 12:5–6), and Jesus' prophecy that the temple would be destroyed (Matt. 24:2).

---

48. For a discussion of this matter, see Roger Mohrlang, *Matthew and Paul: A Comparison of Ethical Perspectives*, SNTSMS 48 (Cambridge: Cambridge University Press, 1984), pp. 42–43.

49. See especially here the reflections on this theme by David E. Holwerda, *Jesus and Israel: One Covenant or Two?* (Grand Rapids: Eerdmans; Leicester: Apollos, 1995), pp. 114–120.

It is difficult to be sure whether Jesus actually contravenes the Sabbath in Matthew (12:1–14). In the account of the man with the withered hand, Matthew stresses that what Jesus did was lawful on the Sabbath (Matt. 12:12). In the narrative of the disciples eating grain on the Sabbath, they are charged with doing what is unlawful (Matt. 12:2). Jesus does not specifically argue that their behaviour was permissible, but appeals to David who ate the bread of presence, which 'was not lawful for him to eat' (12:4). Perhaps Jesus is merely saying that eating the grain is technically not 'lawful', but is permissible in this situation. On the other hand, Jesus claims that he is greater than the temple (12:5–6) and is 'lord of the Sabbath' (12:8). He is the greater David who exercises sovereign authority in interpreting the law – the same kind of authority we witnessed in the matter of the temple tax.

A very illuminating text on Jesus' relationship to the law is found in Matthew 15:1–20. The Pharisees and scribes complain that Jesus' disciples transgress the tradition of the elders by not washing their hands before eating. Jesus excoriates the leaders for exalting their tradition over God's law. The injunction to honour one's father and mother is violated by their tradition, and hence God's law takes second place to their human tradition. Jesus categorically rejects 'the commandments of men' (15:9). Up to this point Jesus upholds a conservative view of the Old Testament law, but the story takes a surprising turn. Jesus proceeds to teach that what enters into a person's mouth does not defile that person. Rather, it is the evil thoughts and actions that flow from our hearts that stain us (15:10–20). Matthew is not as explicit as Mark, for Mark comments that with these words Jesus declared that all foods are clean (Mark 7:19). It seems fair to say that Matthew's wording at least implies the same conclusion. If this is the case (and in Mark it is so without a doubt), we see the same sovereign freedom in interpreting the law that was observed in previous texts. Jesus cites commands from the law that require honouring fathers and mothers and teaches that they are binding on his hearers. Yet he seems to wave aside food laws and to imply that they are no longer applicable for believers.[50] The Matthean view of the law, however, is not arbitrary, but must be interpreted in light of the kingdom of God and the fulfilment that has arrived in Jesus Christ (e.g., Matt. 11:11–13), so Jesus, in Matthew, interprets the law in terms of eschatology.

The texts examined above are instructive for Matthew's most extensive teaching on the law in Matthew 5:17–48. Verses 17–19 might suggest at first

---

50. Perhaps Paul's instructions on purity laws were themselves rooted in Jesus tradition (cf. Rom. 14:14).

glance that the Old Testament law continues to apply to believers down to the last detail. It is important to note, however, the presence of the word 'fulfil' (*plēroō*). Jesus did not come to abolish the law, but to fulfil it (v. 17). The Old Testament laws and commands are fulfilled in Christ, and hence how they apply to believers must be discerned in the light of the Christ event. Such a conclusion seems warranted in light of the three texts examined above. How to interpret the subsequent verses in Matthew 5:21–48 is also quite controversial. I am still convinced that Jesus responds to misinterpretations of the Old Testament law and provides the proper interpretation.[51] The Old Testament law does not command people to hate their enemies, not even in Psalm 139:19–22. Indeed, the Old Testament itself teaches that people are to love their enemies (Lev. 19:17–18; Exod. 23:5; Job 31:29–30). It seems clear that Jesus corrects a wrong interpretation in this passage. That Jesus corrects a wrong understanding of the law is not too difficult to see in the texts on murder and adultery (Matt. 5:21–30). Perhaps some in Jesus' day wrongly concluded that anger and lust were permissible, but the Old Testament itself forbids both unrighteous anger (e.g., Prov. 14:29; 22:24; 29:22) and lust (Job 31:1; Prov. 5:23–25). The divorce saying is admittedly more difficult for my interpretation (Matt. 5:31–32). Many conclude that Jesus actually contravenes the Old Testament law here, and that is a possible reading. There are reasons to think, however, that Jesus corrects an abuse of the Old Testament. Deuteronomy 24:1–4 does not recommend divorce, but regulates it.[52] Some rabbis justified divorce for the most trivial of reasons. Jesus explains that divorce is justified only in the case of sexual immorality (cf. Matt. 19:3–12) and appeals to the Old Testament itself to support his case (Gen. 1:26–27; 2:24). Others think the prohibition against oaths is a clear abrogation of an Old Testament law (5:33–37), but in Matthew 23:16–22 Jesus responds to an abuse of oath-taking, for in the latter text the Pharisees and scribes are criticized for their casuistry whereby they declare some oaths to be binding and others to be breakable. Such abuses became excuses for not speaking the truth. In the rest of the New Testament, the interpretation proposed here seems to be

---

51. For the view that Jesus contravenes the Old Testament law, see Douglas Moo, 'Jesus and the Authority of the Mosaic Law', *JSNT* 20 (1984), pp. 3–49; Robert Banks, *Jesus and the Law in the Synoptic Tradition* (Cambridge: Cambridge University Press, 1975).

52. For a recent and thorough discussion of divorce in the Scriptures, see David Instone-Brewer, *Divorce and Remarriage in the Bible: The Social and Literary Context* (Grand Rapids: Eerdmans, 2002).

supported, for Paul uses oath formulas (e.g., Rom. 1:9; 2 Cor. 1:23) and Hebrews informs us that even God took an oath (Heb. 6:13–18). The same solution applies to the injunction not to resist evil (Matt. 5:38–42). At first glance Jesus seems to sweep away the regulations that require an eye for an eye and a tooth for a tooth. It should be noted, however, that 'an eye for an eye and a tooth for a tooth' is simply a colourful way of saying that the punishment should fit the crime. Indeed, it prevents the injured party from extracting a greater punishment than is warranted and hence is a merciful law! Furthermore, the eye for an eye laws always occur in civil contexts in the Old Testament (Exod. 21:22–25; Lev. 24:17–22; Deut. 19:21). Jesus responds to those who misinterpret these words and use them as an excuse to pay back those who injure them personally. Jesus insists that disciples must not avenge themselves, but should have a spirit of forgiveness and generosity. Interestingly, Paul's words are very helpful in this regard and support the interpretation offered here. Personally, believers are to refrain from avenging themselves and giving in to anger (Rom. 12:17–21), but governing authorities, on the other hand, have the responsibility to wield the sword and to avenge evildoers (Rom. 13:1–7). Perhaps the case is strengthened further by the fact that in Romans 12:17–21 Paul appears to be dependent on traditions about Jesus he has received from earlier disciples.

Conclusion

Several key themes emerge in the biblical teaching on law. First, sinners are unable to keep God's law, and hence no one can stand in the right before God by means of the law. Justification is by faith in both Testaments (Gen. 15:6; Ps. 32:1–2; Rom. 4:1–25). Justification now belongs to believers by virtue of the atoning work of Jesus Christ (Rom. 1:18 – 3:26; Gal. 3:10–14). Second, in the scriptural storyline God did not give the law to establish a relationship with himself. The covenant stipulations were given to those who were already recipients of God's gracious and redeeming work. Obedience to the law was a response to God's grace, not a means of meriting his favour. This pattern is true in both the Old Testament and the New Testament. The parenetic texts in the New Testament are in this sense the same as the injunctions to obey found in the Sinai covenant. Third, the new covenant is superior to the old, for most members of the Sinai covenant were uncircumcised in heart. On the contrary, *all* the members of the new covenant community have received forgiveness of sins through Jesus Christ's death and resurrection, and are transformed by the Holy Spirit.

Fourth, true obedience is always the obedience of faith (Rom. 1:5; 16:26). Faith and obedience may be distinguished, but should not be segregated from one another, as if God summons his people to obey him without trusting in him, or as if faith in him could ever be separated from obeying him. Abraham's obedience, then, flowed from his faith, so we can say of Abraham that he was justified by faith alone, as long as we recognize that such faith always issues in obedience (Jas 2:14–26). Fifth, those who keep God's law are enabled to do so by the work of the Holy Spirit. The Spirit empowers and strengthens God's people to do his will, although this obedience in the interval between the inauguration and consummation of the kingdom is imperfect. When the Scripture refers to the law killing or putting to death, the writers refer to the unregenerate, for when the law comes to those who do not know God it slays them instead of enlivening them. The law is not a source of life, for it provides no ability to keep its prescriptions. The Mosaic covenant, then, produced death because the nation of Israel as a whole was unregenerate. The problem was not with the content of the law, nor was the Sinai covenant legalistic. Except for the remnant, the law was given to people who were stubborn and stiff-necked, who had no inclination to do God's will.

Sixth, the New Testament teaches that the Sinai covenant was a temporary covenant, not intended to be in force for ever. The Sinai covenant separated Israel from the nations as God's special people. With the coming of Christ, the Mosaic covenant is terminated and the distinctions between Jews and Gentiles are erased, and they are now one body if they belong to Christ. Believers are no longer under the prescriptions of the Mosaic law. The Mosaic covenant pointed towards and is fulfilled in the work of Jesus Christ. The new covenant is established by him, so that the law is written on the heart. Seventh, the content of the law for believers is the 'law of Christ'. The law of Christ centres on Jesus Christ himself and his interpretation of the law. Believers fulfil the law of Christ supremely in their love for one another. It does seem to be the case that the moral norms of the Old Testament law are included in the law of Christ, but the focus in the law of Christ is not the Old Testament law but its fulfilment in Christ – in Christ's command to love one another. Still, this love also manifests itself in the keeping of God's commands. Thus Christ's death and the power of the Holy Spirit help *all* members of the new covenant community to do what only the *remnant* of the old covenant did: to love the Lord with all their heart, mind and strength and their neighbours as themselves (Deut. 6:4–9; Lev. 19:17–18; Mark 12:28–32).

3. THE ATONEMENT

Frank S. Thielman

In recent years a long and gruesome list of social horrors has been laid at the doorstep of the substitutionary view of the atonement. Some scholars claim that the image of Christ's willing suffering has forced Christian women into the role of the 'suffering servant', encouraging them to accept their status as victims and become complicit in their own oppression.[1] Others say that the picture of a wrathful Father punishing his Son unavoidably paints God as an abusive parent, and so fuels violence against children.[2] One scholar believes that Great Britain and the United States have patterned their cruel and ineffective penal systems after the image of God's retributive justice contained within the 'satisfaction' view of the atonement.[3] Another scholar claims that the conquistadors used Christ's acceptance of suffering, if not a

1. Joanne Carlson Brown and Rebecca Parker, 'For God So Loved the World?', *Christianity, Patriarchy and Abuse: A Feminist Critique*, eds. Joanne Carlson Brown and Carole R. Bohn (New York: Pilgrim Press, 1989), pp. 1–30, here at pp. 2–3.
2. Ibid., pp. 2, 9, 26; Rita Nakashima Brock, 'And a Little Child Will Lead Us: Christology and Child Abuse', *Christianity, Patriarchy and Abuse*, eds. Brown and Bohn, pp. 42–61, here at pp. 52–53.
3. Timothy Gorringe, *God's Just Vengeance: Crime, Violence and the Rhetoric of Salvation*, CSIR 9 (Cambridge: Cambridge University Press, 1996).

particular theory of the atonement, to encourage the Aztecs to submit to oppression.[4]

Some evangelical theologians are also concerned that the 'penal substitutionary' understanding of atonement is unintelligible to many cultures outside North America and Western Europe, and is increasingly unintelligible even in Western cultures as they move into a postmodern mode of thought.[5] Crude expressions of it dominate popular, evangelical Christianity, they observe, and this both frightens children and gives the impression that God is mean and vindictive.[6]

The implications of these criticisms are clear. To insist on the theological importance of a substitutionary atonement is to become complicit in the oppression of the weak and dispossessed. Depending on how this view is expressed, it may also hinder the progress of the gospel.

These are serious charges. If one of the essentials of evangelical Christianity is its claim to stand under the authority of Scripture,[7] then there is no question that it must be committed to relieving the burdens of the poor, the oppressed and the unevangelized. It must also be committed to the winsome proclamation of the gospel in sensitive ways that do not confuse the ancient cultural medium in which the message is contained with the message itself. But if the central understanding of the atonement in evangelical Christianity both oppresses the weak and hinders the gospel's advancement with a simplistic hermeneutic, then evangelicals face a large problem. Either our understanding of the essential meaning of Jesus' death is flawed, or the teaching of Scripture on atonement is incompatible with the Scriptures' own approach to the poor, the oppressed and the unevangelized. Much more than a short essay is required to sort all this out, but the attempt to do so must begin with the biblical witness.

----

4. David B. Batstone, *From Conquest to Struggle: Jesus of Nazareth in Latin America* (Albany: State University of New York Press, 1991), p. 17. Cf. Joel B. Green and Mark D. Baker, *Recovering the Scandal of the Cross: Atonement in New Testament and Contemporary Contexts* (Downers Grove: InterVarsity Press, 2000), p. 19.

5. Green and Baker, *Recovering the Scandal of the Cross*, pp. 28–30, 153–170.

6. Ibid., pp. 30, 141–142, 147–148.

7. Alister McGrath, *A Passion for Truth: The Intellectual Coherence of Evangelicalism* (Leicester: Inter-Varsity Press; Downers Grove: InterVarsity Press, 1996), pp. 53–117.

The Old Testament

Old Testament texts that explicitly describe substitutionary atonement are relatively rare. The notion occurs outside cultic contexts in several places. After Israel has committed idolatry in the Sinai wilderness, Moses asks God to forgive the people and, if he will not do so, to blot him out of the book of life. He requests this apparently so that his death might substitute for the death of the people. God refuses both options and instead sends 'a plague on the people, because they made the calf, the one that Aaron made' (Exod. 32:35). The text shows the currency of notions of substitutionary atonement in ancient Israel, but, since God both refuses Moses' offer and refuses to forgive, the passage is of little help in determining God's view of substitutionary atonement.

A much more helpful text occups in Deuteronomy 21:1–9 where the law provides a means of atonement for God's people when an unknown person has committed murder. The elders of the town nearest the place where the victim's body was found are to break the neck of a heifer and confess that they themselves had no knowledge of the crime. They must then appeal to God to 'accept atonement . . . for your people Israel, whom you have redeemed, and do not set the guilt of innocent blood in the midst of your people Israel, so that their blood guilt be atoned for' (21:8).

The requirements for the heifer and for the place where the heifer is killed are instructive. The heifer must never have worked and never have worn a yoke (21:3) and she must be killed in a valley 'with running water, which is neither ploughed nor sown' (21:4). It is difficult to say for sure, but it seems reasonable to take these requirements as an indication that the murder has violated the order that God gave to the world when he created it. The heifer's death seems to substitute for the death of the unknown person who committed the crime and thus symbolizes the restoration of order to creation.[8]

At first, it seems as if something similar happens in 2 Samuel 21:1–14 where the Lord reveals to David that the origins of a famine plaguing the land lie in Saul's violation of Joshua's treaty with the Gibeonites (21:1; cf. Josh. 9:3–27). Saul had, it turns out, put them to death. When David summoned the remaining Gibeonites and asked them how he could make reparation for this injustice, they responded that he could give them seven of Saul's male descendants whom they would kill and expose 'before the LORD' (21:6). David agreed to do

---

8. Cf. Hartmut Gese, 'The Atonement', *Essays on Biblical Theology* (Minneapolis: Augsburg, 1981), pp. 93–116, here at pp. 97–98.

this, and the Gibeonites killed the seven and 'hanged them on the mountain before the LORD' just as the barley harvest began (21:9). One of Saul's concubines, Rizpah, piously protected the exposed corpses from the ravages of wild animals and, moved by her piety, David gave all of Saul's deceased family a proper burial in the tomb of Saul's father. 'After that', we read, 'God responded to the plea for the land' (21:14). Does a substitutionary sacrifice here too restore the violated moral order and spare Israel death by famine?

Although the pattern of famine for sin, death for sin, release from famine might at first seem to lead to this conclusion, a closer reading shows this understanding of the text to be a misreading. The text does not say that the Lord lifted the famine because of the death of Saul's sons. It says clearly that the Lord sent the famine to punish Israel for the unjust actions of its king (24:1). It also clearly indicates that the Gibeonites thought they could appease the Lord and stop the famine through killing seven of Saul's sons (21:6). It just as clearly says, however, that God actually ended the famine in response to the piety first of Rizpah, for treating the corpses of Saul's sons with respect, and then of David, who gave Saul and his sons a decent burial (21:14).

The text is helpful, therefore, in a discussion of substitutionary atonement in the Old Testament, but not because it shows how the concept works from God's perspective. It is helpful because it shows the common currency of such notions in Ancient Near Eastern cultures.

This common currency makes it likely that notions of substitutionary atonement are present at least some of the time in contexts of cultic sacrifice, and particularly in the Day of Atonement ritual described in Leviticus 16:1–34. Four animals are involved in this ritual: a young bull, two male goats and a ram. Aaron offers the bull 'as a sin offering for himself and shall make atonement for himself and for his house' (16:6). He sprinkles the blood from this offering both on and before the 'mercy seat' (Heb. *kappōret*) or 'place of atonement' (Septuagint, *hilastērion*) in the Holy of Holies (16:14). He follows the same procedure with one of the two goats, chosen by lot 'for the LORD' (16:8). This time, however, the goat is a sin offering for the people (16:15).

Using blood from the sacrificed bull and goat, Aaron then moves outside the Holy of Holies and sprinkles the blood on an unspecified spot in the Tent of Meeting (16:16). Next he moves even further away from the Holy of Holies to the altar. Here he places blood from the goat and the bull on the horns of the altar and, in addition, sprinkles blood on it (16:18). After this, he lays his hands on the head of the remaining goat, chosen by lot 'for Azazel' (16:8), and confesses 'over it all the iniquities of the people of Israel, and all their transgressions, all their sins'. In this way, he puts these sins 'on the head of the goat' (16:21). He then sends it into the wilderness, and it bears 'all their iniquities on itself to a remote area' (16:22). Aaron then apparently sacrifices the ram as a burnt offering for himself and for the people (16:24).

The whole procedure is designed to 'make atonement' for three broad entities: the places where God comes into contact with his people, the priestly family who mediates this contact, and the people themselves (16:6, 11, 16–18, 20, 24, 30, 33). Atonement for these three entities is necessary because of the 'uncleanness of the people of Israel and because of their transgressions, all their sins' (16:16; cf. v. 21).

Does this complex ritual, however, involve notions of substitutionary sacrifice? If so, do the slain animals accept the punishment due to the priests and the people for 'all their sins'? Occasionally scholars argue that the rite involves no substitutionary concepts, whether penal or otherwise, because the 'goat for Azazel', not the slain goat, makes atonement for Israel's sins. This understanding of the ritual, however, seems to contradict the clear statement in the text that the blood of the bull and the goat make atonement 'for the Holy Place, because of the uncleannesses of the people of Israel and because of their transgressions, all their sins' (16:16). It also conflicts with the text's statements that the the entire ritual, not simply the scapegoat procedure, atones for the sins of the priests and the people (16:24, 29–34).[9]

The argument that the rite nowhere presupposes specifically *penal* substitution has more to be said for it.[10] The text nowhere explicitly says that the slain bull, goat and ram die in the place of those who have sinned, receiving the punishment that sinners deserved. An important purpose of the sacrifices, moreover, was to 'atone' for the *places* that Israel had polluted through its uncleanness and sin, and it is difficult to imagine how the destruction of the animals could somehow take the punishment of these places. Hartmut Gese believes that atonement is effected in this ritual, as in other sin offerings, not through a substitutionary punishment, but through the identification of the individual with the animal and then a devotion of the animal to God through the sacrifice of its life. Gese points to Leviticus 17:11 as evidence for this approach: 'The life of the creature is in the blood, and I have given it to you to make atonement for yourselves on the altar; it is the blood that makes atonement for one's life.'[11]

---

9. For the position that the phrase 'to make atonement for himself and for the people' in 16:24 applies to the whole ritual and not simply to the burnt offering, see Baruch Levine, *Leviticus*, JPSTC (Philadelphia: Jewish Publication Society, 1989), p. 108.

10. See, e.g., Gese, 'The Atonement', p. 114.

11. Ibid., pp. 100–116.

Gese helpfully emphasizes that the ultimate goal of the Day of Atonement ritual is to carve a path from humanity to God – to make fellowship with God possible. His idea that the sacrificial animal's shed blood symbolizes the complete devotion of one's life to God, however, seems unlikely in the light of the wide currency of the notion of substitutionary sacrifice in the Ancient Near East, and in view of the biblical picture of God as one who punishes sin.[12] In the absence of any clear explanation of how the Day of Atonement ritual worked theologically, we should probably assume that the goat sacrificed as a 'sin offering' gave up its life symbolically, in place of the Israelites who had sinned and whose lives were therefore forfeit. We should also probably assume that the scapegoat's banishment to the wilderness symbolizes the removal of Israel's sin and impurity, and the possibility, in the light of their removal, of fellowship with God rather than destruction by his wrath.[13] It is in terms of the aversion of God's wrath that we should read Leviticus 17:11. God has graciously provided animal sacrifice as a means of atoning for the sin of his people without the sacrifice of their own lives. This makes possible the perilous activity of coming into the presence of God.[14]

This conceptual framework of substitutionary sacrifice also provides the most natural understanding of Isaiah 52:13–53:12. Here Isaiah interprets the death of the Servant as a guilt offering (53:10). The guilt offering was made not only in cases where the offence was unintentional (Lev. 5:15–19), as with the sin offering, but also in cases where the offence was wilful, especially in cases of theft and fraud (Lev. 6:1–5; 19:20–22).[15] The offering had to be a ram, sometimes more specifically defined as a male, yearling lamb, and had to be without defect (Lev. 5:15; 14:10, 12; 19:21–22; Num. 6:12). The priest sprinkled the blood of the animal on all sides of the altar, burned the fatty parts of the animal on the altar, and could eat the meat (Lev. 7:1–6; Num. 18:9). None of the relevant texts indicate how the offering worked conceptually, although they mention that the offering is the guilty party's 'compensation' which he brings

---

12. See the comments of Levine, *Leviticus*, p. 115, on 17:11.

13. Cf. the ritual for the removal of skin diseases and mildew in Lev. 14:33–57, involving both a live bird and a slain bird. This ritual also makes atonement for the diseased person or object. See ibid., pp. 250–251.

14. Levine, *Leviticus*, pp. 6–7, 115.

15. The phrase in Lev. 6:3 ('in any of all the things that people do and sin thereby') seems to broaden the scope of the guilt offering from sins involving the theft of someone else's property to any sin, regardless of its nature.

'to the LORD' (Lev. 6:6) and that when the priest slaughters the offering, he makes 'atonement' for the offender 'before the LORD' (Lev. 6:7; 19:22).

Isaiah may have some of these details in mind when he describes the Servant in Isaiah 52:13–53:12. The Servant is 'like a lamb' (53:7), and although he is certainly not without physical defects (52:14), he is without moral defect, for he 'had done no violence, and there was no deceit in his mouth' (53:9). It is possible that Isaiah also conceived of the 'transgressions' and 'iniquities' of Israel as a debt that Israel owed to God and for which the Servant paid the required compensation as a guilt offering. If so, then Isaiah understood the guilt offering generally as substitutionary and described the Servant's suffering within this framework. Just as the year-old male lamb dies in the place of the person who wilfully sinned and so makes atonement for that person with God, so the Servant takes the place of Israel, becoming 'wounded' and 'crushed' (53:5, 11–12) for God's people and so suffering the fate that they deserved because of their rebellion against God.

The New Testament

As we move into the New Testament, the concept of atonement by means of substitutionary sacrifice becomes more explicit, and it is connected specifically with the crucifixion of Jesus. The importance of this understanding of the atonement is clear from its appearance in the three great theological traditions that dominate the New Testament: the Pauline, the Petrine and the Johannine traditions. It is also clear in the relatively independent witnesses of Hebrews and Revelation.

The Pauline tradition
Galatians 3:10–14 and Romans 3:25 are among the clearest expressions of the substitutionary nature of Jesus' atoning death in the New Testament. They are also among the earliest such expressions. In the Galatians text, Paul describes to his readers the penalty that the law exacts for 'everyone who does not abide by all things written in the Book of the Law … '. Transgressors are, Paul says, 'cursed' (3:10). This is a quotation from Deuteronomy 27:26, which in its own context summarizes the curses pronounced from Mount Ebal on those who disobey the law. Since the law also pronounces a curse on 'everyone who is hanged on a tree' (cf. Deut. 21:23), however, Christ was able to free those who lived under the law's curse through his death on the wooden cross. Paul could hardly be more explicit about how this worked: through Christ's death on the cross, he became a curse 'for us' (*hyper hēmōn*, 3:13).

These statements make sense only if they rest on two unexpressed assumptions. First, Paul assumes that no one has done the 'works of the law' and that everyone, whether Jew or Gentile, therefore stands under the law's curse. Second, Paul assumes that Christ was sinless, and that this allowed his death as a common criminal, cursed by God (Deut. 21:22–23), to atone for the sins of all those who had transgressed God's law and therefore deserved the law's curse.

That we are on the right track in making these two assumptions emerges from two considerations. First, the notion that the death of a willing and innocent victim could make atonement with the gods or God for the sins of others was common in antiquity among ancient Greeks, Romans and Jews. A couple of examples must suffice to illustrate the common currency of the notion in the mid-first century AD. Lucan, a contemporary of Paul, puts onto the lips of Cato the following speech to Brutus:

> So may it be: may the strict gods of the Romans receive complete expiation [*piacula
> . . . plena*], and may we not cheat war of any of its victims. If only the gods of heaven
> and the underworld would allow this head to expose itself to all punishment as one
> condemned! The hordes of the enemy cast down Decius, the consecrated one: may
> the two armies [involved in the civil war] pierce me through. May the barbarians from
> the Rhine make me the target of their shots, and exposed to every spear, may I
> receive all the wounds of the whole war. This my blood will ransom [*redimat*] all the
> people; this my death achieve atonement [*luatur*] for all that the Romans have
> deserved through their moral decline. (*Pharsalia* 2.304–309)[16]

The death of the relatively innocent Cato atones for the sins of the Romans by absorbing the devastation of the civil war. Death is required to restore the moral order that the gods have worked into the universe, but Cato hopes that his death will be an adequate substitute for the death of vast numbers of Romans.

Writing at roughly the same time, the author of 4 Maccabees describes the effect of the Maccabean martyrs' deaths this way:

> The tyrant himself and all his council marvelled at their endurance, because of which
> they now stand before the divine throne and live through blessed eternity. For Moses
> says, 'All who are consecrated are under your hands.' These, then, who have been

---

16. From Martin Hengel, *Atonement: the Origins of the Doctrine in the New Testament* (Philadelphia: Fortress, 1981), pp. 23–24, Latin text on p. 88.

consecrated for the sake of God, are honoured, not only with this honour, but also by the fact that because of them our enemies did not rule over our nation, the tyrant was punished, and the homeland purified – they having become, as it were a ransom [*antipsychon*] for the sin of our nation. And through the blood of those devout ones [*eusebōn*] and of the propitiation of their death [*tou hilastēriou tou thanatou autōn*], divine Providence preserved Israel that previously had been afflicted. (4 Maccabees 17:17–22, RSV, modified)[17]

The term *antipsychos* refers to something 'given for life'.[18] Although 'devout' (*eusebēs*) themselves, the martyrs had died, and so their death substituted for the affliction that Israel had deserved and that Israel had, up to that time, experienced. Their death, therefore, was a substitutionary and propitiatory sacrifice, satisfying the requirement that God pour out his wrath upon sin but, at the same time, rescuing Israel from God's wrath by absorbing it themselves. The martyrs themselves had no sins to pay for, and so they could become 'a ransom' for Israel.[19]

In addition to such texts from within a decade or two of the time Paul wrote to the Galatians, one statement from Paul himself reveals that he understood Christ's death as a sinless person to have saving efficacy for the sinful. Paul summarizes in the following words his efforts to be faithful to the 'ministry of reconciliation' that God has given to him:

We act as envoys for [*hyper*] Christ as though God were making an entreaty through us. We plead with you, standing in for [*hyper*] Christ, be reconciled to God. God made him who did not know sin to be sin in place of [*hyper*] us so that we might become the righteousness of God in him. (2 Cor. 5:20–21, my translation)

Here sacrificial language is not explicit, but the language of exchange could hardly be clearer, as Paul's use of the preposition *hyper* demonstrates. Paul uses this preposition in two different contexts within the short space of these lines,

---

17. I am following the text of Codex Sinaiticus rather than Codex Alexandrinus in the last sentence. See Peter Stuhlmacher, 'Recent Exegesis on Romans 3:24–25', *Reconciliation, Law, and Righteousness: Essays in Biblical Theology* (Philadelphia: Fortress, 1986), p. 101.

18. LSJ, p. 166.

19. Cf. 4 Maccabees 6:28–29, where Eleazar prays concerning his own death and the deaths of other Israelite martyrs, 'Be merciful to your people, and let our punishment suffice for [*hyper*] them. Make my blood their purification, and take my life in exchange [*antipsychon*] for theirs' (RSV).

but the way he uses it in each context is similar. As an envoy, he substitutes for the presence of the one who sent him: his acting as an envoy for Christ means that he 'stands in' for Christ. Paul uses *hyper* in the same way with respect to Christ's death on our behalf: God made Christ, although sinless, to be sin, so that God could view us as innocent of sin.[20]

Both the cultural context in which Paul wrote Galatians and Paul's own explicit statement elsewhere make it likely that in Galatians 3:10–14 he means to say that Christ's innocence of legal transgression qualified him to absorb the curse that the law pronounced on transgressors. God poured out his wrath against those who transgress the law upon his innocent Messiah instead, and so the actual transgressors were freed from the curse that they deserved. In this way, Christ became a curse 'for' (*hyper*) us (3:13).

Paul's use of *hyper* in this way in Galatians 3:10–14 and 2 Corinthians 5:20–21 makes it likely that when he says simply in other contexts that Christ died or gave himself up 'for' (*hyper*) us, he often has substitutionary ideas in mind (Rom. 5:8; 8:32; Eph. 5:2; Titus 2:14). If *hyper* is the right reading in 1 Thessalonians 5:10, for example, then we may have an expression of the substitutionary nature of Christ's death in what many believe to be the earliest extant Christian document. We must be careful not to draw this conclusion too definitively, however, since in another letter Paul can speak in the same breath not only of Christ's death, but also of his resurrection as 'for' Christians (2 Cor. 5:15), using *hyper*. In such places as these, substitutionary notions are missing – Christ was not raised in place of us, but as 'the firstfruits of those who have fallen asleep' (1 Cor. 15:20).

In Romans 3:25–26 Paul also portrays the death of Christ as a sacrifice that, because it substitutes for the death of the offender, protects the offender against the justified wrath of God against sin. God redeemed his people by displaying Christ Jesus publicly as a 'means of atonement', or *hilastērion*, the means by which atonement is procured with the deity for sinners.[21] Since this

---

20. Cf. 5:14–15, and on the whole question of the use of *hyper* to refer to the substitutionary nature of Christ's death in the New Testament, see Daniel B. Wallace, *Greek Grammar Beyond the Basics: An Exegetical Syntax of the New Testament* (Grand Rapids: Zondervan, 1996), pp. 383–389.

21. Cf. the opening comment in the article on this word in BDAG, 'In Gr-Rom. lit. that which serves as an instrument for regaining the goodwill of a deity; concr. a "means of propitiation or expiation, gift to procure expiation".' *Hilastērion* could be a masculine singular adjective (as in 4 Maccabees 17:22) rather than a neuter singular noun, but, as Joseph A. Fitzmyer, *Romans*, AB 33 (New York: Doubleday, 1993), p. 349, comments, 'the difference in meaning is only slight'.

term plays such an important role in the Septuagint's translation of the description of the Day of Atonement ritual, it seems likely that Paul was thinking of the Day of Atonement when he used it.

It also seems likely, however, that he knew the word would be heard in the predominantly Gentile context of the Roman church (Rom. 1:13; 15:18, 22) with the kinds of connotation that surrounded such statements as those from Lucan and the profoundly Hellenized author of 4 Maccabees. Jesus died in the place of those who had offended the moral standards of God, and on whom, apart from his propitiatory death, God's wrath would certainly be visited. As with Cato's death, Jesus' death both restores the moral order that God has worked into the universe and allows the ungodly to go unpunished. Jesus' death allows the many to escape God's wrath at the same time as God's justice is preserved.

Once again, however, it is not only the cultural context of the first-century Greco-Roman world that leads to this conclusion, but the literary context of Paul's letters themselves. Paul's statement about the propitiatory nature of Christ's death comes on the heels of a detailed description of human sin that begins with, and is frequently punctuated with, references to God's wrath. Paul begins by saying that 'the wrath of God is revealed [*apokalyptetai*] from heaven against all ungodliness and unrighteousness of men' (1:18). Those who attribute wickedness to others while denying it of themselves are similarly 'storing up' for themselves 'wrath in the day of wrath and revelation [*apokalypseōs*] of the righteous judgment of God', who 'will repay each person according to his works' (2:5–6). This eschatological visitation of God's wrath, moreover, is not unjust; indeed it demonstrates his righteousness (3:5). To speak in such a context of the death of Christ as a *hilastērion* is to invoke the notion, both biblical and Greco-Roman, of substitutionary sacrifice that absorbs the wrath of the deity against human offence.

Some scholars continue to maintain that notions of propitiatory sacrifice are absent from Paul's use of the term in this passage. It is difficult to see, however, how Paul could have used the term *hilastērion* to describe the solution to the justified wrath of God against sin and at the same time expect his Roman readers not to hear propitiatory connotations in it. It is also difficult to see why we should choose between the description of the Day of Atonement in Leviticus 16 as the proper background for the term and Greco-Roman notions of propitiatory sacrifice.[22] It is probable that people like Paul and his

---

22. Both Stuhlmacher, 'Recent Exegesis', pp. 96–103, and Fitzmyer, *Romans*, pp. 349–350, see this choice as necessary. Thomas R. Schreiner, *Romans*, BECNT (Grand Rapids: Baker, 1998), pp. 192, 194, argues persuasively against 'either-or' solutions to this complex text.

Roman audience who stood at the intersection of Jewish and Greco-Roman culture would have understood Leviticus 16 itself in terms of propitiatory sacrifice. Paul clearly understood the effectiveness of Jesus' death as a solution to the problem of human sin in terms provided by the Old Testament sacrificial cult (Rom. 5:8–9; 8:3). He also seems to have understood that cult in largely propitiatory terms.

The Petrine tradition

This is not the place to argue for some connection between Mark's Gospel and the apostle Peter. Martin Hengel has provided a cautious and persuasive case for the basic reliability of traditional accounts of this connection.[23] Since both Mark's Gospel and 1 Peter look very Pauline at different points – and not least in their understanding of Jesus' death – it would be imprudent to assume that their alignment with Peter prohibits their dependence at points upon Paul. Having said all this, however, it is significant for understanding the importance of the notion that Jesus' death was a substitutionary sacrifice that the Pauline and the Petrine traditions, although relatively independent of each other, take a similar perspective.

Mark portrays Jesus' death as the sacrifice of an innocent victim for a sinful people, and he does this primarily through allusions to Isaiah's suffering Servant. By the time we get to the passion narrative of his Gospel, Mark has already subtly identified Jesus as the Servant at his baptism (1:10–11; cf. Isa. 42:1; 64:1).[24] He has also identified Jesus as the physician who comes not for the righteous, but for those sick with sin (2:17; cf. Isa. 53:5). When we arrive at Jesus' statement that 'the Son of Man came not to be served but to serve, and to give his life [*psychēn*] as a ransom for many' (10:45), therefore, we are prepared to understand Jesus as Isaiah's 'Servant' who poured out his 'soul' (LXX, *psychē*) to death and bore the sin 'of many' (Isa. 53:11–12).

The idea that Jesus' death follows the atoning pattern of the Servant's death emerges again in 14:24 where Jesus explains the cup at the final Passover meal with his disciples as 'the blood of the covenant, which is poured out for many'. Here too the concept of Jesus' death as a death for 'many' seems to come from Isaiah 53:11–12. Almost as if to be sure that we do not miss this correlation,

23. Martin Hengel, *The Four Gospels and the One Gospel of Jesus Christ* (Harrisburg: Trinity Press International, 2000), pp. 78–89.

24. On this see Rikki E. Watts, *Isaiah's New Exodus in Mark*, WUNT 288 (Tübingen: Mohr [Siebeck], 1997), pp. 102–118; and Robert A. Guelich, *Mark 1–8:26*, WBC 34a (Dallas: Word, 1989), pp. 39–40.

Mark incorporates into his telling of Jesus' passion a number of allusions to Isaiah's description of the Servant's suffering (Isa. 50:6/Mark 14:65; 15:17–19, 29; Isa. 53:7/Mark 14:60–61; 15:3–5).[25]

Is this suffering 'for many', however, a suffering 'in the place of many', as it was for Isaiah's Servant? Does Mark, in other words, describe Jesus' death as a substitutionary atonement? Two considerations make this likely.

First, in the first of the two places where Mark describes Jesus' death as 'for' many (10:45), he uses the preposition *anti*, and the most natural rendering of *anti* in such a context is 'in the place of'.[26] This makes it likely that when he uses the more ambiguous preposition *hyper* in the second reference (14:24), he also means that Jesus would pour out his blood 'in the place of' his disciples.

Second, Mark is interested in showing us that Jesus was blameless of any wrongdoing when he died (14:56–57; 15:10, 14), in the same way that Isaiah wants us to know that the Servant suffered innocently (Isa. 53:9). In Isaiah the innocence of the Servant is important because the Servant's suffering is not for his own sins, but for the sins of others.[27] It is likely that Mark emphasizes the innocence of Jesus, at least in part, for the same reason. He wants to clarify that Jesus suffered not for his own sins, but for the transgressions of the 'many' sinful, including his obtuse and cowardly disciples.

In 1 Peter, this understanding of Jesus' death is assumed and Peter uses this assumption as a foundation on which to base his exhortation to the persecuted Christians of Anatolia. As part of a strategy designed both to shame their persecutors (2:12a; 3:16) and to win them over (2:12b; 3:1–2), Peter urges Christian slaves neither to wrong their masters nor to retaliate against them when they are wronged, but to follow the example of Jesus in his role as Isaiah's suffering Servant.[28] Peter's indebtedness to Isaiah's portrait of the Servant's suffering runs deep:

---

25. Again, see Watts, *Isaiah's New Exodus in Mark*, pp. 349–365.

26. Wallace, *Greek Grammar Beyond the Basics*, pp. 365–367.

27. 'He has borne our griefs and carried our sorrows' (53:4). 'He was wounded for our transgressions; he was crushed for our iniquities' (53:5). 'The LORD has laid on him the iniquity of us all' (53:6). 'His soul makes an offering for sin' (53:10). 'He bore the sin of many' (53:12).

28. Peter's advice is intended to cover Christians generally and not merely slaves. This is clear from his use of the first person plural in the first part of v. 24. On this, see Leonard Goppelt, *A Commentary on 1 Peter* (Grand Rapids: Eerdmans, 1993), p. 207.

1 Peter 2:22–25	Isaiah 53:9, 4–6 (LXX)
[22] He committed no sin, neither was deceit found in his mouth	[9] And I will give evil people for his burial and wealthy people for his death because he did no lawlessness, neither was deceit found in his mouth.
[24] He himself bore our sins in his body on the tree	[4] This one bears our sins and suffers for us, and we ourselves have reckoned him to be in distress and in calamity and in oppression. [5] And he himself was wounded because of our lawlessness and weakened because of our sins. The discipline that brought us peace was upon him. By his
By his wounds you have been healed.	wounds we have been healed.
[25] For you were straying like sheep, but have now returned to the Shepherd and Overseer of your souls.	[6] All of us have strayed like sheep. Each person has strayed in his way , and the Lord handed him over for our sins. (My translation)

Like the Servant, Jesus did not sin by speaking deceitfully (2:22; Isa. 53:9); his own wound healed us (2:24b; Isa. 53:5); and it did so when we were straying sheep (2:25; Isa. 53:6). Most significantly, Peter glosses his paraphrase of Isaiah 53:4, 'He himself bore our sins', with the phrase 'in his body on the tree' (2:24a). This gloss shows that Peter assumed the substitutionary nature of Jesus' death as Isaiah's Servant. The notion that Jesus died on the 'tree' or the 'wood' (*xylon*) is not a natural way to speak of his death on the 'cross' (*stauros*), unless it is assumed that Jesus was 'hanged on a tree' (LXX, *xylou*) because he was 'cursed by God' according to the pattern laid down in Deuteronomy 21:23.[29] Peter believed, therefore, that when Jesus 'bore our sins' as Isaiah's Servant, he did so as an innocent substitute for God's sinful people. Although innocent of any crime, he bore the curse that they deserved.

If doubt remains that this understanding of the atonement was a basic

---

29. Cf. Gal. 3:13; Acts 5:30; 10:39; 13:29, and the comments of J. N. D. Kelly, *A Commentary on the Epistles of Peter and Jude*, HNTC (New York: Harper & Row, 1969), p. 122.

theological conviction for Peter, then 3:18 should dispel it. Here, too, Peter's primary interest is ethical instruction with an evangelistic goal. Christians should respond to slander before pagan magistrates with a defence of their hope, but their defence should be tempered with 'gentleness and respect' (3:15). The pattern of Christian behaviour ought to follow Christ's behaviour when he atoned for sin: he suffered not for doing evil, but for doing good (3:16). 'For Christ . . . suffered once for sins, the righteous for [hyper] the unrighteous, that he might bring us to God.' The substitutionary nature of Christ's suffering could hardly be clearer: we were unrighteous; Christ was righteous; he suffered in our place; this made it possible for us to enter the presence of God.

In the Petrine tradition, therefore, the atoning nature of Christ's death was explained by means of Isaiah 52:13–53:12. Jesus filled the role of the suffering Servant and in this role he died in the place of sinners. His innocent suffering allowed him to take the curse that they deserved, making forgiveness and entrance into God's presence possible.

The Johannine tradition

Scholars sometimes argue that John was uninterested in Jesus' death as atonement for sin.[30] Jesus' crucifixion was not the way by which God would forgive human sin, it is said, but the path by which Jesus returned to the glory of the Father.[31]

Although this understanding of Jesus' death in John's Gospel correctly emphasizes the distinctiveness of John's narrative on this point, it does not do justice to his acknowledgment that Jesus died as a vicarious atonement for sin.[32] When the Baptist says that Jesus is the 'Lamb [amnos] of God, who takes away the sin of the world' (1:29; cf. 1:36), he probably means that Jesus is the

---

30. The substance and some of the wording of the next several paragraphs are indebted to my *Theology of the New Testament: A Canonical and Synthetic Approach* (Grand Rapids: Zondervan, 2005), pp. 200–201.

31. See, e.g., Ernst Käsemann, *The Testament of Jesus: A Study of the Gospel of John in the Light of Chapter 17* (Philadelphia: Fortress, 1968), pp. 17–21, and cf. William Loader, *The Christology of the Fourth Gospel: Structure and Issues*, BBET 23 (Frankfurt am Main: Peter Lang, 1989), pp. 101–102, who argues that although John acknowledged the tradition of Jesus' atonement for sin, it was not important to his understanding of the significance of Jesus' death.

32. See especially the balanced comments of Andreas J. Köstenberger, *John*, BECNT (Grand Rapids: Eerdmans, 2004), p. 68.

Servant of God who, according to Isaiah, suffered for the sins of others. Isaiah calls the Servant both a 'sheep' (*probaton*) and a 'lamb' (*amnos*) in 53:7, and although John certainly thought of Jesus' death as the slaying of a Passover lamb (John 19:14, 29, 36; cf. Exod. 12:22, 46), the Baptist's reference to the removal of sin recalls most clearly the 'lamb' who in Isaiah bears the sins of many, becomes an 'offering for sin', and suffers not for his own transgressions, but for those of others (Isa. 53:4, 10, 12).[33]

John can also speak of the atoning and substitutionary significance of Jesus' death without borrowing imagery from Isaiah 52:13–53:12. Jesus says, for example, that 'the bread' he gives 'for [*hyper*] the life of the world is [his] flesh' (6:51). Since he begins to speak of his blood immediately after this (6:52–56), it is clear that he refers in this statement to his death. This statement, moreover, resembles closely Jesus' words over the bread in the accounts of the Lord's Supper found in Luke 22:19 and 1 Corinthians 11:24: 'This is my body, which is [given] for [*hyper*] you . . .' A substitutionary significance probably lies behind the preposition *hyper* in that context, and so here too Jesus probably means that he gives his life 'in the place of' the life of the world.[34] When Jesus describes himself as the good shepherd who lays down his life 'for' (*hyper*) the sheep (10:11, 15), or as the one who lays down his life 'for' (*hyper*) his friends (15:13), he probably also has in mind notions of the costly substitution of one's life for that of another. Like a shepherd who endangers his or her own life in order to rescue an endangered sheep, Jesus dies in the place of those he loves so that they might be spared.[35]

This same understanding of Jesus' death probably lies behind the high priest Caiaphas's unwitting explanation of the deeper meaning of Jesus' execution. Frustrated that his fellow council members have failed to come to the point about what to do with Jesus, Caiaphas blurts out, 'You know nothing at all. Nor do you understand that it is better for you that one man should die for the people, not that the whole nation should perish' (11:50). John comments that, although Caiaphas did not know it, he prophesied that Jesus would die both 'for' (*hyper*) the Jewish nation and 'for' (*hyper*) other children of God who would eventually join them (11:51–52). Here, too, Jesus' death substitutes for

---

33. Cf. Raymond E. Brown, *John I–XII*, AB 29 (New York: Doubleday, 1966), pp. 58–63.

34. Cf. Leon Morris, *The Gospel According to John*, NICNT (Grand Rapids: Eerdmans, 1971), p. 374 n. 116. Cf. Köstenberger, *John*, p. 215.

35. D. A. Carson, *The Gospel According to John*, PNTC (Grand Rapids: Eerdmans; Leicester: Apollos, 1991), pp. 386–387.

that of the nation: Jesus' death will occur in the nation's place, and so the nation will be spared.[36]

Why did the nation need sparing? Into what danger had they wandered? The answer comes in John's distinctive allusion to God's cure for the curse of poisonous snakes that God had brought upon his people in the wilderness. Just as God told Moses that he should 'make a fiery serpent and set it on a pole, and everyone who is bitten, when he sees it, shall live' (Num. 21:8), so the Johannine Jesus says that 'as Moses lifted up the serpent in the wilderness', the Son of Man too must 'be lifted up, that whoever believes in him may have eternal life' (John 3:14). By describing Jesus' allusion to this story, John implies that God's people stood under a curse that the crucifixion of Jesus removed.

It is certainly true that John places no special emphasis on the substitutionary and atoning nature of Jesus' death in his Gospel. Other aspects of his death have greater urgency for John. Just as certainly, however, he acknowledges this traditional understanding of Jesus' death as important – important enough that he expresses it not only in the more traditional language of the suffering Servant, but also through his own distinctive idiom.

After the publication of John's Gospel, threats, probably from Gnosticism, made it necessary for John to bring his latent conviction that Jesus' death atoned for sin into the open. In 1 John, John's opponents have seceded from the church (1 John 2:19) and continue to exercise some influence over those they have left behind (2:20, 26–27). The traditions on which the church was founded, these opponents claim, are inadequate and wrong-headed for overcoming sin. The concept of sin itself, they seem to have thought, needed redefining in terms of knowledge and enlightenment rather than transgression (2:3–6, 9–11). As a consequence of this redefinition of the human plight, the secessionists who prompted 1 John apparently denied the necessity of Christ's atoning death: Christ did not need to die for transgression against God's law if this kind of sin was not the human problem.

The secessionists were happy to speak of the redemptive significance of Christ's coming, perhaps focusing on his baptism as the moment at which he assumed his redemptive mission, but they failed to find any significance in Jesus' death. Against this, John reminds his readers that he had seen Jesus die and had himself understood the sacrificial significance of his shed blood (5:6–8; cf. John 19:34–35). Elsewhere, John alludes to the Greek text of

---

36. Ibid., p. 422. Cf. Köstenberger, *John*, p. 351, who observes that the concept of dying 'for the people' recalls the Maccabean martyrs, who died to end God's wrath on 'our whole nation' (2 Maccabees 7:37–38, RSV).

Leviticus to explain Jesus' death, and these allusions place him within the mainstream of the early Christian interpretation of Jesus' death as the climactic and final Day of Atonement sacrifice.

For John, the shedding of Jesus' blood 'cleanses' (*katharizei*) us 'from all sin' (*apo pasēs hamatias*, 1:7).[37] This corresponds with the purpose of the Day of Atonement ritual, according to the Septuagint's rendering: it is to 'cleanse' (*katharisai*) Israel 'from all . . . sins' (*apo pasōn tōn hamartiōn*; Lev. 16:30).[38] For John, sin is clearly defined as 'lawlessness' (*anomia*, 3:4) and 'unrighteousness' (*adikia*, 5:17), and the 'cleansing' (*katharisē*) of people from 'all unrighteousness' (*pasēs adikias*) occurs when they 'confess' their sin (1:9).

At first this notion might seem to contradict the conviction that an atoning sacrifice is necessary as a remedy for sin. If confession brings forgiveness, why is atonement necessary? In Leviticus 16:21, however, the high priest is instructed to 'confess . . . all the iniquities [*pasas tas anomias*] of the people of Israel, and all their transgressions [*pasas tas adikias autōn*]' on the Day of Atonement. Just as the two concepts of confession and atoning sacrifice are held together in the Day of Atonement ritual in Leviticus, so John holds them together.[39] In view of these many verbal correspondences, it is not surprising that John considers Jesus to be the 'atonement' (*hilasmos*) for our sins (2:2; 4:10), the precise term that the Greek rendering of Leviticus uses to describe the Day 'of Atonement' (*hilasmou*, Lev. 25:9).[40]

Nothing here explicitly describes Jesus' atoning sacrifice in substitutionary terms. When we couple the language of atonement in 1 John with the notion of substitution that runs like an undertow through John's Gospel, however, it becomes likely that John intended his references to the sacrificial nature of Jesus' death in 1 John to carry a substitutionary meaning. When we read the Gospel and the first epistle together, they supply one of the clearest articulations of the sacrificial and substitutionary character of Jesus' death in the New Testament.

Hebrews and Revelation
Hebrews and Revelation, each in its own way, affirm the sacrificial nature of Jesus' death, and although the substitutionary nature of this sacrifice is not a

---

37. The substance and much of the wording of this and the next paragraph are indebted to my *Theology of the New Testament*, p. 550.
38. Cf. Hans-Josef Klauck, *Der erste Johannesbrief, EKK* 23.1 (Zurich: Benziger; Neukirchen-Vluyn: Neukirchener, 1991), p. 91.
39. The two concepts also appear together in Lev. 5:5–6.
40. Cf. Klauck, *Erste Johannesbrief,* p. 107.

major issue in either text, both assume it. Hebrews dwells at length on the sacrificial nature of Christ's death in order to demonstrate its superiority to the sacrifices mandated under the 'first covenant' (8:6–7). Christ's sacrifice is superior to that of the levitical priests because it is the blameless (7:27; 9:14; cf. 5:3; 9:7) sacrifice of himself rather than of goats, bulls and a heifer (9:13; 10:4). Because of these superior qualities, it was able to produce not merely the cleansing of the flesh, but the cleansing of the conscience (9:13–14). It provided forgiveness not merely for inadvertent sins, but for all sins (9:7).[41] It established not an old covenant, destined to become obsolete, but a new covenant (8:13; 9:18–25; 12:24; 13:20). It was therefore wholly and finally effective in dealing with sin and needed to be made only once for all time (7:25, 27; 9:26; 10:12, 14; cf. 1:3). It perfected God's people (10:14; cf. 9:9) and opened the way for them to the unmediated presence of God (4:14, 16; 6:19–20). For all these reasons, the death of Jesus was the sacrifice to end all sacrifices.

The author does not tell us precisely how Christ's death accomplished all this. He does provide some hints, however. First, although he does not dwell on the subject, he says explicitly that in his role as high priest, Christ made 'propitiation [*hilaskesthai*] for the sins of the people' (2:17). Scholars are divided about whether the verb *hilaskesthai* refers to dealing with the wrath of God against sin, or simply to dealing with sin in a more general way.[42] The Hellenistic Jewish milieu in which Hebrews was produced, however, makes it likely that the term means here what it means in 4 Maccabees 6 and 17 – that sacrifice lifted the curse of God against his sinful people. It is in this sense, then, that Jesus' death accomplishes redemption (*apolytrōsin*) 'from the transgressions committed under the first covenant' (9:15; cf. Gal. 3:13).

Second, the author of Hebrews repeatedly says that Jesus was a blameless sacrifice (4:15; 7:27; 9:14), meaning by this not that he was without physical defect (the requirement for the sacrifice of flocks and livestock in the Mosaic law), but that he was morally perfect. It is difficult to see why the author would place such stress on Jesus' sinlessness precisely in speaking of his sacrificial death, unless this sacrifice contained a substitutionary element.

This seems to be confirmed when we consider the author's comments on the willing nature of Jesus' sacrifice in chapter 10. The author begins this section of his argument by claiming that the repetition of the levitical

---

41. See Harold Attridge, *Hebrews*, Herm (Philadelphia: Fortress, 1989), p. 239.

42. For the first position, see, e.g., William L. Lane, *Hebrews 1–8*, WBC 47a (Dallas: Word, 1991), p. 66, and for the second position, see, e.g., Attridge, *Hebrews*, p. 96 n. 192.

sacrifices demonstrates their ineffectiveness to take away sin. They would have ceased, the author reasons, if they had really been effective (10:1b–3). The problem is that the bulls and goats offered in the first covenant's sacrifices provided only a blueprint for the truly effective sacrifice that would come when the second covenant was established (10:1a, 9). The second covenant set aside the first and was wholly effective in dealing with sin, says the author, because the sacrificial offering was an unblemished human being willing to offer his body in sacrifice.

When Jesus came into the world, he voiced his intentions in the words of Psalm 39:9 (LXX; MT Ps. 40:8): 'I have come to do your will, O God' (Heb. 10:7, 9). The author explains that it is precisely by means of this 'will' that 'we have been sanctified through the offering of the body of Jesus Christ once for all' (10:10). To be precise, the 'will' of which the author speaks is God's, but the author's point, revealed in his repetition of the statement 'Behold, I have come to do your will' in verse 9, is that Christ and God were of one mind about his sacrifice.[43] The Father wanted his Son to give his body as a sacrifice for sin, and the Son wanted to do so. Precisely this union of wills in Christ's death makes Christ's sacrifice effective 'once for all', bringing all the sacrifices of the first covenant to an end.

This interior, volitional nature of Christ's sacrifice seems to be the quality that allows it to 'sprinkle' the evil conscience of Christians, purifying their own intentions and making it possible for them to 'draw near' to God 'with a true heart in full assurance of faith' (10:22). The purity of Christ's intentions when he offered himself as a sacrifice somehow purifies the intentions of Christians and makes them acceptable to God. The author seems to see in this effect of Christ's sacrifice the fulfilment of Jeremiah's claim that in the new covenant God would 'put my laws on their hearts, and write them on their minds' (10:16; quoting Jer. 31 [38]:33; cf. 9:14; 13:21). This understanding of the effect of Christ's sacrifice may stand behind the author's difficult statement that 'if we deliberately [hekousiōs] continue to sin after receiving the knowledge of the truth, there no longer remains any sacrifice for sin' (10:26, my translation). Those who freely choose a life of sin demonstrate that they have rejected the power of Christ's willing sacrifice to cleanse their own wills. That their wills lack any transformation reveals that the effect of Christ's sacrifice has not really been at work in them.

If this is a correct understanding of the effect of Christ's sacrifice on the believer, then it raises an interesting theological question. Does the author

---

43. Attridge, *Hebrews*, p. 276.

of Hebrews affirm only that Christ's sacrifice purifies the hearts of Christians so that they obey God's will (9:14; 13:21), or does he also mean that Christ's sacrifice renders Christian hearts pure and holy in a 'positional' sense, apart from any moral transformation?[44] If we go back to the author's emphasis on the lack of any moral defect in Christ, and therefore the suitability of his sacrificial death, then we may have an answer to the question. Christ's death was the sacrifice of a morally blameless offering so that the purity of his conscience could become ours in God's sight. His sacrifice resulted not only in a moral purification of our consciences, but in a 'cultic' purification as well. In this cultic purification, the moral blamelessness of the sacrifice was attributed to those for whom the sacrifice atoned. Although they were sinners, Jesus' moral blamelessness made it possible for them to enter the presence of God apart from the actual moral transformation of their lives. To the extent that this is a correct reading of Hebrews, it bears witness not only to the substitutionary nature of Christ's death for our sin (2:17), but also to the imputation of Christ's righteousness to believers through his death.

John the seer, in Revelation, also assumes the substitutionary nature of Christ's sacrificial death, but does so less ambiguously. He says that Jesus 'freed [*lysanti*] us from our sins by his blood' (1:5). He identifies Jesus with God, who sits on the glorious heavenly throne, and describes Jesus as 'a Lamb standing, as though it had been slain' (5:6, 12; cf. 13:8). His slaughter 'bought by [his] blood people for God from every tribe and language and people and nation' (5:9, my translation). By means of the Lamb's blood and their own perseverance within a social environment hostile to their faith, Christians are able to prevail over the accusations of Satan (12:11; cf. 7:14). The picture of people being purchased by the death of a lamb echoes the biblical account of the exodus, and specifically the story of Passover night during which God did not kill the firstborn males of Israelite households because their doorposts and lintels were marked by the blood of a slain lamb (Exod. 11:1–12:32). Since the Israelites were slaves in Egypt, it was natural to speak of God's powerful rescue of his people from bondage in Egypt as an act of 'redemption' (Exod. 6:6; Deut. 7:8; 9:26; 13:5; 15:15; 24:18). By his powerful acts on their behalf, not least by the display of his destructive power to the Egyptians on Passover night, God purchased his people out of their slavery.

---

44. I suppose this is the equivalent in Hebrews of the debate among Pauline scholars about whether, in Paul's letters, righteousness is only imputed, or is also imparted through Christ's death and resurrection.

The Passover sacrifice was not a sin offering, and the Old Testament never claims that the slain Passover lamb substituted for the life of Israelite firstborn males, but it is not unreasonable to think that John the seer used Passover imagery of Jesus to communicate something like this. He understood Jesus' death as the purchase price necessary to 'buy' (*agorazō*) people for God (5:9) and to set them free from their sins (1:5). Since Jesus' death was the purchase price for this result, it substituted for the bondage in which the sins of believers held them. Perhaps this is why John can say that Jesus' death as the Lamb allows believers to prevail over the accusations of Satan (12:10–11): God has purchased them through Jesus' death and therefore Satan has no claim over them.[45]

Hebrews and Revelation, therefore, confirm what we find in the Pauline, Petrine and Johannine traditions. Although the authors of these texts do not fit squarely within any of these large streams of New Testament tradition, they affirm that Jesus' death effected atonement for sin, and they seem to affirm its substitutionary nature.

Back to substitution

The conviction that Jesus died as a sacrifice to propitiate the wrath of God against his sinful people, and that he did so by dying in their place, is both biblical and important. It not only appears in the Bible, but it appears in many places within the Bible. It is anticipated in certain sacrifices that the Mosaic law prescribes for dealing with sin, and in particular in the Day of Atonement sacrifice for the wickedness and rebellion of God's people. It appears explicitly in all three major strains of New Testament tradition and in texts from outside those traditions also. It is especially important to Paul. Certainly, even for Paul, the substitutionary atonement does not exhaust the significance of Jesus' death – and it should not be emphasized to the exclusion of other benefits of Jesus' death – but it is nevertheless an important element of biblical theology. For those who consider the biblical witness to be the primary authority in shaping their own theological convictions, rejecting the substitutionary nature of Christ's death is not a logical option.

---

45. Henry Barclay Swete, *The Apocalypse of St John*, 3rd ed. (London: Macmillan, 1909), p. 156; Gregory K. Beale, *The Book of Revelation*, NIGTC (Grand Rapids,: Eerdmans, 1999), p. 664; Grant R. Osborne, *Revelation*, BECNT (Grand Rapids: Baker, 2002), p. 476.

If this is true, then have Christians who seek to be faithful to the full bibli-cal witness to the significance of Jesus' death become complicit in the oppres-sion of the poor and the weak? Are those who preach that Jesus endured from God the wrath that our sins deserved, and did so in our place, guilty of bur-dening the gospel with Western notions of justice that are foreign to it?

These questions are the subject for another study,[46] but it is possible, even in a short space, to indicate some basic problems with the claims that stand behind them. First, those who claim that a substitutionary view of the atone-ment lies behind violence against women, children and criminals often fail to provide empirical evidence for these dramatic claims.[47] It is possible to see an analogy between a crude form of the so-called 'penal substitutionary' view of the atonement and these horrific social ills, but the ability to describe such an analogy does not prove an organic connection between them. To note the analogy is not to prove that the two structures, one of belief and one of behav-iour, are connected.

To note the analogy in this simple form is also to leave out two critical ele-ments of the Christian view of substitutionary atonement. First, this view of the atonement is interwoven with an orthodox understanding of the Trinity. When God the Father pours out his wrath on his innocent Son in order to be both just and the justifier of the ungodly, God the Father is himself inti-mately involved in the sacrifice. The most vivid expression of the unity between the Father and the Son at this level appears in Revelation 5:6 where John sees 'a lamb as slain standing in the middle [*en mesō*] of the throne' (my translation). Here Jesus continues to bear the marks of his sacrifice in heaven and he stands in the centre of God's throne. Jesus' death is therefore not merely a matter of his own grace and love, but of God's grace and love. We are 'justified by [God's] grace as a gift, through the redemption that is in Christ Jesus' (Rom. 3:24), and 'God demonstrates his own [*heautou*] love for us because while we were still sinners Christ died for us' (Rom. 5:8, my translation).

This crucial element in the biblical teaching on atoning sacrifice sets it apart from the concept as it appears in the Bible's wider cultural environment. Cato takes the initiative, offering himself to the Roman gods as a propitiatory sacrifice.

---

46. See the perceptive and sensitive treatment of them in Richard J. Mouw, 'Violence and the Atonement', in Kenneth R. Chase and Alan Jacobs (eds.), *Must Christianity Be Violent? Reflections on History, Practice, and Theology* (Grand Rapids: Brazos, 2003), pp. 159–182.

47. Batstone, *From Conquest to Struggle*, pp. 17–18, is perhaps an exception, but even here the discussion is brief and general.

The author of 4 Maccabees similarly considered the pious martyrs to be not gifts from God for the propitiation of Israel's sins, but gifts to God, adequate for the propitiation of Israel's sins. It is perhaps not coincidental that God refused to accept Moses' offer to atone for the sins of Israel with his own life and that God did not lift the famine during David's reign because of the deaths of Saul's seven sons. The only atoning sacrifice ultimately adequate to the task of removing the offence of human sin is one that God himself graciously supplies.[48]

Second, the substitutionary atonement is not conceived in the New Testament as an example of the strong (God) urging the weak (Jesus) to undergo hardship (the crucifixion) for the benefit of the strong (God). It is conceived quite differently as the strong (Jesus) giving up his strength (in the crucifixion) in order to come to the aid of the weak (God's people). This pattern, moreover, often forms the basis for an admonition to the strong precisely not to abuse their positions of privilege and power, but instead to look after the concerns of the weak. This is the context in which Jesus explains the substitutionary nature of his death to his disciples in Mark and Matthew:

> And Jesus called them to him and said to them, 'You know that those who are considered rulers of the Gentiles lord it over them, and their great ones exercise authority over them. But it shall not be so among you. But whoever would be great among you must be your servant, and whoever would be first among you must be slave of all. For even the Son of Man came not to be served but to serve, and to give his life as a ransom for many.' (Mark 10:42–45; cf. Matt. 20:25–28)

It is also the context in which Paul articulates the concept in both Galatians and Romans. In both letters, after his clear articulation of the substitutionary nature of Christ's atoning sacrifice, Paul draws from this concept the conclusion that Jews have no priority over Gentiles in salvation and therefore cannot exclude Gentiles from the people of God (Gal. 3:14; Rom. 3:27–30).

---

48. As the author of Hebrews never tires of reminding his readers (7:27; 9:12; 9:26; 10:2; 10:10; cf. 1 Pet. 3:18), this atoning sacrifice has made all other sacrifices unnecessary. This was a point on which Christians in later centuries would stake their lives as they refused to offer any form of sacrifice, not simply to the local deities or the gods of Rome, but even to their own God. On this, see W. H. C. Frend, *Martyrdom and Persecution in the Early Church: A Study of a Conflict from the Maccabees to Donatus* (Oxford: Basil Blackwell, 1965), p. 257, and S. R. F. Price, *Rituals and Power: The Roman Imperial Cult in Asia Minor* (Cambridge: Cambridge University Press, 1984), pp. 220–221.

It is possible that someone somewhere has twisted the account of Jesus' death as a substitutionary sacrifice out of shape and used it to support the oppression of the weak. If so, those who claim a connection between a substitutionary view of the atonement and the oppression of the weak seem to have a very difficult time finding concrete evidence for it.

We can say for certain, however, that the New Testament authors use a correct account of Jesus' sacrificial death on behalf of sinners to remind Christians that they should not abuse their power, but should achieve greatness through service. The New Testament also uses the substitutionary sacrifice of Christ to remind Christians that, because all people equally deserve God's wrath and are made right with God through Christ's death as a free gift, all should be treated equitably. As Paul says in Romans – a letter written in part to quell ethnic tension (Rom. 14:1–15:13) – 'there is no difference' (Rom. 3:22; cf. 2 Cor. 8:9, 14). It would not be hard to locate accounts from popular Christianity down through the centuries that bear witness to precisely this connection between the substitutionary death of Christ and a sense that people should be treated with compassion and equality. It would not be hard, in fact, to find accounts of people in positions of wealth and power who surrendered part or all of their comfort to aid the weak because they took Jesus' death on the cross for the weak as their example.

The notion that Jesus endured the wrath of God in our place on the cross is neither unbiblical nor socially unhealthy. The idea of substitutionary, atoning sacrifice was part of the conceptual fabric of the ancient world generally, and this conceptual fabric is woven into the Bible's teaching on the significance of Christ's death. As both the sacrifice of the heifer in Deuteronomy 21:1–9 and the speech of Cato in Lucan demonstrate, such sacrifices were understood as necessary for the symbolic restoration of the moral order that God or the gods had worked into the universe. In the Bible, however, substitutionary sacrifice for sin, especially the ultimate sacrifice of Jesus, is understood to be a gift from God.[49] God himself supplies the sacrifice by means of which his wrath against sin is propitiated; indeed, in the New Testament, he is in some way identified with the sacrifice itself. This crucial element within the biblical understanding of Christ's atoning death allows the concept to be used as a motivation for the ethical treatment of the

---

49. The Old Testament sacrifices of atonement were understood as God's gift. See, e.g., Lev. 17:11: 'For the life of the flesh is in the blood, and I have given it for you on the altar to make atonement for your souls, for it is the blood that makes atonement by the life.'

weak and oppressed. Jesus and Paul use the notion to urge the powerful within the church to place their power in the service of the weak and to emphasize the importance of equity within God's people.

Only by distorting the biblical concept of substitutionary atonement could it ever be used as conceptual justification for the oppression of the weak. Correctly understood, it has provided, and will continue to provide, an extraordinarily effective incentive within the church for empowering the weak, showing compassion to the needy and providing justice for the oppressed.

© Frank S. Thielman, 2007

4. THE SERVANT OF THE LORD

Stephen G. Dempster

The Servant of the Lord is an important theme in the Christian Bible. It is the dominant subject in only a few passages,[1] yet is one of the major underlying concepts of the biblical message. In his recent comprehensive analysis of biblical theology, Charles Scobie treats it as one of the four major themes of the Bible around which minor theological ideas cluster.[2] There are many individual studies of the theme, but few trace its development throughout the Scriptures. This is the purpose of the following essay. Before outlining this development, however, the main biblical terms for 'servant' are considered, as well as the phrase 'Servant of the Lord' and other equivalent expressions.[3]

The term 'servant'

Hebrew
There are a number of relevant terms in the Hebrew Bible, but the main one that

---

1. See, e.g., Isa. 40–55 and John 13.
2. *The Ways of Our God: An Approach to Biblical Theology* (Grand Rapids: Eerdmans, 2003), pp. 301–466.
3. That is, the term 'servant' with pronominal suffixes indicating divine possession.

is used, *'ebed*, occurs 806 times.[4] The meaning of this word in most cases is that of someone subordinate to a master. Hanson observes, 'Various types of sub-ordinations within natural groupings (those based on birth, social class, residence and nationality) or voluntary associations (based on contracts or competition) in the OT and ancient near eastern literature use servant-lord terminology.'[5] It fre-quently occurs in the context of its cognate verb 'to serve/work' (*'ābad*) and the verbs 'to hear/obey' (*šāma'*) and 'to keep/observe' (*šāmar*). Eli's advice to the young Samuel, when the latter first hears from Yahweh, exemplifies the attitude of a servant before a master: 'Speak, Yahweh, for your servant is listening' (1 Sam. 3:10, my translation). A prophet relays the divine word to Solomon to obey all the laws and keep them just as 'David my servant did' (1 Kgs 11:38). When Abraham needs to procure a wife for his son Isaac, he sends his chief servant to do the task. The emissary is described as the servant of Abraham, the elder of his house, the *ruler* of all his affairs (Gen. 24:2). Thus the longest chapter in Genesis narrates the fulfilment of this responsibility as the servant journeys to Mesopotamia. He, however, remains anonymous; he is simply referred to as a servant fourteen times and as a man nine times.[6] Frequently he is contrasted with his master, who is mentioned explicitly seventeen times.[7] When he finally identifies himself to his master's relatives, there is no equivocation: 'I am Abraham's servant' (Gen. 24:34). He has been entrusted with a mission and he is single-minded in pursuit of accomplishing his master's will.[8]

As was shown in some of the above examples, the use of the word is not necessarily negative: the servant is in fact a 'ruler' in the house of Abraham.[9] Depending on the context, the word 'servant' could mean a trusted emissary or an abject slave, a social superior or inferior.[10] Sometimes it is simply a polite

---

4. For a complete statistical list, see Claus Westermann, "*ebed* Servant', *TDOT* vol. 2, p. 823. For another study which considers the linguistic aspect of the word 'servant', see Walther Zimmerli and Joachim Jeremias, trans. Harold Knight et al., *The Servant of God* (London: SCM Press, 1979).

5. K. Hanson, 'Servant', *ISBE*, vol. 4, p. 419.

6. Servant: Gen. 24:2, 4, 9, 10, 14, 17, 34, 52, 53, 59, 61, 65 (2x), 66; Man: Gen. 24:21, 22, 26, 29, 30 (2x), 32, 58, 61.

7. Gen. 24:12 (2x), 14, 18, 27 (3x), 35, 36, 37, 39, 42, 44, 48 (2x), 49, 65.

8. Cf. Zimmerli's discussion of this striking passage, Zimmerli and Jeremias, *Servant of God*, p. 10.

9. Cf. Joseph in the house of Potiphar (Gen. 39:4–6, 8–9).

10. Callender observes, 'It is used for a wide range of relations, from that of social inferior to a social superior to chattel slavery.' See D. E. Callender Jr, 'Servants of

form of self-address used in a formulaic manner when making a request to a social superior.[11]

A telling usage occurs when Rehoboam's older counsellors advise him to deal wisely with the northern tribes, which had threatened to secede from the United Kingdom: 'If you will be a servant to this people today and serve them, and speak good words to them when you answer them, then they will be your servants forever' (1 Kgs 12:7). This passage stresses mutual submission initiated by the king. Rehoboam's father, Solomon, had created conditions that incited revolt. A policy of domineering kingship had led to a form of enslavement that in a very real sense had returned the nation to Egypt, which was always viewed as the 'house of servitude'. [12] Rehoboam's older counsellors rightly called for mutual service, lest the kingdom divide.

Greek

In the Septuagint a variety of Greek terms are used to translate the Hebrew *'ebed*. Depending on the context, the translators used different equivalents. The word *pais*, which can mean subordinate with respect to physical descent and therefore 'son' or 'child' as well as 'servant', is the most common translation (340 times).[13] The term *doulos*, which carries a primary meaning of subordination, and its variant forms run a close second (327 times). Another choice, *therapon*, may indicate a servant who is given an important task (46 times).

In the New Testament there is some semantic change. The main word used for servant is *doulos* (127 times). The noun *pais* (76 times) is frequently used for 'child', but some semantic overlap occurs with *doulos*.[14] The word *therapōn* occurs only once, and in that instance in a text that is dependent on the

---

God(s) and Servants of Kings in Israel and the Ancient Near East', *Semeia* 83 (1998), p. 73.

11. It therefore does not imply that the addressee is a legal master. Cf. Gen. 19:2; 2 Sam. 9:2, 6, 8, 10, 11; 15:2. Note that Jacob uses this expression when speaking to his brother, but he definitely perceives himself in an inferior position (Gen. 32:5).

12. In the classic text describing Egyptian bondage (Exod. 1:13–14), the linguistic root for such oppressive labour appears repeatedly, 'The Egyptians reduced the Israelites to harsh *slavery* and embittered their lives with severe *service* in clay, and in brick, and in every kind of *labour* in the field; all their *work*, which *they did*, was oppressive' (my translation).

13. For the relevant statistics, see Zimmerli and Jeremias, *Servant of God*, pp. 35–42.

14. For semantic overlap with *doulos*, see Luke 7:7, 10.

Septuagint.[15] Thus by the time of the New Testament writings *doulos* is mainly used, although words like *diakonos* are beginning to share a similar semantic domain.

The term 'Servant of the Lord'

The phrase 'Servant of the Lord' (*'ebed yhwh*) shifts the term 'servant' into the religious sphere, since the phrase refers to a subordinate relationship in which a human being is entrusted with a special task to do God's will.[16] Consequently the expression is an important designation. It occurs 23 times in the Hebrew Bible, describing the following people: Moses (18),[17] Joshua (2),[18] David (2)[19] and probably the nation of Israel (1).[20] The phrase 'servants of the Lord' (6 times) refers to Israelites who have followed Yahweh and not Baal during the time of Elisha (2),[21] to cultic officials in the temple (3),[22] and to those who become the servants of Yahweh after the work of a suffering Servant (1).[23]

The word 'servant' also occurs with possessive pronouns that express divine ownership: my servant(s), his servant(s), and your servant(s). 'My servant' appears 61 times and the main designations are as follows: David (23),[24] Jacob (13),[25] Moses (8),[26] Job (6),[27] and Israel

---

15. The word occurs 46 times – e.g., Moses is the special servant of Yahweh in Exod. 14:31 and Num. 12:7–8. The lone New Testament passage is Heb. 3:5 and it is dependent on the LXX of Num. 12:7–8.

16. Cf. Callender, 'Servants', p. 73.

17. Deut. 34:5; Josh. 1:1, 13, 15; 8:31, 33; 11:12; 12:6 (2x); 13:8; 14:7; 18:7; 22:2, 4, 5; 2 Kgs 18:12; 2 Chr. 1:3; 24:6.

18. Josh. 24:9; Judg. 2:8.

19. Ps. 18:1; 36:1.

20. Isa. 42:19. This blind and deaf servant is most likely the nation of Israel.

21. 2 Kgs 9:7; 10:23.

22. Pss. 113:1; 134:1; 135:1.

23. Isa. 54:17.

24. 2 Sam. 3:18; 7:5, 8; 11:13, 32, 34, 36, 38; 1 Kgs 14:8; 2 Kgs 19:34; 20:6; Isa. 37:35; Jer. 33:21, 22, 26; Ezek. 34:23, 24; 37:24, 25; Ps. 89:4, 21.

25. Isa. 41:8, 9, 19; 43:10; 44:1, 2, 21; 45:4; Jer. 30:10; 46:27, 28; Ezek. 28:25; 37:25.

26. Num. 12:7, 8; Josh. 1:2, 7; 2 Kgs 21:8; 1 Chr. 17:4, 7; Mal. 3:22.

27. Job 1:8; 2:3; 42:7, 8 (3x).

(3).[28] 'His servant' appears 24 times with the main references being David (5)[29] and Moses (4).[30] 'Your servant' occurs 90 times. David appears in the majority of these instances (44),[31] with an unidentified psalmist in second position (15),[32] followed by Solomon (10)[33] and Moses (7).[34]

In the Hebrew Scriptures, then, to be classed as a 'Servant of the Lord' is to have a special relationship to God in which an individual is a subordinate to the divine Lord. Moses and the prophets are good examples, for they are called

---

28. Isa. 49:3, 6, 7. Cf. also an unidentified servant: Isa. 42:1 (Israel in LXX). Cf. Isa. 52:13; 53:11. Cf. also Nebuchadnezzar (Jer. 25:9; 27:6; 43:10), the Branch (Zech. 3:8), Zerubbabel (Hag. 2:23), Eliakim (Isa. 22:20), Isaiah (Isa. 20:3), Abraham (Gen. 26:24), Caleb (Num. 14:24). For 'my servants', see Lev. 25:42, 55; 2 Kgs 9:7; 17:13; 65:8, 9, 13 (3x), 14; Jer. 7:25; 26:5; 35:15; 43:10; 44:4; Ezek. 38:17; Hag. 2:23; Zech. 1:6.

29. 1 Kgs 8:66; 2 Kgs 8:19; Pss. 35:27; 78:70; 144:10.

30. Exod. 14:31; Josh. 9:24; 1 Kgs 8:51; Ps. 105:26. The other occurrences are: Abraham (2x): Ps. 105:6, 42; Ahijah (2x): 1 Kgs 14:18; 15:29; Elijah (2x): 2 Kgs 9:36; 10:13; Israel (2x): Ps. 136:22; 1 Chr. 16:13; Joshua: Josh. 5:14; Jonah: 2 Kgs 14:25; Solomon: 1 Kgs 8:59; Jacob: Isa. 48:20; Hezekiah: 2 Chr. 32:16; Cyrus: Isa. 44:26; unidentified: Isa. 50:10. The term 'his servants' occurs 16 times: prophets (6x): 2 Kgs 17:23; 21:10; 24:2; Jer. 25:4; Dan. 9:10; Amos 3:7; Israel (5x): Deut. 32:36, 43; Isa. 65:14, 66:14; Neh. 2:20 (post-exilic community); psalmists (4x): Pss. 34:23; 69:37; 105:25; 135:14; angel: Job 4:18.

31. 1 Sam. 23:10, 11 (2x); 2 Sam. 7:19, 20, 21, 25, 26, 27 (2x), 28, 29 (2x); 24:10; 1 Kgs 3:6; 8:24; 25, 26; 1 Chr. 17:17, 18 (2x), 19, 23, 24, 25 (2x), 26, 27; 21:8; 2 Chr. 6:15, 16, 17, 42; Pss. 9:12, 14; 27:9; 31:17; 69:18; 86:2, 4, 16; 89:40; 109:28; 132:10; 143:2, 12.

32. Pss. 116:16 (2x); 119:17, 23, 38, 49, 65, 76, 84, 122, 124, 125, 135, 140, 176.

33. 1 Kgs 3:7; 8:28 (2x), 29, 30; 8:52; 2 Chr. 6:19 (2x), 20, 21.

34. Exod. 4:10; Num. 11:11; Deut. 3:24; 1 Kgs 8:53; Neh. 1:7, 8; 9:14. The other occurrences are as follows: Nehemiah (4x): Neh. 1:6, 11 (2x); 9:14; Abraham (3x): Gen. 18:3, 5, 19; Samuel (2x): 1 Sam. 3:9, 10; Isaac (1x): Gen. 24:14; Jacob: Gen. 32:11; Samson: Judg. 15:18; Elijah: 1 Kgs 18:36; Daniel: Dan. 9:17. The reference 'your servants' occurs 27 times with the vast majority referring to the people of Israel (20x): 1 Kgs 8:23, 32, 36; 2 Chr. 6:14, 23, 27; Neh. 1:6, 10, 11; Pss. 79:2, 10; 89:51; 90:13, 16; 102:15, 29; Isa. 37:24; 63:17; Jer. 22:2; 37:18. Other identifications are as follows: patriarchs (2x): Exod. 32:13; Deut. 9:27; prophets (2x): Ezra 9:11; Dan. 9:6; faithful Hebrews (2x): Dan. 1:12, 13; laws: Ps. 119:91.

upon to do a special task for Yahweh. David is also noted as a special case of someone set apart to do Yahweh's will. But it is interesting that the phrase 'Servant of the Lord' is predominantly used for Moses (18 times) or his successor (2 times). David merits the term only twice and Israel only once. Yet at the same time, when the word is considered with its possessive pronouns in the Old Testament, David is most often deemed God's servant (66 times), followed by Moses (19 times).

In the New Testament the phrase only occurs twice.[35] Mary is described this way as she yields herself to the divine will in order to bear the child Jesus (Luke 1:38), and ministers are given a character description that befits 'the Lord's servant' (2 Tim. 2:24). Moses is called 'the servant of God' (Rev. 15:3), as is Paul (Titus 1:1).[36] Paul and Silas are called 'servants of the Most High God' by a demoniac (Acts 16:17). More often, the apostles are termed 'servants of Jesus Christ'.[37] As for the use of the term with possessive pronouns, 'my servant' occurs only five times, referring to a centurion's servant three times, a generic servant of a centurion, and Jesus once;[38] 'his servant' appears five times and refers to Jesus twice, and to Israel, David and Mary;[39] and 'your servant' occurs four times, referring to Jesus (twice), David and Simeon.[40]

Thus, in the New Testament the terminology for divine servant is not used as much as in the Old Testament. Moses and particularly David are designated with the relevant titles most often in the Old Testament. In the New Testament Jesus especially is the divine servant, a usage which depends on the Old Testament.[41] But the apostles and disciples can also be described in this way.

---

35. Unless otherwise noted, the term 'servant' in the New Testament is a translation of *doulos*.

36. For 'servants of God', see 1 Pet. 2:16 and Rev. 7:3; for 'servants of Jesus', see 2 Cor. 4:5.

37. Rom. 1:1; Gal. 1:10; Phil. 1:1; Jas 1:1; 2 Pet. 1:1; Jude 1; cf. Col. 4:12.

38. The term *pais* is used of the centurion's servant (Matt. 8:6, 8, Luke 7:7) and Jesus (Matt. 12:18); doulos is used of the generic servant (Matt. 8:9, Luke 7:8). For 'my servants' see Acts 2:18 and Rev. 2:20.

39. Jesus: Acts 3:13, 26; Israel: Luke 1:54; David: Luke 1:69. The Greek is *pais*. Mary: Luke 1:48. For 'his servants', see Rev. 11:18; 19:2, 5; 22:3, 6.

40. Jesus: Acts 4: 27, 30; David: Acts 4:25. The Greek is *pais*. David: Luke 2:29. For 'your servants', see Acts 4:29 and Rev. 11:18.

41. This is clear for Matt. 12:18; Acts 3:13, 26; 4:27, 30. See below.

The biblical story[42]

With a basic definition of the Bible's main uses of the term 'servant' in place, it is now possible to trace this theme more accurately in the Scriptures. In the following survey of this biblical theme in the Old Testament, the order of the Hebrew Scriptures that Jesus himself may have known will be followed.[43] This order consists of a narrative storyline from Genesis to Kings that is broken by a poetic commentary consisting of prophetic oracles (Jeremiah, Ezekiel, Isaiah and the Twelve 'minor prophets') and the largely poetic works of the Writings (Ruth, Psalms, Job, Proverbs, Ecclesiastes, Song of Songs). The storyline is resumed in Daniel and concludes with Chronicles.

The New Testament consists of a similar pattern, with a storyline (Gospels and Acts) broken by a commentary (Pauline letters and Catholic epistles), followed by the Apocalypse, which brings the entire canonical storyline to a grand conclusion. If one leans on linguistic evidence alone, then the Servant theme does not seem to be as prominent in the New Testament as in the Old. But one should be wary of this type of analysis. For example, two critical passages about the importance of the concept of service in the New Testament are John 13 and Philippians 2:6–11, and the term 'servant' occurs only once in each. Scholars are divided, therefore, as to the importance of this theme in the New Testament. For example, Cullman has argued that 'we come straight to the heart of New Testament Christology with the title *ebed Yahweh*', whose sacrificial death 'is the principle by which the New Testament understands the whole course of *Heilsgeschichte*'.[44] Similarly, Richardson claims that Jesus' adoption of the messianic office of the Servant of the Lord provides the concep-

---

42. In the following account of the biblical evidence, the canonical order of the Hebrew Scriptures will be used, particularly that found in an older source (*baraita*) in the Talmud (*Baba Bathra* 14b). It consists of the following books: Torah (Gen., Exod., Lev., Num., Deut.), Prophets (Josh., Judg., Sam., Kgs, Jer., Ezek., Isa., The Twelve [Minor Prophets]), Writings (Ruth, Ps., Job, Prov., Eccl., Song, Lam., Dan., Esth., Ezra-Neh., Chr.). This order largely consists of a narrative backbone interrupted by a poetic commentary (Jer. through to Lam.).

43. See, e.g., Jesus' allusion to the scope of the canon in Luke 24:27, 44. See also the major study by Roger Beckwith, *The Old Testament Canon of the New Testament Church* (Grand Rapids: Eerdmans, 1984).

44. O. Cullman, *The Christology of the New Testament*, trans. S. Guthrie and C. Hall (Philadelphia: Westminster Press, 1959), p. 51. See also L. Mudge, 'The Servant Lord and His Servant People', *SJT* 12 (1959), p. 115.

tual substructure for the New Testament.[45] On the other hand, many others, most notably Morna Hooker, have presented an alternative understanding in which they maintain that the evidence for such a position is greatly exaggerated.[46] Although attention will be focused on the word 'servant' where it occurs in the biblical text, this will not be done in a literalistic way. The concept of servant may be present even without the explicit wording.[47]

Genesis 1–11: the preface to the biblical story

The preface to the biblical story is found in Genesis 1–11. The term 'servant' does not occur in the creation accounts, but the cognate verb and the concept do (Gen. 2:5, 15). In the Eden story a chief function of humanity is to serve, or work, the ground. As scholars have noted, there is a close association of serving and preserving the creation that is given to Adam.[48] 'To serve' and 'to keep' are closely related, and it has been noted that these terms are later used to describe the work of the Levites in the tabernacle (Num. 3:7–8). Some scholars thus understand these words in this context to mean 'to worship and obey'.[49]

---

45. A. Richardson, *An Introduction to the Theology of the New Testament* (New York: Harper & Row, 1958), pp. 26–27.

46. M. Hooker, *Jesus and the Servant* (Cambridge: SPCK, 1958). See the defence of Hooker's position: J. T. Williams, 'Jesus the Servant – Vicarious Sufferer: A Reappraisal', in T. Ashley, G. Wooden and R. S. Wilson (eds.), *You Will Be My Witnesses* (Macon: Mercer University Press, 2003), pp. 53–80. On the other hand, Alan Richardson (*Christology of the New Testament* [New York: Harper & Row, 1958], p. 135) remarks, 'A radical reinterpretation of current Jewish notions about the Messiah is involved in the Son-of-Man conception in the Gospels, and it was made necessary by the deep spiritual insight expressed in the phrase "the Son of Man must suffer".' It can hardly be doubted that the scriptural basis of this insight was Isa. 53: 'The whole passage including almost every phrase of it, echoes through the New Testament.' See G. Johnston, 'The Servant Image in the New Testament', *Theology Today* 15 (1958), p. 326.

47. Note in particular J. Daniel Hays's caution about the problem with word studies: 'If He Looks Like a Prophet', in Richard Hess and M. Daniel Carroll R. (eds.), *Israel's Messiah in the Bible and the Dead Sea Scrolls* (Grand Rapids: Baker, 2003), pp. 59–60.

48. Gordon J. Wenham, 'Sanctuary Symbolism in the Garden of Eden Story', *PWCJS* 9 (1986), pp. 19–25; William J. Dumbrell, *The Faith of Israel* (Grand Rapids: Baker; Leicester: Apollos, 2002), pp. 21–22.

49. See further, John. H. Walton, 'Eden, Garden of', *DOTP*, ed. T. Desmond Alexander and David W. Baker (Leicester: Inter-Varsity Press; Downers Grove: InterVarsity Press, 2003), pp. 202–207.

Genesis 1 and 2 should be read together as an integrated narrative. In Genesis 1 humanity is created in the image of God, and is given the task of having dominion over the creation (Gen. 1:26–28). These tasks entail both royal and servant overtones. Humanity is entrusted with a responsibility to rule. Furthermore, affiliated with the concept of image is the concept of 'sonship' and 'name'. In the next reference to the expression 'likeness of God', the Sethite genealogy indicates that, after God created humanity in his likeness, Adam had a *son* in his own likeness and image and *named* him Seth (Gen. 5:1–3). In the ancient world these concepts cohered. The king represented the gods and often was described as their son, having been made in their image; he also had the task of serving the deities in the world.

Other texts that stress covenant treaty language make this connection. For example, King Ahaz calls himself both a servant and a son when addressing an Assyrian king with whom he has made a treaty (2 Kgs 16:7). Pharaoh is urged to release the Israelites because Israel is Yahweh's firstborn *son* and therefore must *serve* him (Exod. 4:23). The faithful son is an image of his father and thus displays his name. In Genesis 1 this demonstration of the name occurs through the royal task of exercising dominion. In Genesis 2 this royal function is described by the twin verbs 'to serve and to keep'.[50] Interestingly, Psalm 8 reflects on the meaning of the image of God and declares that to be a human being is to be made a little less than God, crowned with glory and honour and placed over the works of creation. When this happens, the name of God is displayed throughout the earth.[51]

---

50. Gen. 2:15. Note Walton's observation, 'Eden', p. 207.

51. For the royal connotations of the image and likeness, see, among others, John Van Seters, 'The Creation of Man and the Creation of the King', *ZAW* 101 (1989), pp. 333–342. This twofold task of divine servant and king is confirmed in the Tell Fakhariyeh inscription in which there is a remarkable correspondence between the creation of humanity in the image and likeness of God and the construction of a statue of a local governor which is referred to as his own image and likeness. W. Randall Garr demonstrates that the inscription, which is written on the statue, is divided into two parts and that the different words 'image' and 'likeness' are coreferential ('"Image" and "Likeness" in the Inscription from Tell Fakhariyeh', *IEJ* 50 [2000], pp. 227–234). Nevertheless, they have a different pragmatic value. In the first section, which features the word 'likeness', the governor views himself as the servant of the god, in fact as a 'devout worshipper'. In the second, which emphasizes the word 'image', he sees himself as a 'sovereign monarch'. Consequently the image has two different functions: a votive function stressing cultic service and a commemorative function focusing on sovereignty.

When the first human couple defy God's words and seek to live by the word of the serpent rather than by the word of their God, they repudiate their role and task. Their failure to worship and obey leads to disaster. They are banished from Eden to work the ground, but now it is a different type of service – service marked by pain and toil (Gen. 3:17–19). Adam, who was to exercise dominion by working the ground, returns to the ground and is subject to it. Similarly, when Cain murders Abel, the ground will not yield its produce to him (Gen. 4:11). The fall frustrates service. Also, a responsibility linked with service, which was used to describe humanity's role in the garden, is refused by Cain with his rhetorical question, 'Am I my brother's *keeper*?' (Gen. 4:9). Sin now rules Cain and his progeny (Gen. 4:7, 17–24), which implies that they have acquired a new master.[52] The Cainite genealogy confirms this conclusion, for it describes not only the roots of the evolution of culture, but also the devolution of humanity, whose nadir is epitomized in Lamech, the seventh generation from Adam (Gen. 4:17–24).[53] He is the only person in this genealogy who speaks, and his boast to his two wives is marked by cruelty.

Yet God does not give up on his creation. He promises a human seed that will destroy the serpent (Gen. 3:15). This person will exercise proper dominion over the creation again. He will be God's Son and therefore represent him on the earth. This focus on descendants explains the extraordinary emphasis on genealogy in Genesis. It is not just a backward-looking device that traces the roots of a people; it functions to create anticipation for a future descendant. This is why Eve is so happy when she gives birth to Seth after the death of Abel (Gen. 4:25), and why Seth's genealogy (Gen. 5:1–32), in contrast to Cain's, focuses on life, concluding with the birth of a son, Noah, who is regarded as a signal of hope for the future (Gen. 5:29).

Noah is selected to serve God by saving creation from imminent catastrophic divine judgment necessitated because the world is now dominated by sin (Gen. 6:5, 11–13). God makes a covenant with this special servant (Gen. 6:18). This covenant is renewed after the flood and secures the world from total disaster. After the flood, Noah, the divine servant, is recast as a new Adam, who exercises dominion over the new creation. But it is a new world

---

52. It is tempting to say that they are now 'servants of sin'.

53. This is really an anti-genealogy, as has been noted by R. R. Robertson, 'The Literary Functions of the Genealogies in Genesis', *CBQ* 48 (1986), p. 600. On this passage, see also Stephen G. Dempster, *Dominion and Dynasty: A Theology of the Hebrew Bible* NSBT (Leicester: Apollos; Downers Grove: InterVarsity Press, 2003), pp. 70–71.

that is tragically flawed. Human sin is still pervasive (Gen. 8:21). The animal kingdom now fears humanity and human life needs to be protected by the reminder that humans are made in the divine image (Gen. 9:1–6). Noah himself is flawed, as are his sons. Awaking from a drunken stupor, he curses his grandson, Canaan, for the obscene behaviour of his father. Canaan is to be a 'servant of servants' (Gen. 9:25). Particularly noteworthy is the fact that Canaan is to be a slave to his *brothers*. This is far removed from the royal service and dignity that marked humanity's pristine beginnings.

The last few chapters of the primeval history focus on human ambition and its opposite, servanthood. The Nephilim made a name for themselves before the flood (Gen. 6:1–4), but it is Noah, the one who does God's will, who survives the deluge.[54] One of Noah's sons is named Shem, which means 'name', and his genealogy sandwiches a story about humans rebelling against their Creator by trying to make a name for themselves by building a city and tower that would reach the heavens.[55] Their colossal ambitions indicate aspirations of divinity instead of dedication to service.[56] Their scheme fails, and Babylon, a human city noted for pride and oppression, is born. Linguistic confusion and spiritual alienation also result.

The line of Shem continues and implicitly becomes the means by which humanity's name will be preserved and God's declared. Just as the last pre-diluvian genealogy culminated with a father whose son would save the earth,[57] and who was represented as an Adamic figure, so too does this first post-diluvian genealogy. The father is Terah and the son is Abram (Gen. 11:26).

Thus, in the narrative of Genesis 1–11 the concept of a servant is present, and it intersects with other concepts. It is because humans do not obey the divine word that they experience disaster and their work becomes wrought with pain and death. They were servants entrusted with the responsibility of the divine house (the world), and they failed in their responsibility. However, there is a seed that is promised that suggests hope (Gen. 3:15). That seed is traced through the line of Adam through Seth with its accent on the image of God and sonship (Gen. 4:25–26; 5:1–32), down through the line of Shem with its emphasis on name (10:21–32; 11:7–26). This new servant called out by God

---

54. For development of this important theme of 'name', see William Osborne, 'Babel', *DOTP*, pp. 73–75.

55. Gen. 10:21–32 (Shem); 11:1–9 (Babel – false name); 11:7–26 (Shem).

56. Note Nimrod, the mighty hunter before the Lord, who founded Babel (Gen 10:8–10). Nimrod's name means 'rebellion'.

57. Gen. 5:28–29. Lamech is the father of Noah.

will win a great name by obeying the divine word rather than by building a tower. But he too will be involved in building. His God will lower a tower from heaven to earth near the head of one of his sons (Gen. 28:10–15), and his descendants will some day see a city of God built on a mountain which will one day grow to fill the entire earth and bring about linguistic order and spiritual unity instead of confusion and division (Isa. 2:1–5; Dan. 2:35).

Genesis 12 – Deuteronomy 34: from Abraham to Moses

This section moves from a universal history to a national history with universal implications. It begins with Abram and Sarai, the father and mother of the Israelite nation, leaving a homeland in search of the land of God's promise, a true homeland, and ends with their descendants finally about to enter into this rest. As such, Abram is regarded as a true servant of God.

Abraham

The text begins with a command for Abram to leave his homeland and become a great nation, win a great name and be the agent of universal blessing (Gen. 12:1–3). In contrast to the builders of the tower of Babel, Abram and his wife, Sarai, are going to be the means of reversing the curse and thus reuniting heaven and earth. They obey and leave for Canaan. Abram is thus a man on a mission, a servant of God. God makes a covenant with him that promises land (Gen. 15) and descendants (Gen. 17). He receives a new name, Abraham, which indicates the new reality that he will be the father of many nations. He views himself as the servant of the divine visitors who come to announce the birth of a son (Gen. 18:3). His obedience as a servant is established in the last great test of his life – the sacrifice of Isaac – when the covenant is confirmed for him:

> By myself I have sworn, declares the LORD, because you have done this and have not withheld your son, your only son, I will surely bless you, and I will surely multiply your offspring as the stars of heaven and as the sand that is on the seashore. And your offspring shall possess the gate of his enemies, and in your offspring shall all the nations of the earth be blessed, *because you have obeyed my voice*. (Gen. 22:16–18, emphasis added)

This is the supreme model of service, for Abraham is willing to lay down his future – the promise God gave him – in obedience to God. Here Abraham is willing to give up more than his life. He is willing to give up his beloved son in order to obey Yahweh. Here ideas of service and suffering are juxtaposed, suffering not only for Abraham, but also for his beloved son.

After Abraham's death, his beloved son, Isaac, is tempted to go down to Egypt because of a famine. God warns him to remain in Canaan, since he is going to be blessed with land and many descendants because of the obedience of Abraham. As was true with his father, obedience and servanthood are synonymous:

> Do not go down to Egypt; dwell in the land of which I shall tell you. Sojourn in this land, and I will be with you and will bless you, for to you and to your offspring I will give all these lands, and I will establish the oath that I swore to Abraham your father. I will multiply your offspring as the stars of heaven and will give to your offspring all these lands. And in your offspring all the nations of the earth shall be blessed, because Abraham obeyed my voice and kept my charge, my commandments, my statutes, and my laws. (Gen. 26:2–5)
>
> I am the God of Abraham your father. Fear not, for I am with you and will bless you and multiply your offspring for my servant Abraham's sake. (Gen. 26:24)

This is the first time a person is designated by God as 'my servant' in the Bible and it most notably refers to Abraham's obedience in the last great test of his life, a passage that stressed service at the expense of great personal suffering and sacrifice. Nevertheless, the concept of a servant has certainly been present. Even though it is not used to describe Isaac, it can be assumed that he was perceived this way.

Before his name is changed to Israel, Isaac's son Jacob refers to himself as God's servant in a prayer of desperation meant to procure divine help to avert a personal disaster, the death of his family members (Gen. 32:11). He walks away from an ensuing encounter with God personally wounded, but he and his family have survived and he has received a new name, Israel. He has saved his family at great personal cost, for he has been wounded in a fight with God.

Later, his son Joseph is singled out by God to bring blessing to the nations through a famine-relief programme. Thus Joseph partially fulfils the promise made to Abraham (Gen. 12:3). But he can do this only after he has gone through the crucible of intense suffering (Gen. 37 – 50), including persecution by his own family. When an aged Israel dies in Egypt, his sons believe that their brother Joseph will now exact vengeance on them for previous persecution. They beg Joseph for forgiveness, referring to themselves as 'the servants of the God of your father' (Gen. 50:17). These servants receive forgiveness from Joseph, the individual servant, who consoles them. A considerable time later, Moses, another divine individual servant, can successfully intervene on behalf of the sinful national servant of Israel by recalling the covenant made to the patriarchs, who are referred to as divine servants (Exod. 32:13). This action stems the imminent tide of divine judgment. God acts on behalf of his servants.

At the end of the Joseph story there is a fitting genealogical conclusion to a book in which genealogy has been extraordinarily important. The blessing on the tribes singles out not only Joseph, but also Judah, who is regarded as becoming a future ruler to whom will come 'the obedience of the peoples' (Gen. 49:10) and whose reign will produce a virtual paradise again. Thus there is a focus on a king who comes from a line of servants – perhaps a royal servant, from the tribe of Judah.

Israel and Moses

In the exodus story the children of Abraham are reminded of two types of servitude, the servitude of Pharaoh and that of Yahweh.[58] In Egypt divine blessing begins to materialize as the Hebrew population mushrooms (Exod. 1:7). This growth, however, leads to Egyptian oppression; the Hebrews are reduced to slavery. An individual who reluctantly does the divine will, and who later becomes known as the servant of the Lord, liberates the nation from bondage. In his life Moses represents the nation.[59] Like Moses, the Israelites are to find their identity as servants not of Pharaoh, but of Yahweh. Repeatedly, Moses tells Pharaoh to release the Israelites so that they can serve Yahweh.[60]

The Hebrews have been liberated from Egypt to attain the dignity for which they were created: 'I am the LORD your God, who brought you out of the land of Egypt, that you should not be their slaves. And I have broken the bars of your yoke and made you walk erect' (Lev. 26:13). Israelite release from Egyptian bondage becomes the first principle of nationhood, and this release is echoed throughout the Old Testament.[61]

This life-changing fact becomes the basis for a relationship with God and neighbour. Particularly it affects the way Israelites are to view their own kin who have become debt slaves. They are not to view them as abject, since 'they

---

58. Bruce C. Birch, *What Does the Lord Require?* (Philadelphia: Westminster Press, 1985), p. 62. In particular Birch notes that the exodus liberates from the forced labour to build the Pharaoh's cities, while Sinai calls to the covenantal labour to build Yahweh's cities, his just community.

59. E. Fox, *The Five Books of Moses* (New York: Schocken, 1997), p. 253.

60. Exod. 4:23; 7:16, 26; 8:16; 9:1, 13; 10:3, 7, 8, 11, 24; 10:26; 12:31.

61. Exod. 20:2; 21:2; Deut. 5:6; 6:12; 7:8; 8:14; 13:6, 11; Josh. 24:17; Judg. 6:8; Mic. 6:4.

are my servants, whom I brought out of the land of Egypt' (Lev. 25:42, 55). In other words, since the Israelites are now Yahweh's servants, they cannot be sold for the sale price of a slave (Lev. 25:42). Exodus liberation and the subsequent Sinai covenant become the Magna Carta for Israelite existence. Israelites reduced to harsh servitude within Israel are a sign of the return to Egypt in practice if not in theory.[62] When the nation is granted a leader, a king like the rest of the nations, he is not to become the locus of power and wealth like a foreign ruler. Such self-aggrandizement will lead the people back to Egyptian oppression (Deut. 17:14–20, esp. v. 16). Instead, the king must be an *Israelite* ruler, and as such he must read God's word daily, subjecting himself to Yahweh's will. As Yahweh's servant he will guide his nation in a just manner. A king in Israel is nothing more than a royal servant!

At Sinai, the newly constituted nation becomes the royal servant of God (Exod. 19:5–6), called into being as his firstborn son. Pharaoh was told that Israel was Yahweh's firstborn son and was given the command, 'Let *my son* go that he may *serve* me' (Exod. 4:23)! This is clearly covenantal language, as is shown in a later text in which King Ahaz has made a covenant with an Assyrian king and calls himself the foreign king's servant and son (2 Kgs 16:7).

Another way in which the Sinai covenant evokes obedience and sonship is suggested by the covenant rite in Exodus 24:8. The people pledge obedience, and the blood of sacrificial animals is sprinkled on the people and on an altar which represents God. The precise meaning of this ritual is difficult to determine, but it may convey a malediction in which the different parties curse themselves if they break their pledge. However, there is no indication of such a curse in the context. More likely it means that a new relationship, 'a blood relationship', has been established between Israel and God, contingent upon Israelite obedience.[63] It is as if the one blood is put upon the two parties to unite them in a relationship like marriage, so that now Israel is the people of Yahweh and Yahweh is their redeemer. An obedient Israel, a royal servant of Yahweh, has been given the task of mediating blessing to the nations (Exod. 19:5–6).[64]

The covenant, however, is but a month old when the people break it by committing idolatry, thus violating their new constitution (Exod. 32:1–6). It is

---

62. Cf. Jer. 34:13; Neh. 9:36.

63. J. P. Hyatt, *Exodus*, NCB (Grand Rapids: Eerdmans, 1980), pp. 255–258.

64. Note John I. Durham's comments (*Exodus*, WBC [Waco: Word, 1987], p. 263): 'It will be a kingdom run not by politicians depending on strength and connivance but by priests depending on faith in Yahweh, a servant nation instead of a ruling nation.' Perhaps it is better to state that Israel will redefine the nature of ruling.

Moses, the servant of the Lord, who offers his own life as a substitute for the sinful nation-servant. Moses saves the people from annihilation when he pleads for mercy based on the covenant made with Abraham, Isaac and Israel, the divine servants (32:11–14). He descends the mountain and, enraged by the sin, smashes the Ten Commandments, indicating the end of the covenant (32:15–19). He destroys the evidence of idolatry, punishes the people and ascends the mount to make atonement (32:20–35).

The ordeal results in Yahweh's refusal to accompany the people into the land; he decides to send his angel instead (Exod. 33:1–6). The nation has been a disobedient servant. A brief narrative interlude indicates the alienation between God and people, for it is noted that the Tent of Meeting is outside the camp (Exod. 33:7–11). Moses' unique mediatorial powers and the divine alienation are suggested by this passage. After this digression, Moses ascends Sinai again to plead for the accompaniment of the divine presence; he wins a hearing and experiences a revelation, which discloses the meaning of the divine name:

> The LORD, the LORD, a God merciful and gracious, slow to anger, and abounding in steadfast love and faithfulness, keeping steadfast love for thousands, forgiving iniquity and transgression and sin, but who will by no means clear the guilty, visiting the iniquity of the fathers on the children and the children's children, to the third and the fourth generation. (Exod. 34:6–7)

Moses pleads forgiveness for the rebellious people (Exod. 34:8–9). He descends the mountain with a new set of commandments and a face transformed by dialogue with God (34:29–30). Moses has brought about a renewal of the covenant. As the mediator of this new covenant, he has sought to reconcile God and the people and his transformed face suggests an intimate relationship with God, a reflection of the divine likeness in human form, which may echo Genesis 1–2.

It is important to pause and reflect on the uniqueness of Moses as a divine servant, since this emphasis is developed in a few other texts as well. He has a unique relationship with God as a conveyor of the divine will. This singularity is elaborated in Numbers 11–12. The context of this passage is the overwhelming task of dealing with all the needs of the people (11:1–15). An exasperated Moses is told that he will receive help, for the elders of the community will share the burden (11:16–23). The divine Spirit resting upon him is then distributed to seventy elders who prophesy when empowered by the Spirit (11:24–30). Moses is depicted as the channel through which leadership and prophetic charisma are given. Thus he is a type of royal and prophetic figure. Miriam and Aaron then complain that they have as much right to be leaders as Moses, since God also speaks through them (Num. 12:1–3). They appear before the Tent of Meeting and the radical difference between Moses and other prophets is described (12:6–8a).

Kselman shows how the verbal artistry of this text 'showpieces' Moses:

1. If you have a prophet of *Yahweh*
2. *In a vision* to him I will make myself known
3. In a dream *I will speak with him*
4. Not so with **my servant Moses**
4. In all my house **he is faithful**
3. Mouth to mouth *I will speak with him*
2. *In a vision* and not in riddles
1. The form of *Yahweh* he will see[65]

God speaks to all other prophets in dreams and visions, but, 'Not so with *my servant Moses*. He is faithful in all my house' (12:7, emphasis added). God speaks to him clearly and not in riddles. This means that Moses experiences direct communication. Moses is regarded as worthy of this type of revelation, since he is faithful in God's entire house, which is correlative with being 'my servant'. Thus he sees the very form of the Lord.

What does it mean to be faithful in all God's house? The clearest parallel is a reference in which the high priest Ahimelech defends David against Saul's accusations: 'And who among all your servants is so faithful as David, who is the king's son-in-law, and captain over your bodyguard, and honoured in your house?' (1 Sam. 22:14). David is understood to be a faithful person who has distinguished himself as a servant in Saul's household, which refers to the royal court. By analogy, 'God's house' in Numbers 12 refers to the nation of Israel, in particular the administrative apparatus of the elders and prophets. Moses, not Aaron or Miriam or any other, is faithful in the divine house. Moses is *the* faithful servant to be distinguished from all others. He is the equivalent of Eleazar in Abraham's house and Joseph in Potiphar's household.[66]

In the immediate sequel to the story in Numbers 12, the people prove unfaithful once again when they fear to enter the Promised Land. Again, the intercession of Moses, the faithful, individual servant, saves the disobedient, national servant from annihilation. With the exception of two individuals,

---

65. J. S. Kselman, 'A Note on Numbers 12:6–8', *VT* 26 (1976), pp. 500–504.

66. Note particularly the parallel between house and kingdom in 1 Chr. 17:14.

Joshua and Caleb, the adult generation is condemned to a life of aimless wandering in the wilderness. Caleb in particular is contrasted with the rest of the people, who tested God ten times in the wilderness and 'have not obeyed my voice' but 'despised me' (Num. 14:22–23). The text says, 'But *my servant Caleb*, because he has a different spirit and has followed me fully, I will bring into the land into which he went, and his descendants shall possess it' (Num. 14:24, emphasis added). It is because Caleb has these qualities that he merits the designation 'my servant'.

The second text describing the uniqueness of Moses and his relationship with God occurs at the end of the Torah. Moses has led the new generation to the border of Canaan, has given the farewell sermon of Deuteronomy, and is given a view of the land from the peak of Mount Pisgah. He is told that he cannot enter the land. The narrator describes his death in laconic prose: 'So Moses the servant of the LORD died there in the land of Moab, according to the word of the LORD' (Deut. 34:5). This is the first time the expression 'the servant of Yahweh' is used in the Bible, and it is virtually an epitaph for the remarkable prophet. The death of this servant is remarkable, for it is a type of judgment. He dies by virtue of the decree of the Lord. 'He did not enter Canaan because he died; he died because he did not enter Canaan.'[67] At the same time it is significant that this person who receives the designation 'servant of Yahweh' for the first time remains outside the land while his people will enter.

Then the narrative focus shifts to Joshua, who has received the spirit of Moses, and the text concludes with a final eulogy to the great Moses: he was the unique prophet. 'And there has not arisen a prophet since in Israel like Moses, whom the LORD knew face to face, none like him for all the signs and the wonders that the LORD sent him to do ...' (Deut. 34:10–11). This comment alludes to a text within Deuteronomy in which the institution of prophecy is established (Deut. 18:15–22). Prophecy in this latter text is

---

67. Eugene H. Merrill, *Deuteronomy*, NAC (Nashville: Broadman and Holman, 1994), p. 434. Gerhard von Rad sees the parallels clearly between the servant of Yahweh here and the Isaianic servant of Yahweh (*Old Testament Theology*, trans. D. Stalker [New York: Harper and Row, 1962], vol. 1, p. 295, cf. vol. 2, pp. 261–262). Both die so that their people might live. Patrick Miller develops the parallels more fully ('My Servant Moses: The Deuteronomic Portrait of Moses', *Int* 41 [1987], pp. 253–254). Cf. also, R. E. Clements, 'Isaiah 53 and the Restoration of Israel', in W. Bellinger Jr and W. R. Farmer (eds.), *Jesus and the Suffering Servant: Isaiah 53 and Christian Origins* (Harrisburg: Trinity Press International, 1998), pp. 39–54.

regarded as necessary for mediating the divine will to people, since they cannot bear to hear the divine word without such mediation (see Exod. 20:18–21). A prophet such as Moses is needed, a prophet who can mediate the divine words as Moses did at Sinai. What is in view in this text is a succession of prophets. But the text in Deuteronomy 34 indicates that this text has triggered an expectation of a Moses-like prophet who would be mighty in word and deed and concludes that this person has not arrived yet.[68] The Torah concludes, then, with Moses, the unique servant of the Lord, dying outside Canaan, and with the expectation of another servant like him who will do God's will. Perhaps he too will be like Moses in the last respect and suffer for his people.

Conclusion

The biblical story from Genesis 12 to Deuteronomy 34 indicates that the curse inflicted upon the world will be reversed through the descendants of Abraham. Abraham, the patriarchs and particularly Moses are key examples of divine servants who have been chosen to represent God's purposes on the earth, which is ultimately expressed in the nation Israel. Covenant and service are inextricably linked. A relationship is made between God and people that supplies the rationale for service and the means through which God's purposes will be achieved. When God's plans for the future of his people seem jeopardized (e.g. through covenant violation), a number of these servants have been willing to suffer for their people.

Joshua – Kings: from Joshua to David

In the narrative from Joshua to Kings, which constitutes the Former Prophets in the Hebrew Bible, there is a movement from the high point of conquest to the low point of exile. Throughout this section of Scripture there are a number of important occurrences of the title 'servant of Yahweh'. The occurrences start with Joshua, continue through the judges and culminate in King David. Before David appears, however, Saul functions as the first king, and an anti-servant, so he presents a dramatic foil for David.

Joshua

Joshua leads the people to conquer the land, calling them to renewed commitment after the initial phase of the conquest. He is patterned as a new

---

68. See, e.g., J. Blenkinsopp, *Prophecy and Canon* (Notre Dame: University of Notre Dame Press, 1977), p. 77; J. Sailhamer, *An Introduction to Old Testament Theology* (Grand Rapids: Zondervan, 1995), pp. 246–252.

Moses, carrying on the latter's work in his Spirit (Josh. 5:13–15; cf. Exod. 3:1–5). Throughout the book of Joshua, the dead Moses is referred to repeatedly as the servant of Yahweh,[69] and the same title is transferred to Joshua when he dies at the end of the book (Josh. 24:29; cf. Judg. 2:8). The text notes that the people served Yahweh all the days of Joshua, with the implication that without the presence of this divine servant they lapsed.

There are fifty references to 'serving' in the book of Joshua, and eighteen of them are found in the last chapter. At this point it seems as if a critical moment has been reached and the nation must make a decision about continuing as a servant of Yahweh. Joshua narrates a brief history of God's acts for the nation in a type of covenant renewal ceremony and calls on the people to serve the Lord just as he and his family household plan to do. The people accept this challenge because of God's gracious acts on their behalf. Then Joshua responds with a shocking statement: 'You are not able to serve the LORD, for he is a holy God. He is a jealous God; he will not forgive your transgressions or your sins' (Josh. 24:19).[70] The people disagree, answering affirmatively that they will serve Yahweh. But Joshua's words stand like a dark shadow over the rest of Israel's history.

The Judges

In the subsequent narrative in Judges, the main leaders, Joshua at the beginning and Samson at the end, are called the Lord's servants. These quite different individuals suggest a significant disparity between Israel at the beginning and at the ending of the book of Judges.[71] Joshua is designated again as the servant of Yahweh, and his death signals the death of faith in the next generation of Israelites (Judg. 2:8–10). Samson laments that God has wrought such a great salvation through the hand of his servant against Philistine oppression, only to let him die of thirst (Judg. 15:18). In the chequered history occurring between these two leaders, the people's faith is revived by the empowerment of judges through God's Spirit. They serve God and the people. As long as they live they bring stability to the nation, but with each respective death there is an increasing moral devolution. The judges themselves have major moral problems. Towards the end of the book the nation's

---

69. Josh. 1:1, 13, 15; 8:31, 33; 11:12; 12:6 [2x]; 13:8; 14:7; 18:7; 22:2, 4, 5.

70. See Dempster, *Dominion*, p. 130.

71. See, e.g., John H. Stek, 'The Bee and the Mountain Goat: A Literary Reading of Judges 4', in W. Kaiser Jr and J. Youngblood (eds.), *A Tribute to Gleason Archer* (Chicago: Moody Press, 1986), p. 83 n. 41.

ills seem caused by the lack of an effective leader – a king in Israel. This seems
to be part of the difficulty with the judges. Their activity seems to function as
a foil for the kingship. It is temporary, partial and flawed. What is needed is a
dynastic kingship, a perpetual judge or true servant of the Lord in the manner
of Moses and Joshua, so to speak, who will achieve a permanent rest for the
people in their own land.

Samuel

Such a situation provides the background for understanding the continuation
of the narrative in the books of Samuel. The corruption of the Elide priesthood, which seems to inherit the judicial role from the previous judges, dramatically illustrates the problem. Eli is to be judged and his line to be replaced
by a faithful high priest (1 Sam 2:35). Here is a remarkable echo of Numbers
12:7, in which Moses was recognized as the pre-eminent faithful servant of
Yahweh in the nation. Now an unfaithful priest will be replaced by a faithful
one, for whom a faithful house will be built, and this creates a mood of anticipation for the future rejection of Saul, an unfaithful king, and his replacement
by a faithful one, David, who is called 'faithful . . . and honoured' in all Saul's
house (1 Sam. 22:14).

The story of Samuel's birth and call indicates the importance of prophets
and servanthood. His birth preludes a new world order presided over by an
anointed king (1 Sam. 2:10). At the same time, when he is called to be a prophet
he is told that his attitude towards the divine word must be that of a servant:
'Speak, Yahweh, for your servant hears' (1 Sam. 3:9). This word becomes *the*
word that defines the prophetic office in ancient Israel. Prophets become servants of the word or, in the language that will become widespread, his servants
the prophets.[72] Samuel embodies this servant posture not only in his call, but
also in the difficult task of delivering his messages from Yahweh (cf. 1 Sam.
3:10–21).

Saul

When the political challenges of the new nation grow to crisis proportions, the
people desire a king for all the wrong reasons. The text views their desire as a
rejection of divine rule that implies the people's rejection of their servant
status (1 Sam. 8:5–8). The consequences of this rejection are dire. Not to be a

---

72. Or variations using the first- and second-person possessive pronouns: 2 Kgs 17:13,
    23; 21:10; 24:2; Jer. 7:25; 25:4; 26:5; 29:19; 35:15; 44:4; Ezek. 38:17; Amos 3:7; Zech.
    1:6.

servant of Yahweh means enslavement to a human king who is only interested in 'taking' rather than serving.[73] Samuel thus presents the implications in a lengthy discourse entitled the 'the law of the king' (1 Sam. 8:10–18). He concludes by stating, 'You shall be his slaves. And in that day you will cry out because of your king, whom you have chosen for yourselves, but the LORD will not answer you in that day' (1 Sam. 8:17–18).[74] Thus human rule as a replacement for divine rule ends in slavery, precisely because the king does not see himself as a servant of Yahweh, but as a law to himself. The law of this type of kingship is a national rule that will lead back to Egypt, to forced slavery and all the accompanying back-breaking oppression.[75] If kingship can be remedied, it must be by the national law envisioned by Deuteronomy in which the Israelite king sees himself as a divine servant (Deut. 17:14–20), and which anticipates a universal law proclaimed by another such servant (see Isa. 42:1, 3, 4).

When Saul is chosen, initially there is the attempt to understand his kingship differently, to transform an ancient oriental despotism into a more 'Israelite-friendly' rule. Saul is anointed not to be a king (*melek*), but to be a ruler or chieftain (*nagîd*).[76]

---

73. 'The speech of Samuel describing the practices of kings is dominated by the verb *take*' (8:11–18). See B. Birch, W. Brueggemann, T. Fretheim and D. Petersen, *A Theological Introduction to the Old Testament* (Nashville: Abingdon Press, 1999), p. 229.

74. For the formula by which the copula verb is used with 'servant' for people becoming slaves, see further Gen. 44:9; 1 Sam. 17:9 (2x); 2 Sam. 8:2, 6; 2 Chr. 36:20; Jer. 34:16.

75. Birch et al. make the point that 'this slavery will be of the people's own choosing' (*Theological Introduction*, p. 230).

76. See 1 Sam. 10:1. A thorough, recent study of this term concludes, 'In our text the *melek* is one who sees power from Yahweh as susceptible to his own arbitrary manipulation, who obtrudes himself inappropriately and disproportionately between Yahweh and Israel and who treats Israel as little more than the subjects of his monarchic powers. The *nagîd*, on the other hand, is positively portrayed as one who sees his power as a sovereign and inviolable devolvement from Yahweh, who acts strictly under orders from Yahweh for the benefit of Yahweh's people, and holds himself as no more than the willing subject of the divine monarch.' See Donald F. Murray, *Divine Prerogative and Royal Pretension: Pragmatics, Poetics, and Polemics in Narrative Sources about David (2 Samuel 5:17–7:29)*, JSOTSup 264 (Sheffield: Sheffield Academic Press, 1998), p. 299. I am indebted to Peter Gentry for calling my attention to Murray's important work.

But instead of Saul acting like a chieftain, someone who is accountable to both Yahweh and the people, he acts like a pagan king and his reign is a disaster. It is precisely because he does not see himself as fundamentally a divine servant that he is not able, unlike his predecessors the judges, to bring even a modicum of rest to the land. The term 'servant' or 'servant of the Lord' is never applied to him; his height seems to keep getting in the way. The prophetic criticism of Saul is that he is an 'anti-servant'. 'To obey is better than sacrifice,' says Samuel to him, when he pleads innocent to the charge of disobedience (1 Sam. 15:22).[77]

David

As the judges provide a foil for kingship, so Saul provides a contrast for David.[78] David is the quintessential servant. Outward appearance does not distinguish him. In fact, this would certainly disqualify him from kingship (1 Sam. 16:7). When Samuel anoints him, the Spirit rests on David and departs from Saul. He proves himself in battle by saving Israel from the oppression of Goliath (1 Sam. 17). He is characterized by hearing Yahweh's voice and experiencing his favour in the rest of the narrative of 1 Samuel, while Saul is marked by a failure in both respects. In the waning days of the house of Saul, Abner, the military leader of Saul's kingdom, encourages the northern tribes to rally around David since he is the servant of the Lord: 'Now then bring it about, for the LORD has promised David, saying, "By the hand of my servant David I will save my people Israel from the hand of the Philistines, and from the hand of all their enemies"' (2 Sam. 3:18). David functions like the earlier servants, Moses and Joshua: Moses was able to lead Israel out of Egypt, and Joshua was able to lead them into Canaan. As events develop, David becomes officially installed as king and is succeeded by a line of kings, the first one of which is Solomon. But three texts in particular emphasize the importance of his kingship/service: the first is 2 Samuel 7, which describes the Davidic covenant and its promise of the building of the Davidic house or dynasty; the

---

77. Note that when Saul is told that Yahweh is going to appoint a *nagîd* in his place, it is because Saul has not acted like a servant by obeying Yahweh's commandments (1 Sam. 13:14).

78. Note Dan Block's insightful comment: 'The entire narrative of Saul's rise and reign is composed in ironical and farcical terms to serve as a foil against which to present David as Yahweh's anointed' ('My Servant David: Ancient Israel's Vision of the Messiah', in Richard S. Hess and M. Daniel Carroll R. (eds.), *Israel's Messiah in the Bible and the Dead Sea Scrolls* [Grand Rapids: Baker Book House, 2003], p. 38).

second describes catastrophe in Israel's life from which Israel is saved by David and his house (2 Sam. 24); and the third is the description of the completion of the temple or divine house in 1 Kings 8.

In the first text David desires to build a house for God and is told that God is going to build one for him instead. God addresses him through Nathan with the words 'my servant David' twice (2 Sam. 7:5, 8), promising him a great name, a secure kingdom for his people, an enduring kingship and a kingship in which the king would be regarded as a son and God as his father. Interestingly, Yahweh does not use the term 'king' (*melek*) to describe this reign, but that of chieftain or ruler (*nagîd*), who is to shepherd his people (2 Sam. 7:8). Moreover, the next ruler was to build the temple for God's name. Even though David's descendants might sin, God's covenant love would never be removed from his line as it was for Saul.

Accordingly, Yahweh makes an enduring covenant with David; he is both a servant and a son, and the emphasis is placed on his house. If Moses was a servant faithful in God's house, David is both a *servant* and a *son* for whom God will build a house and declare his great *name*. As royalty he will represent God in the world as his *image*. Repeatedly in the text, when David prays to God, he refers to himself as 'your servant', thus understanding himself in the same light. The rhetorical effect of the tenfold repetition of this expression in the text is impressive. David may be a king, but he is supremely God's servant first, so it is most appropriate to view him as a *nagîd*.[79] Echoes of Genesis appear here through the focus on royalty (image), and intimacy (son), name and servant.

In the second text (2 Sam. 24) David acts like a pagan king, which gets him and his nation into serious trouble. He takes a census that assumes the importance of military and economic power in accordance with the law of pagan rulers. This brings about a divine judgment on the land. When David sees the people being destroyed by a plague, he averts the judgment by calling it down on himself and the house of his father (2 Sam 24:17). He is told to build an altar to help stem the tide of judgment. When sacrifices are offered on the altar, the plague ceases (2 Sam. 24:25). Both aspects of the Davidic house are indicated here. David the royal shepherd saves the flock of his people (2 Sam 24:17) by offering his house (the dynasty) as a substitute, and the people are saved by David's construction of an altar for the future house of God (the temple). David is the servant-shepherd who is willing to die for his flock.

In the third text, Solomon's prayer at the completion of the house of God, there is repeated reference to the fact that God has made an eternal covenant

---

79. For the expression 'your servant', see 2 Sam. 7:19, 20, 21, 25, 26, 27 (2x), 28, 29 (2x).

on account of 'David his servant' (1 Kgs 8:24, 25, 26). When Solomon begins
to pray, his self-understanding is the same, for he regularly refers to himself as
'your servant' (1 Kgs 8:28 [2x], 29, 30, 52). The temple is to be the focus of
prayer for help, particularly for forgiveness. Solomon repeatedly prays for forgiveness for Israel, culminating in a prayer for forgiveness when they are far
away in exile (1 Kgs 8:46–53). The chapter concludes with a final reference to
David: 'On the eighth day he sent the people away, and they blessed the king
and went to their homes joyful and glad of heart for all the goodness that the
LORD had shown to David his servant and to Israel his people' (1 Kgs 8:66).

David's legacy

Throughout the remaining history of Kings there is repeated reference to
'David my servant'. This phrase or a variation of it is virtually a leading idea in
this text.[80] The prophet Ahijah announces that Jeroboam will be the leader of
a secessionist northern kingdom, but that God will spare Judah because of
'David my servant' (1 Kgs 11:13). *David's servanthood overshadows other references to
service in the text.* The prophets, who are collectively regarded as 'my servants
the prophets', are sent to Israel, the national servant, to warn of impending
disaster for disobedience.[81] Individual prophets in the narrative are sometimes
called the divine servant: Ahijah (1 Kgs 15:29), Elijah (2 Kgs 9:36; 10:10) and
Jonah (2 Kgs 14:25). But David is the most noteworthy. In two remarkable
texts the divine word comes to Hezekiah that Jerusalem will be saved from the
Assyrian enemy because of God and David, his servant (2 Kgs 19:34; 20:6).
The divine and the Davidic causes coalesce.

Conclusion

The end of Kings concludes with the failure of the nation Israel and the disaster of exile. Joshua's words come true. The constant repetition of the importance of serving Yahweh at the beginning of this sad tale stands as a witness
against the people in exile (Josh. 24). The nation has not served the Lord. Israel
as the divine servant has failed in its task. David, the divine servant par excellence, had saved Israel from disaster by calling judgment down upon his own
house and buying the location for another house, the temple. Solomon has
stressed the importance of the temple as a place for forgiveness. What will be
the end of it all? At the conclusion of Kings the temple is devastated and the
king is in exile with many of the people. There is the terse note that the exiled

---

80. 1 Kgs 11:13, 34, 38; 14:8; 15:4; 2 Kgs 8:19; 19:34; 20:6.
81. 2 Kgs 9:7; 17:13, 23; 21:10; 24:2.

Davidic king, Jehoiachin, is released from prison and given a place at the Babylonian king's table (2 Kgs 25:27–31). This appears to many scholars to signify the last footnote in a history of failure and judgment. But if read in the context of the covenant made with Yahweh's servant David, that his throne would never lack an heir, this points to a future pregnant with possibility and hope.[82] Perhaps a true servant will come and suffer so that the people may live. 'David my servant' still lives.

Jeremiah – Lamentations: poetic commentary focusing on David
The Latter Prophets (Jeremiah – the Twelve) and the first part of the Writings (Ruth – Lamentations) break this narrative sequence, for they serve to reflect on the exile and the post-exilic period before the story is resumed again in the Writings with Daniel, Esther, Ezra-Nehemiah and Chronicles. This poetic section serves as a commentary that sharpens the focus on David begun in Genesis – Kings.

Jeremiah
The book of Jeremiah considers the failure of Israel to live up to the Sinai covenant. The people have not heeded the warning of God's servants, the prophets, throughout their history.[83] Jeremiah 34 provides a window into the worldview of the nation. In the last days of Judah, when surrounded by the Babylonian army, the people are told to liberate their fellow Israelite slaves. They do this as a last-ditch effort to fend off their Babylonian enemy. But when the threat disappears, they re-enslave their brothers and sisters. Consequently they have become like the Egyptian taskmasters who oppressed their forefathers, and thus will be judged.

Beyond the judgment there is a hope for both the northern and the southern kingdoms. There are two servants who are specifically identified in the oracles of hope in Jeremiah. First is the national servant of Israel named 'my servant Jacob'. This servant is told that Yahweh is going to bring him back from exile and defeat his enemies. He will be delivered from serving his enemies so that he can serve God. Jacob's new service will coincide with David being appointed his king (Jer. 30:9–10). Later, David appears in the text

---

82. For a recent, meticulous and exhaustive treatment of Jehoiachin, viewing his release as a signal of hope for the Davidic covenant, see J. Critchlow, 'Looking Back for Jeconiah: Yahweh's Cast-Out Signet' (PhD diss., The University of Edinburgh, 2004).

83. Jer. 7:25; 25:4; 26:5; 29:29; 44:4.

through the promise that a righteous plant will sprout up from his line and bring justice, hope and restoration. This is guaranteed because of 'David my servant', who is explicitly named three times as the reason for God's unbreakable covenant with Israel. The covenant is guaranteed in the same way that God's covenant with creation is certain. If it could be broken, the covenant with David, Yahweh's servant, could also be breached (Jer. 33:20–21). This Davidic covenant guarantees and continues the Abrahamic covenant, since David's seed is promised to become as numerous as the stars, a covenant of shalom (Jer. 33:22–26).

Ezekiel

Ezekiel continues the tradition of naming David 'my servant'. Complaining because of the shepherds who exploited Israel, Ezekiel predicts that there will be a true shepherd, 'David my servant'. When God is finally their God, again 'my servant David' will be a ruler in their midst (Ezek. 34:23). Unity of the nation is promised similarly in Ezekiel 37, where 'my servant David' shepherding them will coincide with purity and reconciliation, forgiveness and the pouring out of the Spirit on the people (Ezek. 37:25). Restoration is granted to 'my servant Jacob', who will dwell in the land securely, and to 'David my servant', who will preside over them.[84]

Isaiah

This distinction between two servants, one identified with the nation and the other with its king, anticipates Isaiah. The future king appears frequently in the first half of the book and 'Jacob my servant' and 'Israel my servant' occur repeatedly in the second half of the book. Servant imagery is absent from the first part of the book, whereas royal imagery is largely absent from the second. Alexander has observed that the first division emphasizes the failure of the Davidic monarchy and contrasts this present failure with someone who will sprout up from the Davidic stump, be born as a child, be equipped by the Spirit and bring justice to the nations, thereby transforming the world into a paradise (Isa. 9:5–6; 11:1–9).[85] The word 'servant' does not apply to this individual, but

---

84. For the development of this theme, see Daniel I. Block, 'Bringing Back David: Ezekiel's Messianic Hope', in P. Sattherwaite and G. J. Wenham (eds.), *The Lord's Anointed, Interpretation of Old Testament Messianic Texts* (Downers Grove: InterVarsity Press, 1995), pp. 177–183.

85. See T. Desmond Alexander, *The Servant King* (Grand Rapids: Baker, 2002), pp. 103–112.

clearly he sits on the throne of David, doing the will of God. In the second half of the book, the disobedient Israelite nation, the unfaithful servant, appears languishing in exile as the result of judgment. This present failure contrasts with a faithful divine servant who will lead the people into freedom from their bondage. The word 'king' is not used of this individual, but his work, like that of the Davidic king of the first division, has a universal scope (Isa. 42:1–4), and it brings about a universal Davidic covenant (Isa. 55:3). Significantly, the word 'ruler' or 'chieftain' (*nagîd*) is used when this has been accomplished (Isa. 55:4), thus invoking the ancient ideal for a leader.

Similarly, the present Jerusalem is contrasted with the future Jerusalem in the book.[86] Jerusalem, which was to be the centre of divine dominion, the rule of justice and righteousness, has become a place of murder and promiscuity (Isa. 1:21–23). But the servant will bring about Yahweh's new world order, elevating this city to its intended divine prominence as a beacon of light to the nations (Isa. 60:1–22).[87]

As for the unfaithful servant Israel, its description echoes portions of earlier material. Isaiah's preaching was to effect blindness and deafness in the people until they were ripe for judgment (Isa. 6:9–10). The servant Israel, described in just such terms in 42:19, has experienced judgment for not obeying the Torah. Such a servant is promised so that Israel will be cleansed and delivered from exile (Isa. 44:19). But alongside this servant named Jacob or Israel, there is another more faithful Israel, one anointed by the Spirit to be a witness to the nations.[88] His success despite all opposition and the rewards for his work are

---

86. Isa. 1:21–23, 24–31; 2:1–5; 3:16–26; 4:2–6; 60:1–22.

87. See in particular the analysis by W. J. Dumbrell, 'The Role of the Servant in Isaiah 40–55', *RTR* 48 (1989), pp. 109–110. Thus clearly the servant is distinguished from the city of Jerusalem. A valiant case is made for their identification by Wilshire, but the city is consistently understood as feminine and the servant as masculine. Moreover, how can Jerusalem be the dim wick and bruised reed of Isaiah 42:2 and be helped by the servant at the same time? See L. E. Wilshire, 'The Servant-City: A New Interpretation of the "Servant of the Lord" in the Servant Songs of Deutero-Isaiah', *JBL* 94 (1975), pp. 356–367.

88. Clearly this is a royal motif, as has been shown by a number of interpreters. See, e.g., W. A. M. Beuken, '*Mišpat*. The First Servant Song and its Context', *VT* 22 (1972), p. 7; J. Jeremias, '*Mišpat* im ersten Gottesknechtslied', *VT* 22 (1972), pp. 33–34. Note the parallels: Ps. 2:7; 1 Sam. 10:24; 16:13–17. J. J. M. Roberts's insightful remark is telling against the many views that at times cavalierly identify Israel and the servant: 'The radically contrasting portrayals of blindly disobedient

themes linking all these particular servant passages, and they stand in contrast to the failure of the national servant.[89] He first appears in 42:1–4, where he has the task of bringing real justice to the nations.[90] He is equipped by the divine spirit to do this, and his method is to work quietly, showing compassion on the weak and condemned, those without hope. This emphasis on virtual invisibility is one of the most striking characteristics about the servant in all these passages.[91] A concluding commentary indicates that he will accomplish his universal mission as the distant isles wait for his Torah. He will bring about a covenant for the people, which will result in light for the nations, opening the eyes of the blind and liberating the captives (Isa. 42:6–7).[92] There are royal

----

Israel who suffers justly for its own sins and the humbly obedient servant who suffers justly for the sins of others makes a simple identification of Israel and the servant highly improbable.' See J. J. M. Roberts, 'Isaiah in Old Testament Theology', *Int* (1982), p. 141. See, e.g., the identification of the two servants in the insightful article by Philip Stern, 'The "Blind Servant" Imagery of Deutero-Isaiah and its Implications', *Biblica* 75 (1994), pp. 224–232. Stern makes the best case I have seen for this identification, but ultimately the argument fails when he states that 'the suffering servant has both its own sins and those of others to contend with' (p. 228). Again the straightforward meaning of Isaiah 53 indicates that the servant was not suffering for his own sins.

89. 'The reward and success of the Servant in his mission becomes a theme linking all four texts (cf. 42:4; 49:4; 50:7–9 with 52:13).' See H.-J. Hermisson, cited in D. P. Bailey, 'The Suffering Servant: Recent Tübingen Scholarship on Isaiah 53', in Bellinger and Farmer (eds.), *Jesus and the Suffering Servant*, pp. 251–259.

90. This contrasts with the order that Cyrus will bring (Isa. 41:1–4). The Hebrew expression is as follows: *mišpāṭ laggôyîm yôṣî*. Indeed, *mišpāṭ* is a crucial word in this text, occurring three times (42:1, 3, 4). This is the mission of the servant. This most likely refers to the task of changing the world order, resulting in a new regime, its regulations and the reign of a new king. See, e.g., the use of the term to describe the new order of a king in 1 Sam. 8:9, 11. Note also Job's attempt to criticize the divine order of the world (Job 40:8). See also the statement by Beuken ('*Mišpāṭ*', p. 7) that the expression 'bring justice forth' refers to 'a situation, an event to be realized, a process and its execution resulting in relations of righteousness, the background obviously being this: that the present situation is devoid of justice'.

91. Kenneth R. R. Gros Louis, 'Isaiah: Chapters 40–55', in K. R. R. Gros Louis (ed.), *Literary Interpretations of Biblical Narratives* (Nashville: Abingdon, 1974), p. 221.

92. The term *běrît 'am* is a notable crux. In the context it is parallel with light to the nations, and in 49:9 it brings about restoration of the land. It would seem that the

motifs here represented by the empowerment of the Spirit and the establishment of justice in the world. A Torah like Moses' will be promulgated not just
to Israel, but also to the world.

When he appears the second time, the universal dimension of his task is
immediately apparent, for the distant isles are urged to listen (Isa. 49:1–7). He
is someone who has been born with a servant destiny. His mouth becomes a
sharp sword, echoing the image of the Davidic king who will slay the wicked
with the rod of his mouth (Isa. 11:4). The servant is named Israel and his
daunting task appears futile. On the verge of giving up, he is told that his
national 'failure' will become a universal success. He will not only restore the
tribes of Jacob, he will also bring God's light to the nations, divine salvation to
the ends of the earth (Isa. 49:4–6).

In his third appearance in the text the title 'servant' is not used, but the
concept is present (Isa. 50:4–9). The prophetic element is salient, as the servant
is someone who is so totally obedient to the divine will that he experiences
uninterrupted communion with God.[93] His compassion is evident, for he
encourages the weary with the divine word. The note of suffering is more pronounced: he does not rebel or turn back as the national servant has done, but
surrenders his body to his persecutors. He willingly experiences pain for the
divine cause.

In his climactic appearance the servant has an international role to play, a fact
which had been mentioned in the first and second songs. The structure of this
fourth song (Isa. 52:13–53:12) is fairly transparent. There is a divine word about
the servant at the beginning and ending of the poem in which the servant is named
('my servant') and exalted and the consequences of his mission described. His
mission is for *the many*, a fact repeated twice in the introduction and four times in
the conclusion (Isa. 52:14, 15; 53:11, 12 [3x]).[94] All the rhetorical 'stops' are being
pulled out. The intervening poem is spoken frequently from the perspective of the
first-person plural, suggesting that *the many* are now speaking.

The first part of the complete poem provides a summary of the servant's
mission: exaltation – humiliation – exaltation (Isa. 52:13–15). First, he has an

---

servant has the task of restoring the covenant with the people and extending it to
the nations.

93. On the significance of this communion, see von Rad, *Old Testament Theology*, vol. 2,
p. 69.

94. The word *'āṣûmîm* in 53:12 should be translated 'numerous' instead of 'mighty',
thus providing better sense in the context. I owe this insight to Peter Gentry in a
personal communication.

extremely elevated social position, one that echoes the majesty of the divine king in Isaiah's prophetic call. Remarkably, the servant is even more exalted than the divine king in Isaiah 6 (cf. Isa 6:1; 53:13).[95] Consequently, the entire context of Isaiah 6 with its description of the blindness and stubbornness of the people is evoked by this text. Second, he is disfigured beyond recognition so that he may sprinkle many nations. There may be an allusion to the Day of Atonement here, but the atonement is not just for the nation but for *many* nations.[96] Finally, he is exalted again so that even kings shut their mouths and gape at this incredible figure. He is recognized now, and he is clearly a royal figure who arrests the attention of the social and political elite.

In the main part of the poem, the emphasis falls on the servant's humiliation by which he is able to bring salvation from sins. Imagery used to describe the servant echoes that of the Davidic king predicted earlier in Isaiah, since he is described as a growing plant. Zimmerli believes that the LXX translation of 53:2 suggests an allusion to Isaiah 9:6. If so, this would be the first external witness to this identification.[97] Nevertheless, the servant was completely misunderstood. The 'many' thought that he was suffering for his own sin when he was suffering for their sin (Isa. 53:1–6). This led to his death (Isa. 53:7–8), although he was innocent (Isa. 53:9). Yahweh crushed him, making his life a guilt offering for others (Isa. 53:10).[98] He is thus described with the unique expression 'the righteous one, my servant'. Unlike other servants, he is able to justify many (Isa. 53:11–12), having emptied his life to the point of death. The term 'many' is an important internal bond in the poem, linking beginning and end. *Many* are astonished at the servant's humiliation, but he is thus able to sprinkle *many* nations (Isa. 52:14–15). As a result of his actions, this righteous servant is able to justify *many* by bearing their sins (Isa. 53:14–15).

---

95. For some striking parallels between the final servant song and the early chapters of Isaiah, see H. Wolff, 'Isaiah's Final Servant Song (52:13–53:12) and Chapters 1–6', in Kaiser Jr and Youngblood (eds.), *A Tribute to Gleason Archer*, pp. 251–259.

96. Dempster, *Dominion*, p. 178.

97. Zimmerli and Jeremias, *Servant of God*, p. 41.

98. The basic characteristic of a guilt offering was its function as a means of reparation. Often, but not always, it was paid because sanctity had been violated. Guilt and the obligation of repayment that comes with it is what this term signifies. See R. Knierim, '*āšām* guilt', *TDOT*, pp. 191–195; G. A. Anderson, 'Sacrifices and Sacrificial Offerings', *ABD* 5, pp. 880–881; J. Milgrom, *Leviticus 1–16: A New Translation with Introduction and Commentary*, AB 3 (New York: Doubleday, 1991), pp. 339–382.

The consequence of this mission is emphatically described in the ensuing chapters. Incredible transformations have taken place. A barren woman has given place to a woman with a tent bursting at the seams, filled with children (54:1–5); a divorced woman rejected by her husband has become newly married, never to be forsaken again (54:6–10). In the first example there are allusions to the Abrahamic covenant through the patriarchs and the promise of children and land. Here the few exiles are promised that their uninhabited cities and desolate land (6:12–13) will be repopulated and the boundaries of their nation enlarged to encompass the entire world as a result of the work of the Servant (54:2–3). The 'divorced woman' recalls the rupture that took place with the violation of the Sinai covenant. But now, through the work of the Servant, the separation is over. God's love will never be removed from the people again, a pledge that echoes the Davidic covenant (54:10).[99] The final transformation is that of the people themselves. They have become like the Servant. As the Servant was taught of Yahweh (50:4), so is everyone in this new covenant (54:13). The people also have become servants of Yahweh (54:17), having received their vindication (cf. 53:11). Indeed, one does not hear of the Servant of Yahweh any more, but of the 'servants of Yahweh'.[100] The Servant has seen his descendants (53:10).

Finally, the stupendous good news is proclaimed to everyone so that they can experience this covenant without paying an exorbitant fee (55:1–2). The only requirement is repentance; God's love is unfathomable (55:6–9). The covenant is now explained as the 'sure mercies of David' (55:3, my translation). This is the first explicit reference to David in the second half of the book, and this new covenant is regarded as based on his mercies, his righteous acts. Since this expression, 'mercies of David', most naturally refers to a subjective genitive (mercies extended by David, cf. 2 Chr. 6:42; 35:26; Neh. 13:14), rather than objective genitive (mercies extended to David), what is to be made of this? These are the mercies that brought about the incredible transformations, the

---

99. Peter Gentry (private communication) first brought to my attention these allusions to the various covenants in Isaiah 54. See also Dumbrell, 'The Role of the Servant', pp. 111–112.

100. Isa. 54:17; 56:6; 63:17; 65:8–9, 13 (3x); 66:14. Cf. the references to servant of Yahweh in the singular. There are twenty references to the servant from Isaiah 40–53 and none after. Beuken observes that the servant of Yahweh has done his work, having seen the prolonging of his seed. He can now fade into the background and his servants can move into the foreground. His mission has been successful. 'The Main Theme of Trito-Isaiah', *JSOT* 47 (1990), pp. 67–68.

mercies of the Servant, who is now referred to as David, a new David, the Davidic servant mentioned in Jeremiah and Ezekiel. Finally, a Davidic king has come who is the perfect servant. By his righteous deeds, his mercies, a covenant can be made with everyone, thereby allowing them to experience the benefits of the covenant.[101] This fact fulfils the Davidic hope and, as the text says, this new David continues in the train of David: he is appointed a witness to the peoples to bring light to the nations (55:4–5). But this hope for a king who would bring about a rejuvenation of nature (55:12–13) is not new. It has been a long-awaited hope going back not only to Isaiah 11:1–10, but to Genesis 49:8–10 as well. Just as snow and water produce the fertile conditions for vegetation to sprout up, so the divine word will accomplish its purposes (55:10–11). The new world order that Israel hoped for (40:27) and which the Servant was anointed to establish (42:1) will finally become a reality.

The Twelve

David is regarded as the future king who will bring Israel hope. At the end of the days he will emerge (Hos. 3:5), restoring his kingdom (Amos 9:11–12) and bringing Bethlehem into prominence once again (Mic. 5:1–3). Haggai sees in the reigning governor a glimpse of the future David when he calls him 'Zerubbabel, my servant', who is made to be Yahweh's signet ring (Hag. 2:23). Similarly, in Zechariah 1–8, Zerubbabel and Joshua the high priest are important. Representing the people, Joshua appears in filthy clothes and is accused by Satan (Zech. 3:1). He is vindicated by receiving new clothes and a new charge, and is told to expect someone called 'my servant, the growth' (of vegetation) (Zech. 3:8, my translation). This person's coming coincides with the removal of sin from the land in one Great Day of Atonement that restores paradisiacal conditions (3:9).

Later, two crowns are fashioned. One is placed on Joshua's head, and the other is put on the head of the Davidic descendant Zerubbabel. Although the latter is not explicitly mentioned, he is probably implied in the text. An oracle comes to Joshua that says, 'Here is the man whose name is the "Growth" and he will "grow up" from this place. He will build the temple of Yahweh and rule upon his throne' (6:12–13, my translation).

In Zechariah 9–14, a servant-king is distinguished by suffering and humility as well as regal majesty. As the result of a death of a major figure in Jerusalem (12:10), there will be an opening up of a fountain in the house of David for

---

101. See the essay by Dan Block ('My Servant David'), which argues that the Isaianic servant is Davidic.

the cleansing of sin and impurity and the abolition of all idols and false
prophets (13:1–2). Next, 13:7–9 may indicate that it is a Davidic leader, a shepherd, who has been struck down. Two thirds of the land perishes along with
him. At the same time a complete communion with God results: 'They will call
upon my name, and I will answer them' (13:7–9).

Psalms

The Psalms continue this theme of David and servanthood. Two psalm titles
call him the servant of Yahweh (Pss. 18:1; 36:1), and two times Yahweh calls
him 'my servant' (Ps. 89:3, 20). Some of the seams of the Psalter suggest that
the Davidic ruler, the viceregent of Yahweh, will some day rule the world,
thereby bringing blessing to the nations (Pss. 2; 72; 89).[102] In fact, the Psalter
begins with 'the only text in the Old Testament that speaks of God's king, as
messiah and son in one place'.[103] He is also referred to by the Aramaic term
for 'son' (Ps. 2:12), which may suggest a link with a figure to be announced later
in the Bible (Dan. 7:13), whom all nations will serve. At the same time, humiliation marks the exalted king. In fact, many of the laments have been called
'Servant Psalms', for in these texts the psalmist is threatened with disaster,
complains to God, petitions to him and either hopes in or experiences deliverance.[104]

Probably the most poignant text is Psalm 89, which affirms the Davidic
covenant by reflecting on the position of the Davidic king as the divine
servant. After God's founding of the created order by vanquishing the forces
of chaos, there is a movement into history in which a mighty warrior is chosen
to do the same. 'David my servant' is found and anointed (89:20). His enemies
are defeated and God adopts him as a son. As such, he is the firstborn of all
the kings of the earth. The covenant is mentioned as being eternal and guaranteed even if David's sons sin. Consequently, there is a stress on the regal
majesty of the king as God's son and God's servant, the firstborn of the kings
of the world. But then comes the problem. The servant is now defiled, his
crown thrown in the dust, the covenant repudiated. This debasement begs the

---

102. See also G. Wilson, *The Editing of the Hebrew Psalter*, SBLDS 76 (Chico: Scholars
     Press, 1985); D. C. Mitchell, *The Message of the Psalter: An Eschatological Programme in
     the Book of Psalms, JSOT*Sup 252 (Sheffield: Sheffield Academic Press, 1999),
     pp. 66–89.

103. Ps. 2:2, 6, 7. J. L. Mays, *Psalms*, IBC (Louisville: John Knox Press, 1994), p. 44.

104. See Charles H. H. Scobie, *The Ways of Our God: An Approach to Biblical Theology*
     (Grand Rapids: Eerdmans, 2003), pp. 404–405.

question of what has happened to the former mercies extended through the Davidic covenant; the suffering of the Davidic king seems unjust. In Psalm 132 the titles 'servant', 'horn' and 'Messiah' all appear, thereby stressing that the Davidic covenant is made on account of David, but the conditional element is more salient. David will always have an heir, *if there is a faithful Davidide on the throne*. In other words, read together, these psalms suggest that a faithful Davidide is needed for the covenant truly to take effect. Perhaps this psalm, with the final praise flurry of the Psalter led by David the choirmaster, suggests a pattern of exaltation – humiliation – exaltation, as David Mitchell has recently suggested.[105] In other words, read together with Isaiah, a picture is emerging of a Davidic servant whose faithfulness in keeping the covenant and suffering for covenant-breakers will maintain the covenant benefits.

Job

In the book of Job, there is further prominence given to a servant of Yahweh, this time a non-Israelite, who undergoes intense persecution from a satanic figure to vindicate both God and humanity.[106] Job is Yahweh's servant, and it is precisely because of this fact that he suffers. In his suffering, he learns that Yahweh's ways for righting the wrongs in the world often pass through the vale of suffering and weakness rather than strength.[107]

Conclusion

The commentary on the biblical storyline provided by the Latter Prophets and the first section of the Writings has developed further the idea of a divine Davidic servant. Such a servant who had suffered for the sake of the people had been adumbrated in the biblical storyline; it has now been developed further. Such a faithful servant saves covenant-breakers from the curses of the covenant by receiving punishment in their stead. This fact explains a key problem in the whole covenant question: 'Is God's promise ended with disobedience or does it endure with disobedience?'[108] The answer is 'no' to the first question and 'yes' to the second, since a faithful covenant-keeper will bring upon himself the curses of the covenant and make atonement for the people's sins.

---

105. Mitchell, *Message*, pp. 267–268.

106. This is the last flurry of references to 'my servant' in the Tanak: Job 1:8; 2:3; 42:7, 8 (3x).

107. See, e.g., Yahweh's statement to Job (40:6–14). It is precisely human strength that does not win the day (cf. Gen. 18:27; Job 30:19).

108. Birch et al., *Theological Introduction*, p. 240.

Daniel – Chronicles: the biblical storyline resumed – the Son of Man and David

The storyline of the Bible last came to an end with the people of God in exile (cf. 2 Kgs 25). It is resumed with the book of Daniel, which describes their dire situation and charts out the final course of their history.

Daniel

In envisioning the future destiny of the world and Israel, Daniel sees a future Son of Man, an Adamic figure, who exercises authority over the animals and to whom all authority and power will be given. At the same time he is somehow involved in the suffering of the saints and yet distinguished from them (Dan. 7:13–14, 21–22). His coming means an end to oppression and persecution of the people of God by a ravenous beast. He defeats this beast and establishes an everlasting kingdom *in which all peoples will serve him.* This vision mirrors an earlier vision in Daniel in which a stone cut from a mountain destroys a huge giant representing all the hostile kingdoms of the earth, and then grows into a huge mountain filling the earth that represents the kingdom of God (2:31–45). Several images that appear here were introduced earlier in the canon: the Adamic servant, the seed that would crush the beast's head, the Davidic king, the Isaianic servant, and the Son of Man. There is an individual and a collective aspect to each.[109]

According to Daniel 12, when the end of the days approaches, many of the pious will bear testimony with their lives and turn many to righteousness as a result of their witness. These people are described in language that echoes the terminology used to describe the servant of Isaiah 53, which indicates a close association between the saints and the servant of Isaiah.[110]

Chronicles

The closing of the Hebrew Bible with Chronicles re-emphasizes the Davidic hope. Genesis, with its focus on genealogy, propelled the text forward to look

---

109. Note P. Stuhlmacher's insight that there is a false dichotomy between individualistic and corporate understandings of the servant. The Israelite ruler both rules over the people and represents them. In the New Testament, the Son of God leads the people of God, but they also comprise his body. See P. Stuhlmacher, 'Isaiah 53 in the Gospels and Acts', in B. Janowski and P. Stuhlmacher (eds.), *The Suffering Servant: Isaiah 53 in Jewish and Christian Sources* (Grand Rapids: Eerdmans, 2004), pp. 161–162.

110. Cf . Dan. 12:1–3; Isa. 52:13; 53:11. So, e.g., von Rad, *Old Testament Theology*, vol. 2, p. 315.

for descendants, particularly one from the tribe of Judah (Gen. 49:8–10). The canonical spotlight has moved from Moses, to Joshua, to the Judges, and finally to David. Now Chronicles keeps that spotlight squarely on David by beginning with nine chapters of genealogies that lead to David's arrival on the historical scene. The theme of his reign and that of his son Solomon then occupy approximately twenty chapters.[111] The focus in these books is on the fact that Israel's hope resides in the temple and David. After describing Judah's judgment and exile, Chronicles concludes with the Persian King Cyrus issuing a decree urging the exiles to return to Judah and rebuild the temple (2 Chr. 36:22–23). This clearly evokes the promises to David. The only person called 'my servant' by God in Chronicles is David, twice in the story of the making of the Davidic covenant (1 Chr. 17:4, 7).

A comparison of the account of the Davidic covenant in Chronicles with the parallel account in Samuel suggests a subtle change. The messianic pulse is increased in Chronicles. For example, 2 Samuel 7:12 predicts that God will raise up for David a seed after him 'who shall come from your body' and God will establish his kingdom. Disobedient heirs will be chastised and punished, but God will establish the Davidic kingdom. But the parallel passage in 1 Chronicles 17:11 states that God will raise up for David one who will not so much issue from his loins as be 'one of your own sons'. This particularizes the promise. There is also no mention of the punishment of disobedient sons for covenant violation, and the divine promise ensures that God will establish the Davidic king in his house and kingdom. Consequently, the canonical spotlight has focused on David in this last book of the Hebrew Scriptures not for antiquarian interest, but for eschatological reasons. 'My servant David' of the past was certainly important, but he pales in comparison before 'my servant David' of the future.

Conclusion

At the beginning of the biblical story there is a focus on servant-rulers, the children of God, his representatives on earth (images), who are responsible for declaring his name through service and obedience. With their fall, and creation's with them, God promised a restoration. This restoration largely begins with the call of Abraham to be the divine servant and the making of a covenant with him. This covenant is further established with his descendants, who become a servant nation at Sinai. Israel fails in its task and is led by Moses, another servant, who saves Israel from judgment and suffers on their account.

---

111. Von Rad, *Old Testament Theology*, vol. 1, p. 350; W. Brueggemann, *David's Truth in Israel's Imagination and Memory* (Philadelphia: Fortress Press, 1985), p. 100.

When the expression 'servant of Yahweh' first appears, Moses is condemned to exile while his people enter the land of promise. As the concept develops, the people largely fail again in their task of serving Yahweh, and David becomes a servant, son and king with whom God makes an everlasting covenant. He also suffers so that his people might live. But he, like Moses before him, dies in many ways a personal failure at the end of his life. The Davidic covenant, however, which stressed that the throne of David would always have a servant king if there was obedience, orients Israel to the future. In the judgment of exile Jehoiachin's release from prison functions as a 'lightning rod' for this hope (2 Kgs 25:27–31), a hope for a new day in which 'my servant David' will come and bring justice not only for Israel, but for the many. Like his illustrious but flawed predecessors, he will also suffer for others, but because he is flawless he will effect a great salvation. Perhaps this is unbelievable now (Isa. 53:1), but some day Jesse's stump will sprout a shoot that will demonstrate the meaning of true servanthood (Isa. 11:1; cf. 53:2).

The Gospels and Acts: the resumption of the biblical storyline – suffering servant, son and king

What should give pause to those who question the prominence of the servant theme in the New Testament (see above, pp. 134–135) is the fact that the New Testament contains forty-eight references (allusions or quotations) to the fourth servant song of Isaiah! This emphasis on the servant is surpassed only by the New Testament's interest in the Son of Man of Daniel 7, to which fifty-nine references are made.[112] The conceptual foundation of the theology of the synoptic Gospels presupposes the schematic structure of Isaiah 40–66 as well as the salvation prophecies of the other prophets:[113] the announcement of good news to Israel, the forgiveness of sins, the end of exile, the restoration of Israel, the kingship of God, and the co-occurrence of these events with a figure who represents the nation, but whose work has universal implications. This figure is the servant, the Davidic king, the Son of Man.

Matthew

Matthew resumes the narrative thread of Chronicles. The exhaustive genealogies of Chronicles came to an end when David arrived on the historical scene.

---

112. Barbara Aland et al. (eds.), *Novum Testamentum Graece*, 27th ed. (Stuttgart: Deutsche Bibelgesellschaft, 1993). I owe this observation to Block, 'My Servant David', p. 44.

113. This is a point that Hooker herself acknowledges, as she indicates in her excellent survey of this material (*Jesus and the Servant*, pp. 30–40, cf. pp. 66–67).

Similarly, the lengthy genealogy with which Matthew begins culminates in the arrival of Jesus (Matt. 1:1–18). This genealogy is structured in three triads of fourteen descendants: from Abraham to David, from David to the exile, and from the exile to Jesus. Jesus is the new David, who will not only lead Israel out of exile, but also be a sin-bearer.[114] As a descendant of Abraham he embodies the goal of the nation Israel, which is to be a blessing to all families of the earth (Matt. 1:1; Gen. 12:3). The visit of the Magi stresses the universal implications of his being 'a light for the nations', since a light in the heavens leads these Gentiles to the child (Matt. 2:9–10). His descent into and ascent from Egypt indicates that he recapitulates in his person the history of Israel. At the beginning of his public ministry, the voice of John the Baptist crying in the wilderness signals the end of Israel's exile and the coming glory of God (Matt. 3:3; Isa. 40:1–3). At his baptism, the divine voice echoes Genesis 22:2, Isaiah 42:1–4 and Psalm 2:7, thereby combining the concepts of suffering, service and Davidic kingship: 'This is my beloved Son, with whom I am well pleased' (Matt. 3:17).[115] The testing narrative with Satan in the wilderness evokes memories not only of Adam, but also of Israel. Whereas both failed to obey God, Jesus as Adam's son and as the new Israel obediently serves God. His final salvo to Satan when offered all the kingdoms of the world (cf. Dan. 7:14) is a reminder of the service owed to God: 'You shall worship the Lord your God, and him only shall you *serve*' (Matt. 4: 10, emphasis added). Jesus is the supreme example of a divine servant.

After this encounter, Jesus immediately goes to Capernaum near the borders of Zebulun and Naphtali, where his mission is cast in the role of the Davidic king in Isaiah 9 who will bring light to the nations (Matt. 4:12–17; cf. Isa. 9:1–2). From that time Jesus begins to call disciples and to engage in preaching and healing. The Sermon on the Mount is a new Torah by a new Servant of God who transcends Moses. In effect, Jesus says, 'Moses said one thing then, but *I* now say to you . . .'[116] This would suggest a radically new

---

114. Matt. 1:1–17, 21. See, e.g., Dempster, *Dominion*, p. 232. The numerical value of the Hebrew name David is fourteen.

115. Hooker argues that there is no clear reference to the Isaianic servant here, since Matthew's quotation 'with whom I am well pleased' differs from the LXX of Isa. 42. However, Matthew may be freely translating this passage. He differs from the LXX significantly in Matt. 12:18–21, but there it is clear that he is translating Isa. 42. Also the conceptual similarities with Isaiah are striking: inauguration to ministry by anointing of the Spirit to bring about justice or righteousness.

116. Matt. 5:21–22, 27–28, 31–32, 38–39, 43–44.

Torah proclaimed by the Servant of Isaiah 42, which will ultimately bring light to the nations.[117] After the sermon, Jesus continues his ministry, healing an outcast leper and a Gentile's servant (Matt. 8:1–13). After Jesus heals many people and exorcizes evil spirits, Matthew identifies his actions with that of the suffering servant of Isaiah who took upon himself Israel's infirmities and sicknesses (Matt. 8:17; cf. Isa. 53:5–6). Jesus continues his ministry by calling the twelve disciples to take the message of the kingdom to the lost sheep of the house of Israel (Matt. 10:1–6). Jesus is depicted as the new Davidic shepherd who has come to restore the nation (Matt. 9:36; 10:6; cf. Ezek. 34:23), which is an allusion to the Isaianic servant whose mission was to restore the tribes of Jacob (Isa. 49:5).

When the Pharisees first decide to kill Jesus, he intentionally avoids the limelight. He counsels those he heals not to publicize their cures. Matthew links this lack of concern for personal fame to that of the Isaianic servant, whose divine mission leads him to shun publicity (Isa. 42:1–4).[118] Matthew's longest citation from the Old Testament follows. As a recent study has shown, it seems that it is not just the immediate context that is in view. Rather, Matthew has cited this scripture 'to validate a particular view of Jesus as royal Messiah, that he was the Spirit-endowed, compassionate servant of the Lord whose words and deeds evinced the justice anticipated with the advent of the Messiah and the inauguration of the Kingdom of God'.[119] Jesus' ministry continues with the healing of a blind man. The crowds cry out in amazement, 'Can this be the Son of David?' (Matt. 12:23). The Isaianic servant is pictured in action once again, since in Isaiah the servant is contrasted with another servant who is both deaf and blind, who represents Israel in its unbelief (Isa. 42:19). It is people who sit in darkness whom the servant of Yahweh has come to save (Isa. 42:7).

As Matthew proceeds, three titles are given to Jesus which emphasize his role: Son of Man, Servant, and Son of David.[120] There is considerable overlap here, but the central image is that of the servant. Jesus declares his intention to go to Jerusalem and face death at the hands of the religious leaders. If the terminology is not explicitly that of Isaiah 53, the conceptual world is still the same: the Son of Man will be going to Jerusalem to be delivered over to torment

---

117. D. Holwerda, *Jesus and Israel – One Covenant or Two?* (Leicester: Apollos, 1995).

118. The Matthean text differs from that of the LXX at many points.

119. Richard Beaton, *Isaiah's Christ in Matthew's Gospel*, SNTSMS 123 (Cambridge: Cambridge University Press, 2002), p. 192.

120. Son of Man: Matt. 16:27; 17:22; Son of David: 15:32; 20:30, 31; Servant: 20:25–29.

and death, but will rise again on the third day (Matt. 17:22–23; 20:18–19; cf. 16:21). Here the term 'Son of Man' is used instead of 'servant', and although there is some similar conceptual material in Daniel 7, it seems better to understand this text as a combination of Daniel 7 and Isaiah 53, in which the prophecy about the Son of Man being served by all peoples of the earth is given a twist (Dan. 7:14).[121] He will first serve them before this happens.

This is followed by the request of James and John to sit on the right and left hand of the Messiah's throne (Matt. 20:21–28). Clearly they have misunderstood Jesus' statement and have missed the allusion to Isaiah 53 and suffering (Matt. 20:19). Nevertheless, they are instructed that this mission is not about reigning; it is about serving, or rather about reigning *through* serving. This is a different type of king. Jesus states that in his kingdom greatness and dominion are found through serving. As if to make the point with the utmost clarity, Jesus remarks that even the Son of Man came not to be served, but to serve and to give his life as a ransom for many (20:28). Many scholars see again a combination of Isaiah 53 with Daniel 7, but this time the terminology is more explicit: a ransom for *many*. The allusion to Isaiah 53, where the term functions as a guiding theme, is impossible to miss. The servant offers his life for many. This episode is followed by Jesus healing blind men while accepting the title 'Son of David'. This healing echoes the commentary on the first servant song that portrays the new servant king opening the eyes of the blind (Isa. 42:7).[122] All nations will serve this Son of Man one day, because he has first served them.

The most significant texts portraying Jesus as the servant are those in which his identity is disclosed as 'the Christ, the Son of the Living God'. Immediately after the revelation of this Davidic figure, Jesus speaks about going to Jerusalem to be killed and raised on the third day (Matt. 16:21). This suggests that his death and resurrection are associated with the death of the suffering servant in Isaiah 53. It also indicates that Jesus' death at the end of the Gospels is not just 'an epilogue but is an integrating essential part of his work', as was the death of the Isaianic servant.[123] The transfiguration follows shortly thereafter (Matt. 17:1–9). The revelation of the divine face to his disciples and the appearance of Moses and Elijah evoke all kinds of Old Testament imagery:

---

121. Craig Evans (personal communication).

122. Richardson (*Theology*, pp. 97–98) comments, 'It is hardly surprising that the opening of blind eyes plays such a prominent part amongst the recorded miracles of Jesus in the Gospels [in light of Isaiah].'

123. Cullman, *Christology*, p. 62.

the mountain, the cloud and the tabernacle. But the divine voice clarifies that Jesus is the ultimate revelation because he is the ultimate servant: 'This is my beloved Son, with whom I am well pleased; listen to him' (17:5). This passage probably brings together Genesis 22:2, Isaiah 42:1 and Deuteronomy 18:15. It means, 'This is the servant, the prophet like Moses. Listen to him.'

Here the Son of Man (Matt. 17:9), who is linked with regal authority, is identified with the Suffering Servant of Isaiah 53. Just before his crucifixion, the term 'many' is repeated when Jesus eats the Last Supper with his disciples (Matt. 26:20–30). He specifically identifies the wine with his blood, calling it the blood of the covenant that is poured out for the forgiveness of sins for the *many* (Matt. 26:28). Afterwards, Jesus is arrested, is silent before his accusers (27:12) and, although considered a criminal, he is buried with the rich (27:28–60).

Finally, at the end of Matthew Jesus is exalted with regal authority, and he sends his disciples as witnesses to all the nations. Here the sure mercies of David are being extended to the nations. Christ is now a ruler and commander of the peoples, who are envisioned as becoming his servants. They are to be taught to *obey* everything he has commanded (Matt. 28:20) and thus become his servants.

Mark

Mark emphasizes Jesus as the divine Son. After the gospel of the Son of God is announced (1:1), it is not long before the divine voice confirms this designation (1:11), as do the demons that are about to be exorcised (1:24, 34; 3:11; 5:7). Jesus' miracles highlight his sonship. He is the transcendent Son of Man, who not only forgives sins (2:10–11), but is Lord of the Sabbath (2:28). He is kin to the one who wishes to do the will of God (3:35). He is not just a teacher, but one whom even the winds and seas obey (4:41). His miracles earn him the commendation that 'He has done all things well. He even makes the deaf hear and the mute speak' (7:37). Throughout the Gospel the disciples are described as hard-hearted and unable to understand what is going on (6:52; 8:17–21; 9:32). It is in one such context that Jesus describes his relationship to children and the importance of serving (9:35–37; 10:14–17, 35–45). Immediately after this, as in Matthew, he heals a blind man and enters Jerusalem on a donkey, clearly indicating that his kingdom is different, showing that he is the servant of Isaiah 42 (11:1–10).

But Jesus is more than simply a Davidic descendant, as indicated by his use of Psalm 110 when he discusses the identity of the coming Messiah. The Roman centurion also bears witness when he sees Jesus die on the cross: 'Truly this man was the Son of God' (15:39). This death was alluded to earlier in terminology evoking the servant songs. In 2:20 Jesus describes himself as a bridegroom who will be taken away, thus providing an appropriate time for his disciples to mourn and fast. The verb 'taken away' may allude to the servant being taken away in Isaiah 53:8. If so, this certainly helps the audience understand Jesus' later statements describing his mission as that of suffering and rejection (8:31).[124]

Luke – Acts

The beginning of Luke emphasizes the importance of the role of God's servants in the coming of the Messiah. The angel promises that John the Baptist is going to be a great servant of the Lord (1:15). Mary is depicted as the Lord's servant when she assents to the virgin birth (1:38). In the Magnificat, she states that God is going to help his servant Israel (1:54), and the aged Simeon, when seeing the newborn Jesus, says that as the Lord's servant he can now die in peace (2:29).

Other unique aspects of servanthood described in this Gospel are few, but nonetheless significant. The disciples are to envision themselves as servants and not to expect any commendations when they fulfil their role (17:7–10). Whereas Mark and Matthew place Jesus' discussion of the critical role of servanthood on the way to Jerusalem, Luke locates it on the eve of the crucifixion, when Jesus and his disciples eat their final meal together (22:24–30). He indicates that he has been with his disciples as a servant, and thus he redefines the notion of 'greatness'. They also ought to become servants so that they can rule with Christ in his coming kingdom. The proximity of this teaching to the crucifixion foreshadows the latter as a final act of servanthood. To confirm the example, Jesus announces that he is soon going to be betrayed and handed over to death to fulfil a scripture: 'And he was numbered with the transgressors' (22:37; cf. Isa. 53:12). He clearly understands himself as the servant of Isaiah 53.[125] Since this teaching about sacrificial service and the citation of Isaiah 53 are situated immediately before the impending death of Jesus, they provide the lens through which that death is to be viewed.[126]

Acts underscores the relationship between Jesus as the servant and the continuation of his work by his disciples. In an early sermon recorded in Acts, Peter preaches at the temple, indicating that a recent healing performed on a

---

124. Johnston, 'Servant Image', p. 324.
125. The next words of Isaiah read, 'Yet he bore the sin of many, and makes intercession for the transgressors' (Isa. 53:12b).
126. Cullman, *Christology*, p. 64.

crippled man was God's way of glorifying 'his servant Jesus' (Acts 3:13), whom the people had killed, although he was holy and righteous. This is a clear allusion to Isaiah 53. Peter proceeds to state that the crippled man's faith in the name of Jesus has led to his healing, which in turn evokes Isaiah 42:4 (LXX), where the prophet indicates that the nations will trust in the 'name' of the servant.

Peter then tells his audience that they crucified Jesus in ignorance, and informs them that it was the destiny of the holy and righteous one to suffer. But through repentance they can experience the forgiveness of sins (3:13–20). Thus he evokes the image of the suffering servant of Isaiah 53 who bore the sins of many. Peter reinforces his argument by proclaiming that this was the one who was to be the blessing to all the nations of the earth. God has sent his servant first to bless them when they turn from their sins in repentance (3:25–26).

After the disciples are persecuted, they regather in Jerusalem to pray and reflect on past events. They conclude that there was a conspiracy to kill God's holy servant Jesus, who was anointed by God (4:27). But this only fulfilled the divine plan. Then the disciples pray for boldness and ask that God will reveal his mighty power through healings, miracles and wonders done in the name of 'your holy servant Jesus' (4:30). These are echoes of Isaiah 53. And if this is not enough, in Acts 8:32–37 Jesus is explicitly identified as the suffering servant in Philip's answer to the Ethiopian eunuch's question concerning the identity of the servant in Isaiah 53.[127]

One of the most interesting developments in Luke's thought is that Paul carries on the work of the servant, particularly as a light to the nations. He is truly 'in Christ'![128] Just as the work of the suffering servant produced many servants in Isaiah 54–66, the suffering of Jesus has transformed Paul into a servant. Paul's conversion is one in which he is blinded with light by the risen Jesus (9:1–3), who is so identified with his persecuted disciples that he identifies their persecutions as his. When Paul preaches his new message at the synagogue in Antioch of Pisidia, he surveys the entire Old Testament to point out the messianic identity of Jesus. He moves to the present to show that the recent death and resurrection of Jesus were predicted in the Scriptures. Paul's message is so interesting that he is invited to return to preach again on the next Sabbath. This time his message is rejected and Paul views

---

127. What confirms these references is Luke's choice of the Greek word *pais* for servant, which resonates more with the Greek used in the LXX.

128. Paul House (personal communication).

this dismissal as enabling the fulfilment of the first and second servant songs, in which God raises up the servant to proclaim his message to the nations (Acts 13:47; Isa. 42:1–6; 49:1–6). The metaphor of the message bringing light to the darkness is also a powerful echo of these songs. Paul is now functioning as a servant.

In his defence before Agrippa at the end of Acts, Paul echoes these texts when he states that God raised him up to be a witness to the nations, to open their eyes and to turn them from darkness to light to experience deliverance from Satan and forgiveness of sins by faith in Jesus, God's servant (26:18). This concluding reference, combined with Simeon's declaration about the child Jesus being a light of revelation to the Gentiles at the beginning of the Gospel (Luke 2:32), binds Luke-Acts into an integrated whole. Thus Luke's portrait of the servant in the Gospel and in Acts indicates that the servant of the Lord may have multiple references.

John

In John's Gospel the servant motif provides a background for many of the texts. Throughout the Gospel loom 'the hour sayings', by which the action of the story moves to the crucifixion as if measured by the ticking of a clock (e.g. 2:4; 7:30; 8:20). Repeatedly the audience hears, 'My time has not come yet.' Finally the clock strikes midnight when at the Passover feast in Jerusalem some Greeks wish to see Jesus. Then Jesus begins to speak of his death, his being lifted up on the cross, an act that will draw *all* people to himself (12:32). There is an allusion to Isaiah 52:13 when the text states that 'my servant will be lifted up high' for all to see and he is someone who will sprinkle many nations. After this Jesus goes into hiding and not many put their trust in him. This disbelief on the part of the majority is interpreted as a fulfilment of Isaiah 53:1, 'Lord, who has believed what he heard from us, and to whom has the arm of the Lord been revealed?' (John 12:36–38).

This passage provides the context for the Upper Room discourse that follows (13:1–38). The Divine One becomes the supreme servant. The footwashing scene is introduced and developed as a unique contribution to the portrait of Jesus. Son and servant are one. It is Jesus cast as a humble footwashing servant that defines the role of his disciples. Just as he is a servant, so are they to become servants of each other. There is to be no separation between the master and his disciples at this point. The motivation to live this way comes from a new commandment that Jesus gives – a commandment to love one another, which finds concrete expression in acts of service one for another (13:34–35). It is after this time that the death of Christ occurs, but this act of foot-washing is the hermeneutical key to understanding the death: he is supremely the Messiah because he is the ultimate servant![129]

Conclusion

The Gospels and Acts depict Jesus as not only God's Son and king, but also his servant. The space devoted to his death by the Gospels and the focus on his death in Acts indicate the importance of his suffering for others and the efficacy of his death as an atoning sacrifice in which a new covenant is instituted. The covenantal significance of Jesus' life and death is crucial for understanding his role. He is the fulfilment of the anticipated servant-king of the Old Testament. Yet his work, his role, is ultimately to produce servants in his likeness. Nowhere is this clearer than in John's reflection on the significance of the action of Jesus in the Upper Room. His role of servant is to be duplicated in the lives of his followers.

The epistles: didactic commentary on the storyline – suffering Servant and exalted Lord

The Pauline and Catholic epistles provide further reflection and commentary on the significance of the complex of events surrounding the death and resurrection of Jesus Christ. They further clarify the mission of Jesus as a servant that precedes his exaltation after his resurrection.

Pauline epistles and Hebrews

As was mentioned above, the apostle Paul viewed himself as continuing the work of the servant of Isaiah, in particular in his role as an emissary to the Gentiles. As the servant of Isaiah made many servants, so the servant Jesus made many servants, one of whom was Paul (Rom. 1:1; Gal. 1:1; Phil. 1:1). In fact, when writing to the Romans Paul formulates his travel plans in order to present the message of the fourth servant song.[130] He plans to go to the Gentiles, even as far as Spain, to preach in order to establish new churches so that he does not build on another's foundation (Rom. 15:20). The reason for this is that he 'has found the guiding light for his missionary work in Isaiah

---

129. Note Mudge's ('Servant Lord', p. 119) perceptive comments: 'The footwashing is recounted as the act of Him who "had come from God and was going to God".' It is thus precisely a messianic act. No theological backtracking is needed to connect an idea of the Suffering Servant with an idea of the Messiah. This is the Messiah in action 'in the form of a servant'.

130. I am indebted to Peter Gentry for this observation.

52:15', in the statement that people will see what they have not seen and hear what they have not heard.[131] And what is this message? It is the story of God's holy servant, whose blameless sacrifice has provided redemption for sinners, taking the curses of the covenant upon himself so that covenant violators could be blessed.

While Paul works with many texts from the Old Testament, the servant of Yahweh text in Isaiah 53 looms large in the background. His terminology assumes such a background: the righteous one dying for the many, and the forgiveness of sinners on the basis of a sacrifice (Rom. 4:25; 5:8). His defence of the resurrection is grounded in the truth that 'Christ died for our sins in accordance with the Scriptures' (1 Cor. 15:3). The idea of substitution receives its classic expression in 2 Corinthians 5–6 when Paul declares that peace has been extended to sinners as a result of Jesus Christ being made sin for sinners while they receive the righteousness of God (2 Cor. 5:21).[132] Immediately after this, the language following the second servant song is used: 'Behold, now is the favourable time; behold, now is the day of salvation' (2 Cor. 6:2; cf. Isa. 49:8).

Another important example occurs in Philippians, where there is an allusion to Isaiah 53. The *Son* of God, the highly exalted one, astonishingly took on the form of a *servant* (Phil. 2:6–11). The form of God the Son and the form of a servant are thrown into radical juxtaposition. As a result, the servant will be highly exalted again. Although the exact linguistic usage of Isaiah 53 is not present, the conceptual thought world is clear.[133] The exaltation – humiliation – exaltation pattern of this servant song mirrors the pattern of the fourth servant song of Isaiah. And, as a result of this humiliation,[134] God honours

---

131. Anders Nygren, *Commentary on Romans* (Philadelphia: Fortress Press, 1949), p. 454.

132. See Otto Betz, 'Jesus and Isaiah 53', in William H. Bellinger, Jr, and William R. Farmer (eds.), *Jesus and the Suffering Servant: Isaiah 53 and Christian Origins* (Harrisburg, PA: Trinity Press International, 1998), pp. 70–87.

133. Although the term *pais* is not used, but rather *doulos*, it is clear that at times the latter term in the servant songs is a virtual synonym for the former. Cf. the LXX's use of this term in Isa. 49:3, 5, and its use of the participle in 53:11 for God's righteous servant. The term *pais* is probably avoided in Philippians to eliminate any ambiguity that it might suggest. Thus Ernst Lohmeyer's view that this pre-Pauline hymn displays a Servant Christology is accurate. See J. L. Price, 'The Servant Motif in the Synoptic Gospels', *Int* 12 (1958), p. 29.

134. Jeremias argues that the expression 'he emptied himself' conveys the meaning of Isa. 53:12 ('he poured out his soul to death'). Consequently, this text is not about kenosis theory, but about servant practice. See Zimmerli and Jeremias, *Servant of God*, p. 97.

his servant in the language of Isaiah, that at the *name* of Jesus every knee will bow (Isa. 45:22–23). Here the 'great name' promised to Abraham for obedience receives its ultimate expression (Gen. 12:2). As a result there is complete unity between heaven and earth again (Gen. 12:3).

At the same time, Paul delivers this profound teaching of Jesus as the servant for a practical reason: to inculcate believers with the same 'mind'. They are to develop a 'servant mindset', acting in humility, considering others better than themselves, looking to each other's interests (Phil. 2:3–4). They must become servants just like their Master.

The servant theme is developed a bit differently in Hebrews. Christ is compared to the greatest servant in the Old Testament, Moses. The supremacy of Christ was being attacked in various ways, so the writer addressed this issue by showing the superiority of the new covenant to the old. Moses is associated with the old covenant and is regarded as the supreme servant. In fact, Numbers 12 is cited, which indicates that Moses was a faithful servant in God's entire house. Jesus deserves greater honour, however, since he is regarded as the builder of the house. Moreover, Moses was a servant and Jesus was a Son (Heb. 3:1–6).

Catholic epistles

In the Catholic epistles, the most striking use of the servant motif is found in 1 Peter, where servants are enjoined to be obedient to their masters, even enduring unfair treatment. The reason is that they have an illustrious predecessor. A flurry of quotations from Isaiah 53 describes Jesus:

> For to this you have been called, because Christ also suffered for you, leaving you an example, so that you might follow in his steps. *He committed no sin, neither was deceit found in his mouth [Isa. 53:9]*. When he was reviled, he did not revile in return; when he suffered, he did not threaten, but continued entrusting himself to him who judges justly *[cf. Isa. 53:7]*. *He himself bore our sins [Isa. 53:12]* in his body on the tree, that we might die to sin and live to righteousness. *By his wounds you have been healed [Isa. 53:5]*. *For you were straying like sheep [Isa. 53:6]*, but have now returned to the Shepherd and Overseer of your souls. (1 Pet. 2:21–25, emphasis added)

This flood of quotations from Isaiah 53 is in no apparent order, but as N. T. Wright has observed, 'Everything is here: servant, Messiah, suffering and vicarious sin-bearing.'[135] Again, Jesus also provides the example for believers to

---

135. N. T. Wright, *Jesus and the Victory of God* (Minneapolis: Fortress, 1992), p. 590.

'follow in his steps' (2:21). The Servant has come to serve and to produce servants.

Conclusion

The epistles further clarify the nature of the work of Jesus as the fulfilment of the Old Testament anticipation of a servant who would suffer for his people and be exalted. Just as the mission of one servant is carried on by many servants in Isaiah, apostles and believers in the New Testament are viewed as servants continuing the mission of Jesus. Just as he was called to serve them, so they are also called to a life of service.

The Apocalypse: the conclusion of the biblical story

The precise nomenclature of Jesus as the Servant of the Lord is absent from the Apocalypse. Nevertheless, there is mention of Jesus as the Lion from the tribe of Judah and the Scion of David in the great throne-room scene (Rev. 5:5). Both are messianic titles and then another one is added, the Lamb that looked as if it was slain (Rev. 5:6). This is probably an allusion to the Suffering Servant, who was led as a lamb to the slaughter and whose vicarious death procured salvation (Isa. 53). He alone is able to unseal the scroll that contains the destiny of the world, of the *many*.[136] And it is his victory that has caused the demise of the dragon, the ancient serpent, called the devil (Rev. 12:9, 15; 20:2, 10; cf. Gen. 3:15).

But perhaps there does not need to be much reference to the Servant any longer, since his work has produced *many servants*. John is a faithful servant (Rev. 1:1), as are the prophets (10:7; 11:18) and the believers in the churches (2:20). In a vision, John sees a complete number – 144,000 members of the various Israelite tribes – as servants, as well as an incredible multitude from every tribe, race and language, before the divine throne singing songs of salvation and praise to their God and the Lamb (7:1–12; cf. Dan. 7:14). The Servant is with his servants!

The Christian Bible concludes with a grand vision of the new Jerusalem, where God and the Lamb are seated on a throne. The people will see them face to face and bow down and serve them. From the throne emanates a river of life. Trees of life on either side of the river show that humanity has not just been returned to Eden – Eden has been transcended. In its place is a royal-servant city in which complete communion takes place between God and his

---

136. See also B. Reicke, 'Der Gottesknecht im Alten and Neuen Testament', *TZ* 36 (1979), p. 349.

people. Consequently, with the divine *name* written on their faces, they will also be *sons and daughters*, and in that capacity they will not only *rule* for ever and ever, they will *serve* for ever and ever.[137] For this is what it means to rule.

Concluding summary of the Bible: from Adam to Jesus and beyond

When the entire Christian Bible is considered, the servant theme is remarkably coherent. Human beings, called to be servant monarchs of creation, fell from that lofty position in an act of treason against their Creator. In grace God began the restoration of his creation through the promise of a seed that would conquer the seductive serpent. God began by calling out servants and establishing covenants with them. Israel was constituted to be God's servant nation to the world, to be a royal priesthood. An individual servant, Moses, was able to intercede successfully for the national servant, Israel, when it sinned, and it

---

137. Consequently, my judgment on Hooker's work and its defence and promotion by Williams is largely negative. While they have done a certain service in forcing scholars not to take the interpretive status quo for granted, they have not demonstrated their case. While traditional understandings of specific passages may be questioned, their cumulative weight points to a particular interpretation. Given the context of the New Testament, and that it largely presupposes the general expectations of the later prophets Jeremiah, Ezekiel and Isaiah 40–66, the servant imagery in the New Testament points in one direction. While Hooker acknowledges this context, she goes to extraordinary lengths to avoid its implications. Indeed, at times her methodology is extremely atomistic and assumes that the New Testament writers were more involved in proof-texting than invoking a larger context for their individual sayings. The same can be said of Williams, who largely accepts Whybray's conclusions regarding Isaiah 53 (*Thanksgiving for a Liberated Prophet: An Interpretation of Isaiah 53*, JSOTSup 4 [Sheffield: Sheffield Academic Press, 1978]). Whybray's method is largely the same as Hooker's: try to find an alternative interpretation for the individual pieces of the puzzle while ignoring the cumulative weight of the evidence. C. H. Dodd's (*According to the Scriptures: The Sub-Structure of New Testament Theology* [London: Nisbet, 1957]) study of the use of the Old Testament in the New is on a much sounder footing. The New Testament authors invoked a much larger context when they cited individual sayings from the scriptures of Israel. See also D. E. Johnson, 'Jesus against the Idols: The Use of Isaianic Servant Songs in the Missiology of Acts', *WTJ* 52 (1990): pp. 343–353.

was allowed to enter the land of promise, while he died on the outskirts of Canaan.

David became an even more dominant servant figure than Moses. A covenant was made with King David and his house that someone of that lineage would eventually rule the world and bring about universal shalom. While David interceded successfully like Moses for his people during a time of catastrophe, it was for his own sin that the nation was being judged. David and his sons were deeply flawed human beings and their sins jeopardized the covenant.

Nevertheless, there was a hope that an individual would come from this line who would bring about the final restoration of creation by meeting the demands of the covenant. This royal servant appears in the prophets and is completely righteous. He suffers for the sins of the covenant-breakers from Israel and from the nations. Thus a new covenant is made by this servant to fulfil this aim. Jesus Christ fulfils this role in the New Testament. By virtue of his death and resurrection, creation will be restored and a great multitude of individuals from every tribe and nation will serve him and each other for ever and ever. In the new world this is what it means to reign for ever and ever (Rev. 22:5).

© Stephen G. Dempster, 2007

5. THE DAY OF THE LORD

Paul R. House

Judgment plays an undeniably important role in biblical theology. A cursory examination of representative biblical theologians affirms this assertion. For instance, John Bright commits one chapter of his classic, *The Kingdom of God*, to judgment in the history of the Israelite kingdom, thereby treating judgment as a vital supporting aspect of his central theme.[1] Geerhardus Vos considers the concept particularly vital to grasping the prophets' understanding of the revelation of God to his people,[2] while H. H. Rowley treats it as a necessary segment of the heart of Israel's faith.[3]

More recently, biblical theologians working at Moore College, Sydney, Australia have stressed judgment's place in the whole of Scripture. For instance, Peter Jensen treats judgment as an integral part of the cluster of themes that comprise 'the gospel', the concept he considers the clearest expression of God's personal revelation in the

---

1. John Bright, *The Kingdom of God* (Nashville: Abingdon, 1953), pp. 45–70.

2. See Geerhardus Vos, *Biblical Theology: Old and New Testaments* (1948; reprinted, Edinburgh: Banner of Truth, 1996), pp. 286–296.

3. H. H. Rowley, 'The Day of the Lord', in *The Faith of Israel: Aspects of Old Testament Thought* (Philadelphia: Westminster, 1956), pp. 177–201. Rowley's chapter is perhaps the best short treatment of the Day of the Lord in the Old Testament.

Scriptures.[4] Graeme Goldsworthy highlights judgment as a consistent part of 'the unfolding revelation of God in the Bible' and of 'preaching the whole Bible as Christian scripture', for he does not believe one can separate judgment from the gospel message.[5] William Dumbrell considers judgment an obviously important facet of Old Testament eschatology.[6] Although the list could be extended to other biblical theologians, Old Testament theologians and New Testament theologians, the point is clear: such broad-based interest in the topic underscores its importance.

It is also interesting to observe that some major works on biblical theology do not discuss the matter or discuss it very briefly. Brevard Childs's *Biblical Theology* fits this description, as do Donald Gowan's *Theology of the Prophetic Books: The Death and Resurrection of Israel* and C. H. H. Scobie's *The Ways of Our God: An Approach to Biblical Theology*.[7] These works all make strong contributions to biblical theology, to be sure, and they present many elements helpful to an understanding of judgment, but they do not offer detailed analyses of the role of the theme in biblical context. Thus this situation indicates that further analysis may be in order.

Although preaching and teaching emphases vary from place to place, it is probably not an overstatement to assert that currently judgment does not have a regular place in pulpit presentations in orthodox/confessing churches, or even in evangelical churches. Thus it does not have a high profile in the minds of rank-and-file churchgoers. This situation hardly resonates with the testimony and preaching of John the Baptist, Jesus and the apostles. As C. H. Dodd points out, the early church kerygma routinely included judgment and the resurrection.[8]

---

4. Peter Jensen, *The Revelation of God* (Leicester: Inter-Varsity Press, 2002), pp. 49–53.

5. See Graeme Goldsworthy, *According to Plan: The Unfolding Drama in the Bible* (Leicester: Inter-Varsity Press; Downers Grove: InterVarsity Press, 1991), pp. 105–107, 135–137, 187–189, and *Preaching the Whole Bible as Christian Scripture* (Grand Rapids: Eerdmans, 2000), pp. 106, 179, 233.

6. See especially *The Search for Order: Biblical Eschatology in Focus* (Grand Rapids: Baker, 1994).

7. B. S. Childs, *Biblical Theology of the Old and New Testaments: Theological Reflection on the Christian Bible* (Minneapolis: Fortress, 1992); D. E. Gowan, *Theology of the Prophetic Books: The Death and Resurrection of Israel* (Louisville: Westminster John Knox, 1998); and C. H. H. Scobie, *The Ways of Our God: An Approach to Biblical Theology* (Grand Rapids: Eerdmans, 2003).

8. C. H. Dodd, *The Apostolic Preaching and Its Development* (London: Hodder and Stoughton, 1936), pp. 11–17, etc.

In fact, an examination of the book of Acts indicates that these themes were at least as pervasive as, if not more pervasive than, statements about the cross. This comment is in no way intended to denigrate the importance of the cross. Rather, it is intended to highlight the significance of recently neglected aspects of apostolic preaching. There may be many reasons for current practices, but perhaps it is more important to focus on remedying the situation than exposing it.[9]

Even if one desires to analyse biblical statements about judgment, however, one faces a daunting task. Judgment appears in every segment of the canon and occurs in a variety of settings and as part of several theological emphases, which explains in part why the theme is treated in so many different ways and in such summary fashion in so many scholarly works. Clearly, it is necessary to limit the scope of this study.

To this end, we will focus our attention on the theme of 'the Day of the Lord', since it is one of the most important, if not the most important, of the biblical portrayals of divine judgment. This theme takes its roots from the Law, and then appears in every subsequent part of the Bible. Such frequency of appearance means that the theme is connected to the major events and elements of salvation history, and its direct connection to the name/nature of Yahweh invites analysis of God's character alongside analysis of the theme itself.

What is 'the Day of the Lord'? William Dumbrell observes that the term is not easy to capture in a few words. Indeed, he writes that 'the concept of the day of the Lord, as considered by the prophets, is not singular in meaning; the connotation can be determined only by examining each context in which the phrase appears'.[10] Nonetheless, when these contexts are examined, some basic elements emerge. Stated simply, 'the Day of the Lord' is the conviction expressed in the Bible that 'at specific times through specific events God's rule will be re-established on earth and the elect will be released from sin's sources, adherents, and effects now and/or forever'.[11] In the Bible 'the Day of the Lord' is one particular way, but not the only way, of discussing judgment. Every 'Day of the Lord' is an instance of judgment, although not every depiction of judgment is called a 'Day of the Lord'.

When reading Day of the Lord texts, readers are compelled to ask, 'What will occur on the Day of the Lord?' The answer is primarily that Yahweh will

---

9. For an excellent call to preach this neglected theme, see D. Broughton Knox, *Selected Work: The Doctrine of God*, vol. 1, ed. Tony Payne (Sydney: Matthias Media, 2000), pp. 189–203.

10. Dumbrell, *The Search for Order*, p. 109.

11. See Rowley, 'The Day of the Lord', pp. 177–179.

intervene directly in human affairs through clear actions to judge sin in Israel and the world.

Readers are also led to ask, 'How will the Day of the Lord occur?' On the one hand, it occurs through evident actions, such as an invasion by a foreign army, a famine or a locust plague. It occurs through unrepeatable acts such as like the death and resurrection of Jesus Christ. On the other hand, it also happens through less obvious actions such as preaching or persecution. In these cases the world at large may not understand these events as Days of the Lord, but God's people do and should. Faith is therefore required to grasp the true significance of what happens.

Finally, readers are prompted to ask, 'When will the Day of the Lord occur?' The Bible clearly states that specific instances of the Day of the Lord punish sin in regular historical time to relieve the creation and the saints from the power and effects of individual, societal and cosmic sins. More importantly, the Bible also asserts that a final, eschatological Day of the Lord will eradicate sin for all eternity. This release from sin is permanent. Both temporal and permanent deliverance from sin reveal God's salvation, so the Day of the Lord is ultimately a positive term. Context determines whether a respite from sin or the complete defeat of sin is in view.

This chapter will utilize the following process to explicate this basic definition. First, significant passages in the Law will be examined to highlight imagery that later writers use to compose Day of the Lord texts. Of course, it could be argued that one has to have read the later texts to know which passages are essential. At the same time, if current readers knew as much about the content of the Law as the biblical writers did, they would pick up on the imagery in later texts without being prompted. Later passages make particular use of imagery found in the creation, flood, Sodom, exodus, golden-calf rebellion and covenant blessing and consequences passages, so those texts will be discussed, albeit briefly.

Second, the chapter will summarize selected passages in the Prophets that use terminology such as 'the Day of the Lord', 'that Day', 'the Day of the Lord's wrath', or 'the Day'. As might be expected, texts that utilize the imagery detailed in the Law to explain God's character and the Day of the Lord will receive the most attention. Given the enormous amount of Day of the Lord material in the Prophets, the selected passages will be drawn from several historical periods.

Third, Lamentations will be examined as a book in the Writings that directly links Day of the Lord imagery and comments about God's character. Thus Lamentations will be used as a representative work that expresses what some post-587 BC writers of Scripture believed and felt about the Day of the Lord and its relationship to the loss of land, capital and Davidic promise. Daniel 7 and 9 will then be noted to demonstrate the connection between Israel's exilic woes and their hopes for a coming powerful Son of Man who will be the ultimate solution to world anarchy that includes Israel's exile.

Fourth, texts in the Gospels that provide insight into the connection between the Day of the Lord, the kingdom of God and the Son of Man will be examined. Texts such as Matthew 23:37–24:51, Mark 13 and Luke 23:26–31 will be noted, since they combine Jesus' compassion for Jerusalem with coming judgment. Luke will be treated as a paradigmatic Gospel at this point because of its links to Old Testament texts and its interest in the ethical component of Day of the Lord teaching. John 12:27–36 will be noted, since it links the Son of Man and judgment and therefore has key affinities with Luke.

Fifth, Paul's use of Day of the Lord imagery in 1 and 2 Thessalonians will be treated. Paul clearly views the Day of the Lord as the day of the Lord Jesus. Like the authors of the Gospels, he considers the Day of the Lord both an exhortation to ethical living and a basis for hope. He at least strongly implies that the Day of the Lord is a present reality, especially for the rebellious inhabitants of Judea, as well as a future one.

Sixth, Peter's use of Day of the Lord imagery alongside statements about God's patience will be examined. Like Paul, Peter uses the coming Day of the Lord as both a reason for hope and a cause for warning. He calls his people to ethical purity even as they wait for deliverance from persecution. His connection to the Old Testament's presentation of the Day of the Lord is even more evident than is the apostle Paul's.

Seventh, a summary of the way the New Testament's use of the Day of the Lord indicates biblical unity will be provided. Taken together, these texts indicate that the Day of the Lord can be either a present or a future reality. It can be either penultimate or final. It highlights the need for purity of life among believers. It requires a coming Lord, and Jesus, the Suffering Servant and Son of Man, is that Lord. It provides hope and salvation for the faithful. Clearly, this chapter can be only a down payment on explicating such concepts, but hopefully it will demonstrate the unity of this theme's purpose throughout Scripture. If so, then it will help illuminate such matters as terminology, timing and results associated with the theme.

Roots of the Day of the Lord theme: the Law

Although neither the phrase 'Day of the Lord' nor its synonyms appear in the Law, later passages certainly build on related concepts found there to formulate Day of the Lord themes. These later texts develop earlier imagery as they divulge the Day of the Lord as divine intervention in human affairs for punishing and cleansing purposes. As was noted above, these concepts are ideas that the later writers knew and expected their readers to know. It makes sense, then, for current readers to have them in mind as well. The following survey will introduce these concepts and their importance for later passages. Only a few later passages will be cited, however, so that the Law can speak on its own terms.

Genesis: creation, flood and Sodom

Genesis 1–2 describes the creation of plant life, animals and human beings. It includes God's declaration to human beings about their role as God's chosen rulers/stewards of creation (1:26–31) and the human beings' first activities (2:4–25). The Creator is the ruler, the king of creation. Thus this human ruling is a mediated role. Some later passages will present judgment as an act of the Creator (see Amos 4:13; 5:8), as an 'uncreation' (see Zeph. 1:2–3), and therefore as an undoing of what God did in creation. Other texts will portray the results of judgment as a new creation (see Isa. 65:17–25). Clearly, later readers either knew or were expected to know the basic elements of the creation account and to understand how the passage at hand reverses or reinstates the original creation.

Genesis 3–9 includes the first accounts of judgment in the Bible. After sinning against God's word owing to believing the word of the serpent instead of their Creator, with whom they had a prior relationship, the human beings are punished by God in 3:14–24. These punishments appear later in the Bible as things that will be put right by God's intervening judgment (see Isa. 51:3; 65:17–25; Matt. 4:1–11; Rev. 20:2). Further, Genesis 6:5–9:17 recounts the Lord's sorrow over human activity, delivering of Noah and his family, punishing the earth by flood, and making of the covenant with Noah. In these episodes the Lord punishes in order to renew. Later texts that utilize imagery or themes drawn from the flood account to discuss the coming Day of the Lord include Isaiah 54:9 and Matthew 24:37.[12]

Genesis 18:1–19:29 describes God's revelation of his plans to overthrow Sodom, Abraham's intercession based on God's righteousness (18:25), God's deliverance of Lot, and God's sudden destruction of Sodom by 'fire from the

---

12. For a discussion of the reuse of this imagery, see Walther Eichrodt, *Theology of the Old Testament: Volume One*, trans. J. Baker (Philadelphia: Westminster, 1961), pp. 459–463.

LORD out of heaven'(19:24). This passage includes, then, a statement on the righteousness of God in judgment and imagery of fire and unexpected over-throwing of a city. Subsequent books use one or both of these concepts (see Lam. 3:19–39; 4:6; Matt. 10:15; 2 Pet. 2:6; Jude 7). 'Overthrowing' is a military image, and many similar military metaphors appear later in Day of the Lord texts (see Exod. 15:1–18; Joel 1–2; etc.).

Exodus: the exodus, the Red Sea and the golden calf

Exodus 5–13 portrays God's deliverance of Israel from Egypt as a judgment on Egypt's defiance of God's word (see Exod. 5:2; 13:15) conducted through a series of plagues. This account highlights the fact that Yahweh will punish other nations for what they believe about him and for what they do to Israel, and that he will use nature in 'abnormal' ways to effect this punishment. Later passages include similar or different plagues as part of God's judgment of the nations, or even of Israel (see Hab. 3:5; Zech. 14:15, 18; Rev. 16:21).[13] It is important to note that in the exodus accounts the Lord warns Egypt before sending the plagues, since this fact indicates that Yahweh does not simply warn the *chosen* people when judgment is coming.

Exodus 15:1–18 celebrates Israel's deliverance from the army sent to force their return to Egypt. In this song the people rejoice in the fact that 'Yahweh is a man of war; Yahweh is his name' (15:3). This divine warrior casts Egypt's warriors into the sea (15:4), and indeed he rules the sea (15:8). His fury spreads out like fire, and this fire consumes its enemies like stubble (15:7; see Isa. 5:24; Mal. 4:1–6). All Israel's enemies tremble at the thought of facing such a warrior (15:15–16). These images combine creation, exodus and divine warrior con-cepts. God can do all the passage confesses because he controls nature, fights for Israel and intervenes in human affairs.[14] Later texts emphasize the fact that the Lord will come as a ruling king who defeats his people's enemies (see Pss. 93–99). He is able to defeat armies as mighty as Babylon's (see Isa. 13:1–22) or the nations that rule the world before the final Day of the Lord (see Rev. 19:11–21).

Exodus 32–34 is critical for grasping the connection between God's char-acter and his judgment in later texts, including some of those in which

---

13. Note the discussion of the reuse of exodus imagery in subsequent texts in Gerhard von Rad, *Old Testament Theology: Volume Two*, trans. D. M. G. Stalker (New York: Harper and Row, 1965), pp. 119–125.

14. F. F. Bruce, *New Testament Development of Old Testament Themes* (Grand Rapids: Eerdmans, 1968), p. 23.

judgment is described as the Day of the Lord. Israel's covenantal infidelity in making the calf leads to an outright rupture between God and Israel that includes God's rejection of Israel, the breaking of the covenant stones that symbolize that covenant and the sending of a plague on Israel (32:1–35). Therefore, the covenant relationship between Yahweh and Israel must be repaired, a 'transaction' Moses mediates in Exodus 33. In Exodus 34:6–7 Yahweh explains why he delays judgment, why he judges, and why he forgives and renews his covenant with Israel. This basic list of propositions about God's character defines his nature as it relates to judgment. Parts of this text are quoted frequently in the Prophets and Writings, and this passage is most likely the basis for New Testament comments about what appears to be God's slowness to judge (see 2 Pet. 3:8–10). It is significant to note that later writers utilize Exodus 34:6–7 when discussing divine punishment of both Israel and the nations (see Joel 2:12–13; Jon. 3:8–10; 4:2).

Leviticus 26 and Deuteronomy 27–28: covenant-breaking and punishment

Leviticus 26 and its sister passage Deuteronomy 27–28 relate the blessings, or benefits, that Israel can expect for covenantal obedience and the curses, or consequences, they can expect for covenantal disobedience. These benefits and consequences relate to national covenantal behaviour. Individuals could be faithful even when the nation as a whole was not, and vice versa. The consequences accrue after a long period of time. They are not quick responses on God's part.

Nonetheless, the consequences are terrible. Their final result is Israel's exile from the Promised Land (see Lev. 26:34–39; Deut. 28:64–68). Since this exile occurs because of military invasion that includes siege warfare, such results as starvation, cannibalism, betrayal and other forms of what are normally considered sub-human behaviour will unfold first (see Lev. 26:23–33; Deut. 28:52–57). Deuteronomy 28:60 states that the diseases that once clung to Egypt, presumably during the exodus episodes, will now cling to Israel. Prior to these siege-related events the Lord will discipline the people (Lev. 26:14–22). He will send such warnings as pestilence, drought, famine and financial loss to make the people come to their senses (Deut. 28:15–24). Yahweh will strike them with madness and blindness. They will grope in darkness (28:28–29).

These passages indicate clearly that the Lord will send persons and circumstances to warn Israel to change their ways prior to punishing them. The purpose of these warnings is to ward off judgment, a fact Josiah grasps once Huldah explains God's word to him (see 2 Kgs 22:8–20). Deuteronomy 30:1–10 asserts that, even after Yahweh judges the people, they can restore the covenant relationship through returning to the Lord with all their hearts, which in turn will guarantee covenantal fidelity. As in Exodus 34:6–7, God's character is defined here by reluctance to judge, determination to offer time for Israel to change, and willingness to punish.

Covenantal disobedience imagery is so pervasive in later passages that it is difficult to choose examples.[15] Jeremiah 39 and 52 represent the fall of Jerusalem as the result of not heeding God's warnings. Amos 4:6–13 claims that the Day of the Lord will come because Israel failed to act on warnings such as those mentioned in Leviticus 26 and Deuteronomy 28, and Lamentations describes Jerusalem's fall and subsequent suffering in terms drawn directly from those passages. Matthew 23:29–39 likewise uses some of this imagery to describe Jerusalem's fall, and Hebrews 12:3–28 invokes discipline language as one of many Old Testament images intended to remind the readers to stay faithful to the Lord in the light of coming judgment.

The Day of the Lord expressed: the Prophets

The prophets inherited the full range of materials found in the Law, as well as the teaching, writings and stock phrases of the prophets who preceded them. Thus it is probably impossible to tell exactly when or under what circumstances the prophets first connected the judgment images noted above with the notion of the Day of the Lord. Still, it is possible to note the various uses of this theme throughout the prophetic literature. This development includes the proclamation of short-term and long-term judgment, the use of imagery drawn from the Law, and an emphasis on judgment in Israel and among the nations. A brief analysis of selected texts will demonstrate these elements. These passages are drawn from the Latter Prophets, although texts from the Former Prophets could just as easily be used (see Judg. 1–2; 2 Kgs 17, etc).

Isaiah 1–4: an anatomy of the Day of the Lord
The Latter Prophets immediately introduce the Day of the Lord as a major way of presenting divine punishment. Interestingly enough, given the criticism of Israel in Isaiah 1:1–31, Isaiah 2:1–22 treats restoration of the nations (2:1–5) before it addresses judgment of Israel (2:6–22). This strategy introduces the book's emphasis on Yahweh as the Holy One of Israel who is also the Creator

---

15. For a list of phrases from Leviticus 26 and Deuteronomy 27–28 that recur in Hosea – Jonah, see Douglas Stuart, *Hosea – Jonah*, WBC 31 (Waco: Word, 1987), pp. xxxii–xlii.

and judge of all persons. It also echoes the Law's emphasis on God the Creator judging all persons when necessary (see Gen. 3–9). This section sets the Day of the Lord in the context of 'latter days' (2:1), and includes images of human terror during the Day of the Lord which are cited in subsequent passages that emphasize final judgment (cf. 2:19 and Hos. 10:8; Luke 23:30; Rev. 6:16). The purpose of this Day of the Lord is to remove the arrogant pride of human beings, which appears as the root of sin here (2:11–17), as well as to remove the most offensive form of that arrogance, idolatry (2:8, 18). In this particular context, then, the Day of the Lord is God's intervention in history at an unspecified point in time for the purpose of finally removing pride and idolatry.

In 3:1–4:1 Isaiah highlights Israel's current spiritual condition and current historical setting. At this or a very near point in time (see the 'behold' and present tense in 3:1), the Lord will take away all Jerusalem's means of support (3:1–5), whether physical, governmental or military. Israel's sin has become as brazen as Sodom's (3:9; see Gen. 18), so the Lord will contend with this brand of arrogance by removing all trappings of wealth (3:13–4:1). The result of the Day of the Lord will be actual defeat, devastation and the emptying of the city (3:25–26), images also used in Lamentations 1:1–10; 4:9–10, etc. These images almost certainly derive from Leviticus 26 and/or Deuteronomy 27–28. This Day of the Lord is *like* the one portrayed in 2:1–22 in that it is an event initiated by God when he judges arrogance and its results (or the arrogant and their deeds). This Day of the Lord *differs* from the first in timing: one is depicted as near and occurring soon or at the present time, while the other is depicted as coming later in time. It is also different in that specific results of arrogance other than idolatry are mentioned. Here oppression and other forms of not loving one's neighbour are highlighted as reasons for this Day of the Lord. It is important to note that Isaiah treats both types of the Day of the Lord within a single context, for later texts follow the same procedure.

Isaiah 1–4 begins and ends with promises related to the aftermath of the two types and instances of the Day of the Lord. In 2:1–5 the prophet emphasizes the nations' turning to the Lord's law and walking in his ways. In 4:2–6 the prophet likewise stresses ultimate results, for the people of God rest in Zion with their God in the absence of sin. This formula (life with God in Zion in the absence of sin and its effects, such as death) becomes the book's way of describing God's (and thus his people's) final victory (see 25:1–12; 65:17–25). Who are God's people in this text? They are those who desire his word and, having that word, walk in his ways because of their relationship with him. They are the people who take to heart the prophet's call in 1:10–20 to return to the Lord.

As the book unfolds, Isaiah 9:1–7 and 11:1–16 introduce the idea that the coming Davidic heir, the Messiah, will have a role in judging on the Day of the Lord. These texts also indicate that this figure will have a role in the renewal of God's faithful ones (see also Jer. 32–33). Judgment becomes increasingly associated with this individual as the canon progresses, culminating in the Gospels' presentation of Jesus as the Son of Man and the judge of all persons, and Revelation's presentation of Jesus as the leader of God's army (see 19:16).

As for God's character in Isaiah 1–4, the prophet reminds readers that if God had not left some survivors in Israel, they would have been as devastated as Sodom and Gomorrah (1:9). This leaving of survivors occurred even though Israel had actually been as wicked as Sodom and Gomorrah (1:10; 3:9). Thus one could even conclude that God's mercy is primary. This conclusion is in keeping with the comment in Isaiah 28:21 that judgment is God's strange, alien act. As Exodus 34:6–7 has already indicated, God is merciful and compassionate, yet he will not clear the guilty. God's righteousness (see Gen. 18:25–26) does not allow him to clear the guilty, although his compassion does not allow him to judge without mercy, and this mercy includes allowing time for the people to change. Readers could conclude that the gap in time between the sin and the judgment reflects God's indifference rather than his patience, but they will do so at their own peril (see Zeph. 1:12–13; Matt. 24:36–44; 2 Pet. 3:1–13).

Clearly, this passage draws on texts found in the Law when making its points. Besides the Genesis 3–9 emphasis on Yahweh as the only God and only judge, the text mentions Sodom twice (1:10; 3:9) and includes punishments specifically designed for the covenant people (see Lev. 26; Deut. 27–28). Israel's covenant relationship with and responsibilities to Yahweh are highlighted, which reminds readers of Exodus 34, Leviticus 26 and Deuteronomy 27–28. Therefore, although there may be few direct quotations of previous texts, there are many concepts present that are direct descendants of those found in the Law.

This summary of Isaiah 1–4 leads to three basic conclusions. First, this text introduces judgment as the Day of the Lord in the Prophets, and it provides a paradigm for future statements on the subject. The nature, purpose, timing and imagery of the Day of the Lord here reflect concepts found in the Law and offer various images that later Old and New Testament writers utilize. Second, this passage clearly places God's mercy, especially as it appears through his revelation of the near and distant future, in the forefront of Day of the Lord passages. It states that the Lord has left Sodom-like Jerusalem with some survivors, which was not the case for Sodom itself. Third, this passage introduces later Isaianic treatments of the Day of the Lord, such as those

found in chapters 13–23 regarding the nations, and chapters 24–27 regarding
the whole earth, to name just two instances. These passages likewise utilize
Law imagery, address both Israel and the nations, describe near and distant
judgment, offer evidence that Yahweh acts mercifully in all circumstances and
indicate that the future is bright for those who trust God and walk in his ways.

The book of the Twelve: contours of the Day of the Lord

The book of the Twelve often serves as the starting point for discussions of
the Day of the Lord.[16] One reason for this tendency is the belief that Amos
and Hosea may well provide the oldest historical references to the Day of the
Lord in the canon. Of course, one can debate the dates of these books in relation to Isaiah 1–4, but the concern for historical continuity is valid enough for
scholars to begin at this point. Nonetheless, it is also legitimate to read the
book of the Twelve in the light of Isaiah, Jeremiah and Ezekiel, since the book
of the Twelve shares the same historical context and many of the theological
themes found in those books.

This section will highlight several aspects of the Day of the Lord as they
appear in Joel, Amos, Zephaniah and Malachi. The other books in the book of
the Twelve discuss the Day of the Lord as well, but the theme is especially
prominent in these books and provides a conclusion for the Prophets in
Malachi. These books also span the centuries included in the book of the
Twelve. As in Isaiah, the Day of the Lord encompasses present and future
events in these books. Also, these books utilize the same type of imagery
drawn from the Law as Isaiah does, and they provide concepts that New
Testament writers use to discuss the subject.

Quite significantly, as Rolf Rendtorff points out, themes related to the
concept of the need for changed behaviour, whether in the form of 'returning to the Lord', 'seeking the Lord' or 'taking refuge in the Lord', precede or
stand alongside the Day of the Lord theme.[17] These connected ideas often
emerge early in the books, develop as the text unfolds, then merge at the end

---

16. See Rowley, *The Faith of Israel*, p. 177; and John D. W. Watts, *Vision and Prophecy in
    Amos, Expanded Anniversary Edition* (Macon: Mercer University Press, 1997),
    pp. 91–100. For a discussion of opinions on the matter, see Gerhard F. Hasel,
    Understanding the Book of Amos: Basic Issues in Current Interpretations (Grand Rapids:
    Baker, 1991), pp. 109–112.

17. Rolf Rendtorff, 'How to Read the Twelve as a Theological Unity', in James D.
    Nogalski and Marvin A. Sweeney (eds.), *Reading and Hearing the Book of the Twelve*,
    SBLSym 15 (Atlanta: Society of Biblical Literature, 2000), p. 86.

of individual books to form a resolution to the problems that they have introduced. Thus the preaching of the Day of the Lord intends to change lives, not just condemn the guilty.

Joel

As is well known, it is virtually impossible to date Joel with precision. It is placed between two eighth-century prophets, however, so it may be best to read the book in view of that context. Very quickly the book settles into its main topic. The text announces an extraordinary, unprecedented locust plague that deserves to be described to future generations (1:2–4). This plague is then compared to a military invasion in chapter 2, and thus becomes the occasion for repeated calls for returning to Yahweh before the Day of the Lord comes. Latter stages of the book indicate that renewal may occur as a result of human response and divine judgment. Thus Hosea and Joel are joined thematically through these emphases.[18]

In 1:5–14, the prophet warns every segment of the populace to awake to what immediately looms on the horizon. They are warned that this locust plague will result in drunkards having no wine, farmers having no crops and priests having no offerings. Due to this coming 'Day of the Lord', their crops will be consumed (1:15–18). As the pastures and trees wilt, the prophet cries to the Lord (1:19–20). No guilt is expressed at this time, but the priests at least acknowledge Israel's need to gain help from the Lord. It is his 'Day' that is coming, so only he can help.

The use of locust imagery to describe the Day of the Lord does not occur just in Joel. As James Nogalski has observed, 'Locust imagery unites diverse material presupposing threats from locust, drought, and enemy attack. Later in the Twelve, several passages (Amos 4:9; Nah. 3:16b, 17; Hab. 1:9; Mal. 3:10) use locust metaphors to refer to divinely-initiated threats to Yahweh's people'.[19] Apparently, locust swarms were a typical part of the prophetic stock phrases for the Day of the Lord. In Exodus 10:1–19 the Lord sends a locust plague on Egypt, and Deuteronomy 28:38 threatens Israel with a locust plague if they persist in sinning against Yahweh, their covenant partner. At this juncture, then, Joel has introduced the notion that the same means of judgment that afflicted non-Israelites can indeed afflict Israel. In this way the prophet

---

18. On this point, see ibid., pp. 94–100.

19. James D. Nogalski, 'Intertextuality in the Twelve', in James W. Watts and Paul R. House (eds.), *Forming Prophetic Literature: Essays on Isaiah and the Twelve in Honor of John D. W. Watts*, JSOTSup 235 (Sheffield: Sheffield Academic Press, 1996), p. 117.

underscores the universal nature of the Day of the Lord, although he does so by stressing the local expressions of that universal truth.

Next, Yahweh announces the nearness and terrible nature of the Day of the Lord by commanding that a trumpet be blown in Zion (2:1). Like the lion's roar, the blowing of the trumpet signals disaster and the need to respond to it (see Hos. 5:8; 8:1). The reference to Zion probably indicates that Judah is the nation under attack.[20] Whereas the first chapter warned of the danger to the countryside, the second chapter depicts the threat against Jerusalem.[21] This danger is immediate, for 'the day of the LORD is . . . near' (2:1; see Obad. 15). It is 'a day of darkness' (2:2; see Amos 5:18; Zeph. 1:14–16), one in which a 'great and powerful' army stands poised to invade (2:2). These invaders will turn a place as verdant as the garden of Eden into a wasteland (2:3). They are a consuming fire (2:3–5) that everyone ought to fear (2:6), for they are fiercely and horribly efficient (2:7–9). Indeed, this is God's army and God's Day (2:11). Who can endure it, and under what conditions?

As in Hosea 6:1–3 and 14:1–9, the only hope for the people is in returning to the Lord, in this instance with their whole hearts, 'with fasting, with weeping, and with mourning' (2:12). They must rend their hearts and not their garments (2:13). God is 'gracious and merciful, slow to anger, and abounding in steadfast love; and he relents over disaster' (2:13). This conviction reminds readers of Exodus 34:6–7, which follows the golden-calf incident, and points to Jonah 4:2, which offers God's reasons for forgiving Nineveh. Thus the Lord may turn and have compassion, as in the golden-calf incident or the Nineveh repentance (2:14). In other words, their returning at the impulse of the prophetic preaching may well lead to God returning to a favourable view of them.

Having expressed the nature of Yahweh in 2:12–14, the prophet calls for prayer and fasting in 2:15–17. In other words, the people should pray in a manner similar to Moses after the golden-calf incident (Exod. 32:11–14). As he did, they should petition God based on his choice of Israel and his reputation among the nations. 'Returning' therefore has a specific content. It means humility, fasting, prayer and intercessory lament based on the nature of their covenant God. It is not simply a psychological response to a harsh crisis.[22]

---

20. Marvin A. Sweeney, *The Twelve Prophets: Volume One*, Berit Olam (Collegeville: Liturgical Press, 2000), p. 161.

21. John Barton, *Joel and Obadiah*, OTL (Louisville: Westminster John Knox Press, 2001), p. 70.

22. Ibid., pp. 78–79.

When the people return in this manner, the Lord will have pity (2:18). Yahweh will restore produce (2:19), expel the invader (2:20), revive livestock (2:21–22), give rain (2:23), fill wine vats (2:24), restore crops (2:25) and feed the people (2:26). This positive agricultural imagery coincides with that found in Hosea 14:4–9.[23] Most importantly, they will know that the Lord is their God and there is no other (2:27), the fundamental tenet of Israelite faith according to Deuteronomy 6:4–9; 32:39; and Isaiah 40–48. Returning will spark renewal, although no time frame is given. Now the text stresses the future aspect of the Day of the Lord. At some future time, which the text simply describes as 'afterward' (2:28), God will pour out his Spirit on all flesh, resulting in prophesying by all groups of people in Israel (2:28–29). Signs will accompany this 'great and awesome day of the LORD' (2:30), a designation that ties this Day of the Lord to the one mentioned in Joel 2:11.[24] But this Day is different in at least one particularly significant way. As James Crenshaw writes, 'Now Joel implies that other nations will undergo that same frightening experience, while God's people will escape the divine fury this time.'[25] Zion will be the place where those who call upon the Lord will come for refuge (2:32). In the rest of the book Zion is the holy place where God dwells (3:16–17, 21; see also Mic. 4:2–13; Zeph. 3:14–16; Zech. 9:9). The other nations, however, will be judged 'in those days' (3:1–8). Whatever army comes against Zion will fail (3:9–12), for 'the LORD roars' (3:16; see Amos 1:2) against the wicked, which means that their day of punishment is 'near' (3:14; see Obad. 15).

The result of this 'day' is at least threefold. First, the nations will join Israel in the knowledge that the Lord alone is God (3:17; see 2:27). Second, Jerusalem and Zion will be holy (3:17), and God will restore the land (3:18; see 2:18–27; Hos. 14:4–9). Third, God will make Egypt and Edom (see Obad.) desolate (3:19), but Judah will be inhabited (3:20), for the Lord dwells in Zion (3:21). These renewal elements become standard in future texts such as Micah 4–5 and Zephaniah 3:6–20. They also remind readers of Deuteronomy 28:1–14, 2 Samuel 7:1–11 and Isaiah 65:17–25. Thus they combine imagery that portrays both imminent and long-term judgment which leads ultimately to the redemption of the faithful.

------

23. On this imagery, see James D. Nogalski, 'Joel as "Literary Anchor" for the Book of the Twelve', in Nogalski and Sweeney (eds.), *Reading and Hearing the Book of the Twelve*, pp. 100–104.

24. James L. Crenshaw, *Joel*, AB 24C (New York: Doubleday, 1995), p. 169.

25. Ibid., p. 196.

Joel's portrayal of the Day of the Lord includes many facets already found
in Isaiah, plus certain aspects of the concept that appear later in the
Scriptures. First, it emphasizes imagery found in the Law. Metaphors based
on the exodus and Exodus 32–34 are particularly evident. Second, Joel portrays the Day of the Lord as twofold. It takes place in the near and distant
future. Third, Joel considers the 'latter days' a time of universal judgment. He
begins with Israel and proceeds to the nations. Thus his emphasis coincides
with Isaiah's. Fourth, Joel indicates that the ultimate result of the Day of the
Lord will be the people of God dwelling in Zion with Yahweh and the wicked
receiving divine wrath.

Amos

Hosea's and Amos's superscriptions place the books in the same era, the latter
half of the eighth century. Although scholars have generally claimed that
Amos was written before Hosea, Jorg Jeremias has argued that the editors of
Amos sought to read the book in the light of Hosea's message.[26] If so, this
audience was interested in the interaction of returning, renewal and the future
of God's people, since Amos continues the emphasis on these subjects begun
in Hosea and Joel. All these themes are intricately connected to the concept of
the Day of the Lord. Israel's sin and need to repent are covenantal concepts
enforced by the threat of judgment. Israel's future renewal will come about
only through repentance or a cleansing 'day'. This day has immediate and
future elements. It calls for an ethical revolution in the life of the people. In
short, it includes both individual and national eschatology.[27]

Amos starts with three connections to Hosea and Joel. First, the book
opens with the Lord roaring from Zion (1:2; see Hos. 3:16). Second, 1:2–2:3
describes the sins of the nations, a theme begun in Joel 3, and 2:4–16 continues with a description of Israel and Judah's sins, a theme that originates in
Hosea 1–3. Third, this rebellious behaviour will bring punishment (2:4, 6) on
'that day' (2:16).

God is angry at the 'whole family' that he 'brought up out of the land of
Egypt' (3:1). He has chosen them out of all the nations of the earth, so their sin
is presented as a breach of relationship, a breaking of covenant (3:2). As in Hosea
and Joel, the lion has roared and the trumpet has blown, both of which indicate
approaching judgment (3:3–8). Why does judgment come? Because Judah and

---

26. Jorg Jeremias, 'The Interrelationship between Amos and Hosea', in Watts and
    House (eds.), *Forming Prophetic Literature*, pp. 185–186.
27. Hasel, *Understanding the Book of Amos*, p. 112.

Israel ignore the prophets (3:7–8; see 2 Kgs 17:13–14). Because the people 'do not know how to do right' (3:10). Such behaviour can only bring an invasion by an 'adversary' that will purge the land (3:11–15; see Hos. 9:7–10:15). Idolatrous altars such as Bethel will be destroyed (3:14; see Hos. 4:15–19; 10:5, 15).

Amos 4:6–13 agrees with Joel 2:1–17 that the key to avoiding terrifying judgment is to return to the Lord (see also Hos. 6:1–3; 14:1–3). Unlike the earlier books, however, Amos states the case negatively. That is, in a passage reminiscent of Deuteronomy 28:15–24, Amos 4:6–13 argues that no matter what the Lord did to awaken the people from their moral slumber, they did not return to the Lord (4:7, 9, 10, 11). Thus the text calls for a lament for fallen Israel (5:1–3; see Deut. 28:45–57). Despite this failure to return to the Lord, however, there remains time to 'seek the LORD and live' (5:4–6, 14; see Hos. 3:5; 5:6, 15; 10:12). In this passage 'seeking' and 'returning' amount to the same thing, since they require forsaking cultic centres such as Gilgal and Bethel (5:4–5) in favour of the Lord. Further, since they are to 'seek good, and not evil' (5:14), to 'hate evil, and love good, and establish justice in the gate' (5:15), and to 'let justice roll down like waters' (5:24), returning to a previous behaviour is more than implied.

Indeed, such covenant-based ethical renewal is required if the Day of the Lord is to be avoided (5:18–20). The people do not realize their danger. They believe that the Day of the Lord will be a day of blessing to them. They consider it a day against their enemies. To some extent they are correct, since 1:2–2:16 indicates that Yahweh will judge sin wherever it exists. Nonetheless, as Willem VanGemeren writes, 'It is a bit much, however, that in spite of their bigotry, they longed for the Day as a deserved era of blessing and prosperity (5:18–20)'.[28] The covenant people need to heed the exhortation to change their behaviour in view of their prior commitment to Yahweh and to one another. The day may yet 'be a day of salvation, provided there is repentance'.[29]

Sadly, Amos 6:1–9:10 offers no indication akin to that found in Joel that returning/seeking occurs. Amos's prayers for mercy delay the judgment for a time (7:1–9), but the book's penultimate promise is that the sword, or military defeat, awaits the disobedient nation (9:10). Israel cannot escape. The nation will go into captivity (9:4). The original readers of Amos knew that this threat came true in 722 BC when Assyria conquered Samaria.

---

28. Willem VanGemeren, *Interpreting the Prophetic Word: An Introduction to the Prophetic Literature of the Old Testament* (Grand Rapids: Zondervan, 1990), p. 134.

29. Elmer Martens, *God's Design: A Focus on Old Testament Theology*, 2nd ed. (Grand Rapids: Baker; Leicester: Apollos, 1994), p. 133.

Having experienced God's wrath, however, Israel will eventually enjoy God's blessing again. As Elmer Martens argues, ultimately the Day of the Lord is part of Yahweh's design for deliverance.[30] 'In that day', Yahweh will restore David's tent and subsume Edom under that authority (9:11–12). 'Days are coming' for the renewal of land (9:13), returning of fortunes (9:14) and restoration of security in the land (9:15). In other words, the text uses language quite similar to that found in Joel 3:18 to describe the people's future. Returning is not mentioned directly in this segment, but by this point in Amos one has to wonder if some form of returning should be assumed.

In Amos, as in Hosea and Joel, the threat of the Day of the Lord brings with it the chance for new beginnings. Those who heed the threats may seek the Lord, return to him and thus find forgiveness and renewal. The prophets who carry the threat may pray and preach in a manner that forges a new beginning for the people. If the prophets' efforts fail due to lack of returning, the Day of the Lord itself will effect a new beginning. The day purges sin from the people and leaves persons like the prophets as representatives of the living God. Postexilic readers of the Twelve could decide for themselves whether their own situation called for new beginnings, and they could also decide by what means they wished that fresh start to come, their repentance or God's judgment.

Amos adds an ethical component to the canonical development of the Day of the Lord that was implicit in the earlier books, but not as prominent. The Day of the Lord will come because of sin, as before, but now it is clear that the covenant people must live in a faithful way if they wish to avert judgment. Yahweh has no desire to punish. Rather, he has gone to great lengths to turn the people from their destructive course of action.

Zephaniah

Zephaniah is set in the seventh century BC during the reign of Josiah. Since no other chronological data appears, it is impossible to settle with certainty whether the prophet ministered before or after Josiah's reform (see 2 Kgs 22–23). Regardless of the exact dating, Zephaniah certainly offers a post-Isaiah, post-Amos and therefore post-eighth-century BC perspective on the Day of the Lord. As the book proceeds, it makes full use of previous Day of the Lord imagery. It employs reversal of creation motifs based on Genesis 1–2 and Genesis 9 (1:2–3). It addresses Gentile nations, not just Israel (2:4–15). When it does speak concerning Israel, it utilizes covenant curses (3:1–5). It also uses concepts associated with new heavens and earth theology (3:1–18; see Isa.

---

30. Ibid., pp. 131–136.

65:17–25). Finally, it connects total destruction, unbelieving scoffers and judgment by fire in a way that New Testament writers found compelling (cf. 1:1–18; 2 Pet. 3:1–18).

Zephaniah 1:1–18 portrays the day as the time when Yahweh will 'sweep away' or 'put an end' to sin.[31] This presentation moves in an increasingly specific direction. In 1:2–3 Yahweh threatens to sweep away human beings and animals from the face of the earth. Yahweh will reverse creation,[32] as he did in the flood narrative, and as he threatened to do in Hosea 4:3. Having expressed the universality of this Day of the Lord, the prophet states that Yahweh will judge Judah and Jerusalem at that time (1:4). Even more specifically, Yahweh will punish apostate priests (1:4–6), oppressive officials (1:7–9), greedy merchants (1:10–11) and scoffers who think Yahweh will do nothing about the current sin-laden situation (1:12–13). The day is near (1:14). It is a day of destruction and darkness (1:15; see Deut. 28:28–29) and a day of battle (1:16). The rich cannot buy their way out of this day (1:17), and on this day the Lord's fiery wrath will consume the earth (1:18). Every wicked person will experience Yahweh's cleansing fire on that day. As in Isaiah 1–4, this day includes the entire family of nations.

Despite the fact that 'the day of the LORD is near' (1:7; see Joel 1:15; 2:1, 11, 15, 31; Amos 5:18; Obad. 15), the prophet calls on the people to 'seek the LORD' (2:3). Here seeking the Lord means 'seek righteousness; seek humility' (2:3). Such seeking may lead to their being 'hidden on the day of the anger of the LORD' (2:3). Interestingly enough, this seeking will not forestall the Day of the Lord, as was true earlier in the Twelve. Now such seeking will merely hide the persons who seek the Lord in the midst of the inevitable Day of the Lord. The 'humble of the land' (2:3) should take refuge in the Lord, but this refuge pertains only to them. They will be preserved, but the nation will not. A text

---

31. Zeph. 1:2 is famous for its difficulty. The BHS note offers the reading 'sweep away', while many scholars read the text as 'gather'. Nonetheless, the meaning is clear enough: Yahweh will embark on an extensive cleansing of creation. For a discussion of the linguistic options, see J. J. M. Roberts, *Nahum, Habakkuk, and Zephaniah*, OTL (Louisville: Westminster John Knox, 1991), p. 167; J. Alec Motyer, 'Zephaniah', in Thomas McComiskey (ed.), *The Minor Prophets: An Exegetical and Expository Commentary* (Grand Rapids: Baker, 2003), pp. 58–62.

32. See Michael De Roche, 'Zephaniah 1:2–3: The "Sweeping" of Creation', *VT* 30 (1980), pp. 104–109. For an argument that the flood is not the only possible background for this text, see Marvin A. Sweeney, *Zephaniah*, Herm (Minneapolis: Fortress Press, 2003), pp. 62–63.

like this one may have helped early readers of the Twelve understand why the 'humble of the land', people like Habakkuk and Jeremiah, for instance, suffered when the land was destroyed.

In swift succession Zephaniah includes Philistia (2:4–7), Moab (2:8–11), Cush (2:12) and Assyria (2:13–15) in the list of those to be punished. These passages mirror longer sections of books such as Isaiah 13–23, Jeremiah 46–51 and Ezekiel 25–32, as well as Amos 1:2–2:3. The reasons for the judgment are likewise similar to those given in previous books: arrogance (2:15) and idolatry (2:11) that result in virtual self-worship (2:15) and the oppression of others.

Sadly, as the book begins its final movement towards the punishment that will bring renewal, the prophet includes Judah in the list (3:1–5). The elect nation has acted like a stranger to Yahweh. Arvid Kapelrud writes, 'What was going on among his people was so lacking in the quality required of a chosen people that the reaction could only be one: death and destruction.'[33] Thus 2:1–3:5 has stated in detail what 1:1–18 states in outline: Judah and the entire world will face Yahweh's wrath due to sin against the Creator and one another. Yahweh will judge because he is righteous (3:5) and because Judah has rejected correction (3:2). Judah's woe could have been avoided (as 2:1–3 has already indicated) if the people had been willing to accept the Lord's correction (3:7). Given their evident eagerness to act corruptly (3:7), the Lord decides to pour out his indignation, with the result that 'all the earth shall be consumed' (3:8).

Through this judgment the Lord will renew both the nations and Judah. The Lord 'will change the speech of the peoples to a pure speech, that all of them may call upon the name of the LORD and serve him with one accord' (3:9). Adele Berlin notes that 'the idea seems to be universal worship of the Lord, reminiscent of, or actually going beyond, the idea in 2:11'.[34] Marvin Sweeney adds, 'Verse 9 . . . emerges as a reversal of the scattering of the nations in the tower of Babel tradition . . . The calling on YHWH by the nations appears ironically to portray YHWH's desire that the nations *call* on YHWH rather than build a tower . . .'[35] Further, 'dispersed ones' shall come from a distance to worship the Lord (3:10), and the Lord will leave in the land 'a people humble and lowly. They shall seek refuge in the name of the LORD' (3:12).

---

33. Arvid Kapelrud, *The Message of the Prophet Zephaniah: Morphology and Ideas* (Oslo-Bergen-Tromso: Universitetsforlaget, 1975), p. 87.

34. Adele Berlin, *Zephaniah*, AB 25A (New York: Doubleday, 1994), p. 133.

35. Sweeney, *Zephaniah*, p. 184.

Yahweh will do great things for these renewed people. He will gather them (3:18), deal with their oppressors (3:19), heal their lame (3:19), remove their shame (3:19) and renew them fully (3:20). Truly the renewal has been as thorough as the punishment. Kapelrud observes, 'The exhortation leaves no room for doubt: another day is coming, when there was no more need for fear, when the enemies were cast out, and shame would be changed to praise.'[36] A truly new beginning has been forged out of the punishment inflicted on the nations and on Judah. This vision is truly eschatological. It refers to a time when purity will reign and sin will no longer affect the people who serve Yahweh.

Two means of renewal unfold in Zephaniah. The people may either seek the Lord or experience the Day of the Lord. The 'humble of the land' are likely those who did seek God. They are the remnant of Israel, and they will be joined by a purified group of international people after the full force of the Day of the Lord has been felt. In this way Zephaniah acts as a summary of how judgment comes to Israel and the nations without that judgment being the final word. Renewal is the final word, and that word may well have encouraged the Twelve's first audience, just as it has the power to encourage waiting persons today.

Malachi

Malachi's superscription offers no information on the prophet's date or family. He is certainly a post-exilic prophet like Haggai and Zechariah, but even this conclusion must be drawn from an analysis of the book's contents rather than from the superscription. These contents portray the people as questioning God's love (1:2–5), offering polluted offerings (1:6–14), countenancing priests who do not instruct them properly (2:1–9), profaning the covenant with God and the covenant made with their spouses (2:10–16), and robbing God in their offerings (3:6–14). Clearly, the glorious renewal described in Zephaniah has not yet occurred.

Scholars have often associated this rather dismal picture with Ezra's and Nehemiah's time,[37] although Paul Redditt rightly concludes that Malachi's contents fix a time span only of 515–445 BC as the possible range for the book's composition.[38] Andrew Hill suggests that the book's linguistic data indicate

---

36. Kapelrud, *The Message of the Prophet Zephaniah*, p. 90.

37. Marvin A. Sweeney expresses this point of view in *The Twelve Prophets: Volume Two*, Berit Olam (Collegeville: Liturgical Press, 2000), pp. 715–716.

38. See Paul Redditt, *Haggai, Zechariah, Malachi*, NCB (Grand Rapids: Eerdmans, 1995), p. 150.

that it was probably written c. 500 BC, so Malachi addresses a situation nearer to the time of Haggai and Zechariah.[39] If Hill is correct, then Malachi deals with the people's early attempts at worship and general disappointment with its failure to usher in the sort of glory promised in Zephaniah, Haggai and Zechariah. He does so in part by issuing calls for change and promises of renewal.

After the messages concerning the people's lack of confidence in the Lord's love for them (1:2–5) and their polluted offerings (1:6–14), the prophet uses new phrases to call for change. He tells them to 'take it to heart' (2:2), which seems to be a near parallel to Haggai's demand that they consider their ways (Hag. 1:7). He follows this command with admonitions to guard their spirits and change their behaviour (2:15, 16). This sort of action must replace false weeping and groaning (2:13). Although not identical with earlier *terms* for change, the *effects* are the same.

As in Joel, Jonah, Haggai and Zechariah, some hearers do respond to the message. As in Haggai 1:12, some persons fear the Lord, take stock of their situation and receive God's forgiveness (3:16–18). These people will be God's special possession (3:17; see Exod. 19:5), and God will spare them 'as a man spares his son who serves him' (3:17; see Hos. 11:1–9). As always, those who obey God's call to turn to him find that judgment is no longer necessary.

Malachi concludes the book of the Twelve with one final reference to the Day of the Lord. Wicked persons should fear the day (4:1; see Amos 5:18–27), but those who fear the Lord – another way of expressing the fact that they turn to God – will be blessed then (4:2–3). One last time the people are told to adhere to the covenant standards (4:4), and they are warned to avoid a future 'utter destruction' prefigured by the appearance of a new Elijah (4:6). As before, the returning and seeking mentioned will be accomplished by the Day of the Lord. Regardless of the people's choice, the Lord will remove sin and restore the humble of the land to their rightful place in Zion. Thus the one who is Israel's father (1:6; 2:10), king (1:14) and judge (3:2–3) has an unshakable love for those who respond to his covenant commitment (1:2–5).[40]

Summary and conclusion

In the book of the Twelve, the Day of the Lord is portrayed as a near or distant, yet certain prospect. It is coming because of Israel's and the nations' sins. The books describe the Day of the Lord as an invasion due to Israel's covenantal

---

39. See Andrew E. Hill, *Malachi*, AB 25D (New York: Doubleday, 1998), pp. 80–84.
40. Redditt, *Haggai, Zechariah, Malachi*, p. 187.

waywardness (Hos. 2:14–23), as a natural disaster that punishes Israel's trans-gressions (Joel 1:15–18), and as an act by the Creator against the sins of the nations (Amos 1:2–2:6; 4:6–13). The authors of the book of the Twelve depict the Day of the Lord as a day of defeat for the nations (Obad. 15), of destruc-tion for Nineveh (Jon.), and of invasion for Israel (Mic.). They consider the destruction of Nineveh (Nah.), Jerusalem (Hab.) and Babylon (Zeph.) this sort of day. Depending on the context, they describe the day as either penultimate or final (see Zeph. and Zech. for books that include both ideas), and promise/threaten that Elijah will come before that terrible day appears (Mal. 4:5–6). They promise that beyond the final Day of the Lord lies renewal of unbelievable proportions (Hos. 14:1–9; Zeph. 3:6–20; Zech. 14:16–21).

Along the way, the book of the Twelve asserts that God's character dictates that he offer repentance as an alternative to punishment. Again, his first offer is of returning to him (Hos. 6:1–3; 14:1–9; Joel 2:12–14; Amos 4:6–13; etc). More specifically, Joel 2:12–14, Jonah 4:2 and Nahum 1:2–8 all quote Exodus 34:6–7. Joel does so in the context of a call to repentance, Jonah does so in an explanation of the prophet's anger, and Nahum does so as an explanation of why God judges Nineveh. The first two texts emphasize Yahweh's compas-sion and willingness to forgive, while the third focuses on the Lord's unwill-ingness to clear the guilty. Taken together, they address the future of Israel and the nations. Placed alongside images such as Yahweh's love for Israel, his stray-ing wife, in Hosea 1–3, and love for Israel, his rebellious child, in Hosea 11:1–9, these themes underscore God's compassion, mercy and justice, both for Israel and for the nations. It is apparent in the book of the Twelve that God will remove sin. It is just as apparent that he may do so through repentance or by means of the Day of the Lord.

As has been implied already, these Day of the Lord texts utilize every type of imagery found in the Law. Creation imagery occurs in Amos 4:13 and 5:8–9. 'Uncreation' imagery occurs in Zephaniah 1:2–6, and new creation/Zion imagery appears in Zephaniah 3:9–20. Reversal of the tower of Babel imagery occurs in Zephaniah 3:8–9. Covenant curse terminology appears in Hosea, Joel, Amos, Micah and Malachi. The list could be extended, but the point is clear: the book of the Twelve, like Isaiah, quite often portrays this day in terms from the foundational covenantal texts found in the Law.

The Day of the Lord experienced: the Writings

The Writings emphasize Israel's service to the Lord through time. These books highlight Israel living in the presence of the Lord. The people of Yahweh worship, suffer, learn and wait in these books. Part of this living before Yahweh involves experiencing the Day of the Lord and expecting the bright future promised in Isaiah 1–4, Zephaniah 3:8–20 and elsewhere. Although one could examine several passages to make these points, one can hardly deny that Lamentations expresses the experience of the Day of the Lord as clearly as any book of the Bible. Also, it is hard to deny that Daniel 7 and 9 contribute mightily to whatever hope and confession those who lived after the destruction of Jerusalem may have had. These two books offer at least two key images to New Testament writers: the fall of Jerusalem as a Day of Yahweh, and the coming Son of Man as the ruler who will give the kingdom of God to the people of God.

Lamentations: the fall of Jerusalem and the Day that Yahweh promised

Scholars have long debated the details of the historical background to the book of Lamentations, but a broad consensus that the setting is the fall of Jerusalem in 587 BC has been reached.[41] Until recently, discussions about Lamentations' theology were shaped by Norman Gottwald's contention that the people lament so fiercely because they wonder why the Lord has judged them when they repented during Josiah's time,[42] as well as by Bertil Albrektson's assertion that the book balances Deuteronomistic and Zion theology.[43] Since these volumes appeared, Claus Westermann has argued that Lamentations helps people find ways to express their anger to God and find their way back to him. Thus the main theological importance of Lamentations is its ability to reclaim lament as a legitimate form of prayer for Christians.[44] Others, such as Tod Linafelt and Kathleen O'Connor, have claimed that the book allows sufferers to speak their mind to God, to cry out against what he has done to them, to decry divine violence against human beings, and to give voice to the senseless pain that stalks the world.[45] In other words, the book

---

41. For a discussion of options, consult Duane Garrett and Paul R. House, *Song of Songs/Lamentations*, WBC 23B (Nashville: Thomas Nelson, 2004), pp. 283–303.

42. Norman Gottwald, *Studies in the Book of Lamentations*, rev. ed., SBT 14 (London: SCM, 1962).

43. Bertil Albrektson, *Studies in the Text and Theology of the Book of Lamentations* (Lund: CWK Gleerup, 1963).

44. Claus Westermann, *Lamentations: Issues and Interpretations*, trans. C. Muenchow (Minneapolis: Fortress Press, 1994).

45. See Tod Linafelt, *Surviving Lamentations* (Chicago: University of Chicago Press, 1999); and Kathleen O'Connor, *Lamentations and the Tears of the World* (Maryknoll: Orbis Books, 2002).

allows the sufferers to question or even denounce God's character openly and without reference to any sense of final hope. They emphasize God's silence in the book to support their viewpoint.

In my opinion, recent analyses of Lamentations' theology have not taken the Day of the Lord sufficiently into account.[46] This theme links the book to the rest of biblical theology in a way that its form (personal and corporate lament) does not. As Barry Webb observes, 'The Book of Lamentations, more than any other Old Testament book, shows us God's wrath as a directly experienced reality.'[47] It is nothing less than a report on the Day of the Lord from those who have experienced it in space and time. Thus its comments on the subject are worth examining to aid whole-Bible analysis of the topic.

In the first two poems the book states that what the people of Jerusalem have experienced is 'the day of his fierce anger' (1:12), 'the day you [Yahweh] announced' (1:21). It is 'the day of his anger' (2:1), the day Jerusalem's enemies longed to see (2:16), the day God threatened (2:17), and the day of terror and 'the anger of the LORD' (2:22). The speakers in the text also state why this 'day' has come. They claim that it has come because of Jerusalem's sin (1:5, 8, 18) and 1:18 admits that God has been righteous in what he has done. They also disclose the results of the Day of the Lord. The city has lost inhabitants, holy sites, opportunities to worship, food, water and essential leadership (see especially 2:1–9). They are eating their children because of the siege of Jerusalem, just as Deuteronomy 28:52–57 warned would happen.

Given the speakers' statements, it is hard to agree with commentators who claim that the book questions the Lord's character for judging, although it is plain that the speakers in the book strongly desire their pain to end. They do not claim innocence, but they do wonder, in normal lament fashion, 'how long' the punishment will last. This desire for punishment to end clearly indicates that the Day of the Lord mentioned in Lamentations has already occurred, although this fact does not preclude other time frames for other types of the Day of the Lord. Indeed, some of the book's prayers at least imply that the people hope that promises like those found in Isaiah 2:1–5 and 4:2–6 will occur now.

Chapter 3 offers the clearest explanation of God's character as it relates to the Day of the Lord in the book. Having already detailed the implications of

---

46. Note my comments in Garrett and House, *Song of Songs/Lamentations*, pp. 357–358, etc.

47. B. G. Webb, *Five Festal Garments: Christian Reflections on The Song of Songs, Ruth, Lamentations, Ecclesiastes, and Esther* NSBT (Leicester: Apollos; Downers Grove: InterVarsity Press, 2000), p. 79.

the Day of the Lord in chapters 1–2, the book now highlights a man who has suffered for his own sins (see 3:1–18; 3:39). Hope has left him (3:17–18), yet recalling Yahweh's faithfulness, covenantal steadfast love and compassion restores that same lost hope (3:19–24). In other words, the traits outlined in Exodus 34:6–7 give reason for hope now. Further, the 'man' states that it is good to bear the yoke of judgment quietly while waiting on the Lord, for Yahweh does not cast off forever (3:31). What occurred was necessary, but not from Yahweh's heart (3:33). In other words, Yahweh is gracious and compassionate, but will not clear the guilty even though this 'not clearing' requires the Day of the Lord in this case. The fact that the speakers in Lamentations pray for renewal indicates that they may also draw on Deuteronomy 30:1–10 as the basis for hope.

Chapters 4 and 5 also utilize imagery from Leviticus 26 and Deuteronomy 28 to describe what the Day of the Lord has been like (see 4:1–17; 5:2–18). They also confess that sin has caused the catastrophe (see 4:13; 5:7; 5:16), consider exile the final result of the Day of the Lord (4:15–16, 22) and realize that only Yahweh can restore their fortunes (4:22; 5:19–22). They compare Jerusalem's conquest to the fall of Sodom (4:6). They confess that restoration resides in a renewed relationship with the sovereign God (5:21–22).

Lamentations serves as an excellent model of the Writings' viewpoint on the Day of the Lord for several reasons. First, it asserts that the destruction of Jerusalem was a Day of the Lord. Such days occur in the midst of human history, not just at the end of time. Second, although it treats a past Day of the Lord, the book in no way ignores the possibility – indeed the inevitability – of more cosmic instances of the Day of the Lord. Thus Lamentations should not be pitted against Daniel, for example. Third, it utilizes images from Leviticus 26 and Deuteronomy 28, a strategy appropriate for describing a Day of the Lord related to the covenant people. Judgment fell because of sin. Ethical conduct matters a great deal to Yahweh. Fourth, its images of Jerusalem's desolation provide a backdrop for some important New Testament passages. Fifth, it notes the presence of innocent parties swept up in the Day of the Lord. Children are particularly vulnerable persons in this regard. Sixth, it reveals that God's character remains as it was explained in Exodus 34:6–7. God warned of punishment long before it unfolded (see Lam. 1:21; 2:17), and the punishment was not from God's heart (3:31–33). It was not his first reaction to the sin. Thus the Day of the Lord occurs because of ingrained, determined sin, in the midst of human history as well as at its end, through the means of divine judgment. The wicked and the righteous alike are affected by the Day of the Lord. Nonetheless, when the 'day' is over a remnant still exists. Yahweh still maintains a covenantal relationship with his people.

Daniel 7 and 9: the Son of Man and the kingdom of God

The authorship and date of the book of Daniel have been debated for decades. Regardless of one's opinion on the book's composition, it is clear that the events in Daniel 1–6 depict the activities of Israelite exiles in Babylon, much as Esther describes the activities of Israelite exiles in Persia. Both books make it clear how difficult it was to be an exile, to be an Israelite living after the Day of the Lord that befell Jerusalem in 587 BC. Daniel 7 includes a key ingredient in the Old Testament's portrait of judgment: the Son of Man to whom the Lord will give the kingdom of God. Daniel 9 adds yet another key component, which is the desire to pray for renewal after the Day of the Lord has come. Although the term 'Day of the Lord' does not appear in the book, the concept is nonetheless present.

Daniel receives the vision described in chapter 7 in the first year Belshazzar receives authority from his father. Therefore the vision occurs c. 556 BC. This vision parallels Nebuchadnezzar's dream in chapter 2, so its contents were applicable to succeeding generations. This occurrence of the vision when a new ruler rises indicates that God's plans for the human race continue constant in the midst of changing circumstances. It may appear that human rulers are in control of international events, but Yahweh remains the ruler of rulers. Such assurances in exilic times were likely intended to hearten Daniel's readers.

The vision commences with Daniel seeing four quarrelling beasts/kings (7:1–8). Two scenes then follow that highlight Yahweh's sovereign rule. First, God, called here 'the Ancient of Days' (7:9), takes his throne in heaven and begins to judge. He takes power from the arrogant beasts and prepares to give authority to someone else. This God is eternal, for he is older than days. Daniel's phraseology connects in content with the 'I am' statement in Exodus 3:14, the declaration that 'from everlasting to everlasting you are God' (Ps. 90:2), and the assertion that the heavens will change, 'but you are ever the same' (Ps. 102:26–27). There is no time when the 'Ancient of Days' did not rule, and this king will rule for ever.

With this true and lasting ruler of rulers presented, Daniel sees the 'Ancient of Days' give the final, everlasting kingdom to one 'like the son of man' (7:13–14). Yahweh may give the kingdom to whomever he wills, for all the kingdoms of earth are his. The 'son of man' is a heavenly being worthy and capable of ruling for ever (7:13–14). No mention of the Davidic promise appears here, but Gerhard von Rad states that only a messianic figure could be given the kingdom of God at this juncture of the Old Testament.[48] Walter

---

48. Von Rad, *Old Testament Theology, Volume 2*, p. 309.

Kaiser claims that this person 'would not only be the true David, but He would also be the true Son of Man, combining in His person the high calling of humanity and the position reserved alone for God'.[49]

When the 'son of man' receives the kingdom he does not keep it for himself. Rather, he shares it with 'the holy ones of the Most High' (7:18, 22, 27, my translation). This group will suffer persecution before they share the kingdom (7:25). They will triumph only because 'the Ancient of Days' comes and sits in judgment (7:26–27). These 'holy ones' are 'the remnant' introduced in earlier texts, and the event mentioned is the Day of the Lord.[50] The fourth kingdom, which is a dreadful and persecuting kingdom, will be succeeded by a permanent kingdom led by the 'son of man' and populated by 'the holy ones'.

This notion of the kingdom of God gave hope to faithful persons waiting for deliverance from exile and from terrible conditions in the Promised Land. Aware of Jeremiah's prediction of a seventy-year exile (Jer. 25:12), Daniel prays for mercy and forgiveness in the light of Israel's sin (Dan. 9:1–9). Yahweh warned the people, yet they rebelled (9:12). The law of Moses promised such things, yet the people ignored the word of God (9:13). Nonetheless, Daniel is certain that Yahweh will restore the city and people (9:16–19). Later, both Ezra (Ezra 9) and Nehemiah (Neh. 9) pray in a similar manner. As the Old Testament ends, the people long for renewal. In or out of the land, the people pray and wait for the kingdom of God to come.

The Day of the Lord and the Son of Man: the Gospels

From its first episodes the New Testament announces imminent judgment. In fact, based on Jesus' identification of John the Baptist as Elijah (see Mal. 4:5–6; Matt. 17:9–13; Mark 9:9–13), 'the great . . . day of the LORD' (Mal. 4:5) is near. It appears, then, that the coming of the 'kingdom of God', which is announced by John and Jesus as at hand (see Matt. 3:1–12; Mark 1:4–8; Luke 3:1–17), and the Day of the Lord are closely related events. This fact is not surprising given the Old Testament's insistence on God's intervention in history for the purpose of establishing his reign on earth (see Pss. 93–99; 103:19; Dan. 7–12; etc). As G. R. Beasley-Murray writes, 'In the Old Testament, the ultimate

49. Walter C. Kaiser Jr, *Toward an Old Testament Theology* (Grand Rapids: Zondervan, 1978), p. 246.

50. Maurice Casey, *Son of Man: The Interpretation and Influence of Daniel 7* (London: SPCK, 1979), p. 23.

purpose of the future coming of the Lord and the day of the Lord is the establishment of the kingdom of God'.[51] This future coming of the kingdom of
God may well equate with idealistic scenes such as those in Isaiah 4:2–6;
65:17–25 and Zephaniah 3:8–20.

The kingdom of God and the Day of the Lord

What is this kingdom of God? Edward Meadors writes that the term 'com-
municates the power, authority, justice, righteousness, eternal nature, and
salvific plan of God'. It 'calls to mind the cosmic rule or kingship which the
Jews exclusively associated with their God YHWH'. Thus it indicates a present
reality. Meadors adds, 'Equally apparent in the Synoptic Gospels, however, is
the idea of the kingdom of God as the future realm to be set up by God at the
end of the age.'[52] Thus it also relates a future reality. Michael Lattke agrees with
this assessment. Following a description of Second Temple sources on the
matter, he concludes:

> What we can say with certainty for the (earlier) period in question is that Palestinian
> Pharisees and the scribes used to talk about God as king and of his royal rule.
> Further, it is clear that this kingdom had a two-fold aspect. Both aspects – of the
> present and of the eschatological future – are grounded in and connected with the
> self-revelation of the one God and of the Torah which this revelation enjoins, and at
> most only secondarily with the concept of creation.[53]

Biblically speaking, it is the Day of the Lord that underscores God's current
rule over the earth and that also brings this future reality to final fruition.

Judgment has begun: the ministry of John the Baptist

John the Baptist's preaching links present and future aspects of judgment. It
also links this judgment to the kingdom of God. Luke may offer the most
succinct account of this link between the kingdom of God and the Day of

---

51. G. R. Beasley-Murray, *Jesus and the Kingdom of God* (Grand Rapids: Eerdmans, 1986),
p. 17.

52. Edward P. Meadors, *Jesus the Messianic Herald of Salvation*, WUNT 2:72 (Tübingen: J.
C. B. Mohr [Paul Siebeck], 1995), p. 154.

53. Michael Lattke, 'On the Jewish Background of the Synoptic Concept, "The
Kingdom of God"', in Bruce Chilton (ed.), *The Kingdom of God in the Teaching of
Jesus*, Issues in Religion and Theology 5 (Philadelphia: Fortress Press, 1984), p. 87.
This volume reprints Lattke's 1975 article.

the Lord. In Luke 3:1–17 (see also Matt. 3:1–10) John calls for repentance, announces the Christ's coming and claims that the Christ will judge sinners. The reason for which they must repent is the fact that they are living in a time of judgment. 'Indeed, the axe is already placed against the root of the trees' (3:9).[54] This fact is true for Abraham's heirs, not just for Gentiles (3:8). Werner G. Kummel notes that such preaching is like that found in Amos. He then adds:

> But John actualizes this traditional preaching of judgment in a twofold fashion. First, he takes away from his hearers any possibility of pushing aside the threat of judgment as far as they themselves are concerned, by saying to them that the judgment has *already* begun . . . Further, the Baptist destroys the elusive hope that God will judge a Jew less strictly . . . Not only is the Baptist's preaching of judgment in this way directed at each individual with the same urgency, but the relationship of man to God in principle is defined solely by his being human, and no longer by his belonging to the Jewish people or to any other human group.[55]

His preaching of immediate danger leads hearers to ask what they must do now (3:10). His response is also Amos-like. They must repent. They must adjust their lives to God's word (3:11–14).

John's preaching in Luke 3:15–17 also draws on several Old Testament images, but particularly on texts where the wicked are promised fire that will remove their sins (see Isa. 13:8; 66:15–16; Zeph. 3:8; etc). A mightier one is coming, and he will baptize with the Holy Spirit and with fire (3:16). This one has the power and will to judge. The wicked will burn like chaff on the Day of the Lord. Thus John places the Christ squarely in futuristic Day of the Lord theology, just as Jesus places John in this context by referring to him as Elijah. Whatever else one may conclude from these identifications, one must deal with Jesus' ministry as part of the Day of the Lord and deal with the implications of this conclusion.

John's linking of repentance to his proclamation of the Day of the Lord underscores the possibility of avoiding wrath. God remains merciful. John's preaching produces disciples who are in effect the new remnant of Israel and of the nations (see Luke 3:11–14). Marius Reiser writes:

---

54. This translation appears in John Nolland, *Luke 1–9:20*, WBC 35A (Nashville: Thomas Nelson, 1989), p. 146.

55. Werner G. Kummel, *The Theology of the New Testament According to its Major Witnesses, Jesus – Paul – John*, trans. J. E. Steely (London: SCM, 1974), p. 28.

Therefore Matthew and Luke were not entirely incorrect in saying that the Baptizer preached 'good news' and the approach of the reign of God (Luke 3:18; Matt. 3:2), even though judgment stood in the forefront of his preaching, and in fact the whole of his preaching can be called 'preaching of judgment.' The judge has already laid on the axe, and has the winnowing shovel in hand. The day of the Lord is near. Repent and be baptized by me, so that you may escape the punishing judgment! That is the message of the Baptizer.[56]

The Son of Man and judgment: the ministry of Jesus

Jesus' preaching and parables indicate that he agreed with John's usage of the Day of the Lord traditions. First, his assertion that 'the time is fulfilled, and the kingdom of God has drawn near' (Mark 1:15, my translation) parallels John's urgent message of repentance. Writing about the intent of 'drawn near', James Dunn argues, 'The force of the verb is also clear: the perfect tense (*engiken*) here indicates an action already performed and resulting in a state or effect which continues into the present. It is not a timeless nearness which is in mind; something had happened to bring the kingdom near.'[57] This 'something' is the sending of Elijah and the Son of Man to declare the time of judgment for the unbelieving wicked and the time of deliverance for the faithful believers.

Second, Jesus' parables emphasize the growth of the kingdom in the world as believers accept and live according to Jesus' teachings. They also indicate that judgment will come at an unspecified point in the future. Both this growth and the time of judgment will seem to come very slowly. Nonetheless, both will occur. Commenting on the 'Parable of the Sower' (Mark 4:16–29), David Wenham writes:

Jesus is explaining . . . that he has indeed brought the kingdom of God, but he is like a farmer who sows the crop and then waits patiently for the harvest. It would be silly for the farmer to hurry or anticipate the harvest. So Jesus implies that his work will lead to the harvest of divine judgment on the last day, but in the meantime there has to be patient waiting in the confidence that the work of the kingdom will come to harvest.[58]

---

56. Marius Reiser, *Jesus and Judgment: The Eschatological Proclamation in Its Jewish Context*, trans. L. M. Maloney (Minneapolis: Fortress Press, 1997), p. 193.

57. James D. G. Dunn, *Jesus Remembered*, Christianity in the Making: Volume 1 (Grand Rapids: Eerdmans, 2003), p. 407.

58. David Wenham, *The Parables of Jesus*, The Jesus Library (Downers Grove: InterVarsity Press, 1989), pp. 51–52.

Many other parables 'speak of a (final?) reckoning which the audiences need to anticipate now: the talent/pounds (Matt. 25:14–30/Luke 19:11–27), the unmerciful servant handed over finally to the torturers/jailers . . . until the unpayable debt is paid in full (Matt. 18:23–25), the unjust steward (Luke 16:1–8), and the uncaring rich man, whose fate to be tormented . . . is simply taken for granted (Luke 16:19–31)'.[59] Clearly, one's response to the message that judgment has 'drawn near' in the sense of 'having already begun' (see above) has implications for the time when judgment will be completed. After all, one can meet final judgment through death at any time.

Jesus makes it clear that the judgment he announces as having 'drawn near' and the judgment he says will come in the future are both executed by the 'Son of Man', a term he applies to himself.[60] Indeed, in Luke 17:22 Jesus warns his disciples that in the future they will 'desire to see one of the days of the Son of Man, and you will not see it'. They will wish for a 'day' of judgment to deliver them from their enemies. To be sure, the Son of Man will judge on 'his day' (Luke 17:24), but first the Son of Man 'must suffer many things and be rejected by this generation' (17:25). Thus Jesus links the Son of Man of Daniel 7:13–14 to the 'Suffering Servant' of Isaiah 50:4–9 and 52:13–53:12. Mark 14:62 indicates that he also does so in his trial before the authorities. Jesus has come 'to cast fire on the earth' (Luke 12:49), which he can do only through the 'baptism' of suffering and death (Luke 12:50).

John's Gospel agrees with this emphasis on the Son of Man and judgment. In 12:27–36, Jesus asserts that his coming death amounts to 'the judgment of the world', for it means that the 'ruler of this world' will be 'cast out' (12:31). It is only as he is lifted up from the earth, a reference to his death (12:32), that he will draw all people to himself (12:32). His exaltation as victor over sin and its ruler requires death on the part of the Son of Man. Those who believe this teaching walk in the light, but those who fail to believe walk in darkness (12:35–36). Everything depends on the Son of Man's judgment of sin through death prior to receiving the kingdom from the Father.

After his suffering Jesus is the Son of Man to whom the Ancient of Days gives the kingdom of God, and the one who gives the 'holy ones of God' the kingdom to share with him. He receives this exalted status by his resurrection

59. Dunn, *Jesus Remembered*, pp. 421–422.

60. For a succinct discussion of the term and its authenticity on the lips of Jesus, consult I. Howard Marshall, *The Origins of New Testament Christology, Updated Edition* (Leicester: Apollos; Downers Grove: InterVarsity Press, 1990), pp. 63–82.

from the dead, an event he predicted in Mark 8:31; 9:31 and Luke 9:21–22.[61]
By the end of the Gospels the Son of Man has preached the onset of judgment, has proclaimed himself both Son of Man and Suffering Servant, has
died to judge sin, and has been raised to receive the kingdom from the Ancient
of Days. Jesus thereby proves himself the one who will and does give the
kingdom to the holy ones, the remnant of God's people. The final giving of
the kingdom will occur when he comes to judge for the last time.

Near the end of his ministry, Jesus makes statements about the future of
Jerusalem and this coming of the end of time. Of course, scholars have long
debated whether Jesus treats these subjects as two events separated by an
unspecified length of time, as two parts of the same event, or through some
other construct. Regardless of their conclusions on these matters, interpreters
typically recognize that Jesus threatens the destruction of Jerusalem in terms
similar to those found in the prophetic literature and in Lamentations. Many
also agree that Matthew 24, Mark 13 and Luke 21 deal with the end of time as
one of their topics.

Using Luke as representative of the other Gospels, Luke 21:5–6 clearly
states that the magnificent buildings the disciples point out to Jesus will some
day be destroyed. Jesus then details the horrors associated with such a destruction in 21:10–24, in language that could just as easily appear in Deuteronomy
28:52–57 or Lamentations 4:1–17. Jesus then refers to the end of time, which
he associates with the coming of the Son of Man introduced in Daniel 7:13–14
(Luke 21:25–28). He concludes with a warning to make sure 'that day', a
common Old Testament abbreviation for the Day of the Lord, does not take
them by surprise (Luke 21:34). He also warns that this day will come on all who
are on the face of the earth (Luke 21:35–36; see Zeph. 1:2–6). As in 21:27, he
states that the Son of Man will be the judge (21:36).

Matthew and Mark contain similar images that have roots in Day of the
Lord texts. For example, Matthew 23:29–39 paints the current scene in terms
very similar to the prophetic era. Indeed, the people kill the prophets and stone
God's messengers. All this happens in spite of Jesus' preaching and teaching.
Because of their rebellion, their house will be left desolate and forsaken,
phraseology common in Old Testament judgment texts (see Isa. 64:11; Jer.
12:7; 22:5), and will remain so until they acknowledge God's anointed one.
Jesus then proceeds to describe the destruction of Jerusalem and the end of
the world in 24:1–35. He concludes by noting that no one knows when 'that

---

61. C. H. Dodd, *The Parables of the Kingdom*, rev. ed. (New York: Scribner's, 1961),
    pp. 73–77.

day', the Day of the Son of Man, will occur, so all must be watchful (24:36–51). Mark 13 follows a process very similar to that in Matthew 24:1–35, then concludes with a warning to watch, lest 'that day' come as a surprise. The term 'that day' refers both to the final judgment and to the destruction of Jerusalem in AD 70.

As has been argued above, using Son of Man imagery raises the stakes for Jesus' hearers. The presence of the Son of Man means that the Day of the Lord has come and the kingdom of God is on earth. Therefore, repentance must occur soon, for destruction associated with these facts may happen at any time. The 'holy ones' (see Dan. 7:18, 21, 27) must place their faith in the Son of Man now, for the one entrusted with the kingdom of God could remove earthly powers and their sinful adherents at any time. With 'Elijah' and the Son of Man on the scene, hearers ought to fear the Lord and repent, the very things the prophets ask their people to do. As the Gospels make clear, however, not all respond. Instead, the people will kill both messengers of judgment. Ironically, this means that at any time they could face the wrath of Jesus Christ, the resurrected Son of God, who is now and always will be the judge of the wicked.

These passages also underscore God's mercy. After all, the very presence of the Christ, God's anointed Son, indicates God's desire to warn and forgive (see Mark 12:1–11, especially 12:6). His preaching, as well as that of John the Baptist and Jesus' disciples, is intended to turn people to God, just as their forebears' preaching was. Christ's grief over Jerusalem in Matthew 23:37–39 demonstrates his personal concern for his hearers. Thus his kindness parallels God's in Exodus 34:6–7 as surely as his unwillingness to clear the guilty does. His first impulse is mercy, not punishment.

Although one has to be cautious at this point, it is possible to state that Jesus speaks in these passages in a manner very much as, for example, Isaiah does in Isaiah 1–4 or Zephaniah does in Zephaniah 1:2–3:20. That is, Jesus, like these prophets, speaks definitively about the demise of Jerusalem. The city will fall, and its mothers and children will suffer greatly. With little if any pause, he then states that the world will be judged. As in Isaiah 2, both near and distant judgment are mentioned in a short space with the expectation that the hearers will know enough about the nature of the Day of the Lord to distinguish judgment that occurs now to punish sin and judgment that will occur to punish sin and remove it forever.

Like the prophets, Jesus also expects his disciples to live in a way that reflects their belief in and adherence to the kingdom of God. This point is especially clear in Jesus' parables. They live in the kingdom he has established, yet they must wait for this kingdom to span the entire earth. Therefore, it is fair to conclude with G. E. Ladd that the Gospels agree with the ethical concerns of the Old Testament writers:

> Therefore the warning of the nearness of the Day of the Lord is more a note of ethical exhortation than it is a chronological reference . . . God *did* act. The Day of the Lord *did* come; and yet, the Day of the Lord continued to be an eschatological event in the future. This tension between the immediate and the ultimate future, between history and eschatology, stands at the heart of the ethical concern of the prophetic perspective. For the important thing is not what is going to happen and when it will happen, but the will of God, who is Lord of both the far and the near future, for his people in the present.[62]

Conclusion

This survey of the Gospels indicates that John the Baptist and Jesus have much in common with the Old Testament writers' conception of the Day of the Lord. First, they agree with the Old Testament writers on the timing of the Day of the Lord. Judgment may occur now, in the near future, and in the distant future as the conclusion of human history. John warned that the time had come, much as Joel warned his people in his era. Jesus foretold the fall of Jerusalem in terms very similar to those Jeremiah offered prior to the first destruction of Jerusalem (see Jer. 7; 26). Both stressed the final Day of the Lord as a time when sin will be burned from the earth, a point made by both Zephaniah and Malachi. They also claimed that Jesus is the one who judges. His presence on earth in the first century AD and in the final century AD means that the Judge/Deliverer is on the scene.

Second, they agree with the Old Testament writers on the recipients of the Day of the Lord. All persons face judgment now and will face judgment at the end of time. Jews and Gentiles are included in these teachings (see Luke 3:1–17). All nations and individuals in this world are at risk. They are all in danger of darkness (John 12:27–36).

Third, they agree with the Old Testament writers on the proper response to the proclamation of the coming Day of the Lord. Hearers and readers must believe the word (John 12:27–36). They must repent and live as God's holy ones (Luke 3:1–17; 13:1–3). They must serve the Lord as they anticipate giving an account of their lives (Matt. 25:31–46). They must wait patiently and faithfully

---

62. G. E. Ladd, *The Presence of the Future: The Eschatology of Biblical Realism* (Grand Rapids: Eerdmans, 1974), p. 75.

for the kingdom to come in all its fullness. Indeed, they must pray in hope for the kingdom to come (Matt. 6:9–13; Luke 11:2–4). For them the kingdom has come, for the Lord Jesus Christ has come. The Son of Man who is also the Suffering Servant has come. Nonetheless, the kingdom awaits the Son of Man's cleansing of the earth. The Ancient of Days has given the kingdom to the Son of Man, but the Son of Man waits to give the kingdom to the holy ones. This future giving of the kingdom is, however, as certain as the Son of Man's victory over death.

The Pauline epistles: the Day of the Lord Jesus (1–2 Thessalonians)

Paul's usage of the Day of the Lord continues to reflect ideas found in the Old Testament and in the Gospels, yet he also fits Jesus into the patterns in distinctive ways. Most of his direct references to the 'day' indicate his interest in the vindication of his ministry and of his people on the final 'day' of judgment. The former concern occurs in 2 Corinthians 1:14 and 2 Timothy 1:18, the latter interest is evident in 1 Corinthians 1:8 and 2 Timothy 1:18, and both are present in Philippians 2:16. Strikingly, in 1 Corinthians 1:8 he calls the Day of the Lord the 'day of our Lord Jesus Christ'. He calls it 'the day of our Lord Jesus' in 2 Corinthians 1:14, and calls it the 'day of Christ' in Philippians 2:16. He utilizes typical Day of the Lord images in 2 Timothy 4:8, yet ascribes to Jesus the judging qualities that the Old Testament assigns to Yahweh. Thus Paul claims for Jesus the name and activities of Yahweh and thereby attributes to Jesus the same type of equality in judgment that he gives him in ruling in Philippians 2:5–11. The Day of the Lord is truly the Day of the Lord Jesus Christ.

Paul's letters to the Thessalonians provide a more detailed glimpse into his views on the Day of the Lord. Here he uses terminology very close to Old Testament and Gospel texts while highlighting Jesus' role as Saviour, Judge and Helper. Scholars have long believed that 1 and 2 Thessalonians are either the earliest or among the earliest of the Pauline corpus, having been written soon after AD 49–50.[63] The first letter begins by reminding readers how they came to Christ and of the basic elements of the faith (1:1–10). Next Paul expresses his relationship to them (2:1–3:13). Then the apostle exhorts the Thessalonians to maintain high standards of Christian living in view of the coming Day of the Lord (4:1–5:11). He finishes the epistle with general exhortations and a conclusion (5:12–28).

---

63. F. F. Bruce, *1 & 2 Thessalonians*, WBC 45 (Waco: Word, 1982), pp. xxxiv–xxxv.

In the second letter Paul gives thanks for the people (1:1–12), then turns once again to the subject of the Day of the Lord, this time to clear up some misconceptions (2:1–12). He then encourages the people (2:13–17), stresses God's faithfulness and the necessity of godly living (3:1–15) and closes the epistle (3:16–18).[64] Even this cursory glance at the letters' contents highlights the centrality of the Day of the Lord in both and the importance of ethical living in the light of this coming day. Thus ethics, the wrath of God and the future all receive vital treatment, just as they do in Old Testament and Gospel passages.

Paul discusses God's wrath in 1 Thessalonians even before the section devoted to the Day of the Lord. Having introduced the concept of Jesus' coming bringing wrath from heaven in 1:10, in 2:13–17 he thanks God that the Thessalonians have believed the gospel. Next he compliments them for being willing to suffer for their faith (2:13–14). He then notes that the Jews have persecuted the church, having already killed Jesus and the prophets (2:15). Now they hinder gospel preaching, but 'God's wrath has come upon them at last', which could also be translated 'has come upon them completely/fully' (2:16), depending on how one interprets *eis telos*.

Leon Morris notes the unprecedented nature of Paul's condemnation of his ethnic people, observes that Paul speaks like an Old Testament prophet, and concludes that the condemnation is 'unqualified, and that the final expression indicative of the eschatological wrath leaves no hope for the future'.[65] Morris decides that the wrath is in the future, even though he observes that the aorist tense 'often denotes past action, but here the wrath is surely eschatological, and therefore future'.[66] John Stott agrees with Morris's reading, although he writes that the interpretation of the events as in the past could indicate that

> Paul may be seeing the arrival of God's judgment in such events as the unprecedented famine in Judea of AD 45–47, the brutal massacre of Jews in the temple precincts at Passover AD 49 (described by Josephus), and in the same year the expulsion of the Jews from Rome by the emperor Claudius. Since 1 Thessalonians was probably written in AD 50, these were all at the time vivid, recent events.[67]

---

64. See L. Morris, *The Epistles of Paul to the Thessalonians: An Introduction and Commentary*, TNTC (Grand Rapids: Eerdmans, 1958), pp. 31, 112.

65. Ibid., p. 57.

66. Ibid., pp. 56–57.

67. J. R. W. Stott, *The Gospel at the End of Time: The Message of 1–2 Thessalonians* (Downers Grove: InterVarsity Press, 1991), p. 57.

F. F. Bruce claims that the verses have strong similarities to Matthew 23:34–36, which means that Paul may be drawing either on the synoptic tradition or on a pre-synoptic tradition.[68] Commenting on 2:15–16, he writes, 'The "wrath" which is here said to have overtaken the [Jews] is an instance of the "coming wrath" (1:10) from which Jesus delivers his people. Without further delay it has come upon these [Jews] already. They have reached the point of no return in their opposition to the gospel and final, irremediable retribution is inevitable; indeed, it has come'.[69] Bruce then notes the problem of considering Paul's assertions of final irremediable wrath here and his statement about a partial hardening of the Jews until a better time, which he propounds in Romans 9–11. Having suggested several solutions to the dilemma, Bruce does not offer a firm resolution.[70] It seems, then, that Bruce also treats the Day of the Lord mentioned here as of necessity meaning final wrath.

David Wenham suggests the past tense is the best way to understand the passage, for he translates the text as 'the wrath has come upon them [the Jews] finally'.[71] He notes that *eis telos* appears in Jesus' teaching in Matthew 24:13 and Mark 13:13, and that those passages denounce the Jews who do not believe in Jesus and who kill God's messengers in terms very much like 2:13–16. He further comments that Matthew, Mark and 1 Thessalonians 2:13–16 all speak of persecution in the light of taking the gospel to the Gentiles. Finally, noting the likeness between Luke 21:23 and 1 Thessalonians 2:16, he asserts that Paul draws on his knowledge of Jesus' teaching to indeed claim that the events of AD 49 mean that wrath has come on his ethnic people.[72] Wenham summarizes his opinion concerning 2:16 by writing:

> Scholars have found the idea incomprehensible and the language un-Pauline, with some therefore suggesting that it is a gloss. However, there is a good case for saying that, if the language is un-Pauline, this is because Paul is here drawing on traditions of Jesus, such as Luke 21:23, which speaks of wrath coming on the Jews. Furthermore, the idea makes very good sense in the historical context of AD 49 when Paul was writing 1 Thessalonians, because disaster had struck Jerusalem and the Jews at that

---

68. Bruce, *1 & 2 Thessalonians*, p. 43.

69. Ibid., p. 48.

70. Ibid., pp. 48–49.

71. D. Wenham, 'From Jesus to Paul – via Luke', in P. Bolt and M. Thompson (eds.), *The Gospel to the Nations: Perspectives on Paul's Mission* (Leicester: Apollos; Downers Grove: InterVarsity Press, 2000), p. 94.

72. D. Wenham, *Paul and Jesus: The True Story* (Grand Rapids: Eerdmans, 2002), p. 105.

very time. The disaster was twofold: first, Claudius had expelled the Jews from Rome, which the historian Suetonius tells us was because they were 'rioting at the instigation of Chrestus' (*Cl.* 25:4) . . . In the same year there was a catastrophe for the Jews in Palestine, as Josephus tells us: a Roman soldier in Jerusalem acted indecently in the temple area, in such a way as to infuriate the Jews, who protested *en masse*. When the Roman governor responded to their protest with violent force, there was mayhem, and Josephus tells us that twenty or thirty thousand people were killed as a result . . . And it seems quite likely that Paul saw the disaster striking the Jews in Rome and Jerusalem . . . as the beginning of what Jesus had predicted – namely the desolation of the city of Jerusalem at the hands of Gentiles.[73]

One can certainly argue the merits of one or the other reading of the verse. What should not be done, however, is to *assume* that the judgment Paul mentions must be final judgment, as Morris, Bruce and Stott may do. After all, Stott observes that the wrath in 1:10 seems to be future, but the judgment in 2:16 seems to be completely or partially past. He then argues that the wrath in 2:16 should be interpreted as future. Morris makes a more detailed linguistic case, yet reaches the same conclusion. Bruce nuances the case still more, but does not then have a way out of the dilemma noted above.

If one concludes that Paul believes the Old Testament teaches that judgment can occur now or later, then one may have another option. Paul cites Jesus' concern with Jerusalem's destruction, as Wenham asserts. Thus Paul views what Jerusalem suffers as birth pangs before the end (see Luke 21:20–24), so there is no compelling need to make the wrath mentioned solely eschatological wrath. Paul can indeed conclude that the day of wrath, the Day of the Lord, has come on a specific group, in this case the Jews. He can at the same time indeed view this Day of the Lord as a serious, yet penultimate, case of judgment. In short, he can treat the Day of the Lord as the Old Testament writers, John the Baptist and Jesus did.

On the other hand, 1 Thessalonians 4:13–5:11 deals primarily with the final judgment.[74] At the same time, this final judgment has present significance for those who must live now in the light of the final Day of the Lord. Paul exhorts these new believers to holy living, particularly in the areas of sexuality and loving Christian brothers and sisters, so that they can command the respect of

---

73. Wenham, 'From Jesus to Paul', pp. 94–95.

74. For an excellent, succinct summary of this passage and of 2 Thessalonians 1:3–12, see T. R. Schreiner, *Paul, Apostle of God's Glory in Christ: A Pauline Theology* (Downers Grove: InterVarsity Press; Leicester: Apollos, 2001), pp. 459–471.

outsiders (4:1–12). Paul then comforts the readers concerning their departed loved ones in 4:13–18, and reminds them that the Day of the Lord will come like a thief, just as Jesus warned in the Gospels (5:1–3; see Matt. 24:43; Luke 17:24). He further asserts that they must be sober, filled with love and committed to faith and hope (5:4–11). Nothing less is fitting for those who are not destined for wrath (5:9), and who are therefore not those mentioned in 1:10 and 2:16.

In 2 Thessalonians, Paul addresses the matter of judgment immediately. He begins with thanks for the church's steadfastness in the face of persecution (1:3–4). Next he asserts that the people's suffering is part of God's 'righteous judgment' (1:5). He claims that it is God's will that this suffering make them worthy of the kingdom of God (1:5), repay those who afflict them (1:6) and grant rest to the afflicted when Jesus comes to earth to judge the wicked and be glorified with his saints (1:7–10). He calls the time of Jesus' coming 'that day' (1:10). Thus God's righteous plan includes *both* making the people fit for the kingdom through their suffering *and* the punishing of 'those who do not obey the gospel of our Lord Jesus' (1:8). Given this situation, Paul prays that the people may prove worthy of their calling to suffering and that they may glorify Christ (1:11–12). Thus God's plan for the church and for unbelievers contains present and future aspects. Once again ethics have a vital place in the application of Day of the Lord teaching, as they have since the Law.

With this theology of judgment in place, Paul clears up the misconception that the Day of the Lord has already come, a mistake one could easily make given the flexible nature of the term. Indeed, it is possible that the Thessalonians misunderstood Paul's first letter in this regard. The particular Day of the Lord that Paul addresses here is clearly final judgment. Paul writes that, before that Day of the Lord comes, 'the man of lawlessness' must emerge (2:3–4; see Dan. 7:23–27). While he was with them, Paul had told them that something or someone was restraining the coming of the lawless one (2:5–6). Lawlessness is already present, he continues, yet not fully realized (2:7). This lawless one will do great signs and will be the messenger of Satan (2:9), and God will send a strong delusion so that those who do not believe the truth will be condemned (2:11–12). Perhaps most importantly, the Lord Jesus will kill the lawless one with 'the breath of his mouth' (2:8). As in the first letter, Paul includes ethical exhortations to live industriously and fruitfully while waiting for that day to come (3:6–15).

This overly brief survey of 1 and 2 Thessalonians yields some vital information about Paul's theology of the Day of the Lord. First, the Day of the Lord is the 'day of the Lord Jesus'. The Lord Jesus is the Son of Man of Daniel

7 and the Gospels. Indeed, he is Yahweh (see Phil. 2:5–11), so the Day of the Lord is his day. He is the one who defeats the lawless one (see Dan. 7:23–27), the one who will lead God's armies (see 1 Thess. 4:16–18; Joel 2:11), the one who will judge and give life (see Ps. 96:10–13). Paul alludes to multiple images from the Old Testament to make these points.

Second, the Day of the Lord occurs now as well as at the end of time. In this viewpoint Paul follows the prophets and Jesus. In particular, like Jesus he teaches that this judgment has already begun for the Jews, and that it will get worse (see Matt. 23:23–39). He claims that persecution is part of the Day of the Lord in that it purifies and identifies the church and begins the process of punishing the church's enemies.

Third, he emphasizes godly living as a response to the day's coming. What the church suffers helps them realize the need for holy living, and it also reminds them that worse things await those who do not trust in Christ and follow his commands. Fourth, he asserts God's sovereignty over life's events and over the future. Fifth, his emphasis on God's restraining of wickedness once again highlights God's mercy and slowness to judge. God's character remains consistent.

These beliefs indicate the apostle's location in time (post-resurrection and post-teachings of Jesus) in that he confesses Jesus as the Lord of the Day of the Lord in obedience to Jesus' teachings. He confesses overtly what Jesus taught humbly about himself. These convictions also indicate that the church's suffering is not random or out of God's realm of control. In fact, current suffering is part of judgment. It is part of the Christian's sanctification from sin and at the same time it is part of the non-believer's experiencing of God's wrath for sin. Paul believes that what is happening now participates in the past and in the future. Judgment and redemption have not just been inaugurated; they have been inaugurated and continue to this day. Eventually they will be consummated. Finally, Paul believes that the coming of Christ, his own preaching and God's restraining of lawlessness underscore God's mercy.

The Day of the Lord Jesus and the life of the church: 1–2 Peter

It is not atypical for scholars to highlight the differences between Paul and Peter more than the beliefs that they share. Of course, part of the problem is that scholars do not agree on what books Paul and Peter wrote, so this fact alone hampers the discussion. It matters whether one includes, for example, the pastoral epistles in Pauline theology and 2 Peter in Petrine theology.

William Mounce's arguments[75] (and others') have convinced me of the authenticity of the pastorals, as have the arguments for the authenticity of 2 Peter that Donald Guthrie and Tom Schreiner offer.[76] Nevertheless, there remains the necessity of working on the nature of the unity and diversity of the two authors' epistles. One area of agreement between the two authors is the Day of the Lord and its role in the church of their day. Both apostles assert its biblical basis, its present role in the life of the church and its future impact on the world. Although this theme pervades both letters, this brief treatment will highlight 1 Peter 4:7–19 and 2 Peter 3:1–18 as representative passages.

In 1 Peter 4:7 the apostle states, 'The end of all things is at hand; therefore be self-controlled and sober-minded for the sake of your prayers.' This assertion comes after the apostle exhorts his readers to live 'for the will of God' instead of 'for human passions' (4:2). It also comes after he states that those who mock the readers for not sinning will 'give account to him who is ready to judge the living and the dead' (4:5). As Paul does in 1 Thessalonians 5:8, Peter presents love and mutual service as the necessary ingredients of the Christian life during times of suffering (4:7–11). Further, like Paul in 1 Thessalonians 1:3–12, Peter considers the suffering they encounter as evidence of the genuineness of their faith and as evidence that judgment has begun, in 4:12–19. He claims that judgment has begun with God's people, a fact that should make readers tremble for those who do not obey the gospel (4:17; see 2 Thess. 1:8). He concludes with a quotation from Proverbs 11:31 and an exhortation to suffer according to God's will while doing good instead of living as evildoers (4:18–19). Thus Peter considers judgment a current and future reality that helps explain what the church's suffering has to do with present believers' relationship to God, to outsiders and to one another. In other words, although details change from one epistle to another, Paul and Peter share these common emphases.

In 2 Peter 3:1–18 the apostle stresses the Day of the Lord as a time of final divine judgment. He anchors his comments on the theme in his readers' situation (suffering), in his experiences with Jesus (see 2 Pet. 1:16–19) and in the Old Testament Scriptures (see 2 Pet. 1:20–21). He begins by stating that both his letters have been written to stir up their 'sincere mind', or, in other words,

---

75. William D. Mounce, *Pastoral Epistles*, WBC 46 (Nashville: Thomas Nelson, 2000), pp. xlvi–cxxxvi.

76. Donald Guthrie, *New Testament Introduction* (Leicester: Inter-Varsity Press; Downers Grove: InterVarsity Press, 1976), pp. 820–848; T. R. Schreiner, *1–2 Peter and Jude*, NAC (Nashville: Broadman Press, 2003), pp. 21–36.

to strengthen them in difficult circumstances (3:1). He then reminds his readers that the prophets, Jesus and their apostles all agree that scoffers will arise in the last days. These scoffers will express doubts about whether God will ever judge (see 3:2–4; Isa. 5:19; Jer. 17:15; Zeph. 1:12; Mal. 2:17).

He writes that such people overlook the fact that God created the world by his word, then destroyed it by flood, and now waits until the appropriate time to consume it with fire (see 3:5–7; Gen. 6–9; Zeph. 1:12–18; Mal. 4:1–6). Zephaniah 1:12–16 indicates that the Lord will come looking for scoffers on the Day of the Lord. None of them will escape on this dark, bitter and frightening day. Zephaniah 1:17–18 states that on the Day of Yahweh 'the fire of his jealousy' will consume the earth suddenly and thoroughly. Just as Isaiah's and Zephaniah's readers could count on Yahweh's justice prevailing and the wicked falling, so Peter's readers could expect the same. Their enemies will not always have the upper hand.

Peter warns his people not to overlook God's fundamentally kind nature, drawn from Exodus 34:6–7, Joel 2:12–14, Jonah 3:8–4:2, Nahum 1:3 and elsewhere. God's character includes incredible patience. A day or a thousand years are the same to him (3:8; Ps. 90:4). Thus he is not slow to judge in the sense that he is unwilling or unable to do so, but because of his compassion (3:9; see Jon. 3:8–4:2). He bears with the ungodly for a time so that they can repent. This bearing with sinners is slowness to wrath, not a lack of justice on God's part. As Richard Bauckham writes, 'God's forbearance creates an interval, a period of respite, while judgment is deferred and a last opportunity for repentance is allowed.'[77] In other words, he is slow to anger (Exod. 34:6–7). But he will not clear the guilty (Exod. 34:6–7; see Nah. 1:3). Eventually the Day of the Lord will come as unexpectedly as a thief does (3:10; see Matt. 24:43), and the heavens and earth will be dissolved (3:10; see Isa. 24:19; Mic. 1:4; Nah. 1:5; Matt. 24:35). No one should mistake God's patience for weakness or indifference. Rather, they should expect every person's works to be exposed (3:10).

Peter concludes this section on the Day of the Lord with a call to holy living. Since these things are all to occur, the people should strive for holiness, wait for the day to come, and wait in hope of the new heaven and new earth where righteousness will dwell (3:11–13). The new heaven and new earth reference reminds readers of Isaiah 65:17–25. This emphasis on holy living signals substantial agreement with the apostle Paul, who stresses godliness in 1 Thessalonians 4:13–18 and 2 Thessalonians 1:3–12 in similar contexts (see also

---

77. Richard J. Bauckham, *Jude, 2 Peter*, WBC 50 (Waco: Word, 1983), p. 312.

Matt. 24:36–51). Both apostles remind readers to live in the midst of inaugurated and continuing judgment with a proper awareness of the implications of
final judgment (3:15–16). Indeed, Peter writes that Paul deals with such things
in his letters, documents Peter calls 'scripture' (3:16). Thus he treats Paul's
letters as 'part of the normative literature or canon of the church'.[78] Such
godly living is the correct response of those who believe that Jesus is the Lord
of the Day of the Lord, the Son of Man, the one who redeems them from the
wrath to come. Such is the response of persons avoiding lawlessness so that
they may grow in grace (3:17–18).

Conclusion

Peter's denunciation of false teachers, his understanding of the Day of the
Lord, his dependence on the authority of Scripture and his convictions about
holy living are all in keeping with earlier scriptures. He anchors his beliefs about
God's character in Exodus 34:6–7 and related passages. From these texts he
asserts that the delay of the consummation of the Day of the Lord stems from
mercy, not a lack of truthfulness in the apostolic teaching. He bases his belief
that God will destroy the world by fire on Genesis 6–9, from which he draws
an analogy to the flood. He also grounds it in Isaiah 5:18–24, Isaiah 65–66 and
Zephaniah 1:1–18, from which he links fire with the destruction of the earth
and the wicked, and on Mark 9:48, Luke 3:17 and 2 Thessalonians 1:9, where
Jesus, John the Baptist and Paul link judgment's suddenness to the world's fiery
end. He bases his warnings about holy living on prophetic calls to repentance.

   He supports his statements about Scripture in 2 Peter 1:16–21 by under-
scoring the accuracy and applicability of past prophetic words. He warns his
readers that a penultimate Day of the Lord can occur now. In short, his
approach to whole-Bible theology slowly buries the false teachers under the
weight of Scripture. As he does so, he provides an excellent summary of the
Bible's teaching on the Day of the Lord.

The New Testament's testimony to the unity of the Bible's presentation of the Day of the Lord

The New Testament writers adapt imagery from and agree with specific Old
Testament teachings about the Day of the Lord. This agreement displays

---

78. Bo Reicke, *The Epistles of James, Peter, and Jude*, AB 37 (Garden City: Doubleday,
   1964), p. 183.

variation and adaptation to the needs of the readers, to be sure, but still maintains close contact with previous scriptures. This unity within diversity manifests itself in several ways.

First, the New Testament writers utilize imagery drawn from creation, the flood, Sodom's destruction, apocalyptic texts and prophetic literature. They treat these prior passages as paradigmatic and authoritative, for they govern their patterns of descriptions as well as their knowledge of what will occur.

Second, the New Testament writers take their beliefs about the timing and purpose of the Day of the Lord from the Prophets and Writings. They conclude that it is possible for the Day of the Lord to be an event in the past, potentially in the present, and future-oriented in time. Current or near-future events (e.g., AD 49 and AD 70) may be part of the Day of the Lord, and the final removal of sin certainly qualifies as a Day of the Lord. Even the church's current suffering may be a judgment on their activities, but is surely the beginning of judgment for the wicked. Thus G. R. Beasley-Murray's definition of the Day of the Lord fits both Testaments. He writes that 'the Day of the Lord is an occasion (1) that involves God acting in the historical sphere, (2) that entails judgment for those for whom the day comes, and (3) that occurs at such time as is determined by the Lord (not necessarily at the end of history)'.[79]

Third, they claim that the Day of the Lord is the Day of the Lord Jesus. He is the Son of Man whose appearance makes it evident that the Day of the Lord is near or has come. He is the one to whom the Ancient of Days has entrusted the kingdom of God. He is the Son of Man who rules after the final Day of the Lord. He is the one that the church's enemies will have to face when he returns or when they die. He is also the one who judges them now. As such, he is Yahweh, since the Day of Yahweh is the Day of the Lord Jesus Christ.

Fourth, they assert that the Day of the Lord is intricately connected with believers' behaviour. They share this conviction with the Prophets, especially Isaiah and Amos, and the Writings. Those who serve God should follow kingdom standards. Otherwise, they will experience the judgment of God in their own lives, as the people in Lamentations discovered and the Thessalonians and recipients of the Petrine letters learn.

Fifth, they agree with Exodus 34:6–7 and Day of the Lord texts such as Joel 2:12–13, Jonah 4:2 and Nahum 1:2–8 that God's mercy precedes judgment. God's patience should not be mistaken for indifference. Neither should God's unwillingness to clear the guilty be mistaken for cruelty and a delight in punishing. The Day of the Lord follows many, many days of mercy.

---

79. Beasley-Murray, *Jesus and the Kingdom of* God, p. 11.

Given these preliminary conclusions, it is fair to state that the presentation of the Day of the Lord in Scripture displays a high degree of unity. In fact, it is an interesting example of unity within a normal and understandable level of diversity. It is also an interesting case study in canonical development of a theme and the application of previous texts to new situations. After all, in 2 Peter the apostle mentions the prophets, the Lord Jesus, the church's apostles and the apostle Paul while discussing the issue. Therefore, this subject plays a strategic role not just in the proclamation of the gospel, its most important role, but also in the construction of a unity paradigm for biblical theology.

6. THE PEOPLE OF GOD

Elmer A. Martens

The Scriptures portray God's activity in the world in many ways. Indeed, it is impossible to state comprehensively all that the biblical writers claim God is doing. Nonetheless, it is clear that one of the Bible's chief claims is that God is shaping a people for himself. This intention is captured among other ways in the often-repeated covenant formula 'I will be your God and you shall be my people'. This chapter explores the various dimensions of this declaration as a way of illustrating the unity of the two Testaments.[1]

There are several possible ways to approach the unpacking of this formula. One way would be to trace the theme as it appears as part of the story of

---

1. Cf. C. H. H. Scobie, who proposes 'God's People' as one of four themes for a wholistic biblical theology: *The Ways of Our God* (Grand Rapids: Eerdmans, 2003), pp. 469–651; cf. his claim, 'Modern BT has shown that for *both* OT and NT "the people of God" is a theme of the first importance,' p. 505 (italics his). See also his earlier essay, 'The Challenge of Biblical Theology', *TynBul* 42 no. 1 (1991), pp. 31–61. Cf. H. Cazelles, 'The Unity of the Bible and the People of God', *Scripture* 18 (1966), pp. 1–10; R. Deutsch, 'The Biblical Concept of the "People of God"', *Southeast Asia Journal of Theology* 13 (1972), pp. 4–12.

salvation.[2] Another way would be to offer several exegetical analyses.[3] Yet another way would be to proceed canonically.[4] Although these methods all have their place, the method adopted here is synchronic. This method seeks to uncover the formula's various nuances and implications and explore their theological underpinnings, sociological meaning and ethical and missional implications. To achieve this goal, the method will employ an intertextual approach.[5] A key presupposition of intertextuality is that texts are a mosaic of earlier texts. In other words, texts reuse and adapt earlier texts. This literary

---

2. E.g., Paul Hanson, *The People Called. The Growth of Community in the Bible* (San Francisco: Harper & Row, 1986); John Goldingay, 'A Contextualizing Study of "The People of God" in the Old Testament', *Theological Diversity and the Authority of the Old Testament* (Grand Rapids: Eerdmans, 1987), pp. 59–96. Cf. his *Old Testament Theology I: Israel's Gospel* (Downers Grove: InterVarsity Press, 2003), pp. 437–474, 530–540, 725–760, 839–850. See also William J. Dumbrell, 'The New Israel', *The End of the Beginning* (Homebush West, NSW, Australia: Lancer Books, 1985).

3. Rolf Rendtorff, *The Covenant Formula: An Exegetical and Theological Investigation*, trans. Margaret Kohl (Edinburgh: T. & T. Clark, 1998).

4. Cf. Frederic Bush, 'Images of Israel: The People of God in the Torah', in R. L. Hubbard Jr, R. K. Johnston and R. P. Meye (eds.), *Studies in Old Testament Theology* (Dallas: Word, 1992), pp. 99–115; Leslie Allen, 'Images of Israel: The People of God in the Prophets', in Hubbard et al. (eds.), *Studies in Old Testament Theology*, pp. 149–168; and John Goldingay, 'Images of Israel: The People of God in the Writings', in Hubbard et al. (eds.), *Studies in Old Testament Theology*, pp. 205–221.

5. For advocacy of intertextuality as a method for pan-biblical theology, see E. A. Martens, 'Reaching for a Biblical Theology of the Whole Bible', *Reclaiming the Old Testament: Essays in Honour of Waldemar Janzen* (Winnipeg: CMBC Publications, 2001), pp. 83–101 [95–101]; cf. Paul R. House, 'Biblical Theology and the Wholeness of Scripture: Steps Toward a Program for the Future', in Scott J. Hafemann (ed.), *Biblical Theology: Retrospect and Prospect* (Downers Grove: IVP; Leiceser: Apollos, 2002), pp. 267–279 [276–77]. Introductory essays on the theory of intertextuality can be found in Donna Noland Fewell (ed.), *Reading Between Texts: Intertextuality and the Hebrew Bible* (Louisville: Westminster John Knox, 1992). Examples of biblical scholars employing the method include Richard Hays, *Echoes of Scripture in the Letters of Paul* (New Haven: Yale University Press, 1989); Robert L. Brawley, *Text to Text Pours Forth Speech: Voices of Scripture in Luke-Acts* (Bloomington: Indiana University Press, 1995); and Benjamin D. Sommer, *A Prophet Reads Scripture: Allusions in Isaiah 40–66* (Stanford: Stanford University Press, 1998).

theory assumes both continuity (something is shared by a present text and its precursors) and discontinuity (the reuse is often a tweaking of the earlier text) between passages. Thus the intertextual method is suited to an exploration of unity.

To be more precise about the way intertextuality will be used here, this chapter will begin with a New Testament text and then move back to its Old Testament precursors. For the most part, a New Testament variation of the formula will be the starting point for the discussion. Rather than highlighting word studies and historical settings, the exposition of the theme will focus on symbols and metaphors.[6] To keep the analysis from becoming too theoretical, the discussion will regularly refer to concrete rituals, stories and practices. Thus the synchronic approach used in this chapter is governed by a set of theological, sociological and literary questions. It is also governed by my own imaginative construal of the way governing metaphors and texts are used in the Bible.

Theologically: a God-connected people

The covenant formula occurs, with variations, more than twenty-five times in the Bible. Using intertextual methodology, we begin with the final occurrence of the formula in Revelation 21:3, where the writer tweaks the standard formula by making 'people' plural: 'they will be his peoples' (Rev. 21:3, my translation).[7] Examined for its more strictly *theological* nuances, this formula, which echoes earlier formulations (e.g., Exod. 6:7), speaks to matters of divine initiative, divine purpose, divine presence and the human response of worship.

Divine initiative

The formula (Rev. 21:3) is followed almost immediately by the assertion 'Behold, I am making all things new' (Rev. 21:5), an assertion which echoes Isaiah 43:19 and is consonant with the biblical message throughout. God, as always in the divine-human relationship, takes the first step, illustrated already

---

6. Studies of etymology, historical contexts and tradition history have their place in exegesis, but here more attention is given to such matters as metaphor and praxis. Cf. L. Perdue, *The Collapse of History: Reconstructing Old Testament Theology* (Minneapolis: Fortress, 1994).

7. UBS text, 4th ed., recognizes the plural as the most likely reading; it lists the singular form as a text variant.

in the initial overture to the formula in God's appearance to Abraham: 'I will ... be God to you' (Gen. 17:7). That initiative is historically verifiable. Joshua explained God's acts to Israel, 'Long ago ... I took your father Abraham from beyond the River ... and made his offspring many' (Josh. 24:2–3). At Sinai God explained, '[I] brought you to myself ... you shall be my treasured possession' (Exod. 19:4–5). Such a statement highlights both election and grace.

The theological reality of God's grace work is made concrete in both Testaments through two closely related rituals: the Passover as observed by the Israelites, and the Lord's Supper as observed by the church. When Israelite children enquired about the meaning of the Passover observance, the answer was, 'It is the sacrifice of the LORD's Passover, for he passed over the houses of the people of Israel in Egypt, when he struck the Egyptians but spared our houses' (Exod. 12:27). The sparing comes at the initiative of Yahweh. That initiative was confirmed with the Passover observances at the times of revival under Hezekiah (2 Chr. 30) and Josiah (2 Chr. 35:1–19).

When the church convenes to observe the Lord's Supper, inaugurated 'coincidentally' at the annual observance of the Passover in Jerusalem (Matt. 26:1–2; 17–19), its members hear about the cup, signifying Christ's blood poured out for the forgiveness of their sins. The symbol of blood as connected to the reality of deliverance is common to both the Passover and the Lord's Supper, and so points to the fundamental understanding that the deliverance is God's work. Whether it is a Passover meal for the Israelite family or the service of Eucharist for the church, each is observed as a remembrance of a prior event, God's action of deliverance.[8] Indeed, at the time of Jesus, the observance of the Passover included partaking of four cups of wine; the fourth cup was called the 'Cup of Praise'. As Robin Routledge explains, 'The fourth cup was associated specifically with God's promise: *I will take you as my own people, and I will be your God*' (Exod. 6:7).[9]

Divine purpose

As the holy city is lowered from heaven to earth in John's final end-time vision, the accompanying loud proclamation conveys the feeling of climax of all that

---

8. Rendtorff lists Exod. 6:6–7 along with Exod. 29:45; Deut. 4:20; 2 Sam. 7:23; Jer. 7:22–26; 11:3–5 to show the link between the exodus and the covenant formula, specifically noting that the covenant formula had its beginning in God's liberating act at the exodus. See *The Covenant Formula*, pp. 45–46.

9. Robin Routledge, 'Passover and Last Supper', *TynBul* 53 no. 2 (2002), p. 220.

has gone before. God's redemption is celebrated at the beginning of the book. Jesus Christ 'freed us from our sins by his blood' (Rev. 1:5). God's redemption, however, is an interim goal; divine redemption is to issue more climactically in the formation of a people. In the decisive scene ushering in the final state, the announcement is about a divine community.

Documentation for this assertion about the formation of God's people as a climactic goal of God's action is found in both Testaments. Early on, God gives Moses an overall statement about his purpose (Exod. 5:22–6:8). In the announcement of his intention, deliverance (i.e., salvation) is listed first, but this purpose statement is followed immediately by 'I will take you to be my people, and I will be your God' (Exod. 6:7; for the same sequence see Exod. 19:4–6).[10] So also Paul explains to Titus: 'he [Jesus Christ] gave himself for us to redeem us from all lawlessness and to purify for himself a people for his own possession' (Titus 2:14).

Indeed, if one broadly periodizes the history of salvation as told in the two Testaments, it is clear that not only the exodus but each of God's major interventions is aimed at shaping a people. Another benchmark event was the return of the exiled people, a deliverance also aimed at the formation of a community. Jeremiah says exiles were to be returned home, built up and given a heart to acknowledge Yahweh: 'and they shall be my people and I will be their God' (Jer. 24:7; cf. Ezek. 11:20). God's intervention in the human story through the incarnation of his Son is the most pointed of all interventions, and that one, like the others, is intended to issue in the shaping of a people: 'I will build my church' (Matt. 16:18; cf. Titus 2:14). Finally, John the Revelator, in describing God's end-time intervention with the holy city, Jerusalem, coming down out of heaven from God, hears a loud voice from the throne announcing, 'Behold, the dwelling place of God is with man. He will dwell with them, and they will be his people, and God himself will be with them as their God' (Rev. 21:3). God's acts of deliverance have as their goal the formation of a God-linked community. Viewed canonically, the covenant formula virtually brackets the biblical story: it occurs, though muted, at the beginning (Gen. 17:7), becomes explicit in Exodus 6:7, and is broadcast as a triumphant victory cry at the end (Rev. 21:3).

---

10. Since elements of the covenant formula are clearly present in Exod. 19:4–6, R. Smend describes this text as a 'softened form' of the covenant formula. R. Smend, 'Die Bundesformel' (1963), reprinted in *Die Mitte des Alten Testaments: Gesammelte Studien*, vol. 1, *BEvTh* 99 (1986), p. 13.

Divine presence

The climactic victory cry in the eschaton announcing the realization of the goals of the covenant formula ('I will be your God; you shall be my people') emphasizes God's commitment to be present with his community via catchwords of 'dwelling'.[11] 'Now the dwelling of God is with men, and he will live with them' (Rev. 21:3 NIV). Such a statement echoes an earlier word in the Gospels, 'The Word became flesh and made his dwelling among us' (John 1:14 NIV), and the much earlier promise about presence, 'And I will walk among you and will be your God' (Lev. 26:12).

The reality of God's presence with his people is graphically captured in the wilderness tabernacle and later in the Solomonic temple. One of the terms for this wilderness structure is 'dwelling' (Exod. 25:9; cf. 25:8).[12] By this designation for the structure, Israel memorialized its understanding that God was among them. So ingrained was the understanding of Yahweh's presence in the temple that by the late seventh century the orthodox teaching had been perverted into a mantra announcing the city's invulnerability: 'This is the temple of the LORD, the temple of the LORD, the temple of the LORD' (Jer. 7:4). The significance of Ezekiel's temple is exemplified in the exclamation that also ends the book, 'The LORD is there' (Ezek. 48:35). 'Tabernacle' and 'temple' were clearly symbols of God's presence with his people (Exod. 40:34; 1 Kgs 8:10–12).

When the tabernacle and the temple are viewed typologically, then the antitype is the incarnation, where God is present in Jesus Christ and indeed has taken up residence 'among us' (John 1:14). A further New Testament correspondence with religious structures of the Old Testament is the concept that the Holy Spirit, not unlike the cloud filling the tabernacle and temple, has come to fill the body of God's people the church. God has taken up residence in the church, the community of God's people (1 Cor. 3:16–17; 2 Cor. 6:16). God's commitment to be a people's God is a commitment to be present with them, a point made in both Testaments.

Assertions of God's initiative, purpose and presence are incorporated into the covenant formula. God elects a people.[13] John Goldingay states, 'The

---

11. Cf. 'dwell', *skēnē*, in the texts: 'Now the dwelling [*skēnē*, 'tabernacle'] of God is with men, and he will live [*skēnōsei*] with them' (Rev. 21:3 NIV). 'The Word became flesh and dwelt [*eskēnōsen*] among us' (John 1:14).

12. Hebrew *miškān*, 'dwelling place'.

13. H. D. Preuss asserts that 'election' is the central theme of the Old Testament. See *Old Testament Theology*, trans. L. G. Perdue (Louisville: Westminster John Knox, 1995), vol. 1, pp. 30–39.

notion of election is a key to understanding the notion of Israel. It is not even that God makes an already existent people his own; he brings a people into being. They only exist as a people because of an act of God.'[14] Critical to God's election of a people is the dimension of grace, for it is out of God's abundant goodwill that he initiates a special relationship with a chosen people (Deut. 7:6–10). That note, sounded loudly in the Old Testament, is repeated in the New Testament by Paul (Eph. 2:8) and by Peter, who writes, 'now you have received mercy' (1 Pet. 2:10).

A worship response

A fitting response to such unmerited favour is thanksgiving, worship and praise. Hence the context for the final mention of the covenant formula in connection with the holy city, the new Jerusalem, is praise. Nations bring their glory into it (Rev. 21:24); John, the recipient of the vision, falls down to worship (Rev. 22:8). To realize that 'we are his people' is alone sufficient prompting to worship the Lord with gladness and to come into his presence with singing (Ps. 100:1). Paul Hanson asks, 'What demarcates the people of God?' and answers by identifying the 'triadic notion': the people of God is characterized as a worshipping, righteous and compassionate community.[15] Doxology is fitting for God's people, as spokespersons Paul and David underscore: 'For from him and through him and to him are all things. To him be glory forever. Amen' (Rom. 11:36). 'Oh come, let us worship ... For he is our God, and we are the people of his pasture' (Ps. 95:6–7).

Sociologically: a bonded people

The covenant formula has a definite sociological dimension. The usual rubrics of family, clan and tribe,[16] nation states, or even clusterings around interests such as vocations and ideologies, apply, but only partially. For a more complete understanding we must address the orientation and composition of the 'people of God', as well as the nature of the group's cohesion. Using intertextuality, we begin by examining the New Testament focal text about those 'not my people' now being called 'sons of the living God' (Rom. 9:25–26).

---

14. John Goldingay, *Theological Diversity and the Authority of the Old Testament*, p. 62.

15. Hanson, *The People Called*, pp. 70–78.

16. Cf. N. Gottwald, *The Tribes of Yahweh: A Sociology of the Religion of Liberated Israel, 1250–1050 BCE* (Maryknoll: Orbis, 1979).

Here Paul draws on texts from Hosea, not quoting them precisely, rather inverting the order (inverting 2:23b and 2:23a; also placing 1:10 after 2:23).

Community orientation

So familiar is the covenant formula, especially from Hosea, with its repeated refrain, 'my people', that its uniqueness is easily overlooked. In the Ancient Near East, gods were usually associated not first with people, but with a given territory, as is indicated by such expressions as 'gods of the lands' (2 Kgs 18:35 NASB), 'gods of Egypt' (Exod. 12:12) and the comment on the Mesha Stone about Chemosh being angry with 'his land'. So also the baals were deities (or extensions of Baal) that claimed cities or regions as their jurisdictions. Daniel Block asserts that ancient deities were largely gods of territories, although people groupings had patron deities as well. Block explains, 'Gods were associated with specific lands as well as peoples. In fact their concern with the geographic entity often appears to have overridden their real interest in the people … [T]he witness of the Old Testament is consistent in its portrayal of Yahweh as a God primarily of the people and only secondarily of the land of Canaan.'[17] Yahweh, Israel's God, is distinctive in that this God attaches himself to a people, more so than to a territory.[18] This God is not bounded by territory; this Yahweh is connected to a community.

Similarly, the competing religions in the New Testament era had an orientation different from that of the Christian faith. It was over against the imperial cults which extolled Caesar as a 'god' that the apostles insisted that Jesus was Lord, Saviour, Righteous One, Peacemaker.[19] This new community was an alternative community, and in some ways even an alternative political entity. Earlier analyses of religion in the first century highlighted mystery religions and Gnosticism as the major challengers to Christianity. Because of their stress on the individual, these religions of the first century AD were not marked by a high consciousness of community. For the mystery religions, the experience

---

17. Daniel Block, *The Gods of the Nations: Studies in Ancient Near Eastern National Theology*, 2nd ed. (Grand Rapids: Baker; Leicester: Apollos, 2000), p. 150; cf. 'This verse [Lev. 25:23] declares unequivocally that the nation's primary association is with Yahweh and not with the land' (p. 82).

18. 'The idea of the election of a people by a deity is a unique expression to this point within the religious history of the ancient Near East' (Preuss, *Old Testament Theology*, vol. 1, p. 38).

19. Richard A. Horsley (ed.), *Paul and Empire: Religion and Power in Roman Imperial Society* (Harrisburg: Trinity Press International, 1997).

of God was an individual affair; it was private and internal. While not dis-
counting the importance of the individual, both the Israelite faith and the
Christian metamorphosis of it were radically different from their surrounding
faiths. Both put an emphasis on community; in this community God (Jesus)
was constitutive.

Who belongs to God's community?

The New Testament repeatedly insists that God's people are not to be defined
by ethnicity. Paul's claim that both Jews and Gentiles comprise God's people
(Rom. 9:22–26) is grounded in Old Testament texts (Hos. 2:23; 1:10 [2:1 MT]),
which have in view all Israel. But, as is common in intertextual usage, Paul
tweaks their meaning, so that for him those formerly not God's people are now
defined as Gentiles, and it is they who are candidates to become God's people.
As Craig Evans observes, 'Paul reasons that if God can reclaim a lost, non-
covenant people once, he can do it again (cf. Isa. 56:1–8, where the prophet
envisions not only the regathering of Israel's exiles, but the gathering of
eunuchs and foreigners to the Temple of Jerusalem)'.[20]

The Jerusalem council, after deliberating on entrance requirements to the
faith community, recognized the legitimacy of Gentiles within the 'people of
God' by quoting Amos (Acts 15:12–21; cf. Amos 9:11–12). Paul is exuberant
about this enlarged compass of God's people (Rom. 15:9, 10, 11, 12, quoting
Ps. 18:49; Deut. 32:43;[21] Ps. 117:1; Isa.11:1, 10).[22] Paul might have added from
Isaiah, 'Blessed be Egypt my people' (Isa. 19:25), or Zephaniah's vision of
nations outside Israel calling on God's name and serving him with one accord
(Zeph. 3:9). Paul's insistence that Gentiles are potentially participants within
the 'people of God' means that qualification for membership in God's people
is not DNA (ethnic Judaism). Rather, it is based on spiritual considerations.

---

20. Craig Evans, 'Paul and the Prophets: Prophetic Criticism in the Epistle to the
    Romans (with special reference to Romans 9–11)', in Sven Soderlund and N. T.
    Wright (eds.), *Romans and the People of God*, (Grand Rapids: Eerdmans, 1999), p. 125.

21. John Sailhamer urges that the Deuteronomy passage be translated, following the
    MT, 'Rejoice, O nations, his people'. See *The Pentateuch as Narrative* (Grand Rapids:
    Zondervan, 1992), p. 476 n. 25.

22. A detailed exposition of Paul's use of Isaiah, with its 'intricately-woven intertextual
    tapestry' and so clearly related to the theme of unity of Old Testament and New
    Testament, is found in J. Ross Wagner, *Heralds of Good News: Isaiah and Paul 'In
    Concert' in the Letter to the Romans* (Leiden: Brill, 2002), pp. 307–340, and his overall
    conclusions on pp. 341–359.

So on what basis does one belong to God's people? Fundamentally by a transition involving several 'moves'.[23] First, other gods are renounced and the true God (known through Christ, beginning in New Testament times) is embraced. In a remarkable statement, Jeremiah announces that Gentiles, Israel's 'evil neighbours', can be 'built up in the midst of my people' when they renounce Baal and swear by Yahweh's name (Jer. 12:16). Paul put it similarly: 'You turned to God from idols ... to wait for his Son from heaven' (1 Thess. 1:9–10). Such a change of loyalty is illustrated by Abraham and also by the motley group at Sinai, which included Egyptians, who declared, 'All that the LORD has spoken we will do' (Exod. 19:8). God's people, beginning with the Egyptians who had joined them at the exodus, continued to include non-Jews: Jethro, Moses' Midianite father-in-law; Rahab, the God-fearing Jericho prostitute; Caleb, a Kenite; and Ruth, described to the point of redundancy as the Moabitess. All these non-Jews are enfolded in the group known as 'people of God' because they believed God. In the words of an Asian intellectual of my acquaintance who converted to Christ, 'They came under the God'. Or, to put the same notion in biblical terms, they are people over whom God's name is called (Acts 15:14–17, quoting Amos 9:11–12). 'The prophet Hosea names one of his sons Lo-Ammi, which means "not my people" (Hos. 1:8), to symbolize that when Israel gives her loyalty to other gods, she cannot call herself God's people.'[24] Conversely, the people of God are people who, renouncing all competitors for their allegiance, yield their allegiance to the one true God. To them God says, 'You are my people' (Hos. 2:23).

The biblical emphasis on 'the remnant' underscores the necessity of believing in God in the sense of making a full interior commitment to God. In Elijah's day it was not national, ethnic Israel who qualified as God's people. Instead, it was the remnant of seven thousand who had not bowed their knee to Baal who had that distinction. They were Yahweh's people because they clung to him by faith rather than joining their fellow citizens in pagan worship. At times they suffered greatly for their faith (cf. 1 Kgs 18:13–14).

Paul focuses on the remnant concept in Romans 9:27 and 9:29, where he quotes Isaiah 10:22 and Isaiah 1:9 respectively. Significantly, in Romans 10:13 he adds to this remnant concept Joel's standard for becoming part of God's

---

23. In what follows I am indebted to Christopher J. H. Wright, 'Implications of Conversion in the Old Testament and the New', *International Bulletin of Missionary Research* 28, no. 1 (2004), pp. 14–19.

24. David Ewert, *The Church, The New People of God* (Abbotsford: HeartBeat Productions, 2004), p. 14.

people. 'Everyone who calls on the name of the LORD shall be saved' (Joel 2:32). Of course, Paul believes 'the name' is 'Jesus'. Thus Köstenberger can rightly assert that, for Paul, 'Faith in Jesus the Messiah, the Good Shepherd *par excellence*, is the bond that unites God's people and makes them his new covenant community'.[25] John E. Toews believes the letter to the Romans answers a series of questions, one of which is, 'What is required to be members of God's people?' The answer, harking back to the remnant, is explained by Toews in this way: 'In ch. 9 the "call of God" constitutes the true Israel. Here [9:14–29; 10:18–21], the people "calling on God" meet the requirement to become members of God's people irrespective of their ethnicity.'[26] The insistence that the definition of the people of God is inclusive of all persons who are committed God-followers, regardless of vocation, ethnicity, gender or race, means that the 'other' is not now defined by ethnicity. The 'other' is no longer Jew or Gentile, but the one who stands outside the community of God's people.

Secondly, an 'outsider' became an 'insider' by becoming part of the worshipping community. The 'mixed multitude' that came out of Egypt was given access to the Passover according to procedures outlined in Exodus 12:43–49. The 'converts' participated in the annual feasts (Deut. 16:11, 14), the Day of Atonement (Lev. 16:29) and the ceremony of covenant renewal and commitment (Deut. 29:11; 31:12). 'For the resident alien, then, conversion – at least according to the ideals of Israelite law – meant complete *inclusion, participation and equality* with the living community of God's people.'[27] Likewise, in the New Testament conversion entailed inclusion in the worshipping community, for now all dividing walls were broken down (Eph. 2:13–22).

Thirdly, a change of allegiance entails an ethical transformation. To belong to God's people means to walk in God's paths (Isa. 2:3). As Wright emphasizes, Elijah's call for people to turn from worshipping Baal to worshipping the true God meant no longer 'trampling on justice ... and confiscation of land by unfettered royal power', but 'an ethic of economic justice and limits on political power'.[28] Zephaniah speaks of a people, humble and lowly, the 'remnant of Israel' who 'seek refuge in the name of the LORD', and who are recognized

25. Andreas Köstenberger, 'Jesus the Good Shepherd Who Will Also Bring Other Sheep (John 10:16): The Old Testament Background of a Familiar Metaphor', *BBR* 12.1 (2002), p. 96.

26. John E. Toews, *Romans*, BCBC (Scottdale: Herald Press, 2004), pp. 365, 269.

27. Wright, 'Implications of Conversion', p. 18 (italics his).

28. Ibid., p. 15.

by their godly behaviour (Zeph. 3:12–13; cf. Isaiah's description of the remnant as 'holy', Isa. 4:3, and Haggai's notation of the remnant as a people who obeyed the voice of the Lord their God, Hag. 1:12). Faith means welcoming God's message. It clearly entails repentance, that is, a reorientation of thinking and conduct, as Peter made clear (Acts 2:38; cf. 11:18; 17:30; Jer. 3:22–4:2). Those who have faith in God turn to God from all other gods. As Goldingay explains, 'Gentiles thus turn to the true God for the first time, while by implication Jews have turned away and must turn back'.[29] In either instance, one can expect ethical transformation.

The somewhat problematic designation of 'God-fearers' found in the New Testament seems to be reserved for people in a liminal state, persons who are on the way into the kingdom, sometimes even at the threshold or in the entryway. So, for example, Cornelius is described as a God-fearer, a 'seeker', to use modern idiom (Acts 10:2). The terminology 'devout', 'fearing God' and the related 'proselyte' as well as the precise religious-social status of such persons has been much debated.[30] It is unclear whether these terms are designations for three (or two) different groups, or whether all three Greek terms refer to the same group (comparing Acts 13:16 with 13:43, one might conclude that 'God-fearers' and 'proselytes' mean the same thing). If we can suppose the latter to be the case, then these are likely Gentiles who were sympathetic to the Jewish faith and were possibly, at least in some instances, converts to it. Ben Witherington sums up the discussion by noting that the three terms likely describe Gentiles 'who worship the true God and are to some degree adherents of Judaism'. These people 'are seen as the most likely of those who are within or associated with the synagogue to be converted to Christianity (see, e.g., 18:7–8)'.[31] Still, one would do well to acknowledge the distinction between conversion and proselytism: 'The vast, global, and cultural diversity of the Christian church today is the legitimate fruit of this essential distinction between conversion (i.e., conversion to *Christ* within any culture) and proselytism (which essentially says, "You must first must *become like us*").'[32]

---

29. Goldingay, *Old Testament Theology I*, p. 843.

30. For an accessible and helpful discussion with ample references to scholarly positions, see Ben Witherington III, *The Acts of the Apostles. A Socio-Rhetorical Commentary* (Grand Rapids: Eerdmans, 1998), pp. 341–344.

31. Ibid., p. 344.

32. Wright, 'Implications of Conversion', p. 19 n. 8, in summing up a conversation with Andrew Walls. Italics his.

John the revelator envisions one redeemed community in God's presence (Rev. 7:9–10), but he also speaks of 'peoples' (Rev. 21:3). In doing so he refers not to nations, but to the 'multi-ethnic composition of the church'.[33] In short, these common sociological categories of nationality, race and ethnicity have become irrelevant, for membership in the people of God is defined in terms other than these. In retrospect we can homogenize the elements essential to belonging to God's people. However, historically, acceptance of these 'conditions' was quite difficult for the first-century church. Were the people of God not the Jews, the descendants of Abraham? In both Testaments, however, the boundaries marking a 'people' are spiritual in nature; in both Testaments the composition of this 'people' depends upon a connectedness to God as Saviour; in both Testaments the worshipping community is critical; and in both Testaments these persons follow a new ethic. In sum, belonging to God's family entails faith, family and following.

Community bondedness

One can rightly say that this 'people' is bonded to God, for God describes them as 'my people'. The New Testament underscores that bondedness with its recurring 'in Christ' language (e.g., Eph. 1:1, 4, 11). But it is also true that as a 'people' each constituent belongs to the other.

When Paul speaks to the Ephesians, largely a Gentile congregation, as 'fellow citizens with the saints and members of the household of God' (Eph. 2:19), he is emphasizing their interconnectedness through their bondedness and solidarity.[34] Paul insists that, although the church has many members, the church is a single unity, just as the human body with its several members is one whole (1 Cor. 12). From that analogy the apostle can urge the notion of bondedness: feet, ears and eyes do not function as detached entities; their function is a 'together' function. These entities are not merely attached, but are organically bonded. That connectedness conceptually echoes the Old Testament notion of 'corporate personality', a way of thinking in which an entire group can be conceived of as a single entity.[35] For example, the 'I' in the Psalms may

---

33. G. Osborne, *Revelation* (Grand Rapids: Baker, 2002), p. 734 n. 9.

34. Cf. the many New Testament references to 'one another' (e.g., Rom. 15:7; Eph. 4:2). See listings in G. Lohfink, *Jesus and Community: The Social Dimensions of the Christian Faith* (Philadelphia: Fortress, 1984), pp. 99–100.

35. H. W. Robinson is responsible for the term 'corporate personality', which for him designates a fluidity about boundaries such that a person's individuality would merge with a group, or the group be viewed as a single entity. See H. W. Robinson, *Corporate Personality in Ancient Israel* (Philadelphia: Fortress Press, 1964).

refer not to an individual, but to a congregation or a nation understood as a single entity. 'Corporate personality' thinking is also illustrated in Achan's story, where one person's sin brought punishment to an entire family, and even, although more indirectly, to an entire nation (Josh. 7).

Such a cultural worldview of 'corporate personality' stressing solidarity becomes the cradle for the language of faith. The people of God are to be understood as an aggregate of individuals, but they are so related to one another that, like a corporation of modern times, they share a bondedness in which the whole collection can be understood as a single integer.

The bondedness that characterizes God's people is also illustrated in covenant-making.[36] To enter into covenant means to enter into the solidarity represented in the covenant formula. It means that God establishes them as his people and himself as their God (Deut. 29:12–13).[37] Given the relational nature of the covenant formula, some scholars have considered 'promise' the central idea in covenant-making, while others have emphasized 'obligation' as the key idea.[38] To be sure, the covenants God makes with Abraham and David include promises, but in the ancient world promises could be made outside covenant structures. The same was true of the stating of obligations, so it may be that God's covenant-making aimed at an even more basic dynamic. The Ancient Near Eastern treaties, after which Israel's covenants seem to be modelled, highlight 'loyalty' as a primary feature. In these documents, promises and obligations help establish and strengthen the bonds of loyalty between parties.

J. W. Rogerson critiques Robinson for some untenable assumptions, but agrees that parts of the Old Testament present a view comparable to Robinson's definition of 'corporate personality'. See *Anthropology and the Old Testament* (Atlanta: John Knox; Oxford: Blackwell, 1978), pp. 55–58.

36. 'The primary and most important OT metaphor for the relationship between God and his people was the covenant (*berit*)' (Bush, 'Images of Israel: The People of God in the Torah', p. 100).

37. R. Rendtorff, in concluding his study, says, 'Indeed, the formula may be positively said to be an exposition of what the word *berit* means' (*The Covenant Formula*, p. 88).

38. Cf. the tenor of P. R. Williamson's 'Covenant', in *Dictionary of the Old Testament: Pentateuch* (Downers Grove: InterVarsity Press; Leicester: Inter-Varsity Press, 2003), pp. 139–155; Walter C. Kaiser Jr, *Toward an Old Testament Theology* (Grand Rapids: Zondervan, 1978); Gerhard F. Hasel and Michael G. Hasel, *The Promise* (Nampa: Pacific Press Publishing Association, 2002); and Steven L. McKenzie, who states, 'The covenantal relationship is best described as "divine commitment and human obligation"' (*Covenant*, UBT [St Louis: Chalice Press, 2000], p. 37).

The same is true in God's covenants with Israel, for loyalty to Yahweh, rather than loyalty to other gods, determines whether Israel believes the promises and performs the obligations contained in the covenants. Because loyalty is the governing principle, the major covenants include (and sometimes conclude with) the covenant formula or variations of it (Gen. 17:8; Deut. 26:16–19; 29:13; 2 Sam. 7:14; Jer. 31:31–34). Covenants emphasize solidarity; covenants are about bondedness as much as, if not more than, promise and obligation.

More concretely, this sociological bondedness was expressed in Israel's festivals. Even prior to the institution of festivals, a meal at the time of covenant-making highlighted the importance of togetherness. Once in the land, the community shared in celebration during three annual festivals: the festival of Passover/Unleavened Bread, the festival of Firstfruits and the festival of Tabernacles. In addition, the Passover was a family event in which people ate together, but the religious nature of the occasion is underlined by the Deuteronomic requirement that it be 'at the place that the LORD will choose, to make his name dwell there' (Deut. 16:2).

Of these festivals, none seems to be practised in the New Testament church except the Passover, now transmuted into the Lord's Supper. The communion commemoration is, among other things, a communal event of solidarity. All believers partake of the bread; all believers partake of the cup. One message from this symbolic action is that members of the community belong together.

Just as the Passover emphasized 'the unity and the common identity of those who share it', so also in the Last Supper 'the unity and fellowship of the participants [was] a significant part of the ongoing celebration of the Lord's supper'.[39] For centuries the various Christian traditions have debated how to understand Christ's presence at the Lord's Supper. Regardless of one's viewpoint, the communal aspect must not be lost. Tim Geddert, who pays special attention to the communal dimension of the service of the Lord's Supper, notes that during the observance,

> We not only look back and remember; we not only look forward and anticipate. We also look around. Jesus is indeed present at communion, but not simply in the elements or in the remembering. He is chiefly present, as he promised, in the *gathering* (Matt. 18:19–20). The church is not a collection of individuals mystically bound by common participation in a sacrament; instead the church is a real, living and interrelating family (Mark 3:34–35).[40]

---

39. Routledge, 'Passover and Last Supper', p. 221.
40. Timothy Geddert, *Mark* (Scottdale: Herald Press, 2001), p. 343.

In sum, the idea of bondedness, embedded in the covenant formula 'You shall be my people', can be fruitfully expounded 1) with metaphors such as 'corporate personality' and 'body', 2) by attention to the purpose of 'covenant', and 3) by the symbolic praxis of the Lord's Supper.

Community identity

N. T. Wright explains that a people's identity derives, at least in part, from their worldview. A worldview, he explains, can be glimpsed by attention to four dimensions, one of which is story.[41]

For Israel the larger story that contributed to their identity included the smaller stories of the patriarchs, Abraham, Isaac and Jacob. Moreover, Israel's identity was forged through suffering as a slave people in Egypt and through the march out from that country under the protective fiery cloud. Their story was one of glorious covenant-making with Yahweh at Sinai, followed, to their shame, by the making of a golden calf. The story continued with the wilderness trek from Sinai to Kadesh Barnea, and it should have proceeded quickly to the conquest of Canaan. Instead, due to disobedience caused by doubt, the people spent forty years in the desert. Next, the story was marked by the great moments of fording the Jordan in miracle fashion, the fall of Jericho, the rule of King David and the message of the prophets, who pointed to a climactic moment imminent in that story: the arrival of the Messiah. The New Testament people of God share the same story as part of their identity, except that for them the story continues by way of fulfilment in Jesus. His death and resurrection were followed by the high moment of Pentecost and the birth of the church. The people of God know who they are; they have a history of God pursuing his purposes through them.[42]

Further, Wright claims, a people's identity is fleshed out via its symbols. The Passover and Last Supper have already been mentioned as comparable rituals that as symbols establish an identity.[43] For the people of God in the Old Testament era one might adduce ritualistic identity badge-markers such as cir-

---

41. Three other identity-making factors are symbol, questions asked/answered, and praxis. See N. T. Wright, *The New Testament and the People of God* (Minneapolis: Fortress, 1992), pp. 122–139.

42. For an elaborate rehearsal of this story, see Wright, *The New Testament and the People of God*, pp. 371–443; for a comprehensive review of Old Testament theology as narrative, see Goldingay, *Old Testament Theology*.

43. For Wright, baptism and eucharist are new forms of religious practice (*The New Testament and the People of God*, p. 361).

cumcision, dietary laws, Sabbath-keeping and observance of festivals. Such rit-ualistic practices provide both continuity and discontinuity between Israel and the church. The church, the New Testament people of God, is marked by the ritual of baptism through which persons signal their death to the old life and their rising with Christ into a new life (Rom. 6:1–23).[44] Matters of diet, although not unimportant for the New Testament people of God, are not its recogniz-able markers. Sabbath was an identity marker for Israel (Exod. 31:16–17); its observance has been construed, because it arises out of creation, as incumbent on humankind (Exod. 20:8–11), and for the Christian it has changed into a com-memoration of the resurrection. For the New Testament church, which sits lightly on Old Testament symbols, the governing symbol is the cross.[45] As for defining markers, for the church there is one clear-cut marker, as Jesus made clear, and that is love. 'By this all people will know that you are my disciples, if you have love for one another' (John 13:35). This explanation of the primary Christian marker was given in conjunction with the service of foot-washing, which some churches regard as an ordinance to be ritually observed.

Wright also claims that the identity of a people revolves around the questions they ask, such as 'Who are we?', 'Where are we?', 'What is wrong?' and 'What is the solution?'[46] These questions and their answers delineate a worldview. Israel asked the question, 'Who is like you, O LORD, among the gods? Who is like you, majestic in holiness?' (Exod. 15:11). They answered their own question in terms of God's action in history (Exod. 15:1–18), his unity (Deut. 6:4) and his charac-ter (Exod. 34:6–7). The New Testament people of God see themselves in con-tinuity with that earlier people of God. 'There is one God; there is also one mediator between God and humankind, Christ Jesus' (1 Tim. 2:5 NRSV).[47] God's

---

44. Some would stress the continuity between the Testaments by regarding New Testament baptism as the counterpart of Old Testament circumcision, a connection that in my opinion the New Testament does not make.

45. Wright notes that the symbols for the Old Testament people of God were temple, Torah, land and an ethnic identity, but that the early Christians did not give allegiance to these. For them, 'The symbol in question is the cross' (*The New Testament and the People of God*, pp. 365–367).

46. Ibid., p. 123. Western civilization has been influenced, for example, by the three crucial questions posed by Immanuel Kant: 'What can I know?', 'What should I do?' and 'What can I hope for?'

47. The correlation between the monotheism of the Old Testament and the Trinity in the New Testament clearly calls for explication, but the two are not contradictory. But the observation underlines the 'newness' that the early Christians faced.

people also enquire about obligation – 'What does the Lord require?' – and answer with language about justice and a humble walk with God (Mic. 6:6–8). Jesus agrees fully with this and other Old Testament scriptures when he declares that the two prime duties are to love God and to love our neighbour (Matt. 22:37–38). The people of God, furthermore, are sustained in both the Old Testament and the New Testament by an eschatological hope, the coming of God/Jesus, an event which, although somewhat differently nuanced, is captured in both Testaments in the expression 'Day of the Lord' (Joel 1–3; 1 Thess. 5:2).

A fourth identity marker, says Wright, is praxis. For Israel the praxis called for was obedience to God's will.[48] The praxis of God's people is never detached from the basic premise of God's holiness, which entails morality and ethics (Lev. 19:2; Matt. 5:48). To be God's people implies membership, bondedness and identity. The ethical dimension cannot be ignored (see next section).

Ethically: a holy people

Much concerning distinctiveness is embedded in the phrase 'You shall be my people'. The people of God are to be distinguished from other peoples. To be *God's* people entails being a certain kind of people, a God-kind of people, whose foremost quality is holiness. The apostle Peter, intent on emphasizing that his readers were once not a people but are now God's holy people (1 Pet. 2:9), addresses them, echoing Exodus 19:5–6 in intertextual fashion: 'You are a chosen race … a holy nation.' Such a claim invites consideration of the 'calling' to and content of the holiness of God's people, no matter in which dispensation.[49]

The calling to holiness
Peter leaves no doubt about the calling to holiness. Moreover, he self-consciously links the call to holiness with the Old Testament exhortation in

---

48. Nicholson, in commenting on 'the people of Yahweh', states: 'Appropriated by Yahweh as his own, Israel is commanded to live in exclusive allegiance and total commitment to him.' See Ernest W. Nicholson, *God and His People: Covenant and Theology in the Old Testament* (Oxford: Clarendon Press, 1988), p. 209.

49. A recent excellent study by Jo Bailey Wells has been most helpful in what follows. See *God's Holy People: A Theme in Biblical Theology*, JSOTSup 305 (Sheffield: Sheffield Academic Press, 2000).

Leviticus 19:2: '[As] he who called you is holy, you also be holy in all your conduct, since it is written, "You shall be holy, for I am holy"' (1 Pet. 1:15–16). Paul likewise considers God's people summoned to holy living. He calls the believers at Corinth 'saints', or 'holy ones' (1 Cor. 1:2). The Christians at Ephesus, Paul notes, were chosen before the foundation of the world to 'be holy and blameless' before God (Eph. 1:4; cf. 'who has saved us and called us to a holy life', 2 Tim. 1:9 NIV). Somewhat odd is the discovery that Jesus, according to the Gospels, did not often employ the language of holiness. Some of his language does resemble the Old Testament. Our Lord's prayer that his disciples be sanctified is like the Old Testament language of God making Israel holy (John 17:17; Ezek. 37:28; cf. Heb. 10:10, 14). An echo of this calling to holiness can also be heard when Jesus speaks of his followers being baptized by the Holy Spirit (Luke 3:16; John 1:33; Acts 1:5). The frequent reference in Acts to being baptized (filled) with the Holy Spirit, while connoting a divine infusion of energy, cannot be divorced from the ethical dimension involved in the word 'holy' (4:31; 8:15–17; 9:17; 10:44–45; 11:16; 19:6).

The calling to holiness, while explicit in the Leviticus passage quoted by Peter, is issued frequently in the Old Testament in conjunction with the formation of a people. Moberly has noted that the Hebrew term for 'holy' does not appear in the 'Older Old Testament', that is, the book of Genesis, except for Genesis 2:3 where God sanctifies the seventh day.[50] But in Exodus the concept appears often as part of God's forming of Israel. The Song of the Sea associates Yahweh and his dwelling place with holiness (Exod. 15:11, 13). The mountain Sinai, where the delivered people gather, is a holy mountain (Exod. 19:23); the tabernacle to be erected and placed at the centre of a gathered people has a holy place, and also a most holy place (Exod. 26:33). The explicit summons to holiness comes early in conjunction with the covenant code, 'You are to be my holy people' (Exod. 22:31 NIV; cf. Lev. 11:44–45). Deuteronomy not only repeats a similar refrain, but ties it to God's election: 'For you are a people holy to the LORD your God, and the LORD has chosen you to be a people for his treasured possession, out of all the peoples who are on the face of the earth' (Deut. 14:2; cf. 26:19). Isaiah, whose favourite designation for the deity is the Holy One, envisions a time when the exiles have returned and 'they shall be called The Holy People' (Isa. 62:12). Ezekiel portrays a future time when 'I will be their God, and they will be my people', and follows this

---

50. R. W. L. Moberly, *The Old Testament of the Old Testament: Patriarchal Narratives and Mosaic Yahwism*, OBT (Minneapolis: Fortress, 1992), p. 99. The Hebrew root *qdš* designates 'holy' and, in the hiphil form, 'to make holy'.

announcement with 'I the LORD make Israel holy' (Ezek. 37:28 NIV). In sum, the God who is marked by holiness establishes a people who are to be marked by holiness. What the Old Testament says of Israel, namely that 'Yhwh's holiness is the starting point for Israel's identity',[51] Peter would also claim as true of the church.

The content of holiness

But the call for God's people to be holy still begs for some explication. What, concretely, does it mean for God's people to be holy? One may argue that the call to be holy is a call to be separate, an argument that is often made linguistically from the meaning of *qdš*. But, as John Hartley correctly asserts, '[S]eparation does not get at the essential meaning of holiness – neither in reference to God, the holy One, nor in reference to the variety of items described as holy – for it fails to provide any content to the concept of being holy. . .'[52] A better understanding of holiness in its concrete manifestations can be found in Leviticus 19, where the call to be holy (19:2) is expounded in a series of statements about ethical behaviour. While it is true that holiness and sanctification may entail matters other than ethical behaviour (such as status and position), a holy people is still best characterized by their way of being and their manner of behaving.[53]

This understanding of the primary content of 'holiness' is evident in Peter's conjoining of holiness and ethical behaviour. Peter contrasts a holy life with the previous unregenerate life in which his readers conformed to their own desires (1 Pet. 1:14). Those who have been purified are to embrace positive attitudes, such as having genuine mutual love for one another (1 Pet. 1:22) and avoiding evil attitudes such as malice, envy and slander (1 Pet. 2:1). Immediately following his citation from Leviticus about a 'holy nation', he elaborates on what this term means ethically. Specifically, holiness means conduct that is honourable (2:12) and the showing of respect to all; God is to be feared; the emperor is to be honoured (2:17). Proper behaviour is pre-

---

51. Wells, *God's Holy People*, p. 115.

52. 'Holy and Holiness, Clean and Unclean', in *DOTP*, ed. T. Desmond Alexander and David W. Baker (Downers Grove: InterVarsity Press; Leicester: Inter-Varsity Press, 2003), p. 420. John Gammie conceptualizes holiness as cleanness, purity, in *Holiness in Israel* (Minneapolis: Fortress, 1989).

53. Hartley properly warns against equating holiness with ethics (given the connections between holiness and righteousness), for holiness encompasses also notions of spiritual force, the numinous. See 'Holy and Holiness', p. 420.

scribed for slaves, wives, husbands and believers in general (2:18–3:22). Thus essentially holiness involves right or clean conduct.

Attuned to intertextuality, one notices that Peter follows the sequence of his prime text, Leviticus 19:2. There, too, the call to holiness is followed at once with an exposition of holiness, namely with attitudes and actions that conform to the divine will. The first attitude mentioned is respect for mother and father (Lev. 19:3). Twice mentioned is the exhortation to fear God (19:14, 32; cf. 1 Pet. 2:17). Hatred of kin is proscribed. The neighbour is to be loved, as is the alien (19:18, 34; cf. 1 Pet. 1:22). Holiness entails certain behaviours, such as keeping God's statutes (19:19), offering acceptable sacrifices (19:5–8), keeping Sabbaths (19:30), attending to the needs of the poor by leaving gleanings at harvest time (19:9–10), and practising uprightness in business transactions (19:35). Prohibitions abound: no making of idols (19:4); no practice of witchcraft (19:26); no stealing, lying, reviling the handicapped or oppressing the alien (19:11, 14, 33; cf. 1 Pet. 2:1).[54] Suffice it to say that a holy people in attitude and behaviour conform to the divine will. Put another way, holiness is living out the covenant stipulations. Ample details are provided so that one is not left without guidance. In the words of Jo Wells, 'Holiness focuses, primarily, on faithful adherence to God's covenant laws in all aspects of worship and life'.[55]

Extensive exposition on the subject of holiness and ethics could be continued by means of closer exegetical work.[56] But in this essay symbolism, metaphor and ritual are given a privileged position when it comes to exposition. Among the symbols of holiness in the Old Testament, two are easily identified: tabernacle/temple and the priesthood.[57] We will examine the second of these, priesthood, since this office is associated with cleansing and ethical modelling.

---

54. Other regulations, such as avoiding animal cross-breeding (19:19) and not marring the edges of the beard (19:28), are included; the rationale is not easily determined. For a discussion, see E. A. Martens, 'How is the Christian to Construe Old Testament Law?', *BBR* 12, no. 2 (2002), pp. 199–216.

55. Wells, *God's Holy People*, p. 14.

56. Cf. Wells, ibid. In Deuteronomy, for example, the call to holiness frames the corpus of ethical and ritual requirements (Deut. 7:6–26:19).

57. 'Jesus recognizes the symbols of Israel's holiness – the Temple, the priesthood, the Sabbath and the Torah – and on one reading he acknowledges their requirements.' Ibid., p. 233. Cf. Wells's claim, 'The priest personifies holiness in human form. He demonstrates what it means to be holy, to belong to God' (p. 123).

A focus on the symbolism of priests as holy can begin with the elaborate rituals of their installation. This ritual included the washing of the body with water, the putting on of sacred vestments, the anointing with oil and blood, and the offering of sacrifice (Exod. 40:12–15; cf. Lev. 8:6–13, 22–30). The ritual of washing reinforces Leviticus's emphasis on the connection between 'cleanness' and 'holiness'. It also connects with language in the New Testament about the people of God (see also the combination of 'washing', 'clean' and 'holy' in Eph. 5:26). Aaron and his sons were then to be clothed with special garments which were carefully embroidered with special yarns and decorated with jewellery (Exod. 39:1–31); the high priest's turban carried the signet inscription 'Holy to the LORD' (Exod. 39:30).

Along with cleanness, ethical correctness was not only becoming for a priest, but was required. The narrative about the priests Korah, Dathan and Abiram is concerned both with ritual (who has access to God) and with ethics (compliance with authority). The insubordination of the Levites is evident in their charge that Moses has gone too far in assuming authority. Their claim is that all the congregation are holy (Num. 16:3). Moses in turn rebukes them, because they have gone too far in that they now seek the priesthood as well (Num. 16:10). Their insubordination is demonstrated by their refusal to come when they are summoned (Num. 16:12). The spectacular judgment of the earth swallowing these unholy priests underscores the seriousness of severing holiness from ethical correctness.

The New Testament emphasizes two of the critical priestly requirements: cleansing and ethical modelling. Cleansing is emphasized in baptism, an observance that symbolizes the removal of the filth of sin. When he writes of baptism in terms other than the removal of dirt from the body, Peter may refer to priestly washings (1 Pet. 3:21).[58] The metaphor of a Christian clothed with garments signifying Christ-like qualities (a reference quite possibly going back to the priestly protocol) capitalizes on the person of the priest as a symbol for holiness, construed as ethical behaviour (Col. 3:12; 1 Pet. 5:5). For the New Testament people of God, the ritual of baptism – the removal of dirty clothes and the putting on of new clean clothes – echoes the Old Testament priestly ritual.

The 'holy nation' of Israel as a people of God has its counterpart – no, its continuation – in the 'holy church', the New Testament saints. 'Holiness', which might otherwise be an abstraction, is earthed in such symbols as a holy priesthood and their rituals of cleansing, and in the ordinance of baptism. Jo

---

58. For the metaphor of sin as blemish and stain, see E. A. Martens, 'Sin, Guilt', in *DOTP*, pp. 764–778.

Wells has correctly concluded, 'There is no doubting that here is a thread [holiness] which may be seen to run throughout Scripture and to contribute to its unity'.[59]

A missionally witnessing people

If holiness as a way of life is critical in being the people of God, so is a missional orientation. The apostle Peter specifies a missional dimension to the covenant formula when he addresses his audience, who were once not a people, as 'a chosen race, a royal priesthood, a holy nation, a people for his own possession, *that you may proclaim the excellencies of him who called you out of darkness into his marvellous light*' (1 Pet. 2:9; emphasis added). In extrapolating the nuances of the covenant formula ('I will be your God, and you shall be my people'), the missional dimension dare not be neglected.[60] C. H. H. Scobie comments, 'The theme of the relation of God's chosen people Israel to the other nations of humankind constitutes a test case and a major challenge to any would-be biblical theologian.'[61] He makes this assertion because he holds that it is the Old Testament eschatological expectation of 'ingathering of the Gentiles' that is the clue for a New Testament theology of mission. As with the other topics, we begin near the end of the New Testament in order to hear intertextual echoes.

A missional trajectory

Several instances of intertextuality are at work in Peter's assertion. He draws on three precursor texts, invoking Exodus 19:6 and combining it with Isaiah 43:21 and possibly Isaiah 61:6. Already the Exodus passage allows a missional interpretation in that Israel's election, which makes her God's treasured possession, is specifically contextualized as 'out of all the

---

59. Wells, *God's Holy People*, p. 16.

60. C. H. H. Scobie states, 'The relationship of Israel and of the church to the nations of mankind should be explored'. See 'The Structure of Biblical Theology', *TynBul* 42 no. 2 (1991), p. 192. For his exploration of the 'New Israel' as 'fulfillment', see *The Ways of our God*, pp. 487–508.

61. C. H. H. Scobie, 'Israel and the Nations: An Essay in Biblical Theology', *TynBul* 43 no. 2 (1992), p. 284. See his chapter on the nations in *The Ways of Our God*, pp. 509–540.

peoples'. W. J. Dumbrell observes that the 'for' in the expression 'for all the earth is mine' (Exod. 19:5) may express a causal role. He writes, 'The aim of her [Israel's] call is that she may be a world influence, a "light for revelation to the Gentiles" (Luke 2:32)'.[62] Following an elaborate exegesis of this passage, Wells notes, 'On the basis of the poetic structure of Exod. 19:3b–6b we have identified the thrust of Yhwh's speech as designating the new position and vocation of the people of Israel, relative to all of Yhwh's other peoples.'[63] Moreover, the very designation of Israel as a 'priestly kingdom' conjures up a role of mediation (see below). True, the 'missionary' role of Israel is not clearly identified, but the formulation of the text (Exod. 19:5–6) means that it is hospitable to a missional-oriented interpretation.

Isaiah 43:20b–21, which Peter joins to Exodus 19:6, announces God's interventionist action of providing water in the wilderness 'to give drink to my chosen people, the people whom I formed for myself that they might declare my praise' (Isa. 43:20b–21). Through the term 'chosen people', the Isaiah text is linked conceptually with Exodus 19:5–6. If the missional dimension is latent in the Exodus text, the Isaiah text is explicit as to God's larger purposes: 'that they might declare my praise'. God, so one might put it, has a penultimate purpose, namely the shaping of a people with a clear identity, but his ultimate purpose is for this people to announce God's mighty acts to others, indeed to people everywhere. So Peter is not himself making a novel statement. Any novelty consists of conjoining two texts in order to specify the identity and the mission of God's people.

Election, as H. H. Rowley said decades ago, points towards responsibility as well as privilege.[64] The responsibility is for God's people to be a voice to the world declaring God's mighty acts, which, George E. Wright noted, included Israel's exodus and Christ's resurrection, two giant events which coalesce to encompass the whole of the biblical story.[65] Judging by the sequencing of ideas, for Peter the mighty act of God includes the shaping of a people, God's own people (1 Pet. 2:10). But beyond this 'act of God' there is to follow an 'act

---

62. W. J. Dumbrell, *The Faith of Israel*, 2nd ed. (Grand Rapids: Baker; Leicester: Apollos, 2002), p. 37.

63. Wells, *God's Holy People*, p. 47.

64. See, for example, H. H. Rowley, *The Faith of Israel: Aspects of Old Testament Thought* (Philadelphia: Westminster Press, 1956), pp. 99–149.

65. George E. Wright, *God Who Acts: Biblical Theology as Recital*, SBT 8 (Naperville: Allenson; London: SCM, 1952), pp. 59–76.

of God's people', namely the witness of a redeemed people to what God has done.[66]

Missional symbolism: the priestly function

If such assertions still have an aura of abstraction, greater concreteness is achieved with the use of a symbol, the priest. Peter not only welds together two Old Testament texts, he tweaks the Exodus text. In the Hebrew that text reads 'a priestly kingdom'. Peter inverts the two words and reads 'a royal priesthood', thereby focusing on the *function* of this 'people' more than on its *identity*. Wells correctly notes that in Exodus the 'special possession' of a people is captured in the terms 'priestly kingdom' and 'holy nation'. Peter, however, shifts the focus from belonging to function, so that belonging in turn 'serves another priority: that of demonstrating God's deeds of salvation publicly'. The shift is towards 'describing an initiative for missionary activity'.[67] With the shift to the priesthood aspect of God's people, Peter implicitly calls attention to the mediating role of the priests, which includes acting on behalf of God. Clearly the church took this calling seriously. As N. T. Wright concludes, 'World mission is thus the first and most obvious feature of early Christian praxis'.[68]

In Old Testament practice, part of this priestly function of acting on behalf of God entailed teaching the ways of God. Malachi writes, 'For the lips of a priest should guard knowledge, and people should seek instruction from his mouth, for he is the messenger of the LORD of hosts' (Mal. 2:7). This statement is an amplification of a preceding assertion about God's covenant with Levi: 'True instruction was in his mouth' (Mal. 2:6; cf. Lev. 10:10–11; Deut. 33:10a). The mediating role of the priest included that of transmitting the tradition, the torah, the teaching. The prophets were persons who brought the fresh word of God into a specific circumstance; the priests, by contrast, were the guardians, but also the transmitters, of an earlier word of God. God's call for Israel as a people to be his priest *may*, even *must*, be understood as Israel, now corporately God's people, called to function as teacher about God to the nations of the world.[69]

---

66. Rendtorff, *The Covenant Formula*, pp. 47–49, shows how the covenant formula is linked to other formulae, especially the 'recognition formula' which points to God's larger purpose, 'And you/they shall know that I am Yahweh', by drawing on Exod. 6:6–7; Jer. 24:7; 31:31–34; and Ezek. 37:26–28.

67. Wells, *God's Holy People*, pp. 244, 245.

68. Wright, *The New Testament and the People of God*, p. 361.

69. 'The people of God are empowered (and obliged) to do what is otherwise reserved for priests: to come near to God and serve him.' See Wells, *God's Holy People*, p. 218.

In no Old Testament book, except perhaps for the Psalms, is this missionary role for Israel more often and more fully stated than in Isaiah. In a passage that casts the people of Israel as a servant, Isaiah waxes expansive about its worldwide mission. It is too small a thing for this servant to be concerned about the well-being of one people. No, 'I will make you as a light for the nations, that my salvation may reach to the end of the earth' (Isa. 49:6). The servant is elsewhere described as the justice-bringer who will not rest till the coastlands have heard his teaching (Isa. 42:4). One can hear in this reference to 'teaching' a job description for priests. God's people in the role of a priest/servant mediate the knowledge of God to the world. So Peter, in keeping with the heightened visibility of Gentiles in New Testament documents, uses priestly symbolism to underscore that to be the people of God entails serving the priestly function of being the broker of God's message to the nations (cf. 1 Pet. 2:9–12). In the future, Isaiah announces, it will be said of Egypt, 'Blessed be Egypt my people,' for the ranks of the 'people of God' will be enlarged (Isa. 19:25). Once alerted to God's larger intention of incorporating Gentiles into the 'people of God', the Bible reader will find ample evidence of this 'beyond Israel factor' within the Old Testament.[70] Of course, the early church required considerable prodding and urging before it embraced the 'beyond Israel factor'.

The implementation of mission

The two Testaments, then, share the vision of a people of God engaged in declaring God's mighty acts so that those as yet not a people might glorify God by becoming 'God's own people'. While in this respect one can trace a continuity, it is also true that methodologies of Israel and the church for implementing that mission apparently differed.

There is truth in the claim that the mission of Israel vis-á-vis other nations was implemented on a centripetal model. That is, the 'outreach' was not usually overt; rather, it consisted more of a kind of magnetic action to attract those

---

While Wells has an excellent discussion of Israel performing a priestly role, she does not capitalize sufficiently on the priests' (i.e., Israel's) teaching function.

70. The literature about God's missionary intent within the Old Testament is growing. Cf. Walter C. Kaiser, *Mission in the Old Testament: Israel as a Light to the Nations* (Grand Raids: Baker, 2000); Eckhard J. Schnabel, 'Israel, the People of God, and the Nations', *JETS* 54 no. 1 (2002), pp. 35–57; and Scobie, 'Israel and the Nations', *TynBul* 43 no. 2 (1992), pp. 283–305.

on the 'outside' to consider what God was doing with his people.[71] Israel itself, as God's exhibit A, was envisioned as drawing outsiders to its God (cf. Isa. 2:1–5). The historical examples of such 'magnetism' include Naaman of Syria coming for help to Israel and leaving as a convert, and the Queen of Sheba visiting Solomon and acknowledging the generosity of Yahweh, fulfilling Isaiah's later vision in part: 'nations shall come to your light, and kings to the brightness of your rising' (Isa. 60:3). Other examples of the blessing of Abraham devolving on others without intentional 'missionizing' efforts include Isaac's wholesome witness to his Canaanite neighbour, Abimelech of Gerar (Gen. 26:28), Joseph rescuing an entire nation from the ravages of drought (Gen. 41–42), Jethro acknowledging the sovereignty of Yahweh (Exod. 18:10–11), and Daniel and his friends inspiring even King Nebuchadnezzar to give allegiance to God (Dan. 3:28–30).

By contrast, so it is said, the New Testament is centrifugal. That is, the people of God are actively on the move outwards to bear witness to others about God's purposes in the world, specifically the gospel's offer of salvation (cf. Jesus' command to reach all nations, Matt. 28:19–20). The book of Acts chronicles how the gospel moved from the centre, Jerusalem, to Judea, to Samaria, and to the outer parts of the world (cf. Acts 1:8).

Yet the distinction between centripetal (Old Testament) and centrifugal (New Testament) is not that absolute.[72] The Old Testament is not a stranger to a centrifugal approach. Jonah, who might be cast as a foreign missionary, deliberately moves cross-culturally to Nineveh. Even if Jonah is disallowed as an example,[73] Schnabel notes that at least two of the Isaiah servant passages

---

71. Schnabel, 'Israel, the People of God, and the Nations', p. 41.

72. Cf. C. H. H. Scobie: 'The basically centripetal movement of the Old Testament is replaced by the centrifugal movement of the New Testament' ('Israel and the Nations', pp. 301–302).

73. Titus Guenther takes issue with Jonah as a 'missionary text' and quotes David Bosch, 'Even the book of Jonah has nothing to do with mission in the normal sense of the word. The prophet is sent to Nineveh not to proclaim salvation to non-believers but to announce doom.' See Titus Guenther, 'Missionary Vision and Practice in the Old Testament', in Gordon Zerbe (ed.), *Reclaiming the Old Testament* (Winnipeg: CBMC Publications, 2001), p. 149. Eckhart Schnabel agrees: 'It is doubtful whether the book of Jonah should be labeled a "missionary text"' ('Israel, the People of God, and the Nations', p. 39). Walter C. Kaiser, noting such objections, nevertheless champions the missionary purpose of the book of Jonah (*Mission in the Old Testament*, pp. 66–71).

(42:1–7; 49:6) envision a deliberate outreach to the non-Jews.[74] However, if one defines 'mission' as 'witness', then not only are there statements of witness to 'nations', but examples of 'testimony' elsewhere (e.g., Abraham, Gen. 21:22–24; Jacob, Gen. 30:27; 26:26–29). Isaiah's 'servant' is described as being endowed by the Spirit with a task of bringing justice, putting matters right between God and humans; he will not waver or desist until 'he has established justice in the earth; and the coastlands wait for his law' (Isa. 42:4; cf. 42:6–7; 49:6; 51:4–5).

Another example of 'outreach' in the Old Testament occurs in the final chapter in Isaiah, where survivors of Israel declare God's glory 'among the nations' (Isa. 66:18–21). It is from these 'converts' that God will elect persons for a priestly function. So there is a centrifugal dimension in the Old Testament as well as in the New Testament, even if the latter is more pronounced. There is also a centripetal dimension in the New Testament. Jesus himself pictured his people, represented by his disciples, as the 'light of the world', urging them to let their light shine so that those seeing their good works might 'give glory to [the] Father in heaven' (Matt. 5:14–16). Peter speaks in a similar vein when he urges godly conduct so that Gentiles 'may see your good deeds and glorify God on the day of visitation' (1 Pet. 2:12). Not accidentally, this exhortation follows on the heels of the assertion that God's people are to proclaim God's mighty acts (1 Pet. 2:9). Peter and Jesus, and the Old Testament less distinctly, all advocate both a centrifugal and a centripetal approach to mission.

Indeed, the missiology of both Testaments affirms as a minimum that (1) God is a missionary God; (2) his people have a missionary responsibility; (3) this responsibility consists of being an exhibit of God's shaping endeavours; but (4) it also includes active witness to God's mighty acts.

Conclusion

An important motif in both the Old and the New Testaments is captured in the covenant formula: 'I will be your God; you shall be my people.' In both Testaments that formula is understood theologically to underscore the divine initiative and long-range intention of shaping a people whom God can call his own. God's people is more than an aggregate of unconnected individuals; rather, this people is a bonded people, sociologically a community with specific

---

74. So Schnabel, 'Isaiah contains the only two statements in Israel's prophetic tradition that portray a "centrifugal" movement from Israel to the nations' ('Israel, the People of God, and the Nations', p. 41).

but common faith denominators. This corporate body, the people of God, is committed to being a God-kind of community, which means, first and foremost, a holy people, a point stressed in both Testaments. Finally, both Testaments affirm a missional responsibility for the corporate body.

Among the many ramifications of the characterizations noted above is a political one. This people of God, not bounded by geography or ethnicity, represents an alternative community formed within the world's peoples. The messianic kingdom is textured very differently from Roman, Marxist and even capitalist forms of government. God's community, in contrast to modern nation states, functions with a worldview where God is at the centre. This community does not give highest allegiance to the state. It is Jesus who is Lord, not Caesar, as the New Testament people of God already understood.[75] Like all people groupings, it is mindful of power; for the people of God, however, it is the power of the crucified and resurrected Jesus that is critical, and that modifies or even overturns other goals of power, such as militarism, as a national dynamic. The ethical norms of God's people are not derived from traditions or culture but from quite another source, the Bible, the word of God. Hence God's people are countercultural. To be a member of this community is to be committed to an 'upside-down kingdom'.[76] The challenge to work out the 'political' dimensions of this gospel within the variegated global setting is huge and ongoing. Other kingdoms of the world will eventually disintegrate, but this kingdom of God's people endures into the eschaton.

Such an entity, the people of God, can be conceptualized and described theoretically. The point should not be missed, however, that such a people actually exists. It is a people located in all sectors of the globe, who, although imperfect, nevertheless sing the praises of a redeeming God, aspire to a God-intended unity, seek to live ethically as God's holy people, which may mean being countercultural, and are self-consciously and joyously missional.[77]

75. Richard A. Horsley (ed.), *Paul and Politics* (Harrisburg: Trinity Press, 2000); Warren Carter, *Matthew and Empire* (Harrisburg: Trinity Press, 2001).

76. Donald B. Kraybill, *The Upside Down Kingdom*, rev. ed. (Scottdale: Herald Press, 1990).

77. I wish to thank my fellow contributors to this book for the synergy of our two face-to-face sessions and for their helpful critique. My appreciation is extended to my seminary colleagues Jon Isaak, Mark Baker, Allen Guenther and especially John E. Toews for his extended observations. He also chaired a colloquium where this paper was discussed at length.

7. THE HISTORY OF REDEMPTION

Roy E. Ciampa

The history of redemption (or salvation history, or *Heilsgeschichte*) has long been a common approach (although also a highly debated one) to biblical theology, especially since Oscar Cullmann wrote on *Christ and Time* almost sixty years ago.[1] Since then, it has been widely recognized as an integrating framework for biblical theology.[2] The history of redemption approach to Scripture

---

1. Oscar Cullmann, *Christ and Time: The Primitive Christian Conception of Time and History*, trans. Floyd V. Filson (Philadelphia: Westminster, 1950). The theme goes back at least as far as the nineteenth century with the work of Gottfried Menken, Johann T. Beck and especially J. Ch. Konrad von Hofmann (cf. Gerhard Hasel, *New Testament Theology: Basic Issues in the Current Debate* [Grand Rapids: Eerdmans, 1978], pp. 36–38).

2. For a discussion of this approach to New Testament theology from Cullmann to the mid-1970s, see Hasel, *New Testament Theology*, pp. 111–132. Some of the more significant contributions in this area include Graeme Goldsworthy, *According to Plan: The Unfolding Revelation of God in the Bible* (Leicester: Inter-Varsity Press; Downers Grove: InterVarsity Press, 1991); Craig G. Bartholomew and Michael W. Goheen, *The Drama Of Scripture: Finding Our Place in the Biblical Story* (Grand Rapids: Baker, 2004); Craig G. Bartholomew and Michael W. Goheen, 'Story in Biblical Theology', in Craig G. Bartholomew, Joel B. Green and Anthony C. Thiselton

seeks to uncover the biblical authors' own understanding of the events and their significance within the unfolding narrative context in which they are found. The expression 'history of salvation' or 'history of redemption' therefore does not refer directly to the facts of world history or to the facts/reports of God's intervention in history as though they were self-interpreting, but to particular ways in which the biblical authors interpreted the key events in the history of the relationship between God and his creation/people by way of the narrative-theological structures that they used or assumed.

It should be clarified from the start that this essay will not argue that 'salvation history' is the key theme of every book or author of the Bible. Nevertheless, even those authors who do not make 'salvation history' an explicit theme of their writing reflect an understanding of a certain salvation-historical context within which their own experience and message is understood. Thus in carrying out biblical theology we must often distinguish between the theological foundation that an author expects to hold in common with his readers and the distinct theological points that the author seeks to make in his own writing. Some biblical authors emphasize a programme of salvation history as the plan that God is working out for the redemption of creation and his people. Others assume that framework and address their readers in other terms, but they do so in the light of an awareness of where they stand in relation to the unfolding of God's redemptive plan.

In particular, the goal of this essay is to further the argument of those scholars who have argued in favour of understanding biblical theology in terms of the narrative structure reflected in the Deuteronomic Sin-Exile-

(eds.), *Out of Egypt: Biblical Theology and Biblical Interpretation*, SHS (Grand Rapids: Zondervan, 2004), pp. 144–171; Robert A. Krieg, *Story Shaped Christology: The Roles of Narratives in Identifying Jesus Christ* (New York: Paulist, 1988); Gerhard Sauter and John Barton (eds.), *Revelation and Story: Narrative Theology and the Centrality of Story* (Aldershot and Burlington: Ashgate, 2000); Robert B. Robinson, 'Narrative Theology and Biblical Theology', in John Reumann (ed.), *The Promise and Practice of Biblical Theology* (Minneapolis: Fortress, 1991), pp. 129–142; Stephen G. Dempster, *Dominion and Dynasty: A Biblical Theology of the Hebrew Bible* (Leicester: Apollos; Downers Grove: InterVarsity Press, 2003); G. K. Beale, 'The New Testament and New Creation', in Scott J. Hafemann (ed.), *Biblical Theology: Retrospect and Prospect* (Downers Grove: InterVarsity Press; Leicester: Apollos, 2002), pp. 159–173.

Restoration pattern.[3] This essay will sketch out a somewhat more elaborate understanding of the way that structure informs the understanding of representative biblical authors.[4]

The two CSER structures in the Old Testament

While the biblical narrative may be understood from the starting point of the Sin-Exile-Restoration (SER) schema, the themes of sin, exile and restoration must be understood in relationship to the prior concept of Covenant or Creation (of a covenant people).[5] The 'sin' of the SER structure is sin against

---

3. See, e.g., Odil Hannes Steck, 'Das Problem theologischer Strömungen in nachexilischer Zeit' (1968), pp. 445–458; Michael A. Knibb, 'The Exile in the Literature of the Intertestamental Period', *Heythrop Journal* 17 (1976), pp. 253–272; Jacob Neusner, *Self-Fulfilling Prophecy: Exile and Restoration in the History of Israel* (Boston: Beacon, 1987), pp. 58–60; James M. Scott, For as Many as are of Works of the Law are under a Curse (Galatians 3.10), in *Paul and the Scriptures of Israel. Studies in Scripture in Early Judaism and Christianity 1, JSNTSup* 83 (Sheffield: JSOT Press, 1993), pp. 187–221; idem, 'Paul's Use of Deuteronomic Tradition', *JBL* 112 (1993), pp. 645–665; idem, 'Jesus' Vision for the Restoration of Israel as the Basis for a Biblical Theology of the New Testament', in Hafemann (ed.), *Biblical Theology: Retrospect and Prospect*, pp. 129–143; idem, 'Restoration of Israel', *DPL*, pp. 796–805; N. T. Wright, *The New Testament and the People of God* (Minneapolis, MN: Fortress, 1992), pp. 139–143, 268–272 (see the literature cited on p. 270 n. 108); C. Marvin Pate, J. Scott Duvall, J. Daniel Hays, E. Randolph Richards, W. Dennis Tucker Jr and Preben Vang, *The Story of Israel: A Biblical Theology* (Downers Grove: InterVarsity Press, 2004).

4. Of course, caution must be exercised in developing such overarching biblical-theological frameworks. Christopher J. H. Wright points out that there is 'a sense in which any framework necessarily "distorts" the text to some degree. The only way not to distort the biblical text is simply to reproduce it as it is' ('Mission as a Matrix for Hermeneutics and Biblical Theology', in Bartholomew, Green and Thiselton (eds.), *Out of Egypt: Biblical Theology and Biblical Interpretation*, p. 138). Wright suggests conceptualizing biblical theology through analogy with a map, reminding us that 'every existing map and any possible map is a distortion to some degree of the reality it portrays' and 'the question becomes one of what to include or exclude from the symbolic representation that all maps are. Not every feature of the real landscape can be on a map, so the question again is, what purpose is the map intended to serve?' (ibid., pp. 138, 139).

5. See the essay by Hafemann in this volume.

the covenant established by God, exile is the result of the execution of the covenant curses, and restoration has to do with the restoration of the covenant relationship that was broken or at least threatened. Therefore it seems more appropriate, as this essay will demonstrate, to refer to a CSER structure rather than simply to a SER structure. Specifically, the thesis of this essay is (1) that the main structure of the biblical narrative essentially consists of two CSER structures, with the second one (a national CSER structure) embedded within the first (a global CSER structure) and serving as the key to resolution of the plot conflict of that global CSER structure, and (2) that God's kingdom intentions and promises are understood in the light of the relationship between these two interlocking CSER structures.

Pentateuch and historical narratives

The biblical story begins with God's creation of the universe, with the creation of humanity as its climactic act. Humankind is created as his vice-regents who are to reflect his glory throughout his creation as they reflect the image of the Great Creator-King through their exercise of dominion over the rest of his creation.[6] This summary of the original creation/covenant represents what would be called the 'setting' in a typical narrative overview such as is suggested by Tremper Longman's diagram reproduced below.[7]

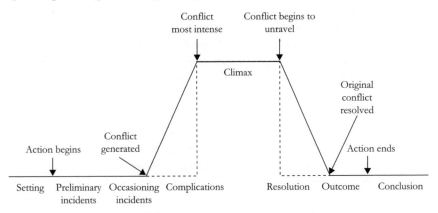

6. See Dan G. McCartney, 'Ecce Homo: The Coming of the Kingdom As the Restoration of Human Vicegerency', *WTJ* 56 (1994), pp. 1–21.

7. Tremper Longman III, *Literary Approaches to Biblical Interpretation*, FCI 3 (Grand Rapids: Zondervan; Leicester: Apollos, 1987), p. 92.

God blesses his vice-regents and places them in a garden paradise that is marked in a special way by God's presence, where they will experience only blessing as long as they faithfully respect his command not to eat of one tree. He warns them that they will die on the day they eat its fruit.[8] The initial exchanges between God and the couple in the garden relate to the beginning of action and the 'preliminary incidents'. Rather than enjoy the tree of life, our protagonists choose to defy the one prohibition given by their Suzerain and eat from the tree of the knowledge of good and evil. Interestingly enough, although curses are pronounced as a result of the sin (and the entry of physical decay and death is no doubt to be understood to begin at that moment), death is not mentioned again until Genesis 5:5, where we are told that Adam died after living 930 years! What we *see* happen, presumably on the same day, is the exile of humanity from their garden paradise (Gen. 3:23–24). This is the 'occasioning incident' in our narrative. The rest of the biblical story revolves around the question of the eventual 'resolution' of the conflict generated by the occasioning incident, that is, the question of the restoration of God's originally intended relationship with his vice-regents and the restoration of their role in reflecting the glory of his reign throughout his realm. Most of the Old Testament will consist of 'complications' on the way to that ultimate resolution.

In this original CSER schema, our protagonists not only lose possession of their special land/place, but they also experience curses in their exilic experience outside that special place. 'Through these chapters the narrator highlights the unravelling of a blessed creation and offers a story of a creation once named "good" but now most certainly gone awry.'[9] The original blessing-based command to multiply is now complicated by the curse of pain in childbearing, and the blessed dominion of the couple will now reflect the ten-

---

8. The theme of God's dominion and presence is highlighted by the implied regularity of theophanic experience and by the temple associations of the garden. See Gordon Wenham, 'Sanctuary Symbolism in the Garden of Eden Story', in Richard S. Hess and D. T. Tsumara (eds.), *I Studied Inscriptions from before the Flood* (Winona Lake: Eisenbrauns, 1994), p. 26; G. K. Beale, *The Temple and the Church's Mission: A Biblical Theology of the Dwelling Place of God* (Leicester: Apollos; Downers Grove: InterVarsity Press, 2004), pp. 66–93; Meredith G. Kline, *Images of the Spirit* (Grand Rapids: Baker, 1980), p. 35. On garden imagery used for the temple, see also T. Stordalen, *Echoes of Eden: Genesis 2–3 and Symbolism of the Eden Garden in Biblical Hebrew Literature* (Leuven: Peeters, 2000), pp. 410–417, 435–437.

9. Pate et al., *The Story of Israel*, p. 31.

sions of fallen relationships (3:16).[10] This suggestion that the Genesis narrative reflects a CSER structure which applies to all of creation obviously entails reading the early Genesis narratives in the light of the covenantal background of their Pentateuchal context, where blessings or curses in the land and the covenantal curse of exile from the land are well-established explicit elements of the narrative.[11] The parallel proposed here between the story of

---

10. Ibid., p. 32.

11. N. T. Wright, *The Resurrection of the Son of God* (Minneapolis: Fortress, 2003), p. 122. Wright 'wonders whether the story in Genesis 3, of Adam and Eve being expelled from the garden, was read in this period as a paradigm of Israel's expulsion from the promised land', but he concludes that 'direct evidence for this connection is lacking'. In view of the clear parallel to the Deuteronomic pattern so essential to so much other Old Testament material, I think it unlikely that readers sensitive to the logic of the narrative development would not read the opening of Genesis in the light of the clear SER patterns found elsewhere. See I. M. Duguid's discussion of the foreshadowing of the exile in Genesis ('Exile', *NDBT*, pp. 475–476): 'The expulsion of Adam and Eve from the garden of Eden is the archetype of all subsequent exile (Gen. 3:24) . . . Throughout the rest of the Bible, the state of God's people is one of profound exile, of living in a world to which they do not belong and looking for a world that is yet to come.' Terence E. Fretheim ('Genesis', in NIB, vol. 3, p. 365) notes that the ending of Genesis 3 'bears some remarkable similarities both to Israel's being sent/driven out of Egypt (Exod. 6:1) and to Israel's exile to Babylon, a banishment from the land (see Lev. 26). The latter, in particular, may have been viewed as a parallel experience to this primeval moment in Israel's eyes.' Kenneth A. Mathews, *Genesis 1–11:26*, NAC 1A (Nashville: Broadman & Holman Publishers, 1995), p. 59, notes the exilic theme of the opening chapters of Genesis: 'Adam and Eve are expelled from Eden (3:24), Cain is exiled from the "LORD's presence" (4:16), and the Babelites are scattered (11:9), all oriented toward the "east", indicating the loss of blessing . . . Without Abraham the primeval history ends on the despairing note of exile.' Looking at the end of chapter 3, Mathews reminds us of the parallel again: 'Moses offered the same choice of life or death, obedience or disobedience, to Israel on the shores of Moab (Deut 30:11–20). Obedience meant life and prosperity in Canaan, but defiance guaranteed expulsion. Israel's parents chose banishment, and Israel itself chose exile' (ibid., p. 255). Furthermore, 'Adam and Eve's exile is decisive and definitive' (ibid., p. 257). Cf. Robert Alter's comments on Genesis 4:9–12 in his *Genesis: Translation and Commentary* (New York/London: W. W. Norton, 1996), p. 18:

humanity and the story of Israel is recognized by much rabbinic literature. As Jacob Neusner put it,

'There are several verbal echoes of Adam's interrogation by God and Adam's curse, setting up a general biblical pattern in which history is seen as a cycle of approximate and significant recurrences. Adam's being driven from the garden . . . is replayed here . . . The biblical imagination is equally preoccupied with the theme of exile (this is already the second expulsion) and with the arduousness or precariousness of agriculture, a blessing that easily turns into blight.' Cf. the discussion of Gary A. Anderson, *The Genesis of Perfection: Adam and Eve in Jewish and Christian Imagination* (Louisville: Westminster John Knox, 2001), p. 120: 'Biblical writers believed that the human condition was best described through what happened to Israel. On the face of it then, we should expect some similarity between what happened to Adam and Eve and what happened to Israel. And this expectation bears fruit. Just as Adam and Eve receive a commandment prior to their entrance into Eden, so Israel is given a set of commandments prior to her entrance into the Promised Land. Just as in the Garden Adam and Eve's well-being is predicated on their obedience, so for Israel. And, most important, just as the tree of life remains a tantalizing reward for Adam and Eve should they be found virtuous, so life itself is offered as a reward to Israel should they be faithful to the covenant.' So then, '[i]n the story of the Fall . . . we have a presentation of Israel's central story in miniature:

Eden	*Sinai*
God creates man	God elects Israel
Command is given	Torah is revealed
Violation	[Should] Israel violate the Torah
Expulsion from Eden	Exile from the Promised Land' (ibid., p. 121).

Finally, Jacob Neusner points out that, according to Genesis Rabbah, 'The message that Scripture yields through Rabbinic Midrash exegesis involves the comparison of Adam and Israel, each having possessed paradise – the Garden of Eden, the land of Israel, respectively – and each having lost it. In the just plan of creation humanity was meant to live in Eden and Israel in the land of Israel in time without end. Humanity sinned and lost Eden, Israel sinned and lost the Land . . . Then, at the other end of time, the eschatological restoration of humanity to Eden, Israel to the Land, will bring about that long and tragically postponed perfection of the world order, sealing the demonstration of the justice of God's plan for creation' ('Genesis in Genesis Rabbah', in Jacob Neusner and Alan J. Avery-Peck (eds.), *Encyclopedia of Midrash: Biblical Interpretation in Formative Judaism* ([Leiden/Boston: Brill, 2005, pp. 966–967]). The entry on 'Ge'ulah' (Hebrew for 'redemption') in *The Routledge*

Adam and Israel, Eden and the Land of Israel – these form the parallel 'histories' that sages in the Halakhah discern in the Torah . . . Scripture tells that story in two parts: (1) the creation of Man to enjoy bliss in Eden, in perfect repose, then his and her rebellion and loss of Eden; and (2) the creation of Israel to enjoy the Land, then Israel's rebellion and loss of the Land. As a matter of fact, that forms the core of the theological system that animates the Halakhah and renders it coherent, proportionate and compelling.[12]

Not only do the rabbis see the parallel between the two narratives, they also understand, according to Neusner, that the resolution of Israel's narrative problem brings about the resolution to the narrative problem of Genesis 1–3, since 'the world's creation commenced a single, straight line of significant events, that is to say, history, leading in the end to the salvation of Israel and, through Israel, of all humanity'.[13]

Although the motifs of the divine curse and judgment are reflected throughout chapters 3–11 of Genesis, there are, nevertheless, many signs of God's grace extended to creation and humanity in the midst of this judgment. Those signs may be seen in the promise of a human triumph over the serpent (Gen. 3:15), in the divine act of clothing the naked couple (Gen. 3:21), in the help God provided in the conception and birth of a son (Gen. 4:1) and in the various ways God blessed and provided for the sons of Adam in the following narrative. The birth of a new generation and of each generation since opens up the possibility that restoration will eventually be achieved. While it has been suggested that 'throughout Genesis 3–11 the story includes elements of sin, exile and restoration',[14] it seems a bit overstated to refer to restoration already in these chapters. The achievement of restoration would presumably herald our arrival at the end, or at least the threshold of the end of the narrative as a whole. Rather, it seems that what we witness are the grace and provision that allow the narrative to move towards a future

---

Dictionary of Judaism (Jacob Neusner and Alan J. Avery-Peck [London: Routledge, 2004], p. 46) suggests it treats 'God's salvation of humanity from the condition of sinfulness; the salvation of holy Israel from the condition of Exile and the restoration of humanity to Eden and of Israel to the land of Israel.'

12. Jacob Neusner, 'Midrash and Halakhic Category Formations', in Neusner and Avery-Peck (eds.), *Encyclopedia of Midrash*, p. 174.

13. Neusner, 'Genesis in Genesis Rabbah', p. 88. See also, 'Theology of Rabbinic Midrash', ibid., pp. 966–967, 971.

14. Pate, et al., *The Story of Israel*, p. 31.

restoration.[15] Throughout this narrative, however, 'Human beings are permanent exiles from the pristine space and time of Eden. There is no way back and the way ahead is uncertain. To its very end the plot of Genesis, and by extension that of the Pentateuchal narrative, will be concerned with the attempt to find another way in which human beings can live with integrity before God, at home on the earth, and within the security of the divine blessing.'[16]

In the following chapters of the Genesis narrative there are a few key texts that reflect back upon the original creation narrative and that provide the reader with clues regarding where we are with respect to God's original intentions for creation and humanity as indicated in the first chapter of the story. Genesis 5:1-3 harks back to 1:26-28, recalling the creation of man and woman in God's likeness and the blessing they received as the context informing the birth of Seth in Adam's own likeness and image. Given the clear allusion to 1:26-28, it is noteworthy that the motif of dominion, which was one of the key themes in 1:26, 28, is not mentioned in 5:1-3 or its context. Death, however, which was last mentioned in chapter 3, is mentioned, as Adam's life comes to an end. The juxtaposition of Genesis 5:1-2 to 5:3 suggests humanity continues to reflect the image of God, but its role in exercising dominion over the rest of the earth is in abeyance.

As a result, the flood narrative of Genesis 6-9 suggests a de-creation and re-creation in which, after destroying the life that had spread on earth, the waters separate once again to let dry land appear (cf. 1:9) so that pairs of the different creatures, and humanity as well, may once again carry on the story of life in God's creation. This took place after the earth had become 'filled with violence' (6:11), rather than filled with a humanity that faithfully reflected the image of God throughout the earth. In chapter 9 Noah becomes a kind of second Adam, and he receives the same command as was given in Genesis 1:28, 'Be fruitful and multiply and fill the earth', with the creatures of the air, earth and water once again mentioned. But there is something different. Noah is not told to subdue the earth and have dominion over all those creatures. He is told that they will fear him and that they are now given to him for food. There is a new start, but we have not been brought all the way back to the clean slate of Genesis 1. Furthermore, Carol Kaminski has persuasively argued that chapters 9-11 reflect

---

15. For the motif of blessing or grace in the Genesis narrative, see Carol M. Kaminski, *From Noah to Israel: Realization of the Primaeval Blessing After the Flood*, JSOTSup 413 (London and New York: T. & T. Clark, 2004), pp. 60-79, 92-123.

16. Thomas Mann, *The Book of the Truth: The Narrative Integrity of the Pentateuch* (Louisville: Westminster John Knox, 1988), p. 19, cited in Pate, et al., *The Story of Israel*, p. 33.

the motif of the 'scattering' of humanity over the face of the earth (9:19; 10:18; 11:4, 8, 9) as a reflection of divine judgment rather than blessing.[17] The verb used in Genesis 10:18; 11:4, 8, 9 is the same used in key passages to refer to the scattering of Israel in the unfolding of its own CSER structure.[18] This strengthens the suggestion that the Genesis narrative reflects the same motifs found in Israel's CSER structure. With the end of the flood we are not back to the blessed state of the garden. We have experienced creation/covenant-sin-exile, but *the narrative goes on because restoration has not been achieved.* The possibility and hope for it continue, but how it might come about is still unclear.

The problem of the conclusion of the global CSER structure provides the context for the introduction of the corresponding CSER structure, which applies to the experience of Israel and is found embedded within the framework of the broader CSER structure applying to all creation (and therefore to the whole of humanity). The CSER structure that applies to Israel serves as the central subplot and key to the plot of the more universal narrative and its complications and resolution.[19] The relationship may be shown in diagram form, as in the following charts.

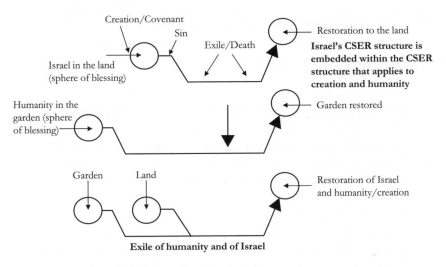

Exile of humanity and of Israel

---

17. Kaminski, *From Noah to Israel*, pp. 10–59, 139–141.

18. Heb. *pûs*, cf. Deut. 4:27; 28:64; 30:3; 2 Kgs 25:5; Neh. 1:8; Jer. 9:15; 13:24; 18:17; 23:1; 30:11; 52:8; Ezek. 11:16–17; 12:15; 20:23, 34, 41; 22:15; 28:25; 34:5–6, 12; 36:19; Zeph. 3:10; Zech. 13:7.

19. Craig Blomberg's discussion of the Old Testament contribution to 'The Unifying Plot of Scripture' skips over the issue of humankind's original role and its

The plight of humanity (and its need for a resolution) serves as the 'setting' for Israel's own narrative. Within that narrative the 'preliminary incidents' would consist of the calling of Israel and God's promises to the patriarchs. The 'occasioning incident' may be discerned in the nation's rebellion in the desert, most prominently in the fiasco with the golden calf, which is followed by a series of 'complications' that ultimately lead to a 'climax', beginning in Israel's exile and moving towards 'resolution' with the return from exile. As we shall see, the climax of Israel's narrative will essentially double as the climax of the universal narrative, since the resolution of the plight of creation and humanity ends up being directly tied to that of Israel.

The relationship between people and land serves as a hermeneutical key to much of this narrative development. Hence, as the narrative advances it develops a remarkable reversal of the original narrative step of separation from a divinely appointed place of blessing when the Creator-Suzerain does not send Abraham *away* from a special habitat, but *to* such a place (Gen. 12:1).[20] The suspicion that a plan of redemption is at work, a *reverse-of-the-curse*, is reinforced by the repeated use of the language of blessing in this episode. As H. W. Wolff has pointed out, the fivefold repetition of the language of blessing in Genesis 12:1–3 suggests the response to the five occurrences of the word 'curse' in Genesis 1–11 (3:14, 17; 4:11; 5:29; 9:25).[21] Thus the promise of blessing to

---

fall: 'The Bible begins with an account of creation and the primeval history of humanity (Gen. 1–11). In Genesis 12:1–3, God singles out the individual Abraham and promises him seed, land and a blessing for the nations' ('The Unity and Diversity of Scripture', *NDBT*, p. 67). Many discussions of biblical theology discuss the exile and restoration, but they often overlook the way in which one SER schema is embedded within another and serves as a key to the completion of the other.

20. As William Dumbrell puts it (*Covenant and Creation: A Theology of the Old Testament Covenants*, BTCL 12 [Carlisle: Paternoster, 2002], p. 72), 'the centrifugal effect of these early Genesis narratives is now arrested by the centripetal potential movement of the world back to an Eden situation through Abram.' Of course, in Genesis 6–11 we have a new creation/covenant episode with Noah (followed by another attempt to usurp divine prerogatives in 11:4; cf. 3:5), following which God – after contemplating the proper response to the sinful action as he did in Genesis 3 (11:6–7) – 'dispersed them from there over the face of all the earth' (Gen. 11:8).

21. H. W. Wolff, 'Kerygma of the Yahwist', *Int* 20 (1966), pp. 145–146, cited in Dumbrell, *Covenant and Creation*, p. 71.

Abram's seed suggests that through him the curses of Genesis 1–11 will be undone.[22] As Michael Fishbane suggests, the three blessings of 'gifts of land, seed and earthly blessing (12:1–3) . . . are, in fact, a typological reversal of the primordial curses in Eden: directed against the earth, human generativity, and human labour'.[23]

God's promises to Abram in Genesis 12:2–3 suggest blessings that one great suzerain might confer upon another. Wenham points out that '[w]hat Abram is here promised was the hope of many an oriental monarch'.[24] He will become a great nation, blessed by his divine Suzerain, including the blessing of the common royal aspiration of a great name,[25] so that he might become 'the mediator of blessing for mankind'.[26] In fact, others will be blessed or cursed depending on their relationship to Abram, as though they were all bound to him by a suzerainty treaty with blessings or curses depending on the attitude taken with respect to Abram as *their* suzerain. This clearly anticipates the later biblical material about the ideal Davidic king (see below), as does God's promise to Abraham in 17:6 that 'kings shall come from you'.[27]

God's intention to bless all nations through Abram confirms the other indications that his calling of Abram did not entail an abandoning of his original intention to govern a world through a human vice-regent who would come to have dominion over and bring blessing to his creation, but a strategy of realizing that very intention. Moreover, God describes the calling of Abraham in terms that parallel the redemptive event his people were to anticipate on the way to the fulfilment of God's great promises: both were experiences of being brought out of a less desirable country into the special land of God's presence and blessing (15:7, 16). As Dumbrell points out, 'Gen. 12:1–3 is the rejoinder to the consequences of the fall and aims at the restoration of the purposes of God for the world to which Gen. 1–2 directed our attention.'[28]

---

22. See Dumbrell, *Covenant and Creation*, p. 71; and N. T. Wright, 'Adam, Israel and the Messiah', in *The Climax of the Covenant: Christ and the Law in Pauline Theology* (Edinburgh: T. & T. Clark, 1992), pp. 21–23.

23. Michael Fishbane, *Biblical Interpretation in Ancient Israel* (Oxford: Clarendon, 1985), pp. 372–373.

24. See the discussion in Gordon J. Wenham, *Genesis 1–15*, WBC 1 (Waco: Word, 1987), p. 275.

25. See, ibid., and *HALOT* on šēm.

26. Dumbrell, *Covenant and Creation*, p. 68.

27. Cf. Fishbane, *Biblical Interpretation in Ancient Israel*, p. 373.

28. Dumbrell, *Covenant and Creation*, p. 68.

Several scholars have observed that the motif evoked by the language of 'being fruitful' and 'multiplying', which is originally tied to the primeval creation narrative (1:28), is 'frequently used in connection with Abraham and his seed', and that 'the primaeval blessing has been *reaffirmed* and *reapplied* to Abraham's progeny'.[29] Here also we have the mirroring of humanity's experience in that of Abraham's family. The promises to Abraham in Genesis 22:17–18 contain the promise of the multiplication and superior military power (cf. dominion in 1:26, 28) of his offspring and reinforce the point that all nations would be blessed through them. That this is also part of the reverse-of-the-curse is suggested by the contrast between the coming of the curse on humanity due to Adam's decision to listen to the voice of his wife (3:17) and the coming of blessing to all humanity thanks to Abraham's decision to listen to the voice of the Lord (22:18).

The patriarchal narratives are filled with episodes that raise questions about the fulfilment of the Abrahamic promises as the likelihood of their fulfilment is threatened over and over again, and as the family's ability to bring blessing rather than curse is put to the test. A family could be wiped out due to famine, or through execution by an offended warlord or political leader, or it could self-destruct. There are times, when reading through the patriarchal narratives, when one could wonder if the heirs of the promises could be any more negligent caretakers of the promises than they are, and yet we still see them rescued from one crisis after another, and we see them being blessed and bringing blessing to others.[30] By the time we get to the end of the book of

---

29. Kaminski, *From Noah to Israel*, pp. 93, 94 (her emphasis). Cf. Gen. 16:10; 17:2, 20; 22:17; 26:4, 15, 24; 28:3; 35:11; 47:27; 48:4; and David J. A. Clines, *The Theme of the Pentateuch, JSOT*Sup 10 (Sheffield: JSOT Press, 1979), p. 79.

30. James Barr, *The Concept of Biblical Theology: An Old Testament Perspective* (Minneapolis: Fortress, 1999), pp. 356–357, asks, 'What, after all, is the "theology" of the stories of Abraham and Isaac with their wives taken into the house of a great potentate (Gen. 12, 20, 26), or of Jacob's manipulations with the sheep and goats of Laban (Gen. 30–31)? Maybe there is a theology there, but one cannot claim that it is obvious, or that it is actually stated by the text. People have been able to think of such a theology, but in order to do so they have had to go outside the text itself, turning either to another passage (which, usually, is more explicit theologically) or to later interpretative tradition.' I would suggest that Genesis 12:1–3 and the other passages regarding the Abrahamic promises are not 'outside the text' or 'other' passages, but the narrative framework within which we are expected to understand the episodes to which Barr refers (especially since one of the episodes he cites

Genesis, we find Joseph functioning as vice-regent over the mighty nation of Egypt and bringing salvation (dare we say blessing?) both to that nation and to his own family in the process.[31] And that happens despite (and through) the wicked actions of his brothers and of Potiphar's wife, etc. The last verses of the book emphasize Joseph's faith that God would fulfil his promises to Abraham (including that of 15:14). That God will raise up a descendant of Abraham who will bring blessing to all the world, perhaps as God's own vice-regent reigning in the land promised to the patriarch, would be an easily imagined scenario, given what God had already done through Joseph while he was in a foreign land.[32]

In the midst of the extended narrative about Joseph we find Jacob's last words to his sons (Gen. 49:1–27). There the reader discovers that while Joseph has provided a model or proleptic view of what God has in mind for his people, the person who will actually realize that dream will come from the line of Judah. In Jacob's words, 'The scepter shall not depart from Judah, nor the ruler's staff from between his feet, until tribute comes to him; and to him shall be the obedience of the peoples' (Gen. 49:10).

Much of the theology of the Pentateuch has to do with the issue of the presence of God. God is present with Adam and Eve in the garden. He appears from time to time in the patriarchal narratives, but one never knows when or where he will appear next. The material regarding the tabernacle and

---

immediately follows the key promise text). It is true that the authors of biblical narratives expect more of their readers than authors of other kinds of text (or is it just that they require more from modern readers than we are used to?). The author of Esther expects the reader to understand something about God's providential working in history, even if God is never mentioned and the point is never stated in so many words. T. Desmond Alexander makes a fine suggestion regarding the role of some of those difficult passages in the wider narrative framework ('Genesis to Kings', *NDBT*, p. 119): 'By tracing the line of "seed" from Seth to Jehoiachin, the narrative [of Genesis – Kings] highlights God's ongoing faithfulness to his promises in spite of many obstacles to their fulfilment.'

31. On the parallels between Joseph and Adam, see, e.g., John H. Sailhamer, *The Pentateuch as Narrative* (Grand Rapids: Zondervan, 1992), p. 215.

32. Perhaps we also have here a foreshadowing of Paul's teaching that the blessing of the nations (through Christ and Paul in the New Testament and through Joseph here) results in blessing to Israel (cf. Rom. 11:11–28). Actually, both probably reflect the idea that the blessing of the nations by a son of Israel results in blessing to Israel, which will then result in even greater blessing to the nations.

sacrificial system, and the return to or entry into the Promised Land in Exodus, Leviticus and Numbers, all relates to the establishment and maintenance of the conditions in which God's presence will be with his people, whether on the way back to the Promised Land or once they have been re-established within the land.[33] The motif of God's presence relates directly to the CSER structure this essay seeks to unpack, in that the whole of the biblical narrative has to do with the loss of God's presence and ultimate restoration of humanity to the fullness of the presence of God (as in the garden and anticipated in the second exodus). The motif of exile relates not only to exile from the garden or Promised Land, since the people's relationship with the garden and Promised Land (the places of God's special dwelling with his people) served as a thermometer indicating the status of their relationship with the God who met with them in those places. To lose the garden or the land was understood to imply the loss of the presence of God. The promise of restoration, in both CSER structures, included at its most fundamental level the promise of the restoration of God's presence in the midst of his people.

The exodus, the dramatic redemptive event which initiated the fulfilment of those promises,[34] was, together with the promises given to Abraham and passed on to his children, the reference point for Israel's self-understanding from that time on. Perhaps the greatest of the blessings given to Israel was the land itself, in which the other blessings were to be experienced. The official entry into the land followed a period of oppression, redemption from which formed the essential background for the establishment of the Mosaic covenant (cf. Deut. 15:15; 24:18). The books of Exodus and Leviticus provide the legal and cultic basis for God's continued covenantal relationship with his people, which was essential to the fulfilment of his promises to Abraham, while the book of Numbers highlights God's continued faithfulness to his promises despite the people's stubborn disobedience. The book of Deuteronomy provides the most influential exposition of the relationship between blessings and curses, the covenant, exile and restoration of Israel. As James A. Sanders points out, the book of Deuteronomy seems to have been placed in its present position in the canon 'to cast its light backward to Genesis

---

33. For a stimulating discussion of the theme of God's presence, see Samuel L. Terrien, *The Elusive Presence: Toward a New Biblical Theology* (San Francisco: Harper & Row, 1978).

34. The promises were initiated in less dramatic fashion in the calling of Abraham and his establishment of altars in the Promised Land (Gen. 12:1–3, 7–8; 13:18; 22:9).

and forward to the Prophets'.[35] The blessings associated with the Mosaic covenant (Deut. 28:1–14) suggest the Promised Land would have been a paradise as long as Israel remained faithful to their Suzerain. If, on the other hand, they were unfaithful to him, they would first lose the experience of blessing in the land and ultimately lose the wonderful blessing of the land itself (Deut. 28:15–68).

Deuteronomy 30 describes the choice between obedience and disobedience, not only as a choice between blessing and curse, but also as a choice between life and death (30:15, 19). That same chapter (30:1–6) predicts that Israel will repeat the primordial history of humanity and find itself choosing disobedience and unfaithfulness, resulting in death and exile.[36] It also hints at the nature of the problem that would lead to such exile and the solution God would provide in the time of restoration. The problem was a hardness of heart that led to constant rebellion and disobedience. The solution would come in an eschatological circumcision of the heart at the time of Israel's restoration.

The history of Israel as recounted in the biblical narratives strongly reflects the Deuteronomic themes of the blessings and curses of the covenant, with the greatest blessings being associated with the reigns of David and Solomon. The books of Joshua, Judges, Samuel and Kings are understood to relate the history of Israel from the conquest to the fall of Judah in terms of the Deuteronomic programme, especially the promises of blessing for faithfulness and judgment for unfaithfulness. The books of Chronicles are heavily dependent upon Kings, while stressing that God still has plans for the post-exilic future of Israel, consistent with the Deuteronomic theme of restoration.[37]

It is during the glory years of David's and Solomon's reigns that a clear development in God's plan to realize his original intention for humanity and creation is revealed by way of the promises of an unending Davidic kingdom, associated with the anticipated establishment of God's presence in the midst of his people through the temple in Jerusalem. That unending kingdom is one in which the Davidic king reigns as God's son (vassal) and vice-regent (2 Sam.

---

35. James A. Sanders, 'The Exile and Canon Formation', in James M. Scott (ed.), *Exile: Old Testament, Jewish, and Christian Conceptions* (Leiden: Brill, 1997), p. 43.

36. For a similar pattern of blessings-curses-restoration, cf. Lev. 26:1–13, 14–39, 40–45.

37. See the helpful discussion of the theology of 'Chronicles' by Martin J. Selman (*NDBT*, pp. 188–195), who argues that the evidence indicates it 'is about the relationship between judgment and exile on the one hand and the restoration of the community around the temple on the other' (p. 192).

7:13–16, as indicated by the fact that this king is the builder and protector of the temple, which serves as the focal point of God's presence on earth). In the view of T. Desmond Alexander, 'The books of Genesis to Kings not only offer an explanation for these traumatic events [associated with the exile] by focusing on the nation's failure to be faithful to Yahweh, but also preserve the hope that God will one day raise up a descendant of David through whom he will bless all the nations of the earth.'[38] David's subjection of the surrounding countries (2 Sam. 8:1–15; 1 Chr. 18:1–14), including Edom, Moab, the Ammonites, the Philistines, Amalek and Zobah, anticipates the extensive reign God has in mind for his kingdom. The narrative of the Queen of Sheba's gifts to Solomon and her recognition of Israel's God (1 Kgs 10:1–13; 2 Chr. 9:1–12) points to the ultimate hope for the Davidic king (although Solomon's heavy-handed use of conscripted workers shows that we have not yet arrived there). We are told, 'King Solomon excelled all the kings of the earth in riches and in wisdom. And the whole earth sought the presence of Solomon to hear his wisdom, which God had put into his mind' (1 Kgs 10:23–24). This motif helps us see one connection between the Old Testament wisdom literature and the motifs being highlighted in this essay. The wisdom given by God to Solomon and his people was to play a significant role in drawing the nations into the sphere of the worship of Israel's God.

In relating the history of the kings of Israel and Judah, the books of Kings and Chronicles continually look to David as the standard by which every other king is to be measured (cf., e.g., 1 Kgs 3:3; 11:4, 6, 33; 14:8; 15:3, 11; 2 Kgs 14:3; 16:2; 18:3; 22:2; 2 Chr. 17:3; 28:1; 29:2, 25, 30; 30:26; 34:2–3). The book of Kings hints at the possibility of restoration in its concluding scene (2 Kgs 25:27–30):

> Evil-merodach king of Babylon . . . graciously freed Jehoiachin king of Judah from prison. And he spoke kindly to him and gave him a seat above the seats of the kings who were with him in Babylon. So Jehoiachin put off his prison garments. And every day of his life he dined regularly at the king's table, and for his allowance, a regular allowance was given him by the king, according to his daily needs, as long as he lived.

The book of Chronicles ends on a similar note by relating the fulfilment of Jeremiah's prophecy of the end of exile through Cyrus's decree that the Jews could return to Jerusalem and rebuild the temple there (2 Chr. 36:22–23).[39]

---

38. Alexander, 'Genesis to Kings', p. 119.

39. The book of Esther does not deal with the Davidic succession, but it does implicitly point to God's faithfulness to Israel. It concludes by pointing out that

The CSER structures in the prophetic literature and the Psalms

Prophetic literature tends to dwell on the upcoming or present exile and on the hope of future salvation and restoration.[40] There are over sixty explicit references to the scattering and gathering of Israel in the Prophets alone.[41] But that is only one of the ways in which the motif is reflected.[42] In addition, the CSER structure is seen in the development of key themes, the most important of which are also developed in the New Testament. Among those themes, I will touch on the second exodus, the new creation, the new covenant, the restored Davidic kingdom and the restored temple. These themes are all interrelated, so that a discussion of any one of them will tend to flow naturally into the other themes as well. I will also look at the ways in which the relationship between the two CSER structures determines the development of each theme and the relationships between them.

God (who is not explicitly mentioned) is able to raise up a faithful Jewish leader to a position of tremendous prominence within the government of the world's greatest power at the time, as Mordecai follows the model set by Joseph in Pharaoh's government, becoming 'second in rank to King Ahasuerus' (Esth. 10:3).

40. As Stephen Dempster puts it ('Prophetic Books', *NDBT*, p. 122), 'The prophetic books record both the largely unheeded prophetic announcement of divine judgment, made to a sinful and self-confident people, and the prediction of salvation beyond the judgment, made to a chastened and discouraged people.'

41. Isa. 11:12; 24:1; 40:11; 43:5; 45:20; 49:5, 18; 56:8; 60:4; Jer. 3:17; 9:15, 21; 10:21; 13:24; 18:17; 23:1–3; 29:14; 30:11; 31:8, 10; 32:37; 40:12; 44:14; 49:36; Ezek. 4:13; 5:10, 12; 6:5, 8; 11:16–17; 12:14–15; 17:21; 20:23, 34, 41; 22:15; 28:25; 34:5–6, 12–13; 36:19, 24; 37:21; 38:12; 39:27–28; Dan. 9:7; Hos. 2:2; Joel 4:2; Mic. 2:12; 4:6; Zeph. 3:20; Zech. 2:2, 4, 10; 7:14; 10:10. Elsewhere in the Old Testament and Apocrypha: Gen. 11:4, 8–9; 49:7; Lev. 26:33; Deut. 4:27; 28:64; 30:3–4; 1 Kgs 14:15; 22:17; 1 Chr. 16:35; 2 Chr. 18:16; Ezra 10:7; Neh. 1:8–9; Pss. 44:12; 74:2; 106:27, 47; 107:3; 147:2; Judith 4:3; 5:19; Tobit 3:4; 13:3, 5, 13; 14:4, 7; 2 Maccabees 1:27; 2:7, 18; Sirach 36:10; 48:15; Baruch 2:4, 13, 29; 3:8; 4:37; 5:5.

42. Cf. Dempster, 'Prophetic Books', pp. 123–124: 'One of the structural arrangements used in the prophetic scrolls is that of judgment and salvation, death and resurrection. Salvation oracles are often juxtaposed to judgment oracles. For example, in the book of Micah an oracle announcing the future exaltation of Zion immediately follows an oracle of doom spoken against the present Zion (3:11–12; 4:1–5); even the book of Amos, which largely consists of judgment oracles, concludes with two salvation oracles (9:11–13, 14–15). This arrangement indicates how the prophets' words functioned as canonical literature.'

Second exodus

As is well known, Isaiah describes the future restoration event as a second exodus (Isa. 11:10–16; 40–66 [esp. 40:3–5, 10–11; 41:17–20; 42:15–16; 43:14–44:5; 51:9–11; 52:7–12; 62:10]; cf. Jer. 16:14–15; 23:5–8; Hos. 2:14–23; Mic. 7:15–17; Zech. 1–8; Ezra 6:19–21), with God playing the part of the divine warrior who leads Israel back to her promised land. The concept of the second exodus serves to associate the redemption of post-exilic restoration with that of the original exodus event. Like the original victory of the exodus, the future eschatological salvation of Israel is described in terms of a height-ened recapitulation/restoration of the military victory over the enemies of God and his people (Hab. 3:2–19; Isa. 52:7–12).[43]

In some texts it becomes clear that Israel's return to the land will end up being seen as merely the first phase of a massive movement of peoples. As the nations of the world see how God has blessed his people, they will go to Zion in order to find blessing for themselves. This is the way some texts picture the role of Israel's CSER structure in bringing about the completion of the universal CSER structure, with the rest of humanity finding its blessing in the context of the eschatological blessing of Israel. This theme is clear in Zechariah 8. Zechariah 8:7–8 contains a promise of the universal ingathering of Israel from exile and verses 21–23 picture the nations grasping onto the last of the returning Jews to go with them to Zion to find blessing for themselves. In Isaiah 2:1–4 and Micah 4:1–5 the nations will flow to Zion in order to be taught the ways of the Lord, so that they might 'walk in his paths', for 'out of Zion shall go the law, and the word of the LORD from Jerusalem' (Isa. 2:3; Mic. 4:2; cf. Isa. 11:10). It seems the flow of the nations *to* Zion is understood to follow the flow of the law and word of Yahweh *from* Zion. The latter may be through the influence of the exiles, or perhaps through the influence of the restored community. Either way, the second exodus is understood to result in the flow of blessing not only to Israel, but also to the nations, bringing about the fulfilment of the promise of Genesis 12:1–3.[44] The theme of Israel's return is frequently associated with that of the coming of the nations to Israel to worship their God or serve the people (Isa. 42:1, 6; 49:5–7, 22; 60:1–16). In

---

43. For a discussion of possible parallels with a victory over chaos in a primordial conflict at the time of creation, see, e.g., Fishbane, *Biblical Interpretation in Ancient Israel*, pp. 354–357; U. Rütersworden, '*rāhab*', *TDOT*, vol. 4, p. 356, who points out that, in Isaiah 51:9–10, 'Yahweh's primeval act is used to interpret the historical event of the exodus, with which it becomes conjoined.'

44. Cf. Ralph L. Smith, *Micah – Malachi*, WBC 32 (Waco: Word, 1984), p. 240.

Isaiah 49:22 the Israelites are carried home on the shoulders of the nations, while in 60:1–16 people come from different nations bringing the Israelites back in ships and also bringing gifts and coming to serve the Israelites.

New creation

Isaiah 2:4 and Micah 4:3 indicate that when the nations flow into Zion after Israel has been judged/purged and restored (see above), they will 'beat their swords into ploughshares, and their spears into pruning hooks'. J. Alec Motyer suggests that '[t]he choice of agricultural implements (ploughshares and pruning hooks) is symbolic of the return to Eden'.[45] Moreover, the restoration of Israel is more explicitly described as a new creation in several prophetic texts. Exile is described as a return to chaos and an undoing of creation (Jer. 4:23–27), whereas restoration is an undoing of the curses of Genesis 3 and of the Mosaic covenant and a re-establishment of the blessings experienced in the garden of Eden (cf. Isa. 51:3–13 [esp. v. 3]; 65:17–25; 66:22–23; Jer. 31:12; Ezek. 31:16–18; 36:35; Hos. 2:18–22). The theme of new creation is also evoked through echoes of the role of the Spirit in creation found in the restoration of the river flowing in the garden (Ezek. 47:1–12;[46] Joel 3:18–21 [4:18–21 MT/LXX]; Zech. 14:8–11), and through echoes of the creation of Adam/humanity in passages referring to the future restoration of Israel (Ezek. 37; Dan. 7:1–14). Ezekiel's description of the restoration of Israel in terms of the resurrection of human bodies which require the breath of life before they actually come to life (Ezek. 37)[47] and Daniel's description of the

---

45. J. Alec Motyer, *The Prophecy of Isaiah: An Introduction & Commentary* (Leicester: Inter-Varsity Press; Downers Grove: InterVarsity Press, 1993), p. 54.

46. On Ezekiel 47 and new creation, see, e.g., Fishbane, *Biblical Interpretation in Ancient Israel*, pp. 370–371; Walther Eichrodt, *Ezekiel: A Commentary*, OTL (Philadelphia: Westminster, 1970), pp. 584–585; Lamar Eugene Cooper, *Ezekiel*, NAC 17 (Nashville: Broadman & Holman, 1994), pp. 411–413 (and his chart on the 'Restoration of Edenic Ideals' in Ezekiel and other biblical texts on p. 349); Daniel I. Block, *The Book of Ezekiel: Chapters 25–48*, NICOT (Grand Rapids: Eerdmans, 1998), p. 696; and Beale, *The Temple and the Church's Mission*, pp. 340–342. On 'The Mountain of Ezekiel's Vision as the Garden of Eden', see Jon D. Levenson, *Theology of the Program of Restoration of Ezekiel 40–48*, HSMS 10 (Missoula: Scholars Press, 1976), pp. 25–36.

47. Cf. Block, *The Book of Ezekiel*, p. 379; Walther Zimmerli, *Ezekiel II: A Commentary on the Book of the Prophet Ezekiel Chapters 25–48*, Herm (Philadelphia: Fortress, 1983), p. 257 (cf. pp. 257–258, 261), points out that Ezekiel's description 'takes as its hidden model the process of the primeval creation of man as this is reported in Gen 2:7'.

human figure who is made to reign over a world previously dominated by beastly kingdoms (Dan. 7:1–14)[48] are two different ways of harking back to the first two chapters of Genesis for an appropriate understanding of the nature and meaning of Israel's restoration.

Both the association of the restoration of Edenic existence with the fulfilment of the Abrahamic promises in Isaiah 51:2–3[49] and the association of the restoration of Israel with the fulfilment of God's mandate to Adam and his promises to Abraham in Ezekiel 36:8–12[50] reflect the relationship between the two CSER structures. As already pointed out, God's covenant with Abram and his gift of the land and promise of blessings within it associated the covenants of Abram and Moses with a return to creation before the fall. Now that original intention for Israel's role in salvation history is achieved in and through the eschatological restoration of Israel. Isaiah 11 describes an Edenic existence (vv. 6–9) which is established under a messianic reign associated with the second exodus (vv. 1–5, 10–12). Thus the establishment of a new creation through the restoration of Israel points to the completion of Israel's CSER structure in the completion of the universal CSER dealing with creation and humanity.

New covenant

We have seen that both Adam's and Israel's relationship with God were understood in terms similar to those of suzerainty treaties in the Ancient Near East, and that Israel's covenant relationship with God was a key to the restoration of humanity's relationship with God. Furthermore, like humanity in general after the fall, Israel's own relationship ended up being in need of restoration, so that the history of creation and of humanity reflected a CSER structure that was dependent upon the positive resolution of the CSER structure governing the relationship between Israel and God. The restoration of Israel, therefore,

---

48. See Dempster, *Dominion and Dynasty*, pp. 216–217; André Lacocque, 'Allusions to Creation in Daniel 7', in John J. Collins and Peter W. Flint (eds.), *The Book of Daniel, Vol. 1, Composition and Reception*, VTSup 83.1 (Leiden: Brill, 2001), pp. 114–131; Ernest C. Lucas, *Daniel*, AOTC (Leicester: Apollos; Downers Grove: InterVarsity Press, 2002), pp. 187, 200.

49. They are to 'look to Abraham your father', since God promised to 'bless him and multiply him', and God will indeed make Israel's 'wilderness like Eden, her desert like the garden of the LORD'.

50. The return and restoration of Israel is described in terms of being fruitful and multiplying, of walking on the land, and of entering into the promised inheritance.

is naturally understood to entail the restoration of the covenantal relationship between God and his people. Our discussion of the new creation and second exodus motifs therefore presupposes the covenant relationships understood to have been established at creation and exodus. Taken together as motifs describing the restoration of Israel, they point to the restoration of God's covenant with Israel as the key to the resolution of both Israel's plight and that of creation.

Deuteronomy 30:5–9 describes the restoration of Israel in terms of the fulfilment of both the blessings promised to Abraham[51] and those of the Mosaic covenant (possibly echoing Eden as well).[52] All of this is in the context of a promise to transform the heart of his people, resulting in a love for God rather than a disdaining of his honour and will. That transformation is described metaphorically as the 'circumcision of the heart' (Deut. 30:6). This concept implies the need for a remedy for something that has gone wrong with human nature – affecting even Israelites!

Jeremiah and Ezekiel develop the same theme. In the context of a discussion of the restoration of Israel, Jeremiah 31 refers to the new covenant that God will make with his people at that time, the distinctive element of which is that he will write his law on their hearts and they will all know him (Jer. 31:31–34). Ezekiel picks up the same theme, but says God will give them a *new* heart and will put his Spirit within them, with the result that they will obey his commands (36:24–27). Although Ezekiel does not explicitly refer to a 'new covenant' (but see his references to 'a covenant of peace' in 34:25 and 37:26), he uses the same covenant formula ('you shall be my people, and I will be your God'; Ezek. 36:28; cf. Jer. 31:33)[53] in detailing the transforming work God would do in the heart of his people at the time of restoration.[54]

---

51. 'God will bring you into the land that your fathers possessed, that you may possess it. And he will make you more prosperous and numerous than your fathers' (v. 5).

52. 'The LORD your God will make you abundantly prosperous in all the work of your hand, in the fruit of your womb and in the fruit of your cattle and in the fruit of your ground. For the LORD will again take delight in prospering you, as he took delight in your fathers' (v. 9).

53. Jer. 31:1, 33; Ezek. 11:20; 36:28. Other texts using the formula (or variations on the theme) include Exod. 6:7; Lev. 26:12; Ruth 1:16; Jer. 7:23; 11:4; 24:7; 30:22; 31:1, 33; 32:38; Ezek. 11:20; 14:11; 34:30; 36:28; 37:23, 27; Hos. 1:9; 2:25; Zech. 8:8; 13:9; Rom. 9:26; 2 Cor. 6:16; Heb. 8:10.

54. On Jeremiah 31 and Ezekiel 36, see Scott J. Hafemann, *Paul, Moses, and the History of Israel: The Letter/Spirit Contrast and the Argument from Scripture in 2 Corinthians 3*

The restored Davidic kingdom

Isaiah looks forward to the proclamation of the good news of the renewed presence of the Lord and the re-establishment of his *kingdom* (Isa. 40:9; 52:7; 61:1; cf. Joel 2:32 LXX; Nah. 1:15).[55] As suggested above, the theme of the kingdom of God goes back to the first chapter of the Bible with God's appointment of mankind to be his vice-regent over the rest of creation.[56] God's glory and honour were to be reflected in all of creation through the righteous dominion of the one(s) created in his image and likeness. Genesis 1 is clearly the subtext for the meditation in Psalm 8, which develops the idea of dominion, alluding to Genesis 1, especially verses 26–28, and develops the theme of God's coronation of humanity with glory and honour.

It is significant that this psalm both begins and ends with the declaration that God's name is magnificent or majestic (*'addîr*) in all the earth (*běkol-hā'āreṣ*). It was over all the earth (*běkol-hā'āreṣ*) that humanity was to exercise dominion on God's behalf. The psalm visualizes God's honour and glory being reflected throughout creation through the presence of the one he had crowned with just that glory and honour. God's determination to establish the monarchy and his promise to establish the throne of David's son for ever (2 Sam. 7) should raise the expectation that this kingdom was somehow to relate to God's original intention for humanity and creation. The father-son relationship between God and the Davidic king reflects the establishment of a suzerain-vassal relationship between the two, consistent with the pattern of relationship suggested by Genesis 2.

Furthermore, several royal psalms suggest that the Davidic kingdom was expected to be not only unending, but also universal (as humanity's reign was intended to be according to Genesis 1). Psalm 2 speaks of the futility of the resistance of 'the kings of the earth' to God's anointed king and builds on the father-son relationship to affirm that upon request the king will be granted 'the nations' and 'the ends of the earth' for his inheritance. Psalm 72 appeals to God to grant the Davidic king 'dominion from sea to sea, and from the River to the ends of the earth' (v. 8) and longs for the day when 'all kings' might 'fall down before him' and 'all nations' might 'serve him' (v. 11).

WUNT 81 (Tübingen: J. C. B. Mohr [Paul Siebeck], 1995; Milton Keynes, UK: Paternoster Press, 2005), pp. 129–135, 156–173. For other new covenant texts, often associated with the establishment of the Davidic king, cf. Jer. 32:40; Ezek. 16:60–62; 20:37; 34:25; 37:26; Hos. 2:18.

55. The theme of God's return to deliver his people is developed in Isa. 40:3–10 and elsewhere.

56. See Wenham, *Genesis 1–15*, p. 33; McCartney, 'Ecce Homo', pp. 1–21.

When might Israel come to see the fulfilment of these expectations of a universal and unending reign of God's representative king? Psalm 89 provides an important key that helps us understand how expectations regarding the Davidic promises wound up being overlaid on the template of the CSER schema. The psalm carefully recounts God's promises to David, including the promise that God would exalt him (v. 24), making him 'the firstborn, the highest of the kings of the earth' (v. 27). The psalm also recalls God's promise to discipline the king in the event of disobedience (vv. 30–32; cf. 2 Sam. 7:14), which is understood to have taken place in and since the time of exile. It also reiterates God's promise that such transgression would not ultimately invalidate his promises of an unending reign (vv. 33–37). The following verses rehearse the terrible plight of Israel since the beginning of exile (vv. 38–45), only to cry out, 'How long, O LORD?' (v. 46), and to ask, 'where is your steadfast love of old, which by your faithfulness you swore to David?' (v. 49). The progression of the psalm makes it clear that expectations regarding the timing of the fulfilment of the promises to David had come to be superimposed on the template of the CSER schema, with the understanding that the ideal realization of that universal Davidic kingdom would be brought about at the time of post-exilic restoration.[57]

---

57. William Scott Green and Jed Silverstein point to a consistent association between the end of exile and the establishment of the ideal Davidic kingdom in Jewish thought: 'The figure of the messiah emerges from the loss of the Davidic dynasty and of Israel's political autonomy. The messiah-theme, therefore, is inextricably bound up with the notion of exile, and the Jews' recovery of the land they regard as theirs inevitably raises unprecedented questions about the religious meaning of return from exile in terms of classic Jewish ideas of the messiah' ('The Doctrine of the Messiah', in Jacob Neusner and Alan Avery-Peck (eds.), *The Blackwell Companion to Judaism* [Oxford: Blackwell, 2003], p. 248). For them, however, the messianic theme is genetically related to the issue of exile: 'Judaism is grounded in the experience of exile. Ancient Jews, certain that they were God's people always, drew creatively on their Israelite culture and heritage to develop two major responses to the twin challenges of national destruction and chronic political oppression. The first was the hope for an ideal national leader – often, but not always, from the royal Davidic dynasty – whose work could range from leading the people home to an ideal kingdom to the establishment of a new cosmic order. The idea of "the messiah," an individual saviour or redeemer of Israel, derives from this conception' (p. 266). In contrast, we suggest that it is genetically rooted in the biblical creation motifs, while the challenges of national destruction and oppression, along with the obvious need for the redemption of creation (and not merely of the nation), also played significant roles in the development of the motif.

That understanding is confirmed in the prophets. Isaiah 9 understands the sequence to require the humiliation and oppression of at least the land of Galilee before the establishment of the Davidic Prince of Peace. Jeremiah 23:3–6; 30:1–11 and 33:15–18 make it clear that it is upon the gathering of God's people from among the nations that he will establish the long-awaited Davidic kingdom in power. Ezekiel 34:2–28 associates the establishment of the Davidic kingdom with restoration to the land and also with the restoration of an Edenic existence. Ezekiel 37:24–25 similarly sees the restoration of the Davidic kingdom following upon the restoration of the nation as depicted by the resurrection of the dry bones. Amos 9:11 reflects a similar understanding.

Like some of the royal psalms, Zechariah too makes it clear that he is not only looking forward to the restoration of the kingdom, but he also expects that kingdom to have universal influence (8:22–23; 9:10; 14:14–19). The establishment of the kingdom comes in the context of 'many peoples and strong nations' coming to seek the Lord in Jerusalem (8:22). Then their humble king will come to them and 'speak peace to the nations', and 'his rule shall be from sea to sea, and from the River to the ends of the earth' (9:10). Daniel's vision of the human-like figure who is given 'dominion and glory and a kingdom', so that 'all peoples, nations, and languages should serve him' (7:14), is made to echo Adam through the association of the other nations and rulers with beastly images (7:3–12). That the fulfilment of the Davidic promises is also in mind is clear from the affirmation that the kingdom of the 'son of man' is 'an everlasting dominion, which shall not pass away . . . one that shall not be destroyed' (cf. 2 Sam. 7:12–16). The description of this dominion is clearly intended to echo descriptions of other world-dominating kingdoms (cf. Jer. 27:5–8; Dan. 2:37–38; 3:4–7; 5:18–19) and it is clear that this kingdom will be (at least) as universal as those of Babylon and Persia. Unlike any previous global domination, however, it would not end up losing its power and influence over time, and through this kingdom glory and honour will redound to the One to whom it is properly due, rather than to those whose arrogance foolishly leads them to attempt to usurp that status.

The universal reign of the Davidic king could be understood in more than one way, of course. Clearly some, as in Qumran, anticipated the extermination or at least the violent subjugation of the pagan nations.[58] Texts such as Zechariah 9 and others, however, described the coming of God's kingdom as something that would bring great blessing to other nations. Isaiah 49 is

---

58. Texts of Yahweh as a warrior are suggestive of such adversarial portrayals. Cf. 1QM I 1–16; XIV 5–8.

crucial for understanding the restoration of Israel and its relationship to the future of the other nations. There it seems the servant of the Lord has a two-pronged commission: first 'to bring Jacob back' and gather Israel to the Lord (that is, 'to raise up the tribes of Jacob and to bring back the preserved of Israel' [49:5–6]), then to serve 'as a light for the nations' so that God's salvation 'may reach to the end of the earth'. That is when 'Kings shall see and arise; princes, and they shall prostrate themselves' (v. 7). Here it becomes clear how God's original intention for humanity and for creation is realized through God's servant as he establishes God's unending reign of righteousness over all creation. That brings tremendous blessing to all the nations and to all of creation. In order for that purpose to be realized, however, Israel must first be restored so that its kingdom might bring blessing to all nations in fulfilment of the promises to Abraham, while simultaneously achieving the original intention for humanity and creation as indicated in Genesis 1.

The restored temple

The relationship between kingdom and cult has already been mentioned, so it comes as no surprise that the theme of the restored temple is related to the themes of new creation and the restoration of the Davidic kingdom. In both the garden narrative and the rest of Israelite history and theology the relationship between king and cult is assumed, so that one would naturally expect the future restoration of God's people to entail a restoration not only of God's intended role for humanity as his vice-regents, but also of the worship and blessings associated with the temple in both the garden and Jerusalem. Establishment of a kingdom is expected to be followed by the building of a temple. In Genesis 1–2 Adam is a royal figure who is given both universal dominion and the privilege of serving God in his garden 'temple'. In 2 Samuel 6–7 it is the king's desire to build a temple for God that leads to God's determination to establish an everlasting kingdom for him. And it is understood by both parties that it would be the king's place to build the temple.

The theme of the restoration of the temple is especially developed by Ezekiel (Ezek. 37:26–28; 40–48; see also Isa. 44:28; 60:13; 62:9), who also makes it clear that he associates the restoration of the temple with the restoration of the Davidic kingdom (Ezek. 37:22–25; 44:3 and *passim* in Ezekiel 44–48) and with the restoration of Eden (Ezek. 47:1–12). Through the establishment of the Davidic kingdom, with its restored temple, blessings flow like a river throughout the rest of creation, recreating an Edenic context.

The two CSER structures and the Psalms and wisdom literature

The question of the relationship between the theology of the Old Testament wisdom literature and that of the rest of the Old Testament has been a persistent problem, one that will not be finally resolved here. The fact that most of the wisdom literature is attributed (or at least dedicated) to David or Solomon suggests that any relationship with the structure proposed here would most likely be found in terms of the role of the Davidic kings in the unfolding of God's plan and purposes for his creation and his people. The role of some of the royal psalms in pointing to the expectation of a universal reign of the Davidic king was discussed above. Those psalms may provide further help in understanding how other psalms and wisdom literature may relate to the themes that have been expounded here. The very psalms that speak of the hope of such a reign reflect an acute awareness that the world in which their authors live is far from the realization of such an ideal! As Paul puts it, 'who hopes for what he sees?' (Rom. 8:24).

Psalms 1, 2 and 8 testify that there are some who support God's reign and righteousness and others who would oppose it. The moral dualism is explicit in the first psalm, seen in the contrast between the righteous and the wicked, that is, between those who follow 'the counsel of the wicked' and those who delight in and meditate on God's law. Psalm 2 speaks of the ultimate triumph of the Davidic Son of God, but it does so in the midst of the raging of the nations and the plotting of the peoples against the Lord and his king (vv. 2–3). Most of Psalm 8 deals with the reign of humanity over the rest of creation, harking back to the original purpose indicated in Genesis 1, but near the beginning (v. 2) we have what seems to be an out-of-place reference to God's foes and to 'the enemy and the avenger'.

The same may be said of several other psalms which testify to the psalmist's commitment to, or hope in, the reign of the Lord himself or of his king (e.g., Pss. 22, 46, 47, 59, 66, 67, 72, 89, 93, 96, 97, 98, 99, 103, 110, 148): usually the very psalms that depict the ultimate hope clearly reflect the fact that at present it is far from being realized. Similarly, psalms of lament, with their standard confession of faith in the Lord's future vindication,[59] also may serve, at least in part, as 'status

---

59. As stressed by Erhard Gerstenberger (*Psalms, Part I: With an Introduction to Cultic Poetry*, FOTL 14 [Grand Rapids: Eerdmans, 1988], p. 256), 'affirmation of confidence constitutes an integral part of complaint'. Cf. John H. Walton and Andrew E. Hill, *The Old Testament Today: A Journey from Original Meaning to Contemporary Significance* (Grand Rapids: Zondervan, 2004), pp. 347–348; Tremper

reports' or 'reports from the field' regarding where the world is actually at with respect to the realization of the vision of God's intention for his people and his creation. Although the authors usually express confidence in God's ultimate vindication, the laments declare that this present world is often far from fair or just. Such psalms reflect the varying degrees to which the ultimate hope has been realized or continues to be thwarted.

The historical psalms (78, 105, 106, 135, 136) tend to expound key points in the history of Israel's relationship with God, often in terms that are explicitly or implicitly dependent upon the Deuteronomic view of history and its emphasis on Israel's recalcitrance in the face of prophetic warnings and divine forbearance.[60]

Recent work on the canonical structure of the Psalter has also suggested that the themes of exile and restoration play a major role in the thinking of the final editors. John Walton has suggested that the Psalms reflect a 'content agenda' that includes an introduction (Pss. 1–2) and then groups of psalms focused sequentially on David's conflict with Saul (3–41), David's reign (42–72), the Assyrian crisis (73–89), the destruction of Jerusalem (90–106) and the final return to the land (107–145), before concluding with a series of psalms of praise (146–150).[61] Stephen Dempster points out that within the

---

Longman, *How to Read the Psalms* (Downers Grove: InterVarsity Press, 1988), pp. 27–28.

60. See Pate, et al., *The Story of Israel*, pp. 71–75. The theme of repentance plays an important role in two phases of the CSER structure of Deuteronomic theology. As summarized by James M. Scott ('Restoration of Israel', *DPL*, pp. 798–799), it 'begins with the affirmation that Israel has been persistently "stiff-necked," rebellious and disobedient during its whole long history'. Having established that, it 'goes on to affirm that God constantly sent his messengers, the prophets, to call his people to repentance and obedience'. However, 'Israel continued in its obduracy and rejected the message of the prophets', in view of which 'the wrath of God burned against Israel; judgment came upon them starting in (722 or) 587 BC; and the people were sent into Exile'. It is important that 'during the protracted exile Israel still has the chance of repenting of sin' and '[i]f the people repent . . . God will restore them to the land and to a covenantal relationship with himself'. Thus repentance is preached before exile as the key to avoiding that consequence, and it is preached during exile as the key to restoration from it.

61. John H. Walton, 'Psalms: A Cantata about the Davidic Covenant', *JETS* 34 (1991), pp. 21–31; cf. Paul R. House, *Old Testament Theology* (Downers Grove: InterVarsity Press, 1998), p. 405.

group that focuses on the return we find 'the bitter lament of exiles in Psalm 137', which 'almost suggests that exile has the final word in the Psalter'. However, 'a final flurry of Davidic psalms (138–144) provides an answer to this lament, concluding with an acrostic psalm of praise in which David calls for all flesh to praise the holy name of Yahweh (145:21). The answer to the problem of exile is David'.[62] As we shall see, Matthew's opening genealogy reflects the same conviction.

Like the Psalms, the wisdom literature of the Old Testament reflects the fact that the Davidic kingdom never came close to achieving the ideal vision that was associated with it. While many proverbs expect there to be some correlation between wise behaviour and prosperity and between foolish behaviour and ruin, it seems that the extent to which those expectations are realized in this world may depend upon the extent to which the ideal culture of the Davidic sage is also realized.[63] Ecclesiastes reflects on the great extent to which that vision continues to go unfulfilled. The author's disarmingly honest look at the human situation 'under the sun' is intended to lead the reader to recognize the superiority of the author's God-given wisdom and to submit to the concluding call to revere the God of Israel (12:13–14). That the practice of wisdom resulted in greater or lesser benefits depending on the situation may be understood as a reflection of the 'already . . . not yet' tension of a world that is to a greater or lesser extent in submission to the reign of wisdom that the sage seeks to transmit to his 'son'.

---

62. Dempster, *Dominion and Dynasty*, p. 201. Psalm 145:21 actually points beyond the restoration of Israel to a world that is caught up in praising and glorifying God. Psalm 147 points to the gathering of 'the outcasts of Israel' (v. 2) and other blessings on the nation (vv. 2–20), while Psalm 148 calls on all creation to praise him (listing the main players from Genesis 1). All creation should praise God, since 'his name alone is exalted; his majesty is above earth and heaven. He has raised up a horn for his people, praise for all his saints, for the people of Israel who are near to him' (Ps. 148:13–14). Psalms 149 and 150 conclude the praises to be sung to the God who redeems Israel and leads her 'to execute vengeance on the nations and punishments on the peoples, to bind their kings with chains and their nobles with fetters of iron, to execute on them the judgment written! This is honour for all his godly ones' (Ps. 149:7–9).

63. Bruce K. Waltke has suggested that some of the proverbs expect us to understand that their fulfilment may not come until after this present life has come to an end. See *Book of Proverbs: Chapters 1–15*, NICOT (Grand Rapids: Eerdmans, 2004), pp. 104–109.

Although the Song of Solomon has its own distinct thematic focus, it also reflects the motif of the Davidic king's role in the (already . . . not yet) restoration of creation through its depiction of David's son, Solomon, enjoying what appears to be a restoration of the Edenic bliss presumably experienced by Adam and Eve. As Tremper Longman suggests, the Song portrays 'the story of sexuality redeemed', following 'a movement from the creation of the sexual relationship, to its distortion, and then finally to its redemption'.[64]

> In the Song of Songs we read about the man and the woman in the garden. They are naked, and feel no shame. Specific poems that support this statement include 1:15–17; 2:1–7, 8–17; 4:10–5:1; 6:1–3; 6:11–12; 7:7–11 (English 7:6–10); 7:12–14 (English 7:11–13). One cannot help but hear echoes of the Garden of Eden while reading these poems. The implication of a canonical reading of the Song is that the book speaks of the healing of intimacy. Not that that healing is fully accomplished. On the one hand, the Song celebrates their union and proclaims that intimacy happens in this world. On the other hand, the cautionary poems show that lapses occur in even the best relationships. The redemption of our intimate human relationships, indeed like the redemption of our relationships with God, is an already – not yet phenomenon.[65]

Thus here again we find wisdom literature subtly leading us to hope for a restoration of the ideal world of the original creation (a restoration associated with an ideal depiction of a Davidic king), while acknowledging that such an ideal often seems like a dream that is never more than partially and imperfectly realized in life as it is now experienced.

On the brink: the two CSER structures in post-exilic and Second Temple literature

The suggestion that the New Testament authors view themselves as the generation that was experiencing the long-awaited initiation of the time of restoration – and the end of the time of exile – raises the question of the self-perception of the authors of the post-exilic literature of the Old Testament. Did they understand that the exile had come to an end by 538 BC

---

64. Tremper Longman, *Song of Songs*, NICOT (Grand Rapids: Eerdmans, 2001), p. 63 (see pp. 63–66).

65. Ibid., pp. 65–66; cf. T. D. Gledhill, 'Song of Songs', *NDBT*, p. 217.

with Cyrus's decree that the Jews could return and rebuild the Jerusalem temple?

As Paul House suggests, 'Haggai, Zechariah and Malachi long for renewal of temple, city and people,'[66] and they 'point toward God's eventual transformation of judgment to glory'.[67] While 'Zephaniah concludes without stating how renewal will occur in history', Haggai, Zechariah and Malachi 'offer a consistent pattern for how final restoration will unfold. These prophecies are perfectly honest about how preliminary and preparatory to complete renewal their era is, but they are hopeful that the foundations that have been laid will be vital for the future'.[68] Haggai emphasizes the need to build the temple in order to 'experience a change of fortune, the blessing of fertility in place of the judgment of hunger (1:7–11; 2:15–19)', and indicates that 'the restored temple would be the scene of the return of Yahweh's presence to dwell in the temple and rule over all nations'.[69] Regarding Malachi, Hill suggests, 'Amid growing skepticism because the "Zion visions" of Second Isaiah, Haggai, and Zechariah and the "Temple vision" of Ezekiel never materialized, the prophet sought to assure the restoration community in Jerusalem that God still maintained covenant love for them.'[70] Thus it has been suggested that Malachi's purpose and message were intended to help his audience come 'to terms, mentally, spiritually and ethically, with the non-appearance of the new eschatological beginning'[71] which had been expected with the return from exile. Malachi 'explains how barriers to restoration may be removed' as well as 'the sins that delay the people's renewal'.[72]

Of course, there was also a significant element of 'realized eschatology' in the post-exilic literature. 'Haggai and Zechariah 1–8 are especially aware that they are living in a new age marked by God's blessing', but, still, 'Haggai contends that full national renewal cannot take place until the temple is rebuilt'.[73]

---

66. House, *Old Testament Theology*, p. 419.

67. Ibid., p. 348.

68. Ibid., p. 383.

69. Rex Mason, 'Haggai: Theology', in *NIDOTTE*, vol. 4, pp. 691, 692.

70. Andrew E. Hill, *Malachi: A New Translation with Introduction and Commentary*, AB 25D (New York: Doubleday, 1998), p. 42.

71. K. Koch, *The Prophets: The Babylonian and Persian Periods*, trans. M. Kohl (Philadelphia: Fortress, 1984), p. 179, cited by Hill, *Malachi*, p. 45 n. 4.

72. House, *Old Testament Theology*, p. 383.

73. Ibid., p. 383.

N. T. Wright has done the most to popularize the idea that many post-exilic and Second Temple Jews believed they were still living in a state of exile, despite the fact that many of them had returned to the land.[74] In his important recent study, Steven M. Bryan has pointed out that 'recent scholarship on Ezra-Nehemiah has brought into focus the importance of seeing the way a partially realized eschatology is at work in the books'.[75] In his view, 'the problem of Ezra-Nehemiah is not so much one of continuing exile but of incomplete restoration'. Furthermore, 'for the author(s) of Ezra-Nehemiah to equate the two, as Wright does, would have been to deny a key moment in the outworking of God's eschatological purposes'.[76] In Bryan's view,

> Wright's equation of bondage to exile reflects his strong emphasis on the storyline of Israel reflected in much of the Old Testament which follows a straight-line trajectory from exile to restoration. That is why prophetic hopes for restoration are framed as hopes for the end of the exile. *But that is only how Israel's story should have turned out, not how it did turn out.* The ensuing history was considerably more complex.[77]

Stephen Dempster, on the other hand, thinks Wright has 'correctly captured the use of the concept [of exile] as a powerful theological metaphor for judgment'.

---

74. See also Craig A. Evans, 'Jesus and the Continuing Exile of Israel', in Carey C. Newman (ed.), *Jesus and the Restoration of Israel: A Critical Assessment of N. T. Wright's 'Jesus and the Victory of God'* (Downers Grove: InterVarsity Press, 1999), pp. 77–100; Pate, et al., *The Story of Israel*, pp. 105–118; Scott, 'Paul's Use of Deuteronomic Tradition', pp. 645–665; idem, 'Jesus' Vision for the Restoration of Israel', pp. 129–143; idem, 'Restoration of Israel', pp. 796–805; Anderson, *The Genesis of Perfection*, pp. 177, 191; Dempster, *Dominion and Dynasty*, p. 219 n. 7. Others have been quite critical of Wright's proposal, e.g., Mark A. Seifrid, 'Blind Alleys in the Controversy over the Paul of History', *TynBul* 45 (1994), pp. 73–95; James D. G. Dunn, *Jesus Remembered*, Christianity in the Making 1 (Grand Rapids: Eerdmans, 2003), p. 473 n. 422; I. H. Jones, 'Disputed Questions in Biblical Studies: 4. Exile and Eschatology', *ExpT* 112 (2000–1), pp. 401–405; M. Casey, 'Where Wright is Wrong', *JSNT* 69 (1998), pp. 95–103; Steven M. Bryan, *Jesus and Israel's Traditions of Judgement and Restoration*, SNTSMS 117 (Cambridge: Cambridge University Press, 2002), pp. 12–20.

75. Bryan, *Jesus and Israel's Traditions of Judgement and Restoration*, p. 16, citing as an example, J. G. McConville, 'Ezra-Nehemiah and the Fulfillment of Prophecy', *VT* 36 (1986), pp. 205–224.

76. Bryan, *Jesus and Israel's Traditions of Judgement and Restoration*, p. 16.

77. Ibid., p. 14 (his emphasis).

He asserts that 'John the Baptist's appearance *in the wilderness directly echoing Isaiah 40* indicates not only that the predicted restoration was understood as incomplete in the postexilic texts of Ezra, Nehemiah and the New Testament but also that the exile continued'.[78] Bryan suggests that Jesus and the Gospels make pervasive use not so much of the exile motif, but of the motif of a new conquest.[79] Dempster responds by asking what such a conquest implies if not disenfranchisement from the land: 'Perhaps this is the worst type of "exile".'[80]

The position defended by Bryan suggests the texts reflect a conviction that eschatological hopes are already being realized, while that defended by Wright and Dempster suggests the texts reflect a conviction that eschatological hopes have not yet been realized. Each side has a valid point, it seems. The texts seem to reflect a tension similar to that traditionally referred to in New Testament theology as the one existing between the 'already' and the 'not yet'.[81]

The penitential prayer tradition, reflected in Ezra 9, Nehemiah 1, 9, Daniel 9, and in several Jewish texts of the Second Temple period, suggests the same sense that the time of exile is coming (or should be coming) to an end, and yet that it is not quite over, or at least that the covenant curses have not yet ceased, and that the sins of the people have not yet been fully forgiven (thus the penitential prayers confessing those sins and seeking that forgiveness). The prayers themselves reflect a theology based on an understanding of the proper response to the curse of exile. 'Writing during the exile, the author of 1 Kings 8 establishes an ideology of prayer especially suited for his nation's situation . . . For 1 Kings 8, penitential prayer will restore exiled Israel.'[82] The

---

78. Dempster, *Dominion and Dynasty*, p. 219 n. 7 (his emphasis).

79. See Bryan, *Jesus and Israel's Traditions of Judgement and Restoration*, pp. 2–34.

80. Dempster, *Dominion and Dynasty*, p. 219 n. 7.

81. Cf. Scott J. Hafemann, *The God of Promise and the Life of Faith: Understanding the Heart of the Bible* (Wheaton: Crossway, 2001), pp. 114–116.

82. Rodney Alan Werline, *Penitential Prayer in Second Temple Judaism: The Development of a Religious Institution*, SBL, Early Judaism and Its Literature 13 (Atlanta: Scholars, 1998), p. 28. Werline is supported by Mark J. Boda: 'It is obvious to all that key to the form under consideration [the traditional penitential prayer] is the belief that prayer is an essential component of authentic penitence that will bring an end to the exile and that such prayer must contain a confession of sin' ('Confession as Theological Expression: Ideological Origins of Penitential Prayer', in Mark J. Boda, Daniel K. Falk and Rodney A. Werline (eds.), *Seeking the Favor of God: The Origin, Development and Impact of Penitential Prayer in Second Temple Judaism*, SBL, Early Judaism and Its Literature (Atlanta: Society of Biblical Literature, forthcoming), p. 8.

penitential prayer tradition is related to the motif of repentance as a prerequisite for restoration after the people failed to repent when warned by the prophets before the exile.[83] Israel continues to confess its sins, since 'the ultimate *ma'al* [sin against God] which led to the exile . . . demanded a penitential confession to restore covenantal relationship'.[84]

In turning our attention to the Second Temple period, Rodney Werline points out concerning the book of Baruch that

> [t]he notion that the nation remains under covenantal curses has important ramifications for the author's view of Israel's history. The author omits a reference to the period of restoration under Persian rule as a sign of the end of God's punishment for Israel's sins. This type of omission occurs elsewhere in the literature of Second Temple Judaism (see e.g., the Apocalypse of Weeks, the *Damascus Document*, and *Jubilees*); the time of restoration under Persia was a period of sin. Therefore, according to Baruch, the restoration as Deuteronomy and the prophets had promised never arrived.[85]

---

83. See n. 60 above.

84. Boda, 'Confession as Theological Expression', p. 15.

85. Werline, *Penitential Prayer in Second Temple Judaism*, pp. 94–95. Cf. Baruch 3:6–8 (NRSV), which presents the following prayer: 'For you are the Lord our God, and it is you, O Lord, whom we will praise. For you have put the fear of you in our hearts so that we call upon your name; and we will praise you in our exile, for we have put away from our hearts all the iniquity of our ancestors who sinned against you. See, we are today in our exile where you have scattered us, to be reproached and cursed and punished for all the iniquities of our ancestors, who forsook the Lord our God.' CD i 3–11 (paralleled in 4QDamascus Document[a] 1 i 10–17 and 4QDamascus Document[b] frag. 2 i 8–15) implies the hope that the Qumran community may begin to experience the end of the exile 410 years after its beginning: 'For when they were unfaithful in forsaking him, he hid his face from Israel and from his sanctuary and delivered them up to the sword. However, when he remembered the covenant of the very first, he saved a remnant for Israel and did not deliver them up to destruction. And at the moment of wrath, three hundred and ninety years after having delivered them up into the hands of Nebuchadnezzar, king of Babylon, he visited them and caused to sprout from Israel and from Aaron a shoot of the planting, in order to possess his land and to become fat with the good things of his soil. And they realized their sin and knew that they were guilty men; but they were like blind persons and like those who grope for the path over twenty years. And God appraised their deeds, because they

The same conclusion may be drawn from 2 Maccabees 1:27–29, which cries out to God to 'Gather together our scattered people, set free those who are slaves among the Gentiles, look on those who are rejected and despised, and let the Gentiles know that you are our God. Punish those who oppress and are insolent with pride. Plant your people in your holy place, as Moses promised.'[86] Israel's continuing experience of the covenantal curses leads those who perpetuate the penitential prayer tradition to conclude that the promised restoration has been delayed.[87] Although Tobit 14:4–7 is not a part of the penitential prayer tradition, it reflects a similar viewpoint and in so doing clarifies an idea that may be implicit in 2 Maccabees 1:27–29. The latter text speaks of God letting 'the Gentiles know that you are our God' by his dramatic restoration of his people from their exile. Tobit's last words to his son and grandsons suggest that the same event would lead those Gentiles to abandon their idols to worship the one true God of Israel:

> I know and believe that whatever God has said will be fulfilled and will come true; not a single word of the prophecies will fail. All of our kindred, inhabitants of the land of Israel, will be scattered and taken as captives from the good land; and the whole land of Israel will be desolate, even Samaria and Jerusalem will be desolate. And the temple of God in it will be burned to the ground, and it will be desolate for a while.
>
> But God will again have mercy on them, and God will bring them back into the land of Israel; and they will rebuild the temple of God, but not like the first one until

---

sought him with a perfect heart and raised up for them a Teacher of Righteousness, in order to direct them in the path of his heart' (Florentino García Martínez (ed.), *The Dead Sea Scrolls Translated: The Qumran Texts in English*, trans. Wilfred G. E. Watson [Leiden & New York: E. J. Brill, 1994]).

86. Quotations from the Old Testament Apocrypha are cited from the NRSV.

87. Cf. Anderson, *The Genesis of Perfection*, p. 177: 'Throughout the Second Temple period – after the return of Ezra, Nehemiah, and many of those banished to Babylon – many Jews continued to pray for an end to the exile. When Israel is finally gathered into the Promised Land, the Messiah will arrive, the Temple will be properly rebuilt, and the nations of the earth will stream to Zion to give honor to God for what he has done.' Furthermore, since the exiles who returned to Jerusalem in 538 in response to the edict of Cyrus 'failed to construct a culture and temple that matched the prophetic promises for this return, many writers believed that the exile never ended . . . To this day, Jewish daily, Sabbath, and festival prayers are punctuated by pleas that God will gather in his peoples from the ends of the world' (ibid., p. 191).

the period when the times of fulfilment shall come. After this they all will return from their exile and will rebuild Jerusalem in splendour; and in it the temple of God will be rebuilt, just as the prophets of Israel have said concerning it. Then the nations in the whole world will all be converted and worship God in truth. They will all abandon their idols, which deceitfully have led them into their error; and in righteousness they will praise the eternal God.

The restoration of Israel at the end of time was, according to Tobit, to lead the nations of the world into the true and proper worship of the God of Israel. That is to say that the restoration of Israel was to lead to the restoration of the rest of the world. The literature of Second Temple Judaism is relevant to our discussion not because it forms part of the biblical corpus, but because it provides crucial background information for understanding how Jewish authors and readers of the New Testament period understood the biblical narrative, and how the New Testament authors themselves would have expected to be understood when they related the life and ministry of Jesus Christ, or their own Christian message, to the backdrop of God's unfolding work of redemption.

Hence, in response to the question of whether Jews of the post-exilic and Second Temple periods (and the authors of the New Testament) would have understood Israel's situation in the first century as one of continuing exile, we have seen that there are significant reasons for understanding Israel's situation as one that entails an incomplete resolution of the original exile.[88]

---

88. The fact that various ancient Jewish authors believed the exile had come to an end through events not far removed from their lifetime is not a decisive argument against the suggestion that other Jews and Christians thought the exile had continued to their day (*pace* James D. G. Dunn, *The Epistle to the Galatians*, BECNT (Peabody: Hendrickson, 1993), p. 171; CD 1:5–8; and Seifrid, 'Blind Alleys in the Controversy over the Paul of History', on similar evidence). What such evidence shows, rather, is that various Jewish groups tended to interpret significant spiritual or political developments as portents or indications of either a barely inaugurated or a highly imminent restoration and end to the exile. CD 1:3–11 shows that the Qumran community believed the restoration was being inaugurated by the establishment of their community and the arrival of the Teacher of Righteousness 390–410 years after the beginning of the exile. This precise understanding of the restoration would obviously have been limited to that community. In a context of expectancy, various developments might have been hailed by some or many Jews as the end of the exile and the beginning of the restoration, only to be seen later as a false hope. According to the New Testament, both John the Baptist and Jesus were

The two CSER structures in the New Testament

Within the New Testament we find a continuing tension between the 'already' and the 'not yet' aspects of God's plan of redemption already discernible in the post-exilic and Second Temple periods. Some New Testament authors seem to place the accent on the idea that Christ has already inaugurated the time of restoration (while still reflecting some sense that the restoration has not been fully realized), while others reflect greater awareness of the exilic (or threshold) state in which Christians continue to exist.

Synoptic Gospels and Acts

In Craig Evans's view, the 'single most important datum that attests to the presence of exile theology in Jesus' thinking is his appointment of the "twelve"', which probably 'was intended to symbolize the reconstitution of the twelve tribes of Israel'.[89] He agrees with E. P. Sanders, who suggests that '"twelve" would necessarily mean "restoration"', and with N. T. Wright, who argues that the 'call of the twelve said . . . this is where YHWH was at last restoring his people Israel'.[90] All four Gospels reflect the same motif, as does Paul.[91]

Evans also points to the allusion to Isaiah 56:7 ('my house shall be called a house of prayer for all peoples [LXX: Gentiles]') which Jesus makes during the

---

seen in the light of this hope. What these documents positively demonstrate is that various groups within early Judaism tended to identify great spiritual turning points as the mark of the end of the exile and the beginning of the restoration. Many of the writings of the New Testament fit this same pattern (cf. Roy E. Ciampa, *The Presence and Function of Scripture in Galatians 1 and 2*, WUNT 2.102 [Tübingen: Mohr Siebeck, 1998], p. 234 n. 35). See the essays in the volumes edited by James M. Scott, *Exile: Old Testament, Jewish, and Christian Conceptions* (Leiden: Brill, 1997), and *Restoration: Old Testament, Jewish, and Christian Perspectives* (Leiden; Boston: Brill, 2001).

89. Evans, 'Aspects of Exile and Restoration in the Proclamation of Jesus and the Gospels', in Scott (ed.), *Exile*, pp. 317–318.

90. Ibid., p. 318, citing E. P. Sanders, *Jesus and Judaism* (London: SCM, 1985), p. 98; and N. T. Wright, *Jesus and the Victory of God*, Christian Origins and the Question of God 2 (Minneapolis: Fortress Press, 1992), pp. 430–431.

91. Cf. Matt. 10:1–2, 5; 11:1; 19:28; 20:17; 26:14, 20, 47; Mark 3:14, 16; 4:10; 6:7; 9:35; 10:32; 11:11; 14:10, 17, 20, 43; Luke 6:13; 8:1; 9:1, 12; 18:31; 22:3, 30, 47; John 6:67, 70–71; 20:24; 1 Cor. 15:5.

temple incident in Matthew 21:13, Mark 11:17 and Luke 19:46 as one that may lead us to 'infer that he has criticized the temple establishment for failing to live up to the eschatological expectations enunciated in Isaiah 56:1–8 and so now stands under the judgment uttered by Jeremiah (esp. in Jer. 7) against the Temple establishment of his day'. Due to their failure, the temple has not become 'a place of prayer for Gentiles and a place for the regathering of Israel's exiles'.[92] This suggests that Israel's anticipated role in the salvation of Gentiles (i.e., the rest of the world) played a significant role in Jesus' thinking about the end time.

John the Baptist preaches impending restoration to his disciples and impending destruction to those who do not respond as they should to his message. Jesus does the same, although in his case the response is as much to Jesus' person as to his message. While the coming of the Messiah would have been expected to be a single coming,[93] it turns out to entail two comings – one has already taken place, while the other is still anticipated. That is, if most Jews anticipated the coming of God or his Messiah to divide history neatly into two parts (as in the first figure below) – this age and the age to come – the New Testament requires that we broaden that dividing line, or look at it as if it were under an electron microscope (as in the second figure below), to see that the two sides of that dividing line are defined by the first and second comings of Christ (or by his resurrection and the general resurrection), which bring about the inauguration and the consummation (respectively) of the age to come.

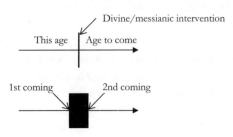

---

92. Evans, 'Aspects of Exile and Restoration', pp. 321, 323–324.

93. That is, by those expecting the coming of a Messiah. A great diversity of views existed within ancient Judaism regarding the possible coming of one or two Messiahs (cf., e.g., Jacob Neusner, William Scott Green and Ernest S. Frerichs (eds.), *Judaisms and Their Messiahs at the Turn of the Christian Era* [Cambridge and New York: Cambridge University Press, 1987]; and John J. Collins, *The Scepter and the Star: The Messiahs of the Dead Sea Scrolls and Other Ancient Literature* [New York: Doubleday, 1995]). But that one Messiah would come, leave and then come again seems to be a unique view for the time.

Thus the coming of Christ brings about the end of exile and the fullness of restoration, but at the moment we find ourselves in the midst of the transition period of that coming, with the recognition that the restoration has not yet been fully realized, so that we continue to live as exiles in this world.

The canonical shape of the New Testament provides a helpful hint regarding the relationship between the Old Testament expectation of restoration and its fulfilment with the twofold coming of Jesus as the Messiah. Jesus' genealogy in Matthew (1:1–17) makes a theological comment on the structure of redemption history and the significance of Christ within that structure. Matthew picks four key turning points in this history and repeats them for emphasis as the key to understanding Christ's coming. The first two points are Christ's relationship to Abraham and David (Abraham is mentioned three times in the passage, David is mentioned five times). That Matthew understands Jesus to be the seed of Abraham and the seed of David, through whom God's promises to both are to be realized, is clear throughout the book. The next key turning point in the genealogy is remarkable for the fact that it is not an expected element in a genealogy, which normally consists merely of a list of names (perhaps, as here, linked together by the same repeating verb [*egennēsen*]). That key turning point is the historical reference to the exile. Indeed, the genealogy mentions the exile *four* different times (v. 11, v. 12, and twice in v. 17)!

Moving further on into the chapter, we come to the naming of Mary's son. He is to be named Jesus, 'for he will save his people from their sins' (1:21). While a traditional understanding of this text takes it to be a reference to the salvation of Christians from their sins, the hermeneutical guidance provided by the opening genealogy suggests that it is a reference to the salvation of Israel ('his people') from the sins that had led it into exile. The follow-up reference to the coming of Immanuel, who restores God's presence to his people, also fits with the theme of Israel's (and humanity's) exile from God followed by the restoration of his presence to his people (and all nations).

When John the Baptist is introduced in chapter 3, he comes preaching the message of Isaiah 40, which foresaw the coming time of restoration. His message of repentance for forgiveness is consistent with the Old Testament teaching regarding the prerequisite for Israel's restoration (3:1–6).

Most of the beatitudes of Matthew 5 refer to the attitudes appropriate for Jews who recognize that they are in need of forgiveness and restoration and who live in anticipation of that restoration.[94] Jesus' prayer in chapter 6 fits the

---

94. The Beatitudes 'are but an expression of the fulfillment of Isaiah 61, the OT promise of the *Heilszeit*, in the person and proclamation of Jesus' (Robert A.

basic pattern of the penitential prayer tradition, where forgiveness of sins is sought in the context of a plea for the in-breaking of the day of salvation and restoration, the coming of God's kingdom and the vindication of the holiness of his name in the eyes of the nations.

Although Matthew has focused on the end of Israel's exile, he does so with full understanding of how Israel's restoration relates to God's intentions for the rest of humanity. The issue of universalism vs. particularism in Matthew's Gospel revolves around Jesus' clear statements that he had come for the sake of 'the lost sheep of Israel' (which, like 'scattered sheep', is an exilic image; Jer. 50:3–6[95]) and sent out his disciples with the same specific focus (Matt. 10:6; 15:24). Although he ministers to others on occasion, his focus remains on Israel, until he has risen from the dead. Then he informs his followers that, in keeping with the vision of Daniel 7, he has been granted all authority over all creation so that he might be obeyed by all nations (Matt. 28:18–20). Now the focus shifts to the discipling of all nations. If his death and resurrection are the key to the restoration of Israel, it is understandable that he can now enter into that long-awaited glorious and universal phase of the Davidic kingdom and that salvation may, or rather must, now go to the ends of the earth.[96] Here

---

Guelich, 'The Matthean Beatitudes: "Entrance-Requirements" or Eschatological Blessings?', *JBL* 95 [1973], p. 433). In Isaiah, '*the poor* becomes more or less synonymous with the exiled people of God (26:6; 49:13; 51:21)', and yet 'the promise of God's vindication of *the poor* in the future emerges in full view as an eschatological hope (cf. Isa 49; 51; 54; 61)' (Robert Guelich, *The Sermon on the Mount: A Foundation for Understanding* [Waco: Word, 1982], p. 68). For 'the poor' as a reference to exiled people within the Qumran community, see CD xix 8–9; 1QM+1Q33 x 13; xiv 6–7; 4QpPs[a] i 20–22; ii 9–10; iii 10; 1QH vi 2–5; 4QMessAp 2 ii 5–7. Carson affirms that 'the godly remnant of Jesus' day weeps because of the humiliation of Israel, but they understand that it comes from personal and corporate sins' (D. A. Carson, 'Matthew', in *Expositors Bible Commentary* (Grand Rapids: Zondervan, 1984), vol. 8, p. 133.

95. Similarly, the conflict between Jesus and the established Jewish leaders (Herod, Pharisees, scribes, etc.) fits the Old Testament prophetic motif of the culpability of the Jewish leadership for the impending or already realized exilic status of the people and God's promise to raise up new leadership in the time of restoration (cf. Jer. 2:8; 3:15; 10:21; 12:10; 23:1; 25:34–36; 31:10; 50:6; Ezek. 34:2–15, 23; 37:24; Zech. 10:2–3; 11:3–16; 11:17; 13:7).

96. This may be reflected in the way each of the synoptic Gospels repeatedly refers to Christ as merely the 'King of the Jews' or 'King of Israel' before his resurrection.

we have the realization of God's original intention for humanity and creation in the person of Christ – the completion of the first and largest CSER structure. It is not realized apart from, but through the restoration of Israel – the completion of the embedded CSER structure. Matthew's understanding of the timing of the fulfilment of the promises to Abraham and David is founded on his understanding of the relationship between those themes and the two interrelated CSER structures.

The motif of the forgiveness of sins (or salvation from sin), placed in the foreground by its role in Matthew 1:21, the Lord's Prayer (6:12–15), the Last Supper (26:28) and the background regarding the need of forgiveness before the coming restoration, suggests that the death and resurrection of Christ have dealt with the issue of the forgiveness of Israel's sin, so that the focus of Christ's ministry need no longer be restricted to his people, but may now be extended to all nations (Matt. 28:18–20). Jesus' interaction with the Canaanite woman in Matthew 15:22–28 reflects his amazement at her understanding that, even though he 'was sent only to the lost sheep of the house of Israel' (v. 24), his ultimate intention is for blessing to flow not only to God's 'children', but also to those who might benefit from the overflow of crumbs that would surely 'fall from their masters' table'. The salvation of the Jews may be Jesus' proper priority, but in the process of meeting their needs those of the rest of the world will also be addressed.

While the final pericope of Matthew's Gospel indicates that the time of restoration has been inaugurated, there are other elements that suggest the restoration is yet to come. It certainly seems that it has not come for Israel in the way that had been imagined. Rather, there are many indications that what Israel (or at least the Jewish establishment) can continue to expect is judgment rather than redemption and restoration (unless they repent and find restoration in Christ).[97] Although Jesus informs the disciples that he has already

---

It may suggest that even if he were a Davidic king he would be like those before him, not yet fitting the description of that Davidic king whose dominion extends far beyond the borders of Israel to include all of creation. After his resurrection no one would think of calling him merely the king of the Jews or of Israel.

97. Bryan, *Jesus and Israel's Traditions of Judgement and Restoration*, passim. This would likely be a shocking (and unacceptable) message for many Second Temple Jews, who would have thought that the nation had already experienced the full measure of judgment from the hand of the Lord, so that it was simply a matter of time before they would experience the tremendous blessings the prophets described for the post-exilic period.

received 'all authority in heaven and on earth' (28:18), they must still wait for the 'the new world, when the Son of Man will sit on his glorious throne' and his disciples 'will also sit on twelve thrones, judging the twelve tribes of Israel' (19:28). Presumably that is when he will 'come with his angels in the glory of his Father' (16:27) and 'he will send out his angels with a loud trumpet call, and they will gather his elect from the four winds, from one end of heaven to the other' (24:31). In fact, all nations will be gathered before him (25:32) and 'the King will say to those on his right, "Come, you who are blessed by my Father, inherit the kingdom prepared for you from the foundation of the world"' (v. 34). The 'gathering' of the chosen people from all corners of the world (24:31) and their inheritance of the kingdom (25:34) are particularly notable for the use of restoration themes, but here they are understood to await Christ's return. Thus the restoration of the rest of humanity is something that seems to begin with the resurrection of Christ, but awaits its completion at the time of his second coming.

Mark's Gospel begins with a composite quotation from Exodus 23:20, Malachi 3:1 and Isaiah 40:3, in which Isaiah 40 provides the framework for understanding the previous first and 'second' exodus passages.[98] The composite quotation is introduced with a reference to 'the gospel of Jesus Christ, the Son of God' (1:1–3). That the Greek word for proclaiming good news (*euangelizō*) is a prominent feature of Isaiah 40 (twice in v. 9; cf. 52:7; 61:1) is unlikely to be a coincidence. Rather, the coming of Jesus, who is the Christ, the Son of God, is understood by Mark to telegraph the inauguration of the fulfilment of Isaiah's prophecy regarding the good news of God's post-exilic forgiveness and restoration of his people. The Baptist's wilderness ministry of calling the people of Israel to prepare 'the way of the Lord' harks back to Isaiah's theme of the promised return of God to his people, and the return of the people to the land, once their sins have been pardoned (Isa. 40:2). In so doing, as Rikki Watts suggests, 'Mark's introductory sentence (1:1–3) indicates his Gospel's conceptual framework.'[99] John's theme of repentance and confession and his ministry of baptizing people in the River Jordan all relate to the prerequisites for the restoration of exilic Israel. In the opinion of Colin Brown,

John was organizing a symbolic exodus from Jerusalem and Judea as a preliminary to recrossing the Jordan as a penitent, consecrated Israel in order to reclaim the land in a

---

98. Rikki Watts, *Isaiah's New Exodus in Mark*, BSL (Grand Rapids: Baker, 2000), p. 61.
99. Ibid., p. 370.

quasi-reenactment of the return from the Babylonian exile. Whereas the waters had parted for Joshua, Elijah, and Elisha, John had no option but to go through them. In short, John waded across, and baptism was effected by heeding John's call to leave the land and follow him in penitence into the Jordan and return as consecrated members of a renewed Israel.[100]

The theme of a second conquest is particularly strong in Mark's Gospel. Watts sees the three main sections of Mark's Gospel following the structure of 'Isaiah's New Exodus schema', in which Yahweh first delivers Israel from 'the power of the nations and their idols', then leads them along the 'Way of the Lord' and finally makes a triumphal entry with them into Jerusalem.[101] The Gospel's focus on the passion and resurrection of Christ in chapters 14–16, as anticipated earlier in the Gospel (e.g., 8:31; 9:9–10, 31; 10:33–34; 14:22–28), suggests to the reader that the fulfilment of Isaiah's vision of the restoration of Israel will be achieved through Christ's passion and resurrection, which serve simultaneously as the climax of Mark's Gospel (as in the other Gospels).

In Luke 1:16–17 Gabriel tells Zechariah that his son John 'will turn many of the children of Israel to the Lord their God' and will turn 'the disobedient to the wisdom of the just, to make ready for the Lord a people prepared'. This turning back of Jews to the God of Israel is based on the preparation that is called for in Isaiah 40, with which John is once again associated (cf. Luke 3:3–6). But Luke wants us to understand that this restoration is the key to the fulfilment of the promises of the Davidic kingdom, since Jesus' fulfilment of those promises is that for which John prepares us (Luke 1:30–33).

Luke's Gospel thus begins with the hope of redemption from exile. Indeed, Zechariah had long been waiting for God to visit and redeem his people (1:68), which Luke understood to be a reference to restoration from exile ('that we should be saved from our enemies and from the hand of all who hate us' [v. 71]) and the fulfilment of God's promise to Abraham (v. 73). Likewise, righteous and devout Simeon was 'waiting for the consolation of Israel', which would be accompanied by the coming of 'the Lord's Christ' (2:25–26), and pious Anna was on the alert for 'all who were waiting for the redemption of Jerusalem' (2:36–38). So, too, at the close of Luke's Gospel, after the death and resurrection of Jesus, the disciples on the road to Emmaus admit that they

---

100. Cf. Colin Brown, 'What Was John the Baptist Doing?', *BBR* 7 (1997), p. 45. Mark 'appears to emphasize the significance of the Jordan' (p. 45 n. 27).

101. Watts, *Isaiah's New Exodus in Mark*, pp. 123–136.

had been hoping 'that he was the one to redeem Israel' (24:21), whereas Jesus clarifies that his passion and resurrection were the prerequisites for the proclamation of 'repentance and forgiveness of sins ... to all nations' (24:47).

Acts also reflects the themes of the restoration of Israel in Christ and, through him, the extension of salvation to the Gentiles. The book reflects the tension between the 'already' and the 'not yet' aspects of eschatological restoration we have found elsewhere. Jesus, the Lord of all, is already seated and reigning at God's right hand and is responsible for the long-awaited out-pouring of the Holy Spirit (2:25–36). The Twelve have been reconstituted (1:12–26) and it seems that Israel's ingathering from the diaspora (2:1–47) has begun. The agenda Jesus sets for his restored community entails witnessing 'to the end of the earth' (1:8), and when we get to the end of the book we find Paul in the centre of the Roman Empire 'proclaiming the kingdom of God and teaching about the Lord Jesus Christ' (28:31). It may be that we are to rec-ognize that Jesus has restored Israel, but not in the way expected, and because he has restored Israel and been established on David's throne, the time has come to publicize the need for universal submission to the kingdom of *this* Lord of the universe. James's interpretation of Amos 9:11–12 LXX in Acts 15:16–18 (' "After this I will return, and I will rebuild the tent of David that has fallen; I will rebuild its ruins, and I will restore it, that the remnant of mankind may seek the Lord, and all the Gentiles who are called by my name," says the Lord, who makes these things known from of old') points in this direction. James perceives that 'the eschatological restoration of God's people was always intended to attract Gentiles to seek God',[102] and they are to find their place in God's kingdom under the reign of the eschatological Davidic king – Jesus.

Other texts suggest the world is on the verge of experiencing the promised restoration, the imminent arrival of which is heralded by Christ's death, resurrection and exaltation. It is not clear when Christ intends 'to restore the kingdom to Israel' (1:6), but, as in other texts intended to prepare Israel for the time of restoration, repentance is called for as a prerequisite for the forgiveness of sins (2:38; 3:19; 5:31; 8:22). Repentance is called for because God is about to judge the world through Christ (17:30–31), and such repentance (and faith) brings a present experience of the Holy Spirit and forgiveness with the understanding that Christ would soon consummate

---

102. Ben Witherington, *The Acts of the Apostles: A Socio-Rhetorical Commentary* (Grand Rapids: Eerdmans, 1998), p. 459.

the restoration and bring in Israel's eschatological 'times of refreshing' (3:19–21).[103] Although many are already experiencing some of the blessings of Christ's reign, most of Israel rejects Christ. Thus, as elsewhere in the New Testament, Christ has inaugurated the restoration and is presently reigning and pouring out some of the initial blessings of his reign, but the proclamation of the gospel is carried out with the understanding that it is part of the preparation for the final consummation of eschatological restoration, which is just around the corner.

Paul

Throughout Paul's letters there is a stress on the fact that the gospel has to do with the salvation of both Jews and Gentiles, which has been achieved through Christ's death and resurrection. Scholars have pointed to numerous texts where this is presented by Paul in terms of a second exodus, that is, the prophetic description of the restoration of Israel in terms of a repeat of the original exodus redemption. Obvious examples include 1 Corinthians 5:7; 10:1–13; and 2 Corinthians 3. Strong cases have also been made for Galatians 3:10–14; 4:1–7; and Romans 8:14–39, among other texts.[104] Furthermore, the fatherhood of God and the adoption of his people as sons,[105] 'redemption' (especially from 'the curse of the law'), slavery followed by sonship or freedom, resurrection (or life following death),[106] the 'new covenant',[107]

---

103. For a careful analysis of Isaiah's new exodus, or the restoration theme, in Acts, see David W. Pao, *Acts and the Isaianic New Exodus* (Grand Rapids: Baker Academic, 2002).

104. On Galatians 3–4, see Scott J. Hafemann, 'Paul and the Exile of Israel in Galatians 3–4', in Scott (ed.), *Exile*, pp. 329–371; and James M. Scott, *Adoption as Sons of God: An Exegetical Investigation into the Background of* ΥΙΟΘΕΣΙΑ *in the Pauline Corpus*, WUNT 2.48 (Tübingen: J. C. B. Mohr [Paul Siebeck], 1992), pp. 121–186. On Galatians 4 and Romans 8, see Sylvia C. Keesmaat, *Paul and His Story: (Re) Interpreting the Exodus Tradition*, JSNTSup 181 (Sheffield: Sheffield Academic Press, 1999). On other texts in Romans (especially chs. 9–11; 15), see J. Ross Wagner, *Heralds of the Good News: Isaiah and Paul in Concert in the Letter to the Romans* (Boston and Leiden: Brill, 2003).

105. On the fatherhood of God and adoption as his sons, see Scott, *Adoption as Sons of God*; Trevor J. Burke, *Adopted Into God's Family: Exploring a Pauline Metaphor* (Nottingham: Apollos; Downers Grove: InterVarsity Press, 2006).

106. On the last three motifs, see Ciampa, *The Presence and Function of Scripture in Galatians 1 and 2*, pp. 61–62, 138–142, 204–209.

107. On the 'new covenant', see Hafemann, *Paul, Moses, and the History of Israel*, pp. 119–156.

receiving an inheritance, bearing fruit,[108] and the edification of a new temple[109] or community have all been identified as some of the many second exodus (or restoration theology) motifs found in Paul's letters.

It was Paul's recognition of Jesus' glory that made it possible for him to accept that Jesus was the Christ and to understand why Christ would send him to preach the message to all nations and not just to Jews. The ultimate Davidic king is reigning, so Israel's restoration has begun and the time has come for salvation to go to the ends of the earth. The CSER structure that applies to humanity is being completed by the resolution of Israel's own CSER structure which had been embedded within it.

When Paul summarizes his understanding of the gospel in Romans 1:1–5, he does so in terms of the relationship between the Davidic promises and the two CSER structures: Jesus is not only 'descended from David' like every other Davidic king, but, unlike any other Davidic king, he has also entered into that long-awaited, glorious and universal phase of the promised kingdom by reason of his Spirit-declared installation on the throne through his resurrection. That such is Paul's understanding of the significance of the resurrection for the current status of the Davidic kingdom is made clear by the logical relationship between Romans 1:4 and Romans 1:5. Since Jesus has been 'declared to be the Son of God *in power*', the time has come 'to bring about the obedience of faith for the sake of his name among all the nations'.

Chapters 1–3 of Romans show that not only Gentiles, but also Jews, have sinned against God and, like Gentiles, Jews have experienced death (1:18–3:20; cf. 3:23). Paul goes on in chapters 3–4 to make the point that 'in the Messiah, Jesus of Nazareth, the God of Israel has been true to the covenant established with Abraham and has thereby brought saving order to the whole world'.[110] Frank Thielman and N. T. Wright have both highlighted the relationship between the story of Israel in the Old Testament and the outworking of Paul's argument in Romans 5–8. According to Thielman, in chapters 5 and 8 'the people of God, newly defined on the basis of faith, are the recipients of God's promises through the prophets to restore Israel's fortunes and make a new covenant with them'.[111] Similarly, Wright summarizes chapters 5–8 in this way:

---

108. On the last two motifs, see Keesmaat, *Paul and His Story*, pp. 81–84, 206–208 (cf. Isa. 32:14–18).

109. On the temple motif, see Beale, *The Temple and the Church's Mission*.

110. N. T. Wright, 'Romans', NIB (Nashville: Abingdon, 2002), vol. 12, p. 405.

111. Frank Thielman, 'The Story of Israel and the Theology of Romans 5–8', SBLSP 32 (Atlanta: Scholars Press, 1993), p. 234.

In the Messiah, Jesus, God has done for this new people what was done for Israel of old in fulfilment of the promise to Abraham: Redeemed from the Egypt of enslavement to sin, they are led through the wilderness of the present life by the Spirit (not the Torah), and they look forward to their inheritance, which will consist of the entire redeemed creation.[112]

While Wright stresses that this is 'the result of God's . . . covenant love expressed completely and finally in the death of Jesus', Paul's logic seems to put at least equal stress on Jesus' role as 'Lord', which in Romans 1:4 and elsewhere is closely tied to Jesus' resurrection from the dead and exaltation (Phil. 2:9–11; Rom. 10:9). In chapters 5–8 key aspects (including peace, reconciliation, life, deliverance and the love of God) of the redemption of both Jews and Gentiles (i.e., the rest of humanity) are directly related to the identity of Jesus Christ as 'Lord' (cf. 5:1, 11, 21; 6:23; 7:25; 8:39). This is all consistent with 1:1–5, where the declaration of Christ as the 'Son of God in power' is related to the calling 'to bring about the obedience of faith for the sake of his name among all the nations'.

There are two passages in particular that make it clear that this extension of salvation to all nations is related to the relationship between the two interrelated CSER structures discussed above. Galatians 3:10–14 refers to the curse that is upon all those who are 'of the works of the law' (a reference to all those who understand the performance of the requirements of the Mosaic covenant to serve as a basis for their relationship with God). Whenever curse is mentioned in such close relationship to the law it is most likely that we are dealing with the covenantal curses which led to Israel's exile. Paul goes on to say that through the crucifixion 'Christ redeemed us from the curse of the law by becoming a curse for us' (v. 13), in order that 'the blessing of Abraham might come to the Gentiles' (v. 14). In the light of the theological pattern seen elsewhere (and the logic of the passage itself), it is best to understand this text in terms of Christ's initial redemption and restoration of Israel as the prerequisite for the extension of salvation to the rest of the world, here explicitly understood as the fulfilment of God's intention to use Abraham and his seed to resolve the problem of (even) non-Abrahamic humanity.

That this is Paul's train of thought becomes even clearer when Galatians 4:4–8 is taken into consideration. There Paul uses a chiastic structure to

112. Wright, 'Romans', p. 405. Cf. N. T. Wright, 'New Exodus, New Inheritance: The Narrative Substructure of Romans 3–8', in S. Soderlund and N . T. Wright (eds.), *Romans and the People of God: Essays in Honor of Gordon D. Fee on the Occasion of His 65th Birthday* (Grand Rapids: Eerdmans, 1999), pp. 26–35.

communicate the logic of the two interrelated CSER structures. Speaking to Gentiles, he says:

God sent forth his Son,
> **A** born of woman,
>> **B** born under the law,
>> **B′** to redeem those who were under the law,
> **A′** so that we might receive adoption as sons. And because you are sons . . .

Here we have – literally – an abbreviated summary of the two CSER structures and the relationship between them. Jesus was human and came to bring adoption even to Gentiles like the Galatians (A:A′), but in order to accomplish that he had first to redeem those who were 'under the law'. The redemption of Israel from her plight is the prerequisite for and key to the redemption of humanity from its plight.

Through the one CSER structure embedded within the other we find a biblical understanding of God's approach to restoring his original intention for humanity and creation, bringing blessing rather than curse through the seed of Abraham. This blessing is experienced under the reign of the promised Davidic king who, in his person and through his people, brings about the originally intended universal reign of God over all creation in such a way that his glory is reflected in the entire universe.

To give just one more example, this time from the letter many consider an exquisite introduction to Paul's thought, the pattern described in this essay is also reflected in Ephesians 1–3. According to Ephesians 1:3–14, the Gentile readers (along with their Jewish brothers in Christ) have inherited an eschatological version of the blessings of Israel. According to 1:10, one of the blessings in which the readers are participating is the unification or harmonization of all creation under the Lordship of Christ. According to Ephesians 2:1–10, both Gentiles and Jews were dead in sin but have been raised up together and seated with Christ, who has brought reconciliation on at least two levels (between Jews and Gentiles and between God and humans). Here we have a proleptic vision of the end of the history of redemption, with humanity being brought back to the role depicted in Genesis 1 as they are made to reign with Christ in a world that has been restored to its original pristine harmony. All of this has been brought about by the death and resurrection of Christ, the events that bring the two parallel narrative plots to their climaxes and lead to the ultimate resolution of their entwined narrative conflicts. At this stage Paul expects us to see clearly where the story is going and how Christ is taking us to that final resolution.

Unrealized aspects of the two CSER structures in the New Testament

While many of Paul's texts suggest that his readers have already entered into the time of restoration, others suggest they are still on their way home. Todd Wilson suggests that Paul's portrayal of the Galatians places them 'in the wilderness, somewhere between an Exodus-like redemption and the inheritance of the "kingdom of God" (5.21)'.[113]

In 2 Corinthians 5:6, 8, 9 Paul uses the language of being 'at home' or 'away' from the body or the Lord. BDAG points out that the word Paul uses for being 'away' (*ekdēmeō*) means 'to be in a strange land' when used in conjunction with the word for 'at home' (*endēmeō*), as it is here, and means 'to live in exile' when used absolutely (as in Plato, *Leg.* 9, 864e).[114] As Ralph Martin puts it, 'Christians are in a strange land' and '[w]hile Christians are in communion with God they are nevertheless in a foreign land, continuing their pilgrimage. As long as one is on the earth, that perfect fellowship desired between the believer and the Lord remains elusive.'[115] Thus, as long as we exist in our pre-resurrection bodies, we are experiencing something of an exile from our ultimate home and destiny and to arrive there requires that we be exiled from our pre-resurrection bodies. As long as the ultimate narrative (the original, universal CSER structure) has not come to an absolute end, we continue to await the consummation of our restoration to God's full presence and the end of any taint of exile.

Paul's understanding of the relationship between the restoration of Israel and the salvation of the Gentiles is further complicated by at least two aspects of his thinking. First, Gentiles who respond to the gospel message are grafted into Israel, so that it becomes extraordinarily difficult to distinguish between the theme of the salvation of Israel and that of the salvation of Jews and Gentiles together. Second, although there is a sense in which the restoration of Israel has already been inaugurated (and thus the Davidic king is reigning and the church as the new temple has been established and is indwelt by the Holy Spirit who has been poured out), there is another sense in which most of 'Israel', that is, most Jews, have rejected the Messiah in this initial phase and will come to recognize him only after an extended time in which they fail to

---

113. Todd A. Wilson, 'Wilderness Apostasy and Paul's Portrayal of the Crisis in Galatians', *NTS* 50 (2004), p. 550.

114. So BDAG, referring to Philo, *Spec. Laws* 4:142, and papyri like P.Mich.Zen. 80, 4; cf. LSJ.

115. Ralph P. Martin, *2 Corinthians*, WBC 40 (Waco: Word, 1985), p. 110.

find reconciliation with God while, ironically, Gentiles find it.[116] Paul also understands this phenomenon in the light of Deuteronomic theology – in view of Deuteronomy 32:21, where God, speaking of the way Israel provoked him to jealousy through their idolatry, says, 'I will make them jealous with those who are no people.'[117] Paul quotes Deuteronomy 32:21 in Romans 10:19 and he expounds on his understanding of its relevance in chapter 11, with clear allusions to the text in 11:11, 14. In the verses following each reference to jealousy in chapter 11 (vv. 11, 14) Paul ties the ultimate salvation of the Gentiles to the final restoration of Israel at the consummation of God's plan. First he exclaims, 'if their trespass means riches for the world, and if their failure means riches for the Gentiles, how much more will their full inclusion mean!' (v. 12), then, 'if their rejection means the reconciliation of the world, what will their acceptance mean but life from the dead?' (v. 15). Each verse suggests an argument *a minori ad maius* (or *a fortiori* – from the lesser to the greater). Since even Israel's failure has proved to be of tremendous benefit to the Gentiles, their inclusion/acceptance by God must be the key to the ultimate resurrection from the dead! Thus, while the biblical schema tied the salvation of the world/Gentiles to the restoration of Israel, Paul sees it happening in at least two waves. In the first wave the inauguration of the restoration of Israel leads to the intermediate salvation of Gentiles (and continued failure on the part of most of Israel). In the second wave the salvation of the Gentiles leads eventually to the conversion and salvation of the rest of Israel which, again, turns out to be the key to even greater benefit for the rest of the world, in that it brings about the resurrection of the dead – the ultimate restoration of creation and humanity.

The use of the language of inheritance in the New Testament also points to unrealized aspects of the restoration of God's people. The language typically goes back to Old Testament references to the gift of the Promised Land as Israel's inheritance and, in Davidic and Messianic contexts based on Psalm

---

116. Wagner, *Heralds of the Good News*, p. 354, recognizes and helpfully describes the tension: 'In terms of Isaiah's larger three-act "plot-line" of rebellion, punishment, and restoration, Paul locates himself and his fellow believers (Jew and Gentile) in the final act of the story, where heralds go forth with the good news that God has redeemed his people. Surprisingly, however, most of Israel remains mired in acts one and two, still rebellious and estranged from God, still blinded to the reality of the redemption God has wrought for Israel and for the world in Christ.'

117. See Richard H. Bell, *Provoked to Jealousy: The Origin and Purpose of the Jealousy Motif in Romans 9–11*, WUNT 2.63 (Tübingen: J. C. B. Mohr [Paul Siebeck], 1994).

2:7–8, to the inheritance of the world, of the kingdom of God, or of eternal life. New Testament texts typically speak of our inheritance as something to be received in the future (Matt. 5:5; 19:29; 25:34; Mark 10:17; Luke 10:25; 18:18; Acts 13:19; 20:32; 1 Cor. 6:9–10; 15:50; Gal. 5:21; Eph. 5:5; Col. 1:12; 3:24; Heb. 1:14; 9:15; 1 Pet. 1:4).

Similarly, Hebrews 2:5–9 applies Psalm 8:4–5 to the life and ministry of Christ, but admits that 'we do not yet see everything in subjection to him' (v. 8). Instead, 'we see him who for a little while was made lower than the angels, namely Jesus, crowned with glory and honour because of the suffering of death, so that by the grace of God he might taste death for everyone' (v. 9). It is *not* the case, however, that the psalm applies to Christ *rather than* to God's intentions for humanity as a whole. The passage goes on to clarify that 'it was fitting that he, for whom and by whom all things exist, in bringing many sons to glory, should make the founder of their salvation perfect through suffering. For he who sanctifies and those who are sanctified all have one origin' (2:10–11). So Christ's humanity was essential to his mission, since his self-sacrifice was not only the key and prelude to his own exaltation and enthrone-ment, but also served as the means of 'bringing many sons to glory'. In Hebrews 8:8–12 the author provides an extended citation of Jeremiah's promise of the new covenant (Jer. 31:31–34). Hebrews 8–9 makes it clear that Christ's sacrifice brings about the fulfilment of that promised covenant and that through the establishment of the new covenant God's intentions for humanity are accomplished.

The book of Hebrews speaks of the innumerable descendants of Abraham as people who died in faith without receiving the things that were promised, 'but having seen them and greeted them from afar, and having acknowledged that they were strangers and exiles[118] on the earth' (11:13). Those kinds of people 'make it clear that they are seeking a homeland' (v. 14). They were seeking 'a better country, that is, a heavenly one' (v. 16).

Making the same point, James addresses his letter to 'the twelve tribes in the Dispersion' (1:1), who are to live in the light of the 'hope for the messianic age and final reward', and he clarifies the 'urgent implications of this for the way life should be lived in the present'.[119] It has been suggested that 'for James the

---

118. Gk. *parepidēmoi* – sojourners or resident aliens (the word does not have the negative connotations of 'exiles').

119. Andrew Chester, 'The Theology of James', in Andrew Chester and Ralph P. Martin (eds.), *The Theology of the Letters of James, Peter, and Jude*, New Testament Theology (Cambridge: Cambridge University Press, 1994), p. 20.

church was the true Israel, eagerly awaiting the call to restoration out of her exile'.[120] Matt Jackson-McCabe agrees. For him, 'The central metaphor that informs James's interest in the figure of Jesus Christ is not, as in the Johannine or Pauline literature, new creation or rebirth, but national restoration'. James 'writes a letter of counsel to the "twelve tribes in the diaspora" to encourage them as they await their promised, and now imminent, restoration'.[121] Andrew Chester explains how the relationship between trials and eschatology in the letter reflects this eschatological framework:

> The themes set out at the start provide an important perspective for the whole work. Thus 1.2–4, set emphatically at the very start of the letter, introduces the theme of trials or testing. This theme belongs, in the framework of Jewish eschatology, to the final tribulation which will usher in the messianic age and final rule of God. Hence, paradoxically, the writer can call on those he addresses to rejoice at the prospect of tribulation, because what awaits them in the end is the positive reward and fulfilment of the final age. This point is made clear by 1.12–13, which speaks of God giving the 'crown of life' (the eschatological reward) to those who endure the trial.[122]

In 1 Peter the theme of continuing exile is suggested in multiple ways. The letter is written to 'those who are elect exiles of the dispersion in Pontus, Galatia, Cappadocia, Asia, and Bithynia' (1:1). They are referred to as 'sojourners and exiles' again in 2:11. Furthermore, the reference to 'Babylon' in 5:13 is taken to be 'a cipher of the exile of God's people whether on the analogy of Israel's captivity in Mesopotamian Babylonia in the sixth century BCE . . . or as the counterpoint to Peter's teaching on the church as residing in the Diaspora as pilgrims and exiles (as in 1:1; 2:11)'.[123] That is, 'Babylon' serves as a 'code-term for the place of Christian exile promising liberation from bondage to freedom in the Zion of the Christian community (1 Pet. 2.1–10)'.[124] In this exilic state our enemy is not so much a pagan empire, but the devil himself who, thanks to the empire-like reach of his power, is causing suffering to our brothers

---

120. E. Randolph Richards, in Pate, et al., *The Story of Israel*, p. 238.

121. Matt Jackson-McCabe, 'The Messiah Jesus in the Mythic World of James', *JBL* 122 (2003), pp. 729–730.

122. Chester, 'The Theology of James', p. 17.

123. Ralph P. Martin, 'The Theology of Jude, 1 Peter, and 2 Peter', in Chester and Martin, *The Theology of the Letters of James, Peter, and Jude*, pp. 93–94.

124. Ibid., p. 94.

'throughout the world' (5:8–9). Nevertheless, 'after you have suffered a little while, the God of all grace, who has called you to his eternal glory in Christ, will himself restore, confirm, strengthen, and establish you' (5:10). The discussion of the purging effect of suffering in 4:1–4 evokes the prophetic understanding of the intended role of Israel's exile under Babylon. E. Randolph Richards has therefore suggested that the message of 1 Peter is dependent upon 'the *original* Diaspora letter, the one by Jeremiah to those in exile in Babylon (Jeremiah 29)'.[125] He suggests that for 1 Peter 'the church was still in exile, living in Babylon, awaiting God's deliverance. This explains the apparent mixed message 1 Peter seems to give: "fit in", but also "don't conform".'[126]

First Peter has other indications that the eschatological restoration has been inaugurated. The readers have been 'born again to a living hope through the resurrection of Jesus Christ from the dead, to an inheritance that is imperishable, undefiled, and unfading, kept in heaven' for them (1:3–4). They are experiencing the fulfilment of what the prophets longed to see (1:10–12). They have already been ransomed (1:18) and they have heard the good news associated with Isaiah 40 (1:24–25). They are 'like living stones . . . being built up as a spiritual house, to be a holy priesthood, to offer spiritual sacrifices acceptable to God through Jesus Christ' (2:5), that is, they are God's new temple and he has called them 'out of darkness into his marvellous light' (cf. Isa. 9:2; 42:16; 60:1–3).

Finally, as Richard Bauckham points out, 'Traces of an interpretation of the saving work of Jesus Christ as bringing about the eschatological exodus can be found in many parts of the New Testament, but it is Revelation that develops the idea most fully.'[127] This is seen in the references to redemption by the blood of the Passover Lamb (5:6, 9–10; 7:14; 12:11) and to the singing of the Song of Moses (15:2–4). Moreover, the antagonistic culture in which they live is referred to as Babylon (Rev. 14:8; 16:19; 17:5; 18:2, 10, 21) and the plagues associated with the seals and trumpets evoke our memory of those that were poured out on Egypt in the process of Israel's redemption in the first exodus. Hence, 'John's own vision of the New Jerusalem has developed from the visions of the prophets of the exile which the actual rebuilding of Jerusalem and the temple after the exile fell far short of realizing'.[128]

---

125. Richards, in Pate, et al., *The Story of Israel*, p. 241.

126. Ibid., p. 244.

127. Richard Bauckham, *The Theology of the Book of Revelation*, New Testament Theology (Cambridge: Cambridge University Press, 1993), p. 70; cf. pp. 20, 70–72, 75, 79, 88, 98–101, 104.

128. Ibid., p. 154.

What is the relationship between the restoration of Israel and the restoration of humanity in Revelation? A clue is offered in chapter 7, where the vision of the sealing of 144,000 saints 'from every tribe of the sons of Israel' (vv. 4–8)[129] is immediately followed by a vision of 'a great multitude that no one could number, from every nation, from all tribes and peoples and languages' (v. 9). The relationship between the two is presumably the same as that between the 'Lion of the tribe of Judah' in 5:5 and the Lamb in 5:6. There it is as a slain Lamb that the Lion 'ransomed people for God from every tribe and language and people and nation' (5:9). Those ransomed people are restored to a new creation, with its new Jerusalem evocative of Eden (21:1–2; 22:1–2). As a kingdom and priests (1:6; 5:10; 20:6) who reign through and with Christ (2:26; 5:10; 20:4–6; 22:5), they have been restored to the role for which they were originally intended.[130] Revelation's depiction of the return to Eden thereby serves as the book's way of concluding by tying together the redemption of Israel[131] and the rest of the world through Christ.

Conclusion

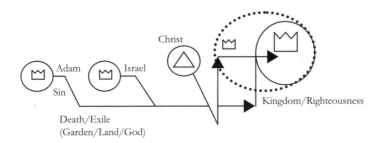

The overview of the biblical narrative proposed here may be represented in the chart above. The crowns found in the first two circles representing the

---

129. The listing of the tribes clearly indicates that it should not be taken literally, since the tribes of Dan and Ephraim are left out, and Levi and both Joseph and Manasseh (the half-tribe descended from his son) are included.

130. The motif of God's people reigning with Christ is found throughout the New Testament. Among passages not commented on in this essay, see Rom. 5:17; 1 Cor. 4:8; 2 Tim. 2:12; Rev. 2:26; 5:10; 20:4–6; 22:5.

131. Noted in a variety of ways, including the multiple references to 'twelve' at the end of the book: gates, angels, tribes, foundations, names, apostles, pearls, kinds of fruit (21:12, 14, 21; 22:2).

garden and the land indicate the dominion for which Adam and Eve (humanity) were created, which was subsequently granted to the Davidic king. The
circle to the right and a bit higher than those circles represents Christ's presence in heaven, which he willingly leaves to identify with his people and with
all humanity in his life on earth and in his death on the cross. The downward
line from the circle does not represent exile due to sin in his case, but his
identification with us in our exile. It penetrates below the original line of death
and exile, since Christ's death goes deeper and accomplishes what human and
Israelite exiles would not be able to accomplish. The upward line represents
the restoration of Israel and of humanity which was accomplished in principle through his resurrection from the dead. It leads to a dotted circle with a
crown that represents Christ's present reign at God's right hand. The two lines
pointing to the right from the vertical line representing Christ's resurrection
and the inaugurated restoration of Israel and creation represent the reality that
we live in the 'time between the times', in which many Jews and Gentiles (all
those who have not entered into Christ) continue in a state of spiritual exile
(represented by the lower of the two right-pointing lines), while those who
have entered into Christ and have participated in his death and resurrection
have entered into the inaugural phase of the ultimate restoration of Israel and
creation. The solid circle within the dotted circle represents the final consummation of the kingdom of God and Christ, when all creation is fully restored
and all peoples and nations recognize that the God of Israel is the only true
God, Creator and Redeemer of heaven and earth. It is the God of Israel and
the nations who therefore receives all the glory that is due him as Christ and
his people exercise dominion under his rule, a dominion which reflects his
righteousness, truth and glory and brings him unending praise.

© Roy E. Ciampa, 2007

INDEX OF SCRIPTURE AND OTHER ANCIENT SOURCES

INDEX OF ANCIENT SOURCES

From the NEW STUDIES IN BIBLICAL THEOLOGY series

Sealed with an Oath
Covenant in God's unfolding purpose
Paul R. Williamson

'Covenant' is a significant biblical theme. Paul Williamson offers fresh readings of Old and New Testament texts that contribute to this theme, highlights its significance for biblical theology, and explores its role within God's unfolding purpose of universal blessing.

978-1-84474-165-6   256 pages

Shepherds after My own Heart
Pastoral traditions and leadership in the Bible
Timothy S. Laniak

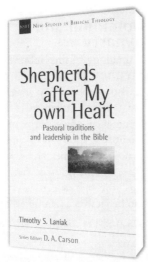

This stimulating biblical theology draws on a wide range of texts to offer a holistic reading of shepherd imagery as it develops across the canon of Scripture, and also highlights principles and implications for contemporary Christian ministry.

978-1-84474-127-4   313 pages

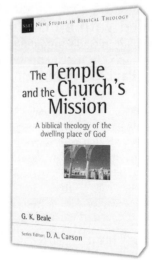

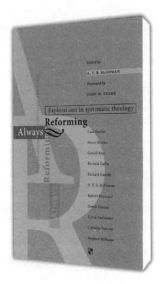

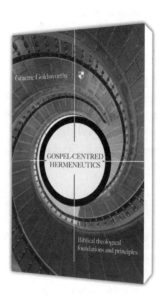